SPERRY
SYMPOSIUM
CLASSICS

SPERRY SYMPOSIUM CLASSICS

The Old Testament

EDITED BY
PAUL Y. HOSKISSON

RSC
BYU

DESERET
BOOK
SALT LAKE CITY, UTAH

Copublished by the Religious Studies Center, Brigham Young University, Provo, Utah, and Deseret Book Company, Salt Lake City, Utah.

© 2005 by Brigham Young University

Library of Congress Cataloging-in-Publication Data
Sperry Symposium classics : the Old Testament / edited by Paul Y. Hoskisson.
    p.   cm.
  Includes bibliographical references and index.
  ISBN-10 1-59038-533-0 (hardbound : alk. paper)
  ISBN-13 978-1-59038-533-3 (hardbound : alk. paper)
  1. Bible. O.T.—Criticism, interpretation, etc. 2. Church of Jesus Christ of Latter-day Saints—Doctrines. 3. Mormon Church—Doctrines.
I. Hoskisson, Paul Y.
  BS1171.3.S64 2005
  221.6—dc22   2005015826

Printed in the United States of America
R. R. Donnelley and Sons, Crawfordsville, IN

10   9   8   7   6   5   4   3   2

CONTENTS

FOREWORD vii

1. REMNANTS GATHERED, COVENANTS FULFILLED
   Elder Russell M. Nelson 1

2. A PRECIOUS AND POWERFUL WITNESS OF JESUS CHRIST
   Elder John M. Madsen 18

3. THE OLD TESTAMENT: A VOICE FROM THE PAST AND
   A WITNESS FOR THE LORD JESUS CHRIST
   Robert J. Matthews 35

4. PROPHETS AND PRIESTHOOD IN THE OLD TESTAMENT
   Robert L. Millet 48

5. MELCHIZEDEK: SEEKING AFTER THE ZION OF ENOCH
   Frank F. Judd Jr. 69

6. THE ABRAHAMIC TEST
   Larry E. Dahl 83

7. THE WIFE/SISTER EXPERIENCE: PHARAOH'S INTRODUCTION
   TO JEHOVAH
   Gaye Strathearn 100

8. JACOB IN THE PRESENCE OF GOD
   Andrew C. Skinner 117

9. THE LAW OF MOSES AND THE LAW OF CHRIST
   Edward J. Brandt 133

10. TRUST IN THE LORD: EXODUS AND FAITH
    S. Kent Brown 154

11. THE PROVOCATION IN THE WILDERNESS AND THE
    REJECTION OF GRACE
    M. Catherine Thomas 164

12. "GREAT ARE THE WORDS OF ISAIAH"
    Hugh W. Nibley 177

13. ISAIAH AND THE GREAT ARRAIGNMENT
    Terry B. Ball 196

14. A LATTER-DAY SAINT READING OF ISAIAH: THE EXAMPLE
    OF ISAIAH 6
    Paul Y. Hoskisson 209

15. OBADIAH'S VISION OF SAVIORS ON MOUNT ZION
    Gary P. Gillum 226

16. CONSIDER YOUR WAYS: THE BOOK OF HAGGAI AND THE
    RESPONSIBILITIES AND BLESSINGS OF TEMPLE WORK
    Ray L. Huntington 236

17. THE PROPHETS OF THE EXILE: SAVIORS OF A PEOPLE
    Richard D. Draper 245

18. "HAST THOU CONSIDERED MY SERVANT JOB?"
    John S. Tanner 266

19. ELIJAH'S MISSION: HIS KEYS, POWERS, AND BLESSINGS FROM
    THE OLD TESTAMENT TO THE LATTER DAYS
    E. Dale LeBaron 283

20. THE LORD WILL REDEEM HIS PEOPLE: ADOPTIVE COVENANT
    AND REDEMPTION IN THE OLD TESTAMENT
    Jennifer C. Lane 298

21. THE RESTORATION AS COVENANT RENEWAL
    David Rolph Seely 311

22. SYMBOLIC ACTION AS PROPHECY IN THE OLD TESTAMENT
    Donald W. Parry 337

    APPENDIX 356

    INDEX 361

FOREWORD

If you believe as I do that variety is the spice of life, this collection of articles will add zest and savor to your study of the Old Testament. In selecting and preparing these essays for this collection, it was my hope to provide a wide range of readings taken from the Sidney B. Sperry Symposium series. Therefore, the articles in this publication touch on a variety of aspects of Old Testament study. Some authors discuss the Old Testament itself, others offer explanations and interpretations, and still others use the Old Testament as a springboard to discuss Restoration theology.

Without any doubt, the best and most important commentary on the Old Testament is the Book of Mormon, with the Pearl of Great Price and the Doctrine and Covenants not far behind. Many of the authors in this collection make extensive use of the latter-day scriptures to help explain Old Testament concepts and themes. Their example demonstrates how we as a people can approach other aspects of the Old Testament using Restoration scripture to guide us.

The prophets of this dispensation also have not been silent about the Old Testament. In fact, without the foundation of the Old Testament, many aspects of the Restoration would not be comprehensible. The prophets of the Restoration have not shied away from pointing out Old Testament grounds for Restoration concepts, and thereby they have provided us with invaluable insights. Therefore, I have also tried to select articles that display a liberal use of prophetic commentary. In our continued study of the Old Testament, as Latter-day Saints, we should pay more than lip service to the prophets, seers, and revelators of this dispensation.

All of us can use a little stretching once in a while. Therefore, though most of the authors' offerings are readily accessible to all Latter-day Saints, a few present more technical material that will give readers a chance to dig deeper and expand their understanding.

For those who would like to read more, I have included a list of all the published lectures, beginning with the 1978 symposium. They represent some of the best Latter-day Saint commentary that has been produced on the Old Testament. Some years the themes were very broad and other years the topics were held within fairly narrow bounds. If you are a serious student of the Old Testament, I encourage you to avail yourself of the entire series, without neglecting the scriptures of the Restoration or latter-day prophetic commentary.

                                                            Paul Y. Hoskisson
                                                                     Editor

CHAPTER ONE

REMNANTS GATHERED, COVENANTS FULFILLED

ELDER RUSSELL M. NELSON

The title of my message is "Remnants Gathered, Covenants Fulfilled." It comes from the Book of Mormon. There the Lord speaks of fulfilling "the covenant which the Father hath made unto his people," the house of Israel. "Then," He continues, "shall the remnants, which shall be scattered abroad upon the face of the earth, be gathered in from the east and from the west, and from the south and from the north; and they shall be brought to the knowledge of the Lord their God, who hath redeemed them" (3 Nephi 20:12–13).

The gathering of those remnants and the fulfilling of that divine covenant are occurring in our day. Yet this big picture is obscure to the eye of many who focus upon bargains at supermarkets and rankings of favorite football teams. Let us examine our place in God's plan for His children and for The Church of Jesus Christ of Latter-day Saints. We are part of a destiny known by relatively few people upon the earth.[1]

During the year 1997, attention across the world was attracted to the history of the Church. Its pioneers arrived at the valley of the Great Salt Lake 150 years ago. Replications of handcarts have been featured from Siberia to Swaziland, from Scandinavia and South America to the isles of the South Pacific. Through theater and stage, printed and electronic media, stories of early converts to the Church have been told.

Elder Russell M. Nelson is a member of the Quorum of the Twelve Apostles.

Generally, writers of these accounts have done well in reporting what these pioneers did. But only a few have captured the reasons why. Even fewer have understood that history in context of the voices of prophets of the Old Testament that link with the great latter-day work that is now being accomplished.

Connections with the New Testament would be no surprise to any who understand the deep commitment to Jesus Christ held by members of this Church that bears His holy name. Its stalwart pioneers opened the period of the Restoration of all things—the promised dispensation of the fulness of times—as prophesied by Peter and Paul (see Acts 3:21; Ephesians 1:10). Those apostolic records and other scriptures of the New Testament are an integral part of the legacy of the restored Church. Its name describes members as Latter-day Saints to distinguish them from those of the Church in the meridian of time. Members were then called *saints,* as they are now. Paul addressed an epistle "to the saints which are at Ephesus, and to the faithful in Christ Jesus" (Ephesians 1:1).[2] To recent converts of that time and place, Paul said, "Now therefore ye are no more strangers and foreigners, but fellowcitizens with the saints, and of the household of God" (Ephesians 2:19; see also 3:17–19).

In that epistle Paul used the word *saint* at least once in every chapter! The term *saint* does not connote beatification or perfection in this life. It simply describes each member of the Church as a believer in Jesus the Christ. It means that members are committed to love God and their neighbor. They are to sacrifice, to serve, and to build the Church as directed by its inspired leaders.

But the connection between the Church and the Old Testament is less apparent. This symposium, which focuses on the voices of the prophets in the Old Testament, is an opportune time to speak of the strong and significant links between ancient and modern Israel. I would like to limit my discussion to five major links that are of immense importance.

As I speak to this theme, you will doubtless think of additional connections. You will also recognize that much more could be said on each segment that I will discuss. That is good. You can explore these interrelationships later without the limitations of time and talent that press upon me now.

THE LINK OF JOSEPH

The first link I shall label as the link of Joseph. This link applies both to Joseph who was sold into Egypt and to the Prophet Joseph Smith. Few men in the Old Testament are of greater importance to Latter-day Saints than is Joseph of Egypt. Many Bible commentators have described him as a type, or shadow, for the Savior. But we also know him as a specific type for the Prophet Joseph Smith and a generic type for all members of The Church of Jesus Christ of Latter-day Saints. Many of the Church's members claim descent from Joseph through his sons, Ephraim or Manasseh.

The importance of Joseph in the book of Genesis is signified by the fact that he figures prominently in sixteen of its fifty chapters (see Genesis 30; 33; 35; 37; 39–50). Joseph's life span from cradle to grave[3] represents only 4 percent of the twenty-seven hundred years covered by the book of Genesis. Yet his life is reported in nearly one-third of its chapters.[4]

In the King James Version, Genesis 50 ends with verse 26, which records the death of Joseph. In the Joseph Smith Translation (JST), that chapter not only adds important information to verses 24 through 26 but provides twelve additional verses that enrich our knowledge of the link of Joseph (see JST, Genesis 50:27–38). Those additions include the following insights, which I paraphrase:

1. A righteous branch would be raised up later out of Joseph's loins (see JST, Genesis 50:24).

2. Israel would be scattered. A branch would be broken off and carried into a far country (see JST, Genesis 50:25).

3. A choice seer would be raised up from Joseph's loins to do work for the fruit of his loins (see JST, Genesis 50:26–29).

4. Writings from the fruit of Joseph's loins would grow together with writings from the fruit of Judah's loins to bring knowledge of their fathers and of everlasting covenants. That knowledge would come in the last days (see JST, Genesis 50:30–32).

5. The promised seer would be called Joseph, after the name of his father, and he would be like unto Joseph, son of Jacob, bringing salvation to the children of the Lord (see JST, Genesis 50:33).

These additions are good examples of "plain and precious" truths that have been restored through the Prophet Joseph Smith (see 1 Nephi 13:40).

He and the ancient Joseph had much in common, as shown by other scriptures that I will cite. From the Book of Mormon we read: "A part of the remnant of the coat of Joseph was preserved and had not decayed. . . . Even as this remnant of garment . . . hath been preserved, so shall a remnant of [Joseph's] seed . . . be preserved by the hand of God" (Alma 46:24).

We are remnants of that precious seed. Joseph Smith had been chosen by the Lord to take up the labors of the tribe of Joseph, son of Jacob. Centuries ago that same Joseph had prophesied of Joseph Smith and described their linkage. Again I quote from the Book of Mormon: "Yea, Joseph truly said: Thus saith the Lord unto me: A choice seer will I raise up out of the fruit of thy loins; and he shall be esteemed highly among the fruit of thy loins. And unto him will I give commandment that he shall do a work for the fruit of thy loins, his brethren, which shall be of great worth unto them, even to the bringing of them to the knowledge of the covenants which I have made with thy fathers. And I will give unto him a commandment that he shall do none other work, save the work which I shall command him. And I will make him great in mine eyes; for he shall do my work" (2 Nephi 3:7–8).

The link of Joseph applied not only to Joseph Smith Jr. but to his father as well. Again I quote from Joseph who was sold into Egypt: "Behold, that seer [Joseph Smith] will the Lord bless; . . . for this promise, which I have obtained of the Lord, of the fruit of my loins, shall be fulfilled. . . . And his name shall be called after me; and it shall be after the name of his father. And he shall be like unto me; for the thing, which the Lord shall bring forth by his hand, by the power of the Lord shall bring my people unto salvation" (2 Nephi 3:14–15).

Joseph and Joseph Smith had more in common than their lineage linking. At age seventeen, Joseph, son of Jacob, was informed of his great destiny (see Genesis 37:2). At that same age, Joseph Smith was informed of his destiny regarding the Book of Mormon: He was seventeen when first visited by the angel Moroni, who told the boy prophet that "God had a work for [him] to do." He was to translate a book written upon golden plates containing the fulness of the everlasting gospel. His "name should be had for good and evil among all nations, kindreds, and tongues" (Joseph Smith—History 1:33; see also 1:34–41).

Both Josephs were persecuted. Joseph in Egypt was falsely accused of a crime he did not commit and was put into prison (see Genesis 39:11–20). Joseph Smith was incarcerated on trumped-up charges and false accusations.[5]

Joseph's coat of many colors was taken from him by his brothers in a cruel attempt to convince their father that Joseph had been killed (see Genesis 37:2–33). Joseph Smith's life was taken from him, largely because of betrayals by false brethren.

Anciently, "when all the land of Egypt was famished, the people cried to Pharaoh for bread: and Pharaoh said unto all the Egyptians, Go unto Joseph; what he saith to you, do" (Genesis 41:55). In the latter days, people starving for nourishment that only the gospel can provide are again to be fed—by Joseph. The Lord declared that "this generation shall have my word through [Joseph Smith]" (D&C 5:10). Today we "feast upon the words of Christ" because of Joseph Smith (2 Nephi 32:3).

This link of Joseph is summarized in lines from the book of Ether:

> The Lord brought a remnant of the seed of Joseph out of the land of Jerusalem, that he might be merciful unto the seed of Joseph that they should perish not. . . .
>
> Wherefore, the remnant of the house of Joseph shall be built upon this land [of America]; and it shall be a land of their inheritance; and they shall build up a holy city unto the Lord, like unto the Jerusalem of old. . . .
>
> . . . and blessed are they who dwell therein, for it is they whose garments are white through the blood of the Lamb; and they are they who are numbered among the remnant of the seed of Joseph, who were of the house of Israel.
>
> . . . and they are they who were scattered and gathered in from the four quarters of the earth, and from the north countries, and are partakers of the fulfilling of the covenant which God made with their father, Abraham. (Ether 13:7–8, 10–11)

THE LINK OF THE BOOK OF MORMON

Link number two I shall identify as the link of the Book of Mormon. In September 1997 I had the extraordinary privilege of seeing portions of the original manuscript and virtually all of the printer's manuscript of the Book of Mormon.[6] That was an incredible experience!

Voices of prophets in the Old Testament foretold of this great book. You are familiar with the prophecy of Isaiah: "Thou shalt be brought down, and shalt speak out of the ground, and thy speech shall be low out of the dust, and thy voice shall be, as of one that hath a familiar spirit, out of the ground, and thy speech shall whisper out of the dust" (Isaiah 29:4).

Could any words have been more descriptive of the Book of Mormon, coming as it did "out of the ground" to "whisper out of the dust" to people of our day?

Other Old Testament passages foretold the Book of Mormon. One such came to mind last January when I attended a prayer breakfast at the White House in Washington D.C., hosted by President Bill Clinton. During an informal reception that preceded the breakfast, I was chatting with a distinguished and scholarly Jewish rabbi from New York. Our conversation was interrupted by another rabbi who asked his colleague from New York if he could recall the scriptural reference to the stick of Judah and the stick of Joseph that would come together one day. My friend paused for a moment, stroked his chin pensively, and then replied, "I think you will find that in the book of Ezekiel."

I could not restrain myself. "You might look in the thirty-seventh chapter of Ezekiel," I interjected. "There you will find the scriptures that you seek."

My rabbi friend was surprised. "How did *you* know that?"

"This doctrine," I said, "is very important in our theology."

Indeed it is. You know it, and I know it. I would like to read it: "Moreover, thou son of man, take thee one stick, and write upon it, For Judah, and for the children of Israel his companions: then take another stick, and write upon it, For Joseph, the stick of Ephraim, and for all the house of Israel his companions: and join them one to another into one stick; and they shall become one in thine hand" (Ezekiel 37:16–17).

Saints of modern Israel in 160 nations across the world are blessed to hold the Bible and the Book of Mormon as one in their hands. The worth of this privilege must never be underestimated.

Keys of authority for the Book of Mormon—the stick of Ephraim—were held by the angel Moroni (see D&C 27:5). The Book of Mormon is the great amplifying, clarifying, and converting scripture. It is indeed "Another Testament of Jesus Christ" (Book of Mormon, title page).

Children of the Lord have ever been admonished to "search the scriptures" (John 5:39; Alma 14:1; 33:2; 3 Nephi 10:14). In addition, we of modern Israel have been specifically commanded to study one particular voice and prophet of the Old Testament. Which one? Isaiah! (see 3 Nephi 20:11; 23:1). The importance of that commandment is underlined by the fact that 433 verses of Isaiah appear in the Book of Mormon. Studying them is not repetitious. Sidney B. Sperry reported that 234 of those verses differ from their biblical counterparts.[7] In addition, the Doctrine and Covenants has more than seventy quotations from or paraphrases of Isaiah.[8] Study the words of Isaiah! Do we get the message?

Other prophets of the Old Testament were quoted to our modern prophets. Malachi's teachings have been repeated.[9] Elijah,[10] Moses,[11] and others have taught people of both ancient and modern Israel (see D&C 27:5–13).

Isaiah described the spirit of the Book of Mormon as "familiar." It resonates with people who know the Old Testament, especially with those who are conversant with its Hebrew language. The Book of Mormon is filled with Hebraisms—traditions, symbolisms, idioms, and literary forms. It is familiar because more than 80 percent of its pages come from Old Testament times.[12]

THE LINK OF THE HOUSE OF ISRAEL

Link number three I shall designate as the link of the house of Israel. It includes doctrines of the Abrahamic covenant and of the scattering and gathering of Israel.

About four thousand years ago, Abraham received a promise from the Lord that blessings would be offered to all of his mortal posterity (see D&C 132:29–50; Abraham 2:6–11). Included were promises that the Son of God would come through Abraham's lineage, that certain lands would be inherited by his posterity, that nations and kindreds of the earth would be blessed through his seed, and more. Knowledge of and reaffirmations of this covenant are evident in scriptures of the Old Testament (see Genesis 26:1–4, 24; 28; 35:9; 48). Although certain aspects of that covenant have already been fulfilled, many have not. The Book of Mormon teaches that we of modern Israel are among the covenant people of the Lord (see 1 Nephi 14:14; 15:14; 2 Nephi 30:2; Mosiah 24:13; 3 Nephi 29:3; Mormon 8:15). And, most remarkably, it teaches that the Abrahamic covenant will be fulfilled only in these latter days (see 1 Nephi 15:12–18). The Lord bestowed this Abrahamic covenant upon the Prophet Joseph Smith for the blessing of him and posterity after him (see D&C 124:56–59). Did you know that Abraham is mentioned in more verses of modern revelation than in all the verses of the Old Testament?[13] Abraham— this great patriarch of the Old Testament—is inextricably linked to all who join The Church of Jesus Christ of Latter-day Saints.[14]

Doctrines relating to the scattering and gathering of the house of Israel were also among the earliest lessons taught in the Book of Mormon. I quote from the first book of Nephi: "After the house of Israel should be scattered they should be gathered together again; . . . the natural branches of the olive-tree, or the remnants of the house of Israel, should be grafted in, or come to the knowledge of the true Messiah, their Lord and their Redeemer" (1 Nephi 10:14).

The Old Testament is replete with prophecies that relate to the scattering of Israel. May I cite one from the book of First Kings: "For the Lord shall smite Israel, as a reed is shaken in the water, and he shall root up Israel out of this good land, which he gave to their fathers, and shall scatter them" (1 Kings 14:15).

In this citation, the word "scatter" was translated from the Hebrew verb *zarah,* which means "to scatter, cast away, winnow, or disperse." The richness of the Hebrew language provides other verbs to describe similar actions. For example, from the book of First Kings we also read: "I saw all Israel scattered upon the hills, as sheep that have not a shepherd" (1 Kings 22:17).

In this instance, "scattered" was translated from the Hebrew verb *puwts,* which also means "to scatter" or "be dispersed."

Isaiah used yet another verb in this prophecy: "He shall set up an ensign for the nations, and shall assemble the outcasts of Israel, and gather together the *dispersed* of Judah from the four corners of the earth" (Isaiah 11:12; emphasis added).

In this case "dispersed" was translated from the Hebrew verb *naphats,* which means "to shatter, break, dash, or beat in pieces."

References to the scattering were also recorded in the New Testament. For example, the book of James begins with these words: "James, a servant of God and of the Lord Jesus Christ, to the twelve tribes which are scattered abroad, greeting" (James 1:1).

In this reference, "scattered" was translated from the Greek feminine noun *diaspora,* which means "dispersed" or "scattered." You may wish to look up the word *diaspora* in the Bible Dictionary (Bible Dictionary, "Diaspora," 657). There the scattering of the house of Israel is succinctly summarized.

Saints of modern Israel know that Peter, James, and John were sent by the Lord with "the keys of [His] kingdom, and a dispensation of the gospel for the last times; and for the fulness of times," in which He would "gather together in one all things, both which are in heaven, and which are on earth" (D&C 27:13).[15]

The travels and travail of our pioneers were of eternal consequence. Their mission was not limited to an international immigration or a transcontinental migration with wagons and handcarts. They were to lay the foundation of an endless work that would "fill the world."[16] They were essential to Jeremiah's prophecy:

"Hear the word of the Lord, O ye nations, and declare it in the isles afar off, and say, He that scattered Israel will gather him, and keep him, as a shepherd doth his flock" (Jeremiah 31:10).[17]

They got the message. Missionaries were sent very early to "the isles afar off" to commence the work of the Lord. As a result, the Church was established in the British Isles and in the islands of French Polynesia years before the pioneers entered the valley of the Great Salt Lake. It has been my privilege to participate in sesquicentennial celebrations in the British Isles in 1987 and in French Polynesia in 1994. Now in 1997, I celebrate this one with you in Utah.

Another aspect of the gathering of Israel reflects back to our first link regarding Joseph. The word *Joseph* comes from the Hebrew masculine personal noun *Yowceph,* the literal meaning of which is "Jehovah has added." *Joseph* also relates to the Hebrew root *yasaph,* which means "to add," and "to *asaph,*" which means both "to take away" and "to gather" (see Genesis 30:24, footnote a).

The Hebrew verbs *yacaph* and *acaph*[18] are used in the Hebrew text of the Old Testament 186 and 180 times respectively. Both words were usually translated into English as "gather" in one of its several forms. For example, in the verse, "David *gathered* together all the chosen men of Israel" (2 Samuel 6:1; emphasis added), the Hebrew verb *yacaph* was used.

Another scripture from Genesis deserves special comment. It reports the naming of Jacob and Rachel's firstborn son: "She called his name *Joseph;* and said, The Lord shall *add* to me another son" (Genesis 30:24; emphasis added).[19] In that verse both the words "Joseph" and "add" were derived from the Hebrew root *yacaph.*

The lineage of Joseph—through Ephraim and Manasseh—is the seed appointed to lead in the gathering of Israel.[20] The pioneers knew—through their patriarchal blessings and from doctrines of the Old Testament, amplified by scriptures and revelations of the Restoration—that the long-awaited gathering of Israel was to commence with them.

THE LINK OF EXODUS

The fourth link connecting ancient and modern Israel I shall name the link of the Exodus. At a Church Educational System fireside satellite broadcast in September 1997, I spoke to the subject of "The Exodus Repeated." Then I spoke of some connections between ancient and modern Israel that will also be relevant to a more comprehensive coverage of the topic, "Remnants Gathered, Covenants Fulfilled." Fascinating are the many parallels between the exodus from Egypt of the Israelites under Moses and the exodus from the United States of the pioneers under Brigham Young.

Both peoples were oppressed by their governments. The ancient Israelites were "bondmen" (Deuteronomy 6:21). The Latter-day Saints were persecuted by their own government.[21]

Moses had been prepared in the courts of Egypt and had gained much experience in military and other responsibilities (see Hebrews 11:24, 27). Brigham Young was likewise prepared for his leadership role. In the march of Zion's Camp, he observed the leadership of the Prophet Joseph Smith under difficult conditions.[22] Brigham Young aided in the removal of the Saints from Kirtland and directed the move of the persecuted Saints from Missouri to Nauvoo.[23]

God preserved ancient Israel from plagues that He sent upon

Egypt (see Exodus 15:26). God preserved the Saints from the plague of the United States Civil War that caused more American deaths due to war than any other war.

Both groups had to leave their homes and earthly possessions. Both had to learn to rely wholly upon the Lord and be sustained by Him during their travels. Both traversed deserts, mountains, and valleys of untamed wilderness. Ancient Israelites left Egypt via the waters of the Red Sea "as by dry land" (Hebrews 11:29). Some pioneers left the United States by crossing the wide waters of the Mississippi River—frozen to become a highway of ice.[24] Both groups endured trials of their faith during which the weak were winnowed away and the strong were empowered to endure to the end (see Ether 12:6; D&C 101:4–5; 105:19).

The children of ancient Israel had a portable tabernacle wherein covenants were made and ordinances were performed to strengthen them on their journey.[25] Originally the tabernacle was intended to be a portable temple, before the Israelites lost the higher law (see D&C 84:23–26; 124:38; JST, Exodus 34:1–2). Similarly, many Latter-day Saints were endowed in the Nauvoo Temple before their trek.

The journey from Egypt to Mount Sinai took about three months (see Exodus 12:2, 3, 6, 18; 13:4; 19:1). The journey from Winter Quarters to the valley of the Great Salt Lake also took about three months.[26]

The promised land for each group also bore similarities. That of ancient Israel had an inland sea of salt water, the inlet to which was the River Jordan. That for the pioneers also had an inland sea of salt water, fed by the Jordan River. The destination of each group was described by the Lord as a land "flowing with milk and honey."[27] The pioneers turned their wilderness into a fruitful field (see Isaiah 32:15–16) and made the desert blossom as a rose (see Isaiah 35:1)—precisely as prophesied by Isaiah.

For both the Israelites and the Saints, civil and ecclesiastical law were unified under one head. Moses bore that responsibility for the early Israelites.[28] Brigham Young—a modern Moses[29] (see D&C 103:16)—led the Latter-day Saints' movement west, with the Lord's blessing (see D&C 136:1–42). Moses and Brigham Young followed parallel patterns of governance (see Exodus 18:17–21; D&C 136:1–4). And each of them endured dissension from their close associates.[30]

Nevertheless, that same unified pattern of government will again prevail when the Lord shall be "King over all the earth" (Psalm 47:2; Zechariah 14:9), and He shall govern from Zion and Jerusalem (see Isaiah 2:1–4).

The Israelites celebrated their exodus from Egypt. The Latter-day Saints commemorated their exodus with the establishment of the world headquarters of the restored Church in the tops of the mountains. Both celebrations acclaimed their miraculous deliverance by God (see Jeremiah 16:15; 23:7).[31] The link of the exodus reminds us of an Old Testament scripture of gratitude: "Moses said unto the people, Remember this day, in which ye came out from Egypt, out of the house of bondage; for by strength of hand the Lord brought you out from this place" (Exodus 13:3).

THE LINK OF THE TIMELESS TRUTHS OF THE GOSPEL

The fifth connection between ancient and modern Israel I shall denote as the link of the timeless truths of the gospel. Those truths are included in the unending priesthood order of Melchizedek, though he is mentioned but twice in the Old Testament (see Genesis 14:18; Psalm 110:4). The Melchizedek Priesthood was removed from ancient Israel shortly after the exodus from Egypt (see JST, Exodus 34:1–2; D&C 84:23–25). Thereafter, ancient Israel functioned under the Levitical Priesthood and the law of carnal commandments (see D&C 84:27).

Timeless truths and principles of the gospel were and are important to people of ancient and modern Israel. The Sabbath day, for example, was honored for different reasons through the generations. From the time of Adam to Moses, the Sabbath was observed as a day of rest from the labor of creation (see Exodus 20:8–11; 31:13; Mosiah 13:16–19). From the time of Moses to the Resurrection of the Lord, the Sabbath also commemorated the liberation of the Israelites from their bondage in Egypt (see Deuteronomy 5:12–15; Isaiah 58:13; Ezekiel 20:20–22; 44:24). In latter days, Saints keep the Sabbath day holy in memory of the Atonement of Jesus Christ.[32]

The restoration of the priesthood rejuvenated the principle of tithing, linking to the Old Testament teachings of Genesis and Malachi (see Genesis 14:20; Malachi 3:8–12). Saints of modern Israel know how to calculate their own tithing from this simple instruction: "Those who have thus been tithed shall pay one-tenth of all their interest annually; and this shall be a standing law unto them forever, for my holy priesthood, saith the Lord" (D&C 119:4).

In contrast, have you ever amused yourself with the thought, on or about April 15th each year, that the filing of income tax returns is a bit more complicated? I'll confess that I have.

Turning our attention again to the timeless truths of the gospel, none are more vital than those associated with temple worship. They compose another link between ancient and modern Israel. The Bible Dictionary states that "whenever the Lord has had a people on the earth who will obey his word, they have been commanded to build temples in which the ordinances of the gospel and other spiritual manifestations that pertain to exaltation and eternal life may be administered" (Bible Dictionary, "Temple," 781).

The best-known temple of ancient Israel was Solomon's temple. Its baptismal font (see 2 Corinthians 4:15) and dedicatory prayer (see 2 Corinthians 6:12–42) provide patterns that are employed for temples today (see D&C 109:1–80). Old Testament scriptures refer to special clothing (see Exodus 28:4; 29:5; Leviticus 8:7–9; 1 Samuel 18:3–4) and ordinances (see Exodus 19:10, 14; 2 Samuel 12:20; Ezekiel 16:9) that are associated with temples (see D&C 124:37–40). How thankful we are that the Lord chose to restore the highest blessings of the priesthood to His faithful sons and daughters! He said: "For I deign to reveal unto my church things which have been kept hid from before the foundation of the world, things that pertain to the dispensation of the fulness of times" (D&C 124:41).

Revealed truth that we know as the Word of Wisdom came to the Prophet Joseph Smith in 1833. Every Latter-day Saint is familiar with it as one of the visible hallmarks of our faith. The final verse of that revelation forges another link back to ancient Israel: "And I, the Lord, give unto them a promise, that the destroying angel shall pass by them, as the children of Israel, and not slay them" (D&C 89:21).

This reference to the Passover shows that the Lord wanted obedient Saints of modern Israel to receive physical and spiritual protection just as He had provided for His faithful followers centuries before.

SUMMARY

Ancient Israel and modern Israel are linked arm in arm. In our day, many Old Testament prophecies are being fulfilled. Isaiah foretold: "And it shall come to pass in the last days, that the mountain of the Lord's house shall be established in the top of the mountains, and shall be exalted above the hills; and all nations shall flow unto it" (Isaiah 2:2; see also 2 Nephi 12:2; JST, Isaiah 2:2).

During the past year, visitors from more than one hundred nations have come to visit world headquarters of The Church of Jesus Christ of Latter-day Saints.[33]

Ancient and modern Israel subscribe to an ageless message of the Old Testament: "Know therefore that the Lord thy God . . . keepeth covenant and mercy with them that love him and keep his commandments to a thousand generations" (Deuteronomy 7:9).[34]

All faithful members of the Church will receive their just reward: "All things are theirs, whether life or death, or things present, or things to come, all are theirs and they are Christ's, and Christ is God's" (D&C 76:59).

I would like to bear my testimony as one with you, my beloved brothers and sisters. We love our Heavenly Father. We love the Lord Jesus Christ. We are His people. We have taken His holy name upon us. We are His remnants now being gathered and gleaned into His eternal garners (see Alma 26:5). We are fulfilling "the covenant which the Father hath made unto his people" (3 Nephi 20:12). We are being brought to the knowledge of our Lord who has redeemed us (see 3 Nephi 20:12–13). We are "children of the covenant" (3 Nephi 20:26; see also Acts 3:25; 3 Nephi 20:25) destined to be as was ancient Israel—"a kingdom of priests, and an holy nation" (Exodus 19:6; see also D&C 76:56–57). We know that Joseph Smith is the great prophet of the Restoration and that President Gordon B. Hinckley is the prophet of the Lord today.

My testimony, my love, and my blessing, I leave with you, in the name of Jesus Christ, amen.

NOTES

1. Ten million members of the Church compose 0.0017 percent of a world population of 5.8 billion.
2. The term *saints* appears in sixty-two verses of the New Testament.

3. Joseph died at the age of 110 years (see Genesis 50:26).

4. Sixteen of fifty chapters equals 32 percent.

5. See J. Reuben Clark Jr., *On the Way to Immortality and Eternal Life* (Salt Lake City: Deseret Book, 1949), 133; Ezra Taft Benson, in Conference Report, April 1954, 58.

6. About 25 percent of the original manuscript is in the historical archives of the Church. The printer's manuscript is owned by the Community of Christ (formerly the Reorganized LDS Church) and was on loan to The Church of Jesus Christ of Latter-day Saints. It is reported to be complete except for two lines of the title page.

7. See Sydney B. Sperry, "The 'Isaiah Problem' in the Book of Mormon," *Improvement Era,* October 1939, 594.

8. Monte S. Nyman, in *Encyclopedia of Mormonism,* ed. Daniel H. Ludlow (New York: Macmillan, 1992), 2:702. Another is mentioned in Joseph Smith—History 1:40.

9. See 3 Nephi 24:1; D&C 110:14; 128:17; 133:64; 138:46; Joseph Smith—History 1:36.

10. See 3 Nephi 25:5; D&C 2:1; 27:9; 35:4; 110:13, 14; 128:17; 133:55; 138:46, 47; Joseph Smith—History 1:38.

11. Moses is mentioned in 1,300 verses of scripture, 515 (40 percent) of which are in modern revelation.

12. Personal communication from Elder Jeffrey R. Holland, June 1997.

13. Abraham is mentioned in 506 verses of scripture, 289 of which are in modern revelation.

14. The covenant may also be received by adoption (see Matthew 3:9; Luke 3:8; Galatians 3:27–29; 4:5).

15. Compare with Paul's prophecy of the Restoration in Ephesians 1:10.

16. Joseph Smith, quoted in Wilford Woodruff, *The Discourses of Wilford Woodruff,* sel. G. Homer Durham (Salt Lake City: Bookcraft, 1946), 39.

17. *Gather* is used to translate the Hebrew verb *qabats,* which means "to gather, assemble."

18. Spellings in James Strong, *The Exhaustive Concordance of the Bible* (1890; reprint, New York: Abingdon, 1965), "Hebrew and Chaldee Dictionary," 50, 15.

19. Joseph was "added" to Rachel's family because her handmaid, Bilhah, had given birth to Dan and Naphtali previously (see Genesis 30:5–8). See also Deuteronomy 33:16–17, which refers to the people of Joseph being pushed together "to the ends of the earth: and they are the ten thousands of Ephraim, and they are the

thousands of Manasseh." JST, Genesis 50:34 also affirms that Joseph's seed would be preserved forever.

20. See Erastus Snow, in *Journal of Discourses* (London: Latter-day Saints' Book Depot, 1854–86), 23:183–84.

21. The pioneers were forced out of Missouri under threat of an order signed by Missouri's governor directing that the "Mormons must be treated as enemies and must be exterminated or driven from the state" (Joseph Smith, *History of The Church of Jesus Christ of Latter-day Saints,* ed. B. H. Roberts, 2nd ed. rev. [Salt Lake City: The Church of Jesus Christ of Latter-day Saints, 1952–51], 3:175). In 1887, the Congress of the United States of America took the unprecedented step of eliminating the Church's legal existence by revoking its corporate charter and authorizing federal receivers to assume ownership of virtually all of the Church's property and other assets, including its most sacred houses of worship—temples in Logan, Manti, St. George, and Salt Lake City (see *The Late Corporation of The Church of Jesus Christ of Latter-Day Saints v. United States,* 136 U.S.[1[1890]). Yet the Saints knew that they were Abraham's seed and heirs to promises and protection from the Lord (see D&C 103:17–20).

22. See Smith, *History of the Church,* 2:6–12, 185; Leonard J. Arrington, *Brigham Young: American Moses* (New York: Knopf, 1985), 58.

23. See Smith, *History of the Church,* 2:529; 3:252, 261; Preston Nibley, *The Presidents of the Church* (Salt Lake City: Deseret Book, 1974), 41.

24. See Orson Pratt, in *Journal of Discourses,* 21:275–77.

25. Ordinances and covenants of ancient Israel are referenced in 1 Corinthians 10:1–3; for modern Israel, see D&C 84:26–27.

26. One hundred and eleven days.

27. For the people of ancient Israel, see Exodus 3:8, 17; 13:5; 33:3; Leviticus 20:24; Numbers 13:27; 14:8; 16:13, 14; Deuteronomy 6:3; 11:9; 26:9, 15; 27:3; 31:20; Joshua 5:6; Jeremiah 11:5; 32:22; Ezekiel 20:6, 15; JST Exodus 33:1. For the pioneers, see D&C 38:18–19.

28. See Joseph Smith, *Teachings of the Prophet Joseph Smith,* sel. Joseph Fielding Smith (Salt Lake City: Deseret Book, 1938), 252.

29. President Spencer W. Kimball wrote of Brigham Young's role in that exodus: "Since Adam there have been many exoduses and promised lands: Abraham, Jared, Moses, Lehi, and others led groups. How easy it is to accept those distant in time as directed by the Lord, yet the ones near at hand as human calculations and decisions. Let us consider for a moment the great trek of the Mormon refugees from Illinois to Salt Lake Valley. Few, if any, great movements equal it. We frequently hear that Brigham Young led the people to make new tracks in a desert and to climb over mountains seldom scaled and to ford and wade unbridged rivers and to

traverse a hostile Indian country; and while Brigham Young was the instrument of the Lord, it was not he but the Lord of heaven who led modern Israel across the plains to their promised land" (*Faith Precedes the Miracle* [Salt Lake City: Deseret Book, 1972], 28).

30. See Numbers 12:1–11 (Aaron and Miriam); for latter-day examples, see Smith, *History of the Church,* 1:104–5 (Oliver Cowdery); and 1:226 (William E. McLellin).

31. Other miracles were shared, such as food provided by the "miracle of the quails." (For ancient Israel, see Exodus 16:13; Psalm 105:40; for the pioneers, see Stanley B. Kimball, "Nauvoo West: The Mormons of the Iowa Shore," *BYU Studies* 18 [Winter 1978]: 142). Protection was provided for ancient Israel by the Lord, who "went before them by day in a pillar of a cloud, to lead them the way; and by night in a pillar of fire" (Exodus 13:21; see also v. 22; Numbers 14:14; Deuteronomy 1:33; Nehemiah 9:19). Similar care has been noted for the pioneers (see Smith, *History of the Church,* 3:34; Thomas S. Monson, in Conference Report, April 1967, 56).

32. See D&C 20:40, 75–79; 59:9; see also Matthew 26:26–28; Mark 14:22–24; Luke 22:19–20; Acts 20:7; 1 Corinthians 16:2; Revelation 1:10.

33. Estimate provided by the Temple Square Mission.

34. See also Deuteronomy 11:1, 27; 19:9; 30:16; Joshua 22:5; 1 John 5:2–3; Mosiah 2:4. Other Old Testament scriptures refer to rewards for those obedient to God's commandments through a "thousand generations" (see 1 Corinthians 16:15; Psalm 105:8).

CHAPTER TWO

A Precious and Powerful Witness of Jesus Christ

ELDER JOHN M. MADSEN

The Old Testament is a precious and powerful witness of Jesus Christ, even though the sacred name and title *Jesus Christ* is not found within its pages today. "Many plain and precious things" were indeed "taken away from the book" (1 Nephi 13:28), but the central and fundamental message of the Old Testament, and indeed of all scripture, is that salvation may be found only in and through His holy name.

ALL SCRIPTURE AND ALL PROPHETS TESTIFY OF CHRIST

Jacob, the brother of Nephi and an Old Testament–period prophet, testified: "We knew of Christ, and we had a hope of his glory many hundred years before his coming; and not only we ourselves had a hope of his glory, but also all the holy prophets which were before us. Behold, they believed in Christ and worshiped the Father in his name, and also we worship the Father in his name" (Jacob 4:4–5; see also 2 Nephi 11:2–4).

President Joseph Fielding Smith taught that "all revelation since the fall has come through Jesus Christ, who is the Jehovah of the Old Testament. In all of the scriptures, where God is mentioned and where he has appeared, it was Jehovah who talked with Abraham, with Noah, Enoch, Moses, and all the prophets. He is the God of Israel, the Holy One of Israel; the one who led that nation out of

---

Elder John M. Madsen serves as a member of the Seventy of The Church of Jesus Christ of Latter-day Saints.

Egyptian bondage, and who gave and fulfilled the Law of Moses. The Father has never dealt with man directly and personally since the fall, and He has never appeared except to introduce and bear record of the Son."[1]

President Spencer W. Kimball declared that "the Old Testament prophets from Adam to Malachi are testifying of the divinity of the Lord Jesus Christ and our Heavenly Father. Jesus Christ was the God of the Old Testament, and it was He who conversed with Abraham and Moses. It was He who inspired Isaiah and Jeremiah; it was He who foretold through those chosen men the happenings of the future, even to the latest day and hour."[2]

I know of no more powerful and wonderful summary of the identity and role of the Lord Jesus Christ than the statement published to the world January 1, 2000, by the First Presidency and the Quorum of the Twelve Apostles entitled "The Living Christ," from which I quote some key phrases:

> [Jesus Christ] was the Great Jehovah of the Old Testament, the Messiah of the New. Under the direction of His Father, He was the creator of the earth. . . .
>
> He gave His life to atone for the sins of all mankind. . . .
>
> He was the Firstborn of the Father, the Only Begotten Son in the flesh, the Redeemer of the world.
>
> He rose from the grave to "become the firstfruits of them that slept" (1 Corinthians 15:20). . . .
>
> He will someday return to earth. . . . He will rule as King of Kings and reign as Lord of Lords, and every knee shall bend and every tongue shall speak in worship before Him. Each of us will stand to be judged of Him. . . .
>
> His duly ordained Apostles [bear testimony] that Jesus is the Living Christ, the immortal Son of God. He is the great King Immanuel, who stands today on the right hand of His Father. He is the light, the life, and the hope of the world.[3]

JEHOVAH WAS JESUS CHRIST

Jesus Christ was the Great Jehovah of the Old Testament. Where can we find this truth in the scriptures? We begin with Father Adam, who learned about salvation through Jesus Christ and was commanded, "Wherefore teach it unto your children, that all men, everywhere, must repent, or they can in nowise inherit the kingdom of God, for no unclean thing can dwell there, or dwell in his presence; for, in the language of Adam, Man of Holiness is his name, and the name of his Only Begotten is the Son of Man, even Jesus Christ, a righteous Judge, who shall come in the meridian of time" (Moses 6:57; see also v. 52).

Enoch was shown the Crucifixion of the Lord Jesus Christ: "And the Lord said unto Enoch: Look, and he looked and beheld the Son of Man lifted up on the cross, after the manner of men; and he heard a loud voice; and the heavens were veiled; and all the creations of God mourned; and the earth groaned; and the rocks were rent; and the saints arose, and were crowned at the right hand of the Son of Man, with crowns of glory" (Moses 7:55–56).

When the priests of Elkanah were about to offer up Abraham as a sacrifice to their "dumb idols" (see Abraham 1:7–15), he lifted up his voice to God. And to Abraham the Lord Jesus Christ declared, "Abraham, Abraham, behold, my name is Jehovah, and I have heard thee, and have come down to deliver thee" (Abraham 1:16; see also 2:7–8).

Abraham could forever afterward testify that His Savior and Redeemer and Deliverer was the Great Jehovah. Abraham understood that Jehovah would come to earth and minister among men as their Savior and Redeemer, as we learn from the following:

"And it came to pass, that Abram looked forth and saw the days of the Son of Man, and was glad, and his soul found rest, and he believed in the Lord; and the Lord counted it unto him for righteousness" (Joseph Smith Translation, Genesis 15:12, Bible appendix; see also Genesis 22:14; Helaman 8:13–23).

To Moses the Lord declared: "I am the God of thy father, the God of Abraham, the God of Isaac, and the God of Jacob. . . . I Am that I Am: and he said, Thus shalt thou say unto the children of Israel, I Am hath sent me unto you. . . . Thus shalt thou say unto the children of Israel, The Lord God of your fathers, the God of Abraham, the God of Isaac, and the God of Jacob, hath sent me unto you" (Exodus 3:6, 14–15).

Then, according to the King James Version, the Lord declared to Moses, "I am the Lord: And I appeared unto Abraham, unto Isaac, and unto Jacob, by the name of God Almighty, but by my name Jehovah was I not known to them" (Exodus 6:2–3).

The Joseph Smith Translation of this same verse reads differently: "And I appeared unto Abraham, unto Isaac, and unto Jacob. I am the Lord God Almighty; the Lord Jehovah. And was not my name known unto them?" (Exodus 6:3, Joseph Smith Translation in footnote *c*).

Also in the Joseph Smith Translation, we read, "For thou shalt worship no other god; for the Lord, whose name is Jehovah, is a jealous God" (Exodus 34:14, Joseph Smith Translation in footnote *c*).

And in Psalms we read, "Let them be confounded and troubled for ever [speaking of the enemies of God]; yea, let them be put to shame, and perish: that men may know that thou, whose name alone is Jehovah, art the most high over all the earth" (Psalm 83:17–18; see also 3 Nephi 11:14).

In the New Testament, John records the words of the Savior, which confirm His identity as the Great Jehovah, or I Am: "Your father Abraham rejoiced to see my day: and he saw it, and was glad. Then said the Jews unto him, Thou art not yet fifty years old, and hast thou seen Abraham? Jesus said unto them, Verily, verily, I say unto you, Before Abraham was, I am" (John 8:56–58). His testimony so offended the Jews that they took up stones to kill Him (see John 8:59).

In these latter days, the Lord Jesus Christ also has confirmed His identity as the Great Jehovah, or I Am, who spoke to Abraham and Moses. To the Prophet Joseph Smith in September 1830, the Lord declared, "Listen to the voice of Jesus Christ, your Redeemer, the Great I Am, whose arm of mercy hath atoned for your sins" (D&C 29:1).

And in a subsequent revelation through the Prophet Joseph, the Lord again declared, "Hearken and listen to the voice of him who is from all eternity to all eternity, the Great I Am, even Jesus Christ— the light and the life of the world; a light which shineth in darkness and the darkness comprehendeth it not; the same which came in the meridian of time unto mine own, and mine own received me not" (D&C 39:1–3; see also 38:1).

Then, when the Lord appeared in majesty and glory to the Prophet Joseph Smith and Oliver Cowdery in the Kirtland Temple, Joseph testified: "We saw the Lord standing upon the breastwork of the pulpit, before us; and under his feet was a paved work of pure gold, in color like amber. His eyes were as a flame of fire; the hair of his head was white like the pure snow; his countenance shone above the brightness of the sun; and his voice was as the sound of the rushing of great waters, even the voice of Jehovah, saying: I am the first and the last; I am he who liveth, I am he who was slain; I am your advocate with the Father" (D&C 110:2–4; see also Revelation 1:13–18).

The Lord Jesus Christ was indeed the Great Jehovah of the Old Testament and the Messiah of the New. He is the "Living Christ, the immortal Son" of the Living God, the Savior and Redeemer of the world.[4]

SALVATION COMES ONLY THROUGH JESUS CHRIST

Let us consider scriptures that reveal the central and fundamental message of the Old Testament—that salvation is obtained only in and through the name of Jesus Christ.

The book of Moses, which is Joseph Smith's translation of Genesis, reveals that all of the prophets from Adam to Noah understood the plan of salvation, or the gospel (see Moses 5:58–59). They understood that salvation is "only in and through the name of Christ" (Mosiah 3:17). For example, the Lord said to Adam, "If thou wilt turn unto me, and hearken unto my voice, and believe, and repent of all thy transgressions, and be baptized, even in water, in the name of mine Only Begotten Son, who is full of grace and truth, which is Jesus Christ, the only name which shall be given under heaven, whereby salvation shall come unto the children of men, ye shall receive the gift of the Holy Ghost, asking all things in his name, and whatsoever ye shall ask, it shall be given you" (Moses 6:52; see also 6:57–62; 7:45–47; 8:19–24).[5]

The Book of Mormon, most of which is essentially an Old Testament record, confirms that prophets in Old Testament times knew the plan of redemption and knew that salvation is only in and through the name of Jesus Christ. Nephi, son of Lehi, said: "According to the words of the prophets, the Messiah cometh in six hundred years from the time that my father left Jerusalem; and according to the words of the prophets, and also the word of the angel of God, his name shall be Jesus Christ, the Son of God. And now, my brethren, I have spoken plainly that ye cannot err. And as the Lord God liveth that brought Israel up out of the land of Egypt, . . . there is none other name given under heaven save it be this Jesus Christ, of which I have spoken, whereby man can be saved" (2 Nephi 25:19–20; see also 10:3; 31:2–21).

King Benjamin testified:

> Salvation cometh . . . through repentance and faith on the Lord Jesus Christ.
>
> And the Lord God hath sent his holy prophets among all the children of men, to declare these things to every kindred, nation, and tongue, that thereby whosoever should believe that Christ should come, the same might receive remission of their sins, and rejoice with exceedingly great joy, even as though he had already come among them. . . .
>
> And moreover, I say unto you, that there shall be no other name given nor any other way nor means whereby salvation can come unto the children of men, only in and through the name of Christ, the Lord Omnipotent. (Mosiah 3:12–13, 17; see also 5:7–8; 13:32–35; 1 Nephi 6:4; Alma 38:9; Helaman 5:9–11)

Before turning again to the Old Testament, we should note that ancient prophets referred to Jesus Christ by various names or titles, including God, Jehovah, Messiah, Savior, Redeemer, Deliverer, the God of Israel, the Holy One of Israel, and many others. We should also note that the Hebrew word for the name *Jehovah* was almost always translated in the King James Version of the Old Testament as "Lord," or "the Lord."[6] It appears thousands of times in the Old Testament.

A few representative passages from the Old Testament indicate that salvation is to be found only in and through the Lord Jesus Christ, whom we have shown to be the Great Jehovah. In most of the passages that follow, we may appropriately add the sacred name and title *Jesus Christ* after each use of the title *Lord* or *the Lord*.

From Psalms we read:

"The Lord [Jesus Christ] is my rock, and my fortress, and my deliverer; my God, my strength, in whom I will trust; my buckler, and the horn of my salvation, and my high tower" (Psalm 18:2; see also 27:1).

"O come, let us sing unto the Lord [Jesus Christ]: let us make a joyful noise to the rock of our salvation" (Psalm 95:1).

"I will take the cup of salvation, and call upon the name of the Lord [Jesus Christ]" (Psalm 116:13).

"I have longed for thy salvation, O Lord [Jesus Christ]; and thy law is my delight" (Psalm 119:174).

"For the Lord [Jesus Christ] taketh pleasure in his people: he will beautify the meek with salvation" (Psalm 149:4).

From the prophet Isaiah we read:

"Behold, God is my salvation; I will trust, and not be afraid: for the Lord Jehovah is my strength and my song; he also is become my salvation. Therefore with joy shall ye draw water out of the wells of salvation" (Isaiah 12:2–3).

"The Lord [Jesus Christ] is our judge, the Lord [Jesus Christ] is our lawgiver, the Lord [Jesus Christ] is our king; he will save us" (Isaiah 33:22).

"I, even I, am the Lord [Jesus Christ]; and beside me there is no saviour" (Isaiah 43:11; see also vv. 3, 15).

"For thy Maker is thine husband; the Lord of hosts is his name; and thy Redeemer the Holy One of Israel; The God of the whole earth shall he be called" (Isaiah 54:5; see also 41:14; 44:24; 48:17; 60:16; compare 3 Nephi 11:14).

Other Old Testament prophets bore similar testimony (such as we find in Job 19:25; Jeremiah 50:34; Hosea 13:4; Jonah 2:9; Micah 7:7; Habakkuk 3:8; Zechariah 9:9), for they knew, as have all the prophets from the beginning, to whom they should look for salvation.

In the New Testament, we read these powerful words of testimony spoken by the Apostle Peter, who had just healed a man in the name of Christ: "Be it known unto you all, and to all the people of Israel, that by the name of Jesus Christ of Nazareth, whom ye crucified, whom God raised from the dead, even by him doth this man stand here before you whole. This is the stone which was set at nought of you builders, which is become the head of the corner. Neither is there salvation in any other: for there is none other name under heaven given among men, whereby we must be saved" (Acts 4:10–12; see also 10:43; Psalm 118:22; Matthew 16:13–16).

John the Beloved, our Savior's disciple, summarized the purpose of his own writings and of all scripture when he testified, "These are written, that ye might believe that Jesus is the Christ, the Son of God; and that believing ye might have life through his name" (John 20:31; see also 2 Nephi 11:2–4; Jacob 7:10–11; Alma 33:14; Moses 6:63).

In Doctrine and Covenants, section 18, the Lord declares: "Take upon you the name of Christ, and speak the truth in soberness. And as many as repent and are baptized in my name, which is Jesus Christ, and endure to the end, the same shall be saved. Behold, Jesus Christ is the name which is given of the Father, and there is none other name given whereby man can be saved" (D&C 18:21–23).

And from section 20 of the Doctrine and Covenants, we read:

> As many as would believe and be baptized in his holy name, and endure in faith to the end, should be saved—
>
> Not only those who believed after he came in the meridian of time, in the flesh, but all those from the beginning, even as many as were before he came, who believed in the words of the holy prophets, who spake as they were inspired by the gift of the Holy Ghost, who truly testified of him in all things, should have eternal life,
>
> As well as those who should come after, who should believe in the gifts and callings of God by the Holy Ghost, which beareth record of the Father and of the Son; . . .
>
> And we know that all men must repent and believe on the name of Jesus Christ, and worship the Father in his name, and endure in faith on his name to the end, or they cannot be saved in the kingdom of God. (D&C 20:25–27, 29; see also 76:1; 109:4)

From the foregoing passages (as well as others that could be cited), we see that the central and fundamental message of the Old Testament, and indeed of all scriptures, is that salvation is only in and through the name of Jesus Christ.

THE OLD TESTAMENT BEARS WITNESS OF JESUS CHRIST

Let us consider how the Old Testament bears further witness of Jesus Christ. Perhaps the following account of the resurrected Lord speaking with two of His disciples as they journeyed to Emmaus (Luke 24:13–27) will illustrate: "Then [Jesus] said unto them, O fools, and slow of heart to believe all that the prophets have spoken: Ought not Christ to have suffered these things, and to enter into his glory? And beginning at Moses and all the prophets, he expounded unto them in all the scriptures the things concerning himself" (Luke 24:25–27).

That the Old Testament bears witness of the Lord Jesus Christ and His great mission of redemption is further illustrated in the account of what occurred when the risen Lord appeared to His disciples later that same evening. Luke records: "And [Jesus] said unto them, These are the words which I spake unto you, while I was yet with you, that all things must be fulfilled, which were written in the law of Moses, and in the prophets, and in the psalms, concerning me. Then opened he their understanding, that they might understand the scriptures, And said unto them, Thus it is written, and thus it behoved Christ to suffer, and to rise from the dead the third day" (Luke 24:44–46; see also vv. 33–43).

These words spoken by Peter on the day of Pentecost indicate that he understood that the Old Testament bears clear and powerful witness of Jesus Christ: "Those things, which God before had shewed by the mouth of all his prophets, that Christ should suffer, he hath so fulfilled" (Acts 3:18).

The Apostle Paul also confirms that the Old Testament bears clear and certain witness of Jesus Christ. He wrote to the Corinthian Saints, saying, "I delivered unto you first of all that which I also received, how that Christ died for our sins *according to the scriptures;* and that he was buried, and that he rose again the third day *according to the scriptures*" (1 Corinthians 15:3–4; emphasis added).

The Law of Moses, the Prophets, and the Psalms

We can only imagine what it would have been like to be among His disciples when the resurrected Lord appeared and "opened . . . their understanding, that they might understand the scriptures" (Luke 24:45). The Lord reminded His disciples that all things had to be fulfilled that were written "in the law of Moses, and in the prophets, and in the psalms" (Luke 24:44). Let us briefly consider what is written in the law of Moses, the prophets, and the Psalms concerning Jesus Christ.

THE LAW OF MOSES

What was the spirit and intent of the law of Moses, as recorded in the Old Testament? Nephi, son of Lehi, explains:

> Notwithstanding we believe in Christ, we keep the law of Moses, and look forward with steadfastness unto Christ, until the law shall be fulfilled.
>
> For, for this end was the law given; wherefore the law hath become dead unto us, and we are made alive in Christ because of our faith; yet we keep the law because of the commandments.
>
> And we talk of Christ, we rejoice in Christ, we preach of Christ, we prophesy of Christ, and we write according to our prophecies, that our children may know to what source they may look for a remission of their sins.
>
> Wherefore, we speak concerning the law that our children may know the deadness of the law; and they, by knowing the deadness of the law, may look forward unto that life which is in Christ, and know for what end the law was given. And after the law is fulfilled in Christ, that they need not harden their hearts against him when the law ought to be done away. (2 Nephi 25:24–27)

King Benjamin testified: "The Lord God saw that his people were a stiffnecked people, and he appointed unto them a law, even the law of Moses. And many signs, and wonders, and types, and shadows showed he unto them, concerning his coming; and also holy prophets spake unto them concerning his coming; and yet they hardened their hearts, and understood not that the law of Moses availeth nothing except it were through the atonement of his blood" (Mosiah 3:14–15; see also 2 Nephi 11:4; Jacob 4:5).

Abinadi declared:

> And now I say unto you that it was expedient that there should be a law given to the children of Israel, yea, even a very strict law; for they were a stiffnecked people, quick to do iniquity, and slow to remember the Lord their God;
>
> Therefore there was a law given them, yea, a law of performances and of ordinances, a law which they were to observe strictly from day to day, to keep them in remembrance of God and their duty towards him.

But behold, I say unto you, that all these things were types of things to come.

And now, did they understand the law? I say unto you, Nay, they did not all understand the law; and this because of the hardness of their hearts; for they understood not that there could not any man be saved except it were through the redemption of God. (Mosiah 13:29–32)

In Alma 25 we read:

Yea, and they did keep the law of Moses; for it was expedient that they should keep the law of Moses as yet, for it was not all fulfilled. But notwithstanding the law of Moses, they did look forward to the coming of Christ, considering that the law of Moses was a type of his coming, and believing that they must keep those outward performances until the time that he should be revealed unto them.

Now they did not suppose that salvation came by the law of Moses; but the law of Moses did serve to strengthen their faith in Christ; and thus they did retain a hope through faith, unto eternal salvation, relying upon the spirit of prophecy, which spake of those things to come. (Alma 25:15–16; see also 34:10–14)

We learn more about the law of Moses from the risen Lord, who declared to the Nephites: "Behold, I say unto you that the law is fulfilled that was given unto Moses. Behold, I am he that gave the law, and I am he who covenanted with my people Israel; therefore, the law in me is fulfilled, for I have come to fulfil the law; therefore it hath an end" (3 Nephi 15:4–5).

THE PROPHETS

As we have seen, all prophets—including Old Testament prophets—testify of Jesus Christ. Representative of all their words are passages from Isaiah. Let us consider a few of them. For example: "Therefore the Lord himself shall give you a sign; Behold, a virgin shall conceive, and bear a son, and shall call his name Immanuel" (Isaiah 7:14). Matthew testifies that the birth of Jesus to the virgin Mary is in fulfillment of Isaiah's prophecy regarding Immanuel: "And she shall bring forth a son, and thou shalt call his name Jesus: for he shall save his people from their sins. Now all this was done, that it might be fulfilled which was spoken of the Lord by the prophet, saying, Behold, a virgin shall be with child, and shall bring forth a son, and they shall call his name Emmanuel, which being interpreted is, God with us" (Matthew 1:21–23; see also D&C 128:22–24).

Now we turn to the immortal words of Isaiah that are familiar to unnumbered millions through the music of Handel's *Messiah:* "For unto us a child is born, unto us a son is given: and the government shall be upon his shoulder: and his name shall be called Wonderful, Counsellor, The mighty God, The everlasting Father, The Prince of Peace" (Isaiah 9:6).

Who is this "child"? "Whose Son is He?" (Matthew 22:42). Who is this "mighty God, The everlasting Father, The Prince of Peace" spoken of by Isaiah? The scriptures reveal clearly who He is.

He is Jesus Christ, born into this world as the "Only Begotten Son" (Jacob 4:5, 11)[7] of God "the Eternal Father" and the son of Mary "after the manner of the flesh" (1 Nephi 11:21, 18).[8]

He is Jesus Christ, the long-awaited "Messiah," the "Savior" and "Redeemer of the world" (1 Nephi 10:4–5),[9] of whom all "the prophets testified" (3 Nephi 11:10).[10]

He is Jesus Christ, the "Lamb of God," who was "judged of the world; . . . lifted up upon the cross" (1 Nephi 11:32–33)[11] and "crucified" (1 Nephi 19:10)[12] to "atone for the sins of the world" (Alma 34:8).[13]

He is Jesus Christ, who, before condescending to "come down from heaven" to dwell "among the children of men" (Mosiah 3:5),[14] was none other than the Great Jehovah, who gave "the law" unto Moses on the mount (3 Nephi 15:5).

He is Jesus Christ, "the Father of heaven and earth, the Creator of all things from the beginning" (Mosiah 3:8),[15] whose "infinite atonement" (2 Nephi 9:7)[16] brings "the resurrection of the dead" (Helaman 14:15).[17]

He is Jesus Christ, "the Eternal Judge of both [the] quick and [the] dead" (Moroni 10:34).[18]

He is Jesus Christ, "the Lord Omnipotent who reigneth, who was, and is from all eternity to all eternity" (Mosiah 3:5).[19]

Isaiah 53 is another glorious prophecy. It fulfills the very purpose and spirit of prophecy as explained by the Apostle John when he declared, "The testimony of Jesus is the spirit of prophecy" (Revelation 19:10). Isaiah eloquently describes and bears testimony of the life and mortal ministry and of the infinite Atonement wrought by the Lord Jesus Christ. He prophesies that Christ will be "despised and rejected of men" (Isaiah 53:3), that He will "[bear] our griefs, and [carry] our sorrows" (v. 4) and heal us with His "stripes" (v. 5). Isaiah also foresaw that despite being "oppressed, and . . . afflicted, yet he opened not his mouth, . . . as a lamb to the slaughter" (v. 7). Latter-day prophets and New Testament writers alike testify that Isaiah's prophecy refers to the mission and death of Christ.[20]

Perhaps the most compelling evidence confirming that Isaiah 53 is a prophecy of the Lord Jesus Christ is the testimony of Abinadi, which, like the Book of Mormon itself, cries from the dust to all the world (see 2 Nephi 26:12–17; 33:4–13; Mormon 8:14–24; Moroni 10:27).

Abinadi, facing a martyr's death at the hands of King Noah and his priests, quoted the whole of Isaiah 53 (see Mosiah 14) and explained its meaning (see Mosiah 15), thus confirming his witness that the Messiah who would come and atone for the sins of mankind was the very same Lord of whom Isaiah bore such powerful and prophetic witness!

It is noteworthy that Abinadi, in the face of death, testified of Christ, who would come to break the bands of death, as if He had already come. Abinadi declared:

> And now if Christ had not come into the world, speaking of things to come as though they had already come, there could have been no redemption.
>
> And if Christ had not risen from the dead, or have broken the bands of death that the grave should have no victory, and that death should have no sting, there could have been no resurrection.
>
> But there is a resurrection, therefore the grave hath no victory, and the sting of death is swallowed up in Christ.
>
> He is the light and the life of the world; yea, a light that is endless, that can never be darkened; yea, and also a life which is endless, that there can be no more death. (Mosiah 16:6–9; see also vv. 10–15)

We would all do well to examine our own testimony of the Lord Jesus Christ in light of the testimony of Abinadi.

Finally, from Isaiah 61 we read, "The Spirit of the Lord God is upon me; because the Lord hath anointed me to preach good tidings unto the meek; he hath sent me to bind up the brokenhearted, to proclaim liberty to the captives, and the opening of the prison to them that are bound; to proclaim the acceptable year of the Lord, and the day of vengeance of our God; to comfort all that mourn" (Isaiah 61:1–2).

Jesus leaves absolutely no doubt about the meaning of these prophetic words. Having commenced His mortal ministry, He returned to Nazareth and "went into the synagogue on the sabbath day, and stood up for to read." He then read Isaiah 61:1 and 2. Then, having closed the book, He sat down and said, "This day is this scripture fulfilled in your ears" (see Luke 4:16–21).

THE PSALMS

Now we shall consider a few selected passages from the Psalms. It is significant to note that the Savior and other New Testament writers quoted more frequently from the Psalms than from any other book in the Old Testament.

We begin with the psalm containing some of the very words spoken by the Savior from the cross, as He hung in unspeakable agony: "My God, my God, why hast thou forsaken me? why art thou so far from helping me, and from the words of my roaring?" (Psalm 22:1; see also Matthew 27:46).

Now consider these prophetic words which so graphically describe the feelings, the humiliation, the suffering, and the agony endured by the Savior during His Crucifixion:

"All they that see me laugh me to scorn: they shoot out the lip, they shake the head, saying, He trusted on the Lord that he would deliver him: let him deliver him, seeing he delighted in him" (Psalm 22:7–8; see also Matthew 27:39–43).

"I am poured out like water, and all my bones are out of joint: my heart is like wax; it is melted in the midst of my bowels. My strength is dried up like a potsherd; and my tongue cleaveth to my jaws; and thou hast brought me into the dust of death. For dogs have compassed me: the assembly of the wicked have inclosed me: they pierced my hands and my feet. I may tell all my bones: they look and stare upon me. They part my garments among them, and cast lots upon my vesture" (Psalm 22:14–18; see also Matthew 27:35; Mark 15:24–25; John 19:37).

"Reproach hath broken my heart; and I am full of heaviness: and I looked for some to take pity, but there was none; and for comforters, but I found none. They gave me also gall for my meat; and in my thirst they gave me vinegar to drink" (Psalm 69:20–21; see also John 19:28–30).

In the following psalm, we see clear reference to the betrayal of Jesus by Judas: "Yea, mine own familiar friend, in whom I trusted, which did eat of my bread, hath lifted up his heel against me" (Psalm 41:9; see also 55:12–13; Matthew 26:20–23; John 13:18–19).

Verses from the Psalms also give us references to scenes from the ministry and teachings and Resurrection of Jesus Christ:

"He shall give his angels charge over thee, to keep thee in all thy ways. They shall bear thee up in their hands, lest thou dash thy foot against a stone" (Psalm 91:11–12; see also Matthew 4:5–6; 26:53; Luke 4:10–11).

"Then they cry unto the Lord in their trouble, and he bringeth them out of their distresses. He maketh the storm a calm, so that the waves thereof are still" (Psalm 107:28–29; see also 89:8–9; Matthew 8:24–27).

"The stone which the builders refused is become the head stone of the corner" (Psalm 118:22; see also Matthew 21:42; Acts 4:10–12).

"And [God] had rained down manna upon them to eat, and had given them of the corn of heaven" (Psalm 78:24; see also vv. 25–27; John 6:31–35).

"I have said, Ye are gods; and all of you are children of the most High" (Psalm 82:6; see also Matthew 5:48; John 10:34–36).

"Therefore my heart is glad, and my glory rejoiceth: my flesh also shall rest in hope. For thou wilt not leave my soul in hell; neither wilt thou suffer thine Holy One to see corruption" (Psalm 16:9–10; see also Acts 2:22–32).

"The Lord said unto my Lord, Sit thou at my right hand, until I make thine enemies thy footstool" (Psalm 110:1; see also Matthew 22:41–45).

Conclusion

From the passages cited, and a host of others that could be, we can see that the Old Testament is a precious and powerful witness of Jesus Christ. Prophets ancient and modern bear solemn witness that salvation is possible only in and through His holy name.

Notes

1. *Doctrines of Salvation,* comp. Bruce R. McConkie, 3 vols. (1954–56), 1:27.

2. In Conference Report, April 1977, 113; or *Ensign,* May 1977, 76.

3. *Ensign,* April 2000, 2–3.

4. *Ensign,* April 2000, 3.

5. It should be noted that in Moses 6:52 and 59 (as also in D&C 29:1, 41–46), the Lord Jesus Christ speaks as if He were God the Father. By the law of divine investiture, the Son represents the Father in all matters here upon the earth, so He may speak as if He were God the Father. For a better understanding of this principle, see "The Father and the Son: A Doctrinal Exposition by the First Presidency and the Twelve," in James R. Clark, comp., *Messages of the First Presidency of The Church of Jesus Christ of Latter-day Saints,* 6 vols. (1965–75), 5:26–34; reprinted in James E. Talmage, *The Articles of Faith,* 12th ed. (1924), 465–73.

6. See James E. Talmage, *Jesus the Christ,* 3rd ed. (1916), 36–37.

7. See also John 1:14, 18; 1 John 4:9; 2 Nephi 25:12; D&C 49:5; 76:13; 93:11; Moses 5:57.

8. See also Galatians 4:4; 2 Nephi 32:6; Mosiah 3:8.

9. See also John 1:41; 4:42; Revelation 5:9; 1 Nephi 1:19; 10:6–17; 2 Nephi 2:6–10; D&C 13; 18:47; 43:34; 93:7–9.

10. See also Mosiah 3:13; Helaman 8:13–23.

11. See also John 1:29; Moses 7:47.

12. See also Matthew 28:5; Acts 2:36; 1 Nephi 19:9, 13–15; 2 Nephi 6:9; Mosiah 3:9; 15:7–9; D&C 20:23; 45:52.

13. See also 1 Peter 3:18; Mosiah 3:11–18; Alma 22:14; 33:22–23; D&C 35:2; 46:13; 53:2.

14. See also John 1:14; 6:38; Hebrews 2:9; Mosiah 3:6–8; D&C 88:6.

15. See also John 1:3; Hebrews 1:2; 2 Nephi 9:6; Alma 11:39; Helaman 14:12; 3 Nephi 9:15; D&C 38:1–3; 76:24; Moses 1:33.

16. See also 2 Nephi 2:6–10; Alma 34:8–16; 36:17–18; D&C 76:40–42, 69.

17. See also Philippians 3:21; 1 John 3:2; 2 Nephi 9:9–13, 21–22; Jacob 4:11–12; Alma 11:42–45; 40:23; Helaman 14:16–19; D&C 88:16–17.

18. See also John 5:22; Acts 10:34–42; Romans 2:16; 14:10; 2 Nephi 9:13–17, 41; Mosiah 3:10, 18; 3 Nephi 27:13–15; Mormon 3:20–22; Moses 6:57.

19. See also Matthew 28:18; Ephesians 1:22; Revelation 19:6; Mosiah 3:6–8, 18; 5:15.

20. See *Doctrines of Salvation,* 1:23–25; *Jesus the Christ,* 47, 655; Matthew 8:17; John 12:38; Acts 8:27–35; 1 Peter 2:24–25.

CHAPTER THREE

THE OLD TESTAMENT: A VOICE FROM THE PAST AND A WITNESS FOR THE LORD JESUS CHRIST

ROBERT J. MATTHEWS

Many well-known phrases from the Old Testament have entered our current language: a good old age (Genesis 25:8); the apple of his eye (Psalm 17:8); a mother in Israel (Judges 5:7); a land of milk and honey (Joshua 5:6); the windows of heaven (Malachi 3:10); the valley of decision (Joel 3:14); a still, small voice (1 Kings 19:12); precept upon precept, line upon line (Isaiah 28:10); a drop in the bucket (Isaiah 40:15); in the hollow of his hand (Isaiah 40:12); trodden the winepress alone (Isaiah 63:3); the rose of Sharon, the lily of the valley (Song of Solomon 2:1); can a leopard change its spots (Jeremiah 13:23); I was saved by the skin of my teeth (Job 19:20); my hair stood on end (Job 4:15); handwriting on the wall (Daniel 5:24); nothing new under the sun (Ecclesiastes 6:1); a coat of many colors (Genesis 37:32); mantle of the prophet (2 Kings 2:13–14); a mess of pottage (Genesis 25:34); and God save the king (1 Samuel 10:24).

The Old Testament offers some help in rearing teenagers. The records say that when Jacob first met Rachel he kissed her. Seminary students are usually quick to point out that this was a first date.

The next verse says she brought her father to meet Jacob,

Robert J. Matthews, who has served as dean of Religious Education, is professor emeritus of ancient scripture at Brigham Young University.

whereupon Jacob also kissed *him*. The moral of the story: You can kiss the girl if you are also willing to kiss her father (see Genesis 29:10–14).

The purpose of the scripture is to bear witness of Jesus Christ, and that it does very well. You recall the statement of Jesus: "Search the scriptures, . . . for they are they which testify of me" (John 5:39). The Old Testament testified of Jesus even better in its original condition.

THE LAW, THE PROPHETS, AND THE WRITINGS

The Old Testament is not a single book but a collection of books, covering events from the Creation of the world until just before the time of Jesus. In the present King James Version this consists of thirty-nine books. In the editions of the Bible used by the Catholic Church, there are forty-six Old Testament books, because they include seven books commonly called the Apocrypha. Early editions of the King James Version also contained the Apocrypha, but for the past one hundred years or so, the majority of the printings of the King James Version have not included the apocryphal books. The King James Old Testament Apocrypha consisted of fifteen books, but it is the same material as the seven in the Catholic Bible, just divided and distributed differently. The Old Testament Apocrypha are primarily books of history rather than doctrine and are not equal to such great works as Genesis, Deuteronomy, or Isaiah.

Hebrew editions of the Old Testament generally contain the same thirty-nine books as the King James Version but are sometimes given different titles.

The way in which these books are arranged, however, differs greatly in the Hebrew, King James, and Catholic Old Testament. For example, in the King James Version the arrangement of the thirty-nine books is according to literary style and content. First are the history books, then the poetical or "wisdom" books, then the prophetic books. Thus, Genesis is the first book, 2 Chronicles is about in the middle, and Malachi is the last book in the Old Testament. In the introductory pages of the Bible, you will find a chart showing the names and order of all the books of the Old Testament. From Genesis through Esther are the history books. Job through Song of Solomon are the wisdom books. These also include Psalms, Proverbs, and Ecclesiastes. Then from Isaiah through Malachi are the books of the prophets. This follows a somewhat chronological order, although it is not strictly chronological. The Catholic Bibles have the same literary arrangement as the King James but with the added apocryphal books inserted at various places.

If you examine a Hebrew Old Testament, you will find the books in a much different order, emphasizing the importance of the books; hence they are grouped as the Law, the Prophets, and the Writings. Thus the five books of Moses are first, since they constitute the Torah, or Law. Next are the Prophets; those from Joshua to Kings being called "early prophets" and from Isaiah through Malachi being called the "later prophets." In the third place are the Writings, being the wisdom books, and also Ruth, Ezra, Nehemiah, Daniel, and Chronicles. Therefore, in the Hebrew editions of the Old Testament, Malachi is about in the middle, and the last book is 2 Chronicles. As Latter-day Saints, being so familiar with quoting Malachi about the coming of Elijah, we would have a little difficulty getting used to looking for Malachi in the middle instead of at the end of the Old Testament. Among the ancient rabbis and scholars, this order of the sacred books was zealously guarded and great deference was given to the Law, or as it was called, the Torah.

Bible scholars have frequently identified the prophets as major or minor prophets, this having reference to how large the book is, not how important the person is. Thus, Isaiah and Jeremiah would be "major" prophets, whereas Jonah and Joel would be "minor" prophets. It is a designation that could be easily misunderstood, and we generally do not use that terminology in the Church.

THE OLD TESTAMENT AS A WITNESS FOR JESUS CHRIST

This threefold arrangement—the Law, the Prophets, and the Writings—is reflected in the New Testament in the words of Jesus. Let us turn to Luke 24. On the road to Emmaus, Jesus, newly resurrected, walked a few miles with two disciples who were sad that their Master had been crucified. He asked them the cause of their sorrow. They, not recognizing Him, told Him that Jesus was crucified and that there was a rumor that He had risen from the dead but they were not so sure of it. Then Jesus opened the scriptures (the Old Testament) to them: "Then he said unto them, O fools, and slow of heart to believe all that the prophets have spoken: Ought not Christ to have suffered these things, and to enter into his glory? And beginning at Moses and all the prophets, he expounded unto them in all the scriptures the things concerning himself" (Luke 24:25–27).

You see the order—Moses, then the Prophets. Later that day, reflecting on how they felt, they said one to another, "Did not our heart burn within us, while he talked with us by the way, and while he opened to us the scriptures?" (Luke 24:32). The purpose of the scripture is to bear witness of Jesus Christ, and when we read it properly, and with understanding, our hearts are warmed and our soul is thrilled by it.

Later that same day, Jesus met with the Twelve and showed them His perfect, resurrected body of flesh and bone, and He ate with them and then "he said unto them, These are the words which I spake unto you, while I was yet with you, that all things must be fulfilled, which were written in the law of Moses, and in the prophets, and in the psalms, concerning me. Then opened he their understanding, that they might understand the scriptures, And said unto them, Thus it is written, and thus it behoved Christ to suffer, and to rise from the dead the third day" (Luke 24:44–46).

You notice how clearly the purpose of the Old Testament is explained as a witness for the Messiah. We see also the order of the books as they were in that day—the Law, the Prophets, and the Writings. Note also the great spiritual effect the scriptures had upon their feelings.

The Old Testament truly is a witness for Jesus Christ. Because of latter-day revelation in the Book of Mormon, Doctrine and Covenants, Pearl of Great Price, and the Joseph Smith Translation of the Bible, we are able to see that all of the ancient prophets were Christian prophets, and every dispensation was a gospel dispensation. Thus, from Adam to John the Baptist, the so-called Old Testament prophets were acquainted with the gospel and with the plan of salvation, and the coming of Jesus Christ as the one and only Savior and Messiah of all mankind. Let us cite just a few examples:

In John 1:45 we read that when Philip first met Jesus he went to get his friend Nathanael and said to him: "We have found him of whom Moses in the law, and the prophets, did write."

In John 5:45–47 we hear Jesus saying to the Jewish rulers: "Do not think that I will accuse you to the Father: there is one that accuseth you, even Moses, in whom ye trust. For had ye believed Moses, ye would have believed me: for he wrote of me. But if ye believe not his writings, how shall ye believe my words?"

There are many more examples, such as 1 Corinthians 10:1–4; 2 Corinthians 3:12–16; Hebrews 4:2; 11:24–26. In the Book of Mormon we find Jacob saying at about 544 B.C.: "We knew of Christ, and we had a hope of his glory many hundred years before his coming; and not only we ourselves . . . but also all the holy prophets which were before us" (Jacob 4:4), and later Jacob declared, "None of the prophets have written, nor prophecied, save they have spoken concerning this Christ" (Jacob 7:11).

And finally in Helaman 8:16–19:

> And now behold, Moses did not only testify of these things, but also all the holy prophets, from his days even to the days of Abraham.
>
> Yea, and behold, Abraham saw of his coming, and was filled with gladness and did rejoice.
>
> Yea, and behold I say unto you, that Abraham not only knew of these things, but there were many before the days of Abraham who were called by the order of God; yea, even after the order of his Son; and this that it should be shown unto the people, a great many thousand years before his coming, that even redemption should come unto them.
>
> And now I would that ye should know, that even since the days of Abraham there have been many prophets that have testified these things.

Time will not permit us to multiply evidences on this point, except one from the Doctrine and Covenants 20:25–26: "That as many as would believe and be baptized in his holy name, and endure in faith to the end, should be saved—not only those who believed after he came in the meridian of time, in the flesh, but all those from the beginning, even as many as were before he came, who believed in the words of the holy prophets, who spake as they were inspired by the gift of the Holy Ghost, who truly testified of him in all things, should have eternal life."

LATTER-DAY REVELATION CLARIFIES THE OLD TESTAMENT

In view of these declarations, it is evident that the Old Testament, as it has come to us today, is not as clear, not as complete, as it was anciently. Many plain and precious things have been taken from it, even entire books have been removed, and also many deletions have occurred in the books that we do have. Thus we need the benefit of latter-day revelation such as the Book of Mormon, the Doctrine and Covenants, the Joseph Smith Translation, the Pearl of Great Price, and the teachings of the Prophet Joseph Smith to give us a perspective and understanding of the Old Testament. Without latter-day revelation, a correct and thorough viewpoint of the Old Testament cannot be achieved, and hence I am bold to declare that the Latter-day Saints can have a more correct understanding of the Old Testament than anyone else upon the face of the earth. We may not always have as much cultural and linguistic appreciation, but we have a clearer doctrinal and spiritual perception of the Old Testament than anyone else. Without these latter-day scriptures and the personal witness of the Holy Ghost, the Old Testament is a sealed book.

GENESIS INTRODUCES THE WORK OF GOD ON THE EARTH

Each book of the Old Testament has a unique and special contribution, and offers something valuable to our understanding. For example, the name Genesis means the beginning, or "beginnings" (plural). I used to think it meant only the beginning of the earth, since the Creation is outlined there. However, as I became more familiar with it, I came to realize that Genesis is an indispensable book for understanding all the scriptures. Elder Bruce R. McConkie called Genesis a "book of books."[1] Since we now have the Joseph Smith Translation of Genesis, we have a very good concept of what the book of Genesis originally contained. It really is a book of several "beginnings." It tells of the beginning of this earth on which we live. It says that God deliberately and intentionally created it. It tells of the beginning of life on the earth; the beginning of man; the beginning of sin, introduced by Satan, and the Fall of Adam introducing mortality; and the beginning of death, both physical and spiritual death. It tells of the beginning of the gospel being taught on the earth to the first man and the first woman. It describes the beginning of the tribes and families and nations of mankind. Among the many beginnings is mentioned the beginning of a covenant people—the beginning of the house of Israel.

It is interesting how the book of Genesis allots various space to each of its topics. The Creation is covered in two chapters. The early years of man are also covered rather quickly. The time from Adam's Fall to Abraham is recorded in only eight chapters. The story of Abraham, who lived 175 years, requires at least a dozen chapters alone, (that ought to tell us something of his importance), and the story of Jacob and Joseph and the founding of the house of Israel (totaling probably two hundred years) requires all the way from Genesis chapters 27 to 50—twenty-four chapters for only two hundred years. You can see that the purpose of Genesis is to get the idea clearly before us of the importance of the Abrahamic covenant, the house of Israel, and the prominence of Joseph.

LATTER-DAY ISRAEL

A majority of Church members are descendants of Abraham through Joseph and Ephraim. Brothers and sisters, the Old Testament is your book! The book of Genesis, which tells of all these beginnings, tells of your beginnings. When we read the Old Testament, we rejoice in the promises and the covenants of the Lord and reflect on our beginnings. The book of Genesis is the indispensable introduction to the rest of the Old Testament and to the New Testament and to all of the standard works.

The Book of Mormon speaks of the Old Testament in these terms:

> And the angel said unto me: Knowest thou the meaning of the book?
>
> And I said unto him: I know not.
>
> And he said: Behold it proceedeth out of the mouth of a Jew. And I, Nephi, beheld it; and he said unto me: The book that thou beholdest is a record of the Jews, which contains the covenants of the Lord, which he hath made unto the house of Israel; and it also containeth many of the prophecies of the holy prophets; and it is a record like unto the engravings which are upon the plates of brass, save there are not so many; nevertheless, they contain the covenants of the Lord, which he hath made unto the house of Israel; wherefore, they are of great worth unto the Gentiles. (1 Nephi 13:21–23)

If we will listen, read, study, and pray, we can gain a greater understanding and a stronger commitment as to who we are and what God wants us to do than we have ever before had in our lives. The Old Testament teaches emphatically the law of obedience, the law of sacrifice, the law of retribution, and the law of compensation. It is a book about faith and the consequences of right and wrongdoing. It teaches that God fulfills His promises and keeps His covenants.

GOD'S PURPOSES AND PLANS

The following is an excerpt from an editorial in the *Deseret News* for February 7, 1852. Although it is unsigned, it sounds very much like President Brigham Young:

> Some have supposed that it would make but little difference with them whether they learned much or little, whether they attained to all the intelligence within their reach or not while they tarry in this world, believing that if they paid their tithing, went to meetings, said their prayers, and performed those duties which were especially commanded, that . . . as soon as they lay off this mortal body all would be well with them. But this is a mistaken idea and will cause every soul to mourn who embraces and practices upon it. When they arrive in the world of resurrected bodies, they will realize, to their sorrow that God required of them in this world not only obedience to His revealed will, *but a searching after His purposes and plans.* (Emphasis added)

You note the phrase "searching after His purposes and plans." I am reminded of a statement by Elder Sterling W. Sill, who said, "It isn't enough just to obey the Lord; we ought to agree with Him."[2] Agreeing with God has something to do with having a knowledge of His purposes and plans for the earth and the people on this earth. Isaiah was a master at this, and that is one reason his book is so valuable. When we read the Old Testament, the Book of Mormon, the Doctrine and Covenants, and the Pearl of Great Price, we begin to get a feeling for the work of God on this earth and for our own individual destiny. There is not anything else in the world like that feeling! What does it mean to be a child of God? What does it mean to be a member of The Church of Jesus Christ of Latter-day Saints? What does it mean to bear the holy priesthood? What does it mean to be part of the covenant of Abraham? What does it mean to be of the house of Israel? These are all answered in the holy scriptures.

A NEED FOR SCRIPTURE STUDY

Sometimes we get so burdened and weary with the problems of every day that we momentarily lose sight of our beginnings and our eternal destiny. We forget to study, and we lose perspective. I will share a few words from some of the Brethren.

President Spencer W. Kimball:

> I hope that you teachers will involve students heavily in scripture reading. I find that when I get casual in my relationships with divinity and when it seems that no divine ear is listening and no divine voice speaking, that I am far, far away. If I immerse myself in the scriptures, the distance narrows and the spirituality returns. I find myself loving more intensely those whom I must love with all my heart and might and mind and strength. And loving them more, I find it easier to abide their counsel. We learn the lessons of life more readily and surely if we see the results of wickedness and righteousness in the lives of others. . . . All through the scriptures every weakness and strength of man has been portrayed, and rewards and punishments have been recorded. One would surely be blind who could not learn to live properly by such reading.[3]

And from Elder Orson Pratt:

> We are commanded over and over again to treasure up wisdom in our hearts continually—to treasure up the words of eternal life continually, and make ourselves acquainted not only with the ancient revelation, but with the modern; to make ourselves acquainted not only with things pertaining to time, but with things pertaining to eternity. . . . [The faithful and diligent Saint] is not the ill-instructed scribe, . . . not the person who does not study, . . . not the person who suffers his time to run to idleness, but . . . that man that instructs himself in all things within his reach, so far as his circumstances and abilities will allow.[4]

While reflecting upon the constant effort and diligence required to learn great truths, Elder Pratt concluded:

> We need not be discouraged upon this subject; for if we do the best we can according to the position in which we are placed, and the opportunities which we have, we do all that the Lord requires; and by and by we shall be placed in a condition in which we can learn much faster than we can now. . . . Perhaps the man who, under a sense of discouragement, gives up and does not make the best of his present limited opportunities, will be limited hereafter in the life to come, and will not be allowed to progress very fast, because of his laziness and his want of desire, courage and fortitude to pursue certain channels of knowledge that were opened up to him here in this life. But when we see individuals not only willing to receive some few of the simple principles of the Gospel of Christ, but are willing to press onward towards perfection as far as opportunities present themselves, we may rest satisfied that they will be honored of the Lord according to their diligence, perseverance, fortitude and patience in striving to understand the laws which he has given to all things.[5]

And once again from Elder Orson Pratt: "[In the scripture we find] information, expressed so simply that a common mind can, in some degree, grasp it, and yet so sublime and so great that when we come to investigate its depths, it requires greater powers and greater understanding than what man naturally possesses."[6]

Elder John A. Widtsoe: "It is a paradox that men will gladly devote time every day for many years to learn a science or an art; yet will expect to win a knowledge of the gospel, which comprehends all sciences and arts, through perfunctory glances at books or occasional listening to sermons. The gospel should be studied more intensively than any school or college subject."[7]

The Jewish rabbis, ancient and modern, study the Torah—the Law. They say everyone should study Torah. The question may be asked, "Why?" "Because God studies Torah." That is, "Learning is a sacred and divine activity." As we progress in the things of God, our status changes. At first we are strangers and foreigners, but when we accept the gospel and are baptized and commit ourselves to Christ, we are "no more strangers and foreigners, but fellowcitizens with the saints, and of the household of God; and are built upon the foundation of the apostles and prophets, Jesus Christ himself being the chief corner stone" (Ephesians 2:19–20). We then become servants of God and of Christ. Continued faithfulness leads to even greater privileges and joys. Jesus said, "Ye are my friends, if ye do whatsoever I command you. Henceforth I call you not servants; for the servant knoweth not what his lord doeth, but I have called you friends; for all things that I have heard of my Father I have made known unto you" (John 15:14–15). In other words, friends are made privy to God's purposes and plans.

You see, our responsibility is not simply to go to a lot of tiring meetings and just stay out of trouble. We have the privilege and the invitation from the Savior to learn of His purposes and to share in His plans. That is what He wants us to do.

LATTER-DAY REVELATION EXPLAINS WHY

I mentioned earlier that the Old Testament, because of its present imperfect state, glorious as it is, must be supplemented by latter-day revelation. I will give one quick example. I have found that by and large, the Bible tells *what* but not always *why*. The plain and precious parts taken away have omitted many of the *whys*. For example, Genesis plainly says that "in the beginning God created the heaven and the earth" (Genesis 1:1). That tells *what*. But Genesis does not elaborate on *why*. If we turn to Abraham 3:24–25, we read that God created the earth as a place whereon His spirit children could come and dwell and be proved. In 1 Nephi 17:36 we find Nephi saying that the Lord "created the earth that it should be inhabited." These are statements of purpose. They tell why. Then in D&C 49:16–18 we read that marriage is ordained of God and that the bearing of children is a divine accomplishment, so that "the earth might answer the end [purpose] of its creation." Then in D&C 88:17–20, we read that this earth was made as a home for people not only in mortality, but forever as a celestial home. Thus, from latter-day revelation we learn not only what God did but also why.

Teaching Aids

With this point in mind, as to how latter-day revelation clarifies and supplements the Old Testament, I call your attention to the teaching aids in the Latter-day Saint edition of the Bible. The chapter headings are the commentary; the footnotes help us to find their related scriptures and explain Hebrew terms and idioms. The Joseph Smith Translation gives us much additional information. The Topical Guide makes it possible to look up 3,495 gospel subjects and find many scriptures from each of the standard works that bear upon each topic. The scriptures in the Topical Guide are always arranged in the order of Old Testament, New Testament, Book of Mormon, Doctrine and Covenants, and the Pearl of Great Price for each subject. Having them arranged this way permits them to bear a forceful and repeated witness that there is unity in the scriptures. When you can look up a single subject and find passages from the Old Testament, New Testament, the Book of Mormon, the Doctrine and Covenants, and the Pearl of Great Price that all bear upon that single subject, and then do that on thousands of subjects, you come to realize that there is a great harmony in the word of the Lord. It also soon becomes apparent that latter-day revelation generally says it better than does the Bible, due to the faulty biblical transmission.

The Latter-day Saint edition of the Bible contains the following study aids: (1) the text of the King James Version; (2) cross-references to latter-day scriptures such as the Book of Mormon, the Doctrine and Covenants, and the Pearl of Great Price; (3) excerpts from Joseph Smith's translation of the Bible; (4) explanatory footnotes showing alternate readings from Hebrew; (5) clarifications of obsolete words and idioms in the English language; (6) all-new interpretive chapter headings; (7) a Topical Guide, and (8) a Bible Dictionary. The Latter-day Saint edition was not to make of a bad edition a good one but to make of a good one an even better one. Thus is brought together the best of three worlds. It combines source material available today through (1) secular scholarship and (2) through latter-day revelation. Furthermore, (3) this edition was made possible only through modern technology such as improved printing presses and computers and high-quality paper and ink. Today thousands of sheets can be printed in one hour. Compare that with Mr. Gutenberg's experience when it took seven years to print just one Bible. The modern computer made the cross-referencing and footnoting possible.

DOCTRINAL RESTORATION AND TECHNOLOGICAL IMPROVEMENTS

The increase of technical know-how in the past century is tremendous. And at the same time there has come an equally great increase of spiritual learning and doctrinal clarification. With the Restoration of the gospel through the Prophet Joseph Smith, there was as much improvement in spiritual and doctrinal knowledge compared to the dark ages as there was in the technical improvement of printing presses and industrial equipment compared to Gutenberg's day. Thus, we can understand the Old Testament better today than ever before because of the insights from latter-day revelation, and we can make source materials about it more readily available because of improved industrial processes.

In religious circles, prophets supersede scholars, and divine revelation has greatly enlarged our fund of source material over the limited knowledge secular scholarship provided in the days before the Restoration of the gospel. And it is not an either-or situation. We have the knowledge of divine revelation and also the benefit of secular scholarship and industrial technology. We could not have had the Latter-day Saint edition if it had not been for the Protestant Reformation, the invention of printing, the Restoration of the gospel, and modern technology such as the computer, Xerox machine, printing press, the telephone, and photography.

NOTES

1. Bruce R. McConkie, *New Witness for the Articles of Faith* (Salt Lake City: Deseret Book, 1993), 392.
2. Sterling W. Sill, in Robert Matthews, *Selected Writings of Robert J. Matthews* (Salt Lake City: Deseret Book, 1999), 110.
3. Spencer W. Kimball, address to seminary and institute personnel at Brigham Young University, July 11, 1966.
4. Orson Pratt, in *Journal of Discourses* (London: Latter-day Saints' Book Depot, 1855–56), 7:74–75.
5. Orson Pratt, in *Journal of Discourses,* 17:329.
6. Orson Pratt, in *Journal of Discourses,* 17:324.
7. John A. Widtsoe, *Evidences and Reconciliations* (Salt Lake City: Bookcraft, 1960), 16–17.

CHAPTER FOUR

Prophets and Priesthood in the Old Testament

ROBERT L. MILLET

The prophetic voice is a voice of authority, divine authority. Those called to speak for the Lord Jehovah are empowered by Jehovah and ordained to His holy order. Thus it seems appropriate to devote some attention to the nature of prophetic authority—the power of the holy priesthood among the prophets in ancient Israel.

Joseph Smith the Prophet wrote in 1842, "We believe in the same organization that existed in the Primitive Church, namely, apostles, prophets, pastors, teachers, evangelists, and so forth" (Articles of Faith 1:6). When the time was right, when God the Eternal Father elected in His infinite wisdom to reestablish His kingdom on earth, He began to restore the basic priesthoods, offices, quorums, and councils that had been put in place by Jesus in the meridian of time. The "marvellous work and a wonder" foreseen by Isaiah (Isaiah 29:14) would also entail a restoration of the Church of Jesus Christ that had existed in the centuries preceding the mortal ministry of Jesus (see D&C 107:4). That restoration would consist of Old Testament truths, powers, priesthoods, covenants, and ordinances, such that "a whole and complete and perfect union, and welding together of dispensations, and keys, and powers, and glories should take place, and be revealed from the days of Adam even to the present time. And not only this, but those things which never have been revealed from the foundation of the world, but have been kept

Robert L. Millet is a professor of ancient scripture and has served as dean of Religious Education at Brigham Young University.

hid from the wise and prudent, shall be revealed unto babes and sucklings in this, the dispensation of the fulness of times" (D&C 128:18).

The Melchizedek Priesthood, that "Holy Priesthood after the order of the Son of God" (D&C 107:3), is, like its Author, infinite and eternal (see Alma 13:7–9). "The Priesthood is an everlasting principle," Joseph Smith explained, "and existed with God from eternity, and will to eternity, without beginning of days or end of years."[1] It is about that holy priesthood that we shall speak—more specifically, the Melchizedek Priesthood, through which this divine authority operated from Adam to Malachi. Sadly, the Old Testament is almost silent in regard to the high priesthood. Thus we must rely heavily upon the doctrinal teachings of Joseph Smith as set forth in his sermons, revelations, and translations. Further, we will turn to clarifications and expansions provided by those who knew Brother Joseph firsthand, as well as those apostolic and prophetic successors to whom is given the divine mandate to build on the doctrinal foundation he laid.

ADAM AND THE PRIESTHOOD

Once the church of God is organized on earth with legal administrators, there is the kingdom of God. "The kingdom of God was set up on the earth from the days of Adam to the present time," the Prophet Joseph Smith explained, "whenever there has been a righteous man on earth unto whom God revealed His word and gave power and authority to administer in His name. And where there is a priest of God—a minister who has power and authority from God to administer in the ordinances of the gospel and officiate in the priesthood of God—there is the kingdom of God."[2]

From the days of Adam to the time of Moses, men and women lived under the patriarchal order of the Melchizedek Priesthood. That is, they lived in a family order presided over by a patriarch. It includes the new and everlasting covenant of marriage.[3] "Adam held the priesthood," Elder Russell M. Nelson observed, "and Eve served in matriarchal partnership with the patriarchal priesthood."[4] President Ezra Taft Benson explained that "Adam and his descendants entered into the priesthood order of God. Today we would say they went to the House of the Lord and received their

blessings. The order of priesthood spoken of in the scriptures is sometimes referred to as *the patriarchal order* because it came down from
father to son. But this order is otherwise described in modern revelation as an order of family government where a man and woman
enter into a covenant with God—just as did Adam and Eve—to be
sealed for eternity, to have posterity, and to do the will and work of
God throughout their mortality."[5]

Though we are uncertain as to the precise organization of the
Church during the so-called pre-Christian times, the priesthood leaders among the ancients sought to follow the will of God in all matters. Such persons as Adam, Seth, Enos, Cainan, Mahalaleel, Jared,
Enoch, Methuselah, Lamech, and Noah were all high priests; they
governed the Church and kingdom in righteousness and by virtue of
their civil (kingly) and ecclesiastical (priestly) positions. Other worthy men held the higher priesthood, but these patriarchs were the
presiding officers and held the keys or right of presidency.[6] "Adam,
our father, the first man, is the presiding high priest over the earth
for all ages," Elder McConkie observed:

> The government the Lord gave him was patriarchal, and . . .
> the righteous portion of mankind were blessed and governed
> by a patriarchal theocracy. This theocratic system, patterned
> after the order and system that prevailed in heaven, was the
> government of God. He himself, though dwelling in heaven,
> was the Lawgiver, Judge, and King. He gave direction in all
> things both civil and ecclesiastical; there was no separation of
> church and state as we know it. All governmental affairs were
> directed, controlled, and regulated from on high. The Lord's
> legal administrators on earth served by virtue of their callings
> and ordinations in the Holy Priesthood and as they were guided
> by the power of the Holy Ghost.[7]

Adam was earth's first Christian. He was baptized, confirmed, born
of the Spirit, quickened in the inner man, ordained, and received
into the holy order of God (see Moses 6:64–68). "The priesthood was
first given to Adam; he obtained the First Presidency, and held the
keys of it from generation to generation."[8] In the book of Moses,
Joseph Smith's inspired translation of the early chapters of Genesis,
the Prophet recorded the revelation of the gospel to Adam. We read

there of Adam's baptism and spiritual rebirth. "And he heard a voice out of heaven, saying: Thou art baptized with fire, and with the Holy Ghost. This is the record of the Father, and the Son, from henceforth and forever." And now note the language of the scripture: "And thou art after the order of him who was without beginning of days or end of years, from all eternity to all eternity. Behold, thou art one in me, a son of God; and thus may all become my sons. Amen" (Moses 6:66–68).

Adam was born again and became through adoption a son of Christ. President Joseph Fielding Smith wrote: "To Adam, after he was driven from the Garden of Eden, the plan of salvation was revealed, and upon him the *fulness* of the priesthood was conferred."[9] Truly, as Elder John Taylor wrote, "Adam was the natural father of his posterity, who were his family and over whom he presided as patriarch, prophet, priest, and king."[10]

The account of Cain and Abel's offerings in Genesis 4 is brought to life and given a doctrinal context by the Prophet's inspired translation. We learn that God had commanded Adam, Eve, and their posterity to "offer the firstlings of their flocks" as an offering in "similitude of the sacrifice of the Only Begotten of the Father" (Moses 5:5–7). Cain, one who "loved Satan more than God" (Moses 5:18), turned away from his parents' teachings and entered into league with the father of lies. At Satan's urging, and in what seems to be a defiance of the command to offer a blood sacrifice,[11] Cain "brought of the fruit of the ground an offering unto the Lord." On the other hand, Abel "hearkened unto the voice of the Lord" and "brought of the firstlings of his flock." The Lord "had respect unto Abel, and to his offering; but unto Cain, and to his offering, he had not respect." Cain then entered into an unholy alliance with Satan, plotted and carried out the death of his brother Abel, and instigated secret combinations in the land (see Moses 5:18–51).

The Prophet Joseph explained that by faith in the Atonement of Christ and the plan of redemption:

> Abel offered to God a sacrifice that was accepted, which was the firstlings of the flock. Cain offered of the fruit of the ground, and was not accepted, because he could not do it in faith, he could have no faith, or could not exercise faith contrary to the plan of heaven. It must be shedding the blood of

the Only Begotten to atone for man; for this was the plan of redemption; and without the shedding of blood was no remission [see Hebrews 9:22] and as the sacrifice was instituted for a type, by which man was to discern the great Sacrifice which God had prepared; to offer a sacrifice contrary to that, no faith could be exercised, because redemption was not purchased in that way, nor the power of atonement instituted after that order; consequently Cain could have no faith; and whatsoever is not of faith, is sin.

The Prophet went on to say that however varied may be the opinions of the learned "respecting the conduct of Abel, and the knowledge which he had on the subject of atonement, it is evident in our minds, that he was instructed more fully in the plan than what the Bible speaks of. . . . How could Abel offer a sacrifice and look forward with faith on the Son of God for a remission of his sins, and not understand the Gospel?" Now note what the Prophet asks: "And if Abel was taught of the coming of the Son of God, was he not taught also of His ordinances? We all admit that the Gospel has ordinances, and if so, had it not always ordinances, and were not its ordinances always the same?"[12]

Almost seven years later, Brother Joseph stated that God had "set the ordinances to be the same forever and ever, and set Adam to watch over them, to reveal them from heaven to man, or to send angels to reveal them." That Adam "received revelations, commandments and ordinances at the beginning is beyond the power of controversy; else how did they begin to offer sacrifices to God in an acceptable manner? And if they offered sacrifices they must be authorized by ordination."

The Prophet then quotes from the Apostle Paul: "By faith Abel offered unto God a more excellent sacrifice than Cain, by which he obtained witness that he was righteous, God testifying of his gifts; and by it he being dead yet speaketh" (Hebrews 11:4). "How doth he yet speak?" Joseph asked. "Why he magnified the Priesthood which was conferred upon him, and died a righteous man, and therefore has become an angel of God by receiving his body from the dead, holding still the keys of his dispensation; and was sent down from heaven unto Paul to minister consoling words, and to commit unto him a knowledge of the mysteries of godliness."

And then, as a type of summary on these matters, the Prophet spoke concerning Cain and Abel: "The power, glory and blessings of the Priesthood could not continue with those who received ordination only as their righteousness continued; for Cain also being authorized to offer sacrifice, but not offering it in righteousness, was cursed. It signifies, then, that the ordinances must be kept in the very way God has appointed; otherwise their Priesthood will prove a cursing instead of a blessing."[13]

We know little concerning the keys of Abel's dispensation, spoken of above, except for the fact that a modern revelation indicates that one line of the priesthood descended "from Noah till Enoch, through the lineage of their fathers; and *from Enoch to Abel,* who was slain by the conspiracy of his brother, who received the priesthood by the commandments of God, by the hand of his father Adam, who was the first man" (D&C 84:15–16; emphasis added). With the murder of Abel and the defection of Cain to perdition, God provided another son for Adam and Eve through which the blessings of the evangelical priesthood or patriarchal order would continue. Seth was "ordained by Adam at the age of sixty-nine years, and was blessed by him three years previous to his (Adam's) death, and received the promise of God by his father, that his posterity should be the chosen of the Lord, and that they should be preserved unto the end of the earth; because he (Seth) was a perfect man, and his likeness was the express likeness of his father, insomuch that he seemed to be like unto his father in all things, and could be distinguished from him only by his age" (D&C 107:42–43; compare Moses 6:10–11).

ENOCH AND HIS CITY

Enoch, the son of Jared, was the seventh from Adam. Jared "taught Enoch in all the ways of God" (Moses 6:21). "Enoch was twenty-five years old when he was ordained under the hand of Adam; and he was sixty-five and Adam blessed him" (D&C 107:48). He was called by God as a prophet and seer to declare repentance to a wicked generation. Because Enoch was obedient and submissive, Jehovah transformed a shy and hesitant young man into a mighty preacher of righteousness. The Lord put His Spirit upon Enoch, justified all his words, and walked with him (see Moses 6:26–34). "And so great was the faith of Enoch, that he led the people of God, and their enemies came to battle against them; and the mountains fled, even according to his command; and the rivers of water were turned out of their course; and the roar of the lions was heard out of the wilderness; and all nations feared greatly, so powerful was the word of Enoch, and so great was the power of the language which God had given him" (Moses 7:13). That is to say, Enoch was faithful to the covenant of the Melchizedek Priesthood, which allowed God to swear an oath unto him, an oath that granted unto Enoch godlike powers (see Joseph Smith Translation, Genesis 14:27–31; compare Helaman 10:4–10; D&C 84:33–44).[14]

Because of his own righteousness and the power of his witness, Enoch established a society of the pure in heart. He established Zion, a people who "were of one heart and one mind, and dwelt in righteousness; and there was no poor among them" (Moses 7:18; compare D&C 97:21). Zion represents the pinnacle of human inter-action, the ideal community, or, as President Spencer W. Kimball taught, "the highest order of priesthood society."[15] Through preach-ing righteousness and incorporating the doctrines of the gospel into all they did, including applying the pure love of Christ into their social relations and thereby consecrating themselves completely, Enoch and his people founded a holy commonwealth and were eventually translated or taken into heaven without tasting death. The people of Enoch "walked with God, and he dwelt in the midst of Zion; and it came to pass that Zion was not, for God received it up into his own bosom; and from thence went forth the saying, Zion is fled" (Moses 7:69). "And men having this faith, coming up unto this [priesthood] order of God, were translated and taken up into heaven" (Joseph Smith Translation, Genesis 14:32). "And [Enoch] saw the Lord, and he walked with him, and was before his face continually; and he walked with God three hundred and sixty-five years, making him four hundred and thirty years old when he was translated" (D&C 107:49). Enoch's society became the pattern, the prototype, for all faithful men and women who lived thereafter. The Apostle Paul could therefore write of Abraham as one of many who "looked for a city which hath foundations, whose builder and maker is God" (Hebrews 11:10).

The Prophet Joseph Smith explained that translation is a power that belongs to the Melchizedek Priesthood, a dimension of the holy order of God.[16] President John Taylor added that "the translated residents of Enoch's city are under the direction of Jesus, who is the Creator of worlds; and that he, holding the keys of the government of other worlds, could, in his administrations to them, select the translated people of Enoch's Zion, if he thought proper, to perform a mission to these various planets, and as death had not passed upon them, they could be prepared by him and made use of through the medium of the holy priesthood to act as ambassadors, teachers, or messengers to those worlds over which Jesus holds the authority."[17]

NOAH AND THE PRIESTHOOD

Noah, the tenth from Adam, was ordained at the age of ten years (see D&C 107:52). "God made arrangements beforehand," Elder John Taylor explained, "and told Methuselah that when the people should be destroyed, that a remnant of his seed should occupy the earth and stand foremost upon it. And Methuselah was so anxious to have it done that he ordained Noah to the priesthood when he was ten years of age. Noah then stood in his day as the representative of God."[18]

Noah was thus more, far more, than a weather prophet; he was a legal administrator, one empowered by God to call a wicked generation to repentance. "And *the Lord ordained Noah after his own order,* and commanded him that he should go forth and declare his Gospel unto the children of men, even as it was given unto Enoch. And it came to pass that Noah called upon the children of men that they should repent; but they hearkened not unto his words." Further, his call to repentance was not just a warning of impending disaster; it was a call to come unto Christ and be saved. "Believe and repent of your sins," Noah said, "and be baptized in the name of Jesus Christ, the Son of God, even as our fathers, and ye shall receive the Holy Ghost, that ye may have all things made manifest" (Moses 8:19–20, 24; emphasis added). In speaking of the patriarchal order of the Melchizedek Priesthood in the days of Noah, President John Taylor stated that "every man managed his own family affairs. And prominent men among them were kings and priests unto God."[19]

The Prophet Joseph Smith explained the position of Noah (the angel Gabriel) in the priesthood hierarchy. Noah "stands next in authority to Adam in the Priesthood; he was called of God to this office, and was the father of all living in this day, and to him was given the dominion."[20] The Prophet also observed that "the keys of this Priesthood consisted in obtaining the voice of Jehovah that He talked with him [Noah] in a familiar and friendly manner, that He continued to him the keys, the covenants, the power and the glory, with which He blessed Adam at the beginning."[21]

MELCHIZEDEK AND ABRAHAM

Abraham, known to us as the "father of the faithful," sought for the "blessings of the fathers" and the right to administer the same (see Abraham 1:1–3). He "was not only a prince on the earth but a prince in the heavens, and by right came to the earth in his time to accomplish the things given him to do. And he found by tracing his genealogy that he had a right to the priesthood, and when he ascertained that, he prayed to the Lord, and demanded an ordination."[22] His father, Terah, was an idolater, so Abraham's blessings could not come to him in father-to-son fashion. And so it was that he looked to Melchizedek, the great high priest of that day, for counsel, direction, and authority. In his discussion of the ancients who entered the rest of the Lord, Alma chose Melchizedek to illustrate his doctrine: "And now, my brethren," he said, "I would that ye should humble yourselves before God, and bring forth fruit meet for repentance, that ye may also enter into that rest. Yea, humble yourselves even as the people in the days of Melchizedek, who was also a high priest after this same order [the holy order of God] which I have spoken, who also took upon him the high priesthood forever" (Alma 13:13–14). God swore the same oath to Melchizedek that he had sworn to Enoch and granted him the same godlike powers. Melchizedek obtained peace in Salem, "and his people wrought righteousness, and obtained heaven, and sought for the city of Enoch which God had before taken (see Joseph Smith Translation, Genesis 14:25–36).

The Saints of God who lived at this time, "the church in ancient days," called the holy priesthood after the name of Melchizedek (see D&C 107:2–4). A modern revelation informs us that "Esaias . . . lived in the days of Abraham, and was blessed of him—which Abraham received the priesthood from Melchizedek, who received it through the lineage of his fathers, even till Noah" (D&C 84:13–14). Further, it appears that Abraham received additional rights and privileges from Melchizedek. The father of the faithful sought for the power to administer endless lives, the fulness of the powers of the priesthood. According to Elder Franklin D. Richards, the Prophet Joseph explained that the power of Melchizedek was "not the power of a prophet, nor apostle, nor patriarch only, but of a king and priest to God, to open the windows of heaven and pour out the peace and law of endless life to man. And no man can attain to the joint heirship with Jesus Christ without being administered to by one having the same power and authority of Melchizedek."[23]

James Burgess recorded a sermon by Joseph Smith, a kind of doctrinal commentary on Hebrews 7, in which he spoke of three orders of the priesthood: the Aaronic, the patriarchal (the new and everlasting covenant of marriage, that which Abraham held), and the fulness of the priesthood (the realization of the blessings promised in the eternal marriage covenant). The Prophet is reported to have said:

> Paul is here treating of three different priesthoods, namely, the priesthood of Aaron, Abraham, and Melchizedek. Abraham's priesthood was of greater power than Levi's [Aaron's], and Melchizedek's was of greater power than that of Abraham. . . . I ask, Was there any sealing power attending this [Levitical] Priesthood that would admit a man into the presence of God? Oh no, but Abraham's was a more exalted power or priesthood; he could talk and walk with God. And yet consider how great this man [Melchizedek] was when even this patriarch Abraham gave a tenth part of all his spoils and then received a blessing under the hands of Melchizedek, even the last law or a fulness of the law or priesthood, which constituted him a king and priest after the order of Melchizedek or an endless life.[24]

In summary, Joseph the Prophet explained, "Abraham says to Melchizedek, I believe all that thou hast taught me concerning the priesthood and the coming of the Son of Man; so Melchizedek ordained Abraham and sent him away. Abraham rejoiced, saying, Now I have a priesthood."[25] The keys of the priesthood then continued through Isaac, Jacob, Joseph, Ephraim, and so on through the centuries, down to the time of Moses. To what degree the Melchizedek Priesthood and its powers were utilized among the people of Israel during their Egyptian bondage is unclear.

FROM MOSES TO CHRIST

We learn from modern revelation that Moses was ordained to the high priesthood by his father-in-law, Jethro the Midianite. That priesthood line then traces back from Jethro through such unknown ancient legal administrators as Caleb, Elihu, Jeremy, Gad, and Esaias. The revelation then speaks of the divine authority coming through Abraham, Melchizedek, Noah, Enoch, Abel, and Adam (see D&C 84:6–16). That the priesthood had been given to Jethro through Midian implies—once again, as was the case with the priesthood descending through Abel, in addition to Seth (see D&C 84:6–16; 107:40)—that there was more than one line of authority. It may be that the priesthood was transmitted through several lines but that the keys or right of presidency remained with and were passed on by the ordained patriarchs.

In speaking of the children of Israel, the Prophet stated: "Their government was a theocracy; they had God to make their laws, and men chosen by Him to administer them; He was their God, and they were His people. Moses received the word of the Lord from God Himself; he was the mouth of God to Aaron, and Aaron taught the people, in both civil and ecclesiastical affairs; they were both one, there was no distinction."[26] Moses sought diligently to bring the children of Israel to a point of spiritual maturity wherein they could enjoy the highest blessings of the priesthood—the privilege of entering into the rest of the Lord, into the divine presence. Jehovah's desire was that the Israelites become "a kingdom of priests, and an holy nation" (Exodus 19:6). "But they hardened their hearts and could not endure his presence; therefore, the Lord in his wrath, for his anger was kindled against them, swore that they should not enter into his rest while in the wilderness, which rest is the fulness of his glory. Therefore, he took Moses out of their midst, and the Holy Priesthood also; and the lesser priesthood continued" (D&C 84:19, 24–26; compare D&C 107:18–19). That is, Israel's unwillingness to enter the Lord's presence (see Exodus 20:19) signaled their lack of preparation as a nation to see God and thus the need to bear the holy priesthood and enjoy its consummate privileges. For one thing, as Abinadi pointed out, many of the children of Israel did not comprehend the place of the law of Moses as a means to a greater end. "And now," he asked, "did they understand the law? I say unto you, Nay, they did not all understand the law; and this because of the hardness of their hearts; for they understood not that there could not any man be saved except it were through the redemption of God" (Mosiah 13:32).

> And the Lord said unto Moses, Hew thee two other tables of stone, like unto the first, and I will write upon them also, the words of the law, according as they were written at the first on the tables which thou brakest; but it shall not be according to the first, for *I will take away the priesthood out of their midst;* therefore my holy order, and the ordinances thereof, shall not go before them; for my presence shall not go up in their midst, lest I destroy them.
>
> But I will give unto them the law as at the first, but it shall be after the law of a carnal commandment; for I have sworn in my wrath, that they shall not enter into my presence, into my rest, in the days of their pilgrimage. (Joseph Smith Translation, Exodus 34:1–2; emphasis added; see also Joseph Smith Translation, Deuteronomy 10:1–2)

When Moses was translated, the keys of the Melchizedek Priesthood were taken from among the Israelites as a body and the patriarchal order of priesthood ceased. True, there were still men like Aaron, his sons, and the seventy elders of Israel who bore the Melchizedek Priesthood. But no longer did the Melchizedek Priesthood pass from father to son. Thereafter, the priesthood of administration among the people generally was the Aaronic Priesthood. The ordination of men to the Melchizedek Priesthood and the bestowal of its keys came by special dispensation.[27]

President Joseph Fielding Smith therefore pointed out:

> In Israel, the common people, the people generally, did not exercise the functions of priesthood in its fulness, but were confined in their labors and ministrations very largely to the Aaronic Priesthood. The withdrawal of the higher priesthood was from the people as a body, but the Lord still left among them men holding the Melchizedek Priesthood, with power to officiate in all its ordinances, so far as he determined that these ordinances should be granted unto the people. Therefore Samuel, Isaiah, Jeremiah, Daniel, Ezekiel, Elijah, and others of

the prophets held the Melchizedek Priesthood, and their prophesying and their instructions to the people were directed by the
Spirit of the Lord and made potent by virtue of that priesthood
which was not made manifest generally among the people of
Israel during all these years.

President Smith adds this detail: "We may presume, with good
reason, that never was there a time when there was not at least one
man in Israel who held this higher priesthood (receiving it by special
dispensation) and who was authorized to officiate in the ordinances."[28] Or, as he wrote on another occasion:

> The Lord, of necessity, has kept authorized servants on the
> earth bearing the priesthood from the days of Adam to the pres-
> ent time; in fact, there has never been a moment from the
> beginning that there were not men on the earth holding the
> Holy Priesthood. Even in the days of apostasy, . . . our Father in
> heaven held control and had duly authorized servants on the
> earth to direct his work and to check, to some extent at least,
> the ravages and corruption of the evil powers. These servants
> were not permitted to organize the Church nor to officiate in
> the ordinances of the gospel, but they did check the advances
> of evil as far as the Lord deemed it necessary.[29]

Joseph Smith was asked: "Was the Priesthood of Melchizedek
taken away when Moses died?" The Prophet stated—and this principle guides our understanding of who held the High Priesthood
from the translation of Moses to the days of Christ—that "all
Priesthood is Melchizedek, but there are different portions or degrees
of it. That portion which brought Moses to speak with God face to
face was taken away; but that which brought the ministry of angels
remained." Now note this important clarification: "All the prophets
had the Melchizedek Priesthood and were ordained by God himself,"[30] meaning that God Himself performed the ordination or sent a
divine messenger to do so. In a meeting of the First Presidency and
Quorum of the Twelve on April 22, 1849, Elder John Taylor asked
President Brigham Young, "If Elijah, David, Solomon and the
Prophets had the High Priesthood, how it was," inasmuch as "the
Lord took it away with Moses." After much discussion, President
Young "said he did not know, but wished he did." Elder Taylor, who

had not been with the Prophet Joseph when the answer was first given in 1841 (he was in England), "thought perhaps the Lord conferred it himself upon some at times whom he had considered worthy, but not with permission for them to continue it down upon others."[31]

And so we operate from a perspective that all the Old Testament prophets held the Melchizedek Priesthood. Exactly how Isaiah and Micah, who were contemporaries, related to one another or who supervised whom, we cannot tell. Who was in charge when Jeremiah, Ezekiel, Habakkuk, Obadiah, or Lehi ministered in the prophetic office, we do not know. It is inconceivable to me that they went about their prophetic labors independent of one another. That Lord who called and empowered them is a God of order and not of confusion (see D&C 132:8), and we would suppose that their labors were coordinated and directed by one holding the appropriate keys of the kingdom—the right of presidency, the directing power (see D&C 107:8). These principles are, unfortunately, nowhere to be found in the Old Testament record.

It is from modern revelation that we learn that the ordinances of the house of the Lord have been delivered from the beginning. The book of Abraham speaks of "the grand Key-words of the Holy Priesthood, as revealed to Adam in the Garden of Eden, as also to Seth, Noah, Melchizedek, Abraham, and all to whom the Priesthood was revealed" (Facsimile No. 2, Explanation, Fig. 3). Modern revelation tells us, further, that sacred ordinances such as washings and anointings were carried out in ancient temples, which, the Lord said, "my people are always commanded to build unto my holy name" (D&C 124:39) and that "Nathan, my servant, and others of the prophets" held the keys of the sealing power associated with eternal marriage and the everlasting union of families (D&C 132:39). Surely if and when God elected to make available the ordinances of the priesthood to certain individuals—including the endowment and sealing blessings—he could do so in the wilderness or on mountaintops.

The scriptural passages quoted also seem to imply that the ancient tabernacle and temples allowed for more than Aaronic Priesthood sacrificial rites. The exact relationship between the prophet (who held the Melchizedek Priesthood) and the literal descendants of

Aaron (who held the keys of the Levitical ordinances) is unclear. Elder Bruce R. McConkie has, however, made the following clarification: "Do not let the fact that the performances of the Mosaic law were administered by the Aaronic Priesthood confuse you. . . . Where the Melchizedek Priesthood is, there is the fulness of the gospel; and all of the prophets held the Melchizedek Priesthood." He continues: "The Melchizedek Priesthood always directed the course of the Aaronic Priesthood. All of the prophets held a position in the hierarchy of the day."[32] In short, "in all ages of the world, whenever the Lord has given a dispensation of the priesthood to any man by actual revelation, or any set of men, this power has always been given" (D&C 128:9).

The Lehite colony, a branch of ancient Israel that was brought by God to the Americas, took the priesthood to the New World. Lehi was a prophet, and, as we have seen, would have held the Melchizedek Priesthood. The Nephites enjoyed the blessings of the fulness of the everlasting gospel, a gospel that is administered by the higher priesthood. There were no Levites among the Nephites, and so we would assume that they offered sacrifice and carried out the ordinances and ministerial duties as priests and teachers by virtue of the Melchizedek Priesthood.[33] President John Taylor explained that the higher priesthood was held by "Moroni, one of the prophets of God on this continent. Nephi, another of the servants of God on this continent, had the gospel with its keys and powers revealed unto him."[34]

ELIJAH AND THE KEYS OF THE PRIESTHOOD

A statement from Joseph Smith seems, to some extent at least, to contradict what has been said heretofore in regard to the keys of the priesthood in ancient Israel. The Prophet Joseph stated: "Elijah was the last Prophet that held the keys of the Priesthood, and who will, before the last dispensation, restore the authority and deliver the keys of the Priesthood, in order that all the ordinances may be attended to in righteousness."[35] Elijah lived about 850 B.C. If this statement were taken at face value, then no prophet after Elijah, at least in the Old Testament or Book of Mormon, would have held the keys of the holy priesthood. That would include such men as Elisha, Joel, Hosea, Jonah, Amos, Isaiah, Micah, Nahum, Jeremiah,

Zephaniah, Obadiah, Daniel, Habakkuk, and Ezekiel, as well as Lehi and the American branch of Israel. Are we to understand that none of these men held keys? Was there no right of presidency, no directing power in regard to the covenants and ordinances of the gospel?

The troublesome statement is from a discourse on priesthood delivered at a conference of the Church held in Nauvoo in October 1840. The Prophet Joseph began by defining the priesthood and then observed that the Melchizedek Priesthood "is the grand head, and holds the highest authority which pertains to the priesthood, and the keys of the Kingdom of God in all ages of the world to the latest posterity on the earth; and is the channel through which all knowledge, doctrine, the plan of salvation and every important matter is revealed from heaven." He went on to say that "all other Priesthoods are only parts, ramifications, powers and blessings belonging to the same, and are held, controlled, and directed by it. It is the channel through which the Almighty commenced revealing His glory at the beginning of the creation of this earth, and through which He has continued to reveal Himself to the children of men to the present time, and through which He will make known His purposes to the end of time."[36]

The Prophet then discussed the role of Michael or Adam as the one designated to oversee the revelations and ordinances of God to his people, stressing, as Joseph did so often, that the ordinances of the gospel are forever the same.[37] He went on to describe the descent of priesthood powers and rites to Abel, Cain, Enoch, Lamech, and Noah. The Prophet provided very important information regarding Enoch and the doctrine of translation. "Now the doctrine of translation," he taught, "is a power which belongs to this Priesthood. There are many things which belong to the powers of the Priesthood and the keys thereof, that have been kept hid from before the foundation of the world; they are hid from the wise and prudent to be revealed in the last times."[38]

Joseph Smith then began to discuss at length the restoration of sacrificial offerings as a part of the restitution of all things, for "all the ordinances and duties that ever have been required by the Priesthood . . . at any former period, shall be had again, bringing to pass the restoration spoken of by the mouth of all the Holy Prophets. . . . The offering of sacrifice has ever been connected and forms a part of the duties of the Priesthood. It began with the Priesthood, and will be continued until after the coming of Christ, from generation to generation. We frequently have mention made of the offering of sacrifice by the servants of the Most High in ancient days, prior to the law of Moses; which ordinances will be continued when the Priesthood is restored with all its authority, power and blessings." Then came the statement: "Elijah was the last Prophet that held the keys of the Priesthood, and who will, before the last dispensation, restore the authority and deliver the keys of the Priesthood, in order that all the ordinances may be attended to in righteousness. It is true," the Prophet continued, "that the Savior had authority and power to bestow this blessing; but the sons of Levi were too prejudiced. 'And I will send Elijah the Prophet before the great and terrible day of the Lord,' etc., etc. Why send Elijah? Because he holds the keys of the authority to administer in all the ordinances of the Priesthood." He added once again that "these sacrifices, as well as every ordinance belonging to the Priesthood, will, when the Temple of the Lord shall be built, and the sons of Levi be purified, be fully restored and attended to in all their powers, ramifications, and blessings. This ever did and ever will exist when the powers of the Melchizedek Priesthood are sufficiently manifest; else how can the restitution of all things spoken of by the Holy Prophets be brought to pass?"[39]

Remember, this sermon was delivered in October 1840, more than four years after Elijah had come to the Kirtland Temple (see D&C 110). But Joseph Smith stated that Elijah "will, before the last dispensation"—meaning, presumably, before the dispensation is complete—"restore the authority and deliver the keys of the Priesthood, in order that all the ordinances may be attended to in righteousness." It could well be that the Prophet was referring to a past event as though it was yet to come. On the other hand, the context of the sermon may suggest that a part of Elijah's role as one who would restore the "fulness of the priesthood"[40] is to restore the keys associated with all the ordinances, including animal sacrifice, an event prophesied by Malachi (4:5–6), quoted by Jesus to the Nephites (3 Nephi 25:5–6), rendered differently by Moroni (D&C 2), and described in modern revelation (D&C 84:31–32). One wonders whether Elijah will not deliver those particular keys at the Council of Adam-ondi-Ahman, that grand gathering of priesthood leaders—those who have held keys of authority in all ages—just before the coming of the Lord in glory.[41]

I am grateful to my friend and colleague Robert J. Matthews for suggesting the following principles, each of which adds somewhat to our understanding of this matter of the keys of the priesthood:

1. It is evident that a person who holds the keys can "give" them to another without losing them himself.

2. There is a difference between holding the keys sufficiently to function and being the person designated to convey those keys to others. Both Moses and Elijah gave keys to Peter, James, and John on the Mount of Transfiguration,[42] yet it was still Moses and Elijah who brought them to Joseph Smith and Oliver Cowdery in 1836. No doubt Peter had sufficient of "Elijah's keys" to operate the Church during the meridian dispensation, yet the Lord did not use Peter to convey those sealing keys to Joseph and Oliver.

3. It is clearly stated in the Book of Mormon, more than once, that the Twelve in the Western Hemisphere were subject and would be subject to the Twelve in Jerusalem (see 1 Nephi 12:9; Mormon 3:18–19). This suggests, again, that a people may have sufficient keys of the priesthood to operate the Church without having the right to pass those keys to future dispensations.

4. Truly, all of the keys and powers of the priesthood have not yet been delivered to us in our day; much lies in futurity, including the keys of creation, translation, and resurrection.[43]

In summary, the keys of the kingdom of God have always been on earth when the higher priesthood was on earth; there must be order in the house of God. Those keys would have been held by the Lord's anointed after the time of Elijah. Elijah was not the last man to hold keys in the Old Testament period, since many did after him, but he was the last one in the Old Testament commissioned to return in the dispensation of the fulness of times to see to it that "all the ordinances may be attended to in righteousness."[44]

CONCLUSION

Ammon explained to King Limhi that "a seer is a revelator and a prophet also; and a gift which is greater can no man have, except he should possess the power of God, which no man can; yet a man may have great power given him from God. But a seer can know of things which are past, and also of things which are to come, and by them shall all things be revealed, or, rather, shall secret things be made manifest, and hidden things shall come to light. . . . Thus God has provided a means that man, through faith, might work mighty miracles; therefore he becometh a great benefit to his fellow beings" (Mosiah 8:16–18).

As Latter-day Saints we love the Old Testament. We cherish the lessons and language of its sacred pages. We know, however, that it has not come down to us in its pristine purity. Many plain and precious truths and many covenants of the Lord have been taken away and kept back by designing persons (see 1 Nephi 13:20–32). The understanding that the fulness of the gospel of Jesus Christ was once among the ancients is missing. The insight that prophets in the Old Testament were Christians who taught Christian doctrine and administered Christian covenants and ordinances is lacking. But thanks be to God that a seer has been raised up, even a "choice seer" (2 Nephi 3:6–7), Joseph Smith, who began the work of restoring many of those plain and precious truths to the Bible. Jehovah instructed Moses to write the things that would be spoken to him. "And in a day when the children of men shall esteem my words as naught and take many of them from the book which thou shalt write, behold, I will raise up another like unto thee; and they shall be had again among the children of men—among as many as shall believe" (Moses 1:40–41).

A study of the Old Testament by the lamp of the restored gospel ties the Latter-day Saints to the former-day Saints. Such a study becomes far more than a lesson in history, for as the revelation declares, "Now this same Priesthood, which was in the beginning, shall be in the end of the world also" (Moses 6:7). What was true for the ancients is true for us. What inspired and motivated them can and should entice us to continuing fidelity and devotion to our covenants. The same authority by which they were baptized, confirmed, endowed, washed, anointed, married, and sealed unto eternal life—that same authority has been delivered to Joseph Smith by heavenly messengers. That we will believe, accept, and rejoice in the treasure house of doctrinal understanding delivered to us through modern revelation is my sincere prayer.

NOTES

1. Joseph Smith, *Teachings of the Prophet Joseph Smith,* comp. Joseph Fielding Smith (Salt Lake City: Deseret Book, 1976), 157.

2. Smith, *Teachings,* 271.

3. See D&C 131:1–4; Bruce R. McConkie, in Conference Report, October 1977, 50.

4. Russell M. Nelson, *The Power within Us* (Salt Lake City: Deseret Book, 1988), 109.

5. Ezra Taft Benson, "What I Hope You Will Teach Your Children about the Temple," *Ensign,* August 1985, 9; emphasis added.

6. See Joseph Fielding Smith, *The Way to Perfection* (Salt Lake City: Deseret Book, 1970), 73.

7. Bruce R. McConkie, *A New Witness for the Articles of Faith* (Salt Lake City: Deseret Book, 1985), 35.

8. Smith, *Teachings,* 157.

9. Joseph Fielding Smith, *Doctrines of Salvation,* 3 vols., comp. Bruce R. McConkie (Salt Lake City: Bookcraft, 1954–56), 3:81; emphasis added.

10. John Taylor, "Patriarchal," *Times and Seasons,* June 1, 1845, 921.

11. See John Taylor, in *Journal of Discourses,* 26 vols. (Liverpool: Latter-day Saints' Book Depot, 1854–86), 22:301; Charles W. Penrose, in *Journal of Discourses,* 25:47–48, 339.

12. Smith, *Teachings,* 58–59.

13. Smith, *Teachings,* 168–69.

14. Joseph Fielding Smith, in Conference Report, April 1970, 59; Boyd K. Packer, *The Things of the Soul* (Salt Lake City: Bookcraft, 1996), 153.

15. Spencer W. Kimball, in Conference Report, October 1977, 125.

16. Smith, *Teachings,* 170–71.

17. John Taylor, *The Gospel Kingdom,* comp. G. Homer Durham (Salt Lake City: Bookcraft, 1964), 103; see also Smith, *Teachings,* 170–71.

18. Taylor, *Gospel Kingdom,* 103–4.

19. Taylor, *Gospel Kingdom,* 139.

20. Smith, *Teachings,* 157.

21. Smith, *Teachings,* 171.

22. Taylor, *Gospel Kingdom,* 104.

23. Andrew F. Ehat and Lyndon W. Cook, eds., *Words of Joseph Smith* (Provo: BYU Religious Studies Center, 1980), 245.

24. Ehat and Cook, *Words of Joseph Smith,* 245–46; spelling and punctuation standardized.

25. Smith, *Teachings,* 322–23.

26. Smith, *Teachings*, 252.

27. See Bruce R. McConkie, *The Mortal Messiah*, 4 vols. (Salt Lake City: Deseret Book, 1979–81), 1:60.

28. Smith, *Doctrines of Salvation*, 3:85.

29. Joseph Fielding Smith, *Answers to Gospel Questions*, 5 vols. (Salt Lake City: Deseret Book, 1957–66), 2:45.

30. Smith, *Teachings*, 180–81.

31. In Ehat and Cook, *Words of Joseph Smith*, 82–83.

32. Bruce R. McConkie, "The Bible: A Sealed Book," in *Church Educational System Religious Educators' Symposium* (Salt Lake City: The Church of Jesus Christ of Latter-day Saints, 1985), 6.

33. See Smith, *Doctrines of Salvation*, 3:87; Bruce R. McConkie, *The Promised Messiah* (Salt Lake City: Deseret Book, 1978), 412, 421, 427.

34. Taylor, *Gospel Kingdom*, 140.

35. Smith, *Teachings*, 172.

36. Smith, *Teachings*, 166–67.

37. Smith, *Teachings*, 59–60, 264, 308.

38. Smith, *Teachings*, 168–71.

39. Smith, *Teachings*, 171–73.

40. Smith, *Teachings*, 337.

41. Smith, *Teachings*, 157; Joseph Fielding Smith, *The Progress of Man* (Salt Lake City: Deseret Book, 1964), 479–82; Bruce R. McConkie, *The Millennial Messiah* (Salt Lake City: Deseret Book, 1982), 578–88.

42. Smith, *Teachings*, 158.

43. Spencer W. Kimball, in Conference Report, April 1977, 69–72; see also John Taylor, in *Journal of Discourses*, 23:32.

44. Smith, *Teachings*, 172.

CHAPTER FIVE

MELCHIZEDEK: SEEKING AFTER THE ZION OF ENOCH

FRANK F. JUDD JR.

The shadowy figure of Melchizedek entices the student of the scriptures. Next to Enoch, Melchizedek is perhaps the most enigmatic figure in the Bible. His life and mission are covered in only a few brief verses in the Bible, yet of all God's holy high priests, "none were greater" (Alma 13:19). What made Melchizedek such a great high priest? The debates are endless about the few verses in Genesis that speak of him. Many scholars come to erroneous conclusions about Melchizedek, king of Salem. For example, some believe that Melchizedek worshipped not Jehovah but a different god named *El Elyon,* or *Most High God.*[1] This and other false conclusions result from a lack of adequate sources and information.

Latter-day Saints, however, are blessed with scriptural insights provided through the Prophet Joseph Smith. For instance, in the Book of Mormon, Alma the Younger delivered a masterful discourse devoted in part to the life and ministry of Melchizedek. Several sections of the Doctrine and Covenants discuss important biographical facts relating to Melchizedek. The Joseph Smith Translation of the Bible (JST) provides valuable knowledge not found in the Old and the New Testament concerning the role of the priesthood in Melchizedek's life. Modern prophets also supply pertinent doctrines relative to Melchizedek and the priesthood. As we study the Bible in light of these Restoration scriptures, a significant pattern emerges.

Frank F. Judd Jr. is an assistant professor of ancient scripture at Brigham Young University.

Just as we seek to emulate our Savior by following the examples of righteous leaders today, those who lived anciently also sought to emulate their promised Messiah by following the patterns set by their righteous predecessors and peers. It is possible that Melchizedek used the pattern set by Enoch and his people as a pattern for seeking after the Lord and establishing a Zion society. On that subject, Elder Bruce R. McConkie said: "Enoch built Zion, a City of Holiness, and Melchizedek, reigning as king and ministering as priest of the Most High God, sought to make Jerusalem [Salem], his capital city, into another Zion. As we have seen, Melchizedek himself was called by his people the Prince of peace, the King of peace, and the King of heaven, for Jerusalem [Salem] had become a heaven to them."[2]

Joseph Smith's translation of Genesis states that Melchizedek was ordained after the same order of the priesthood as Enoch and that "every one being ordained after this order" (JST, Genesis 14:30) had the power to do the things that Enoch did (see JST, Genesis 14:27). Thus, Elder McConkie observed, "Abraham, Isaac, and Jacob sought an inheritance in the City of Zion, as had all the righteous saints from Enoch to Melchizedek."[3] As Melchizedek and his people "sought for the city of Enoch which God had before taken" (JST, Genesis 14:34), Melchizedek was privileged to lead a life remarkably similar to Enoch's. Both of these great men held the same priesthood authority, performed similar miracles, received temple blessings, established Zion communities, and were, along with their people, eventually translated and taken up to heaven.

THE ORDER OF THE PRIESTHOOD

Melchizedek and Enoch were both ordained after the order of the greater priesthood. In addition, Melchizedek and his priesthood authority have a closer tie to Enoch than may be seen at first glance. The Doctrine and Covenants states that "Abraham received the priesthood *from Melchizedek,* who received it through the lineage of his fathers, even till Noah; and from Noah *till Enoch,* through the lineage of their fathers" (D&C 84:14–15; emphasis added). This greater priesthood was originally called *"the Holy Priesthood, after the Order of the Son of God"* (D&C 107:3; emphasis in original). To avoid disrespect for the Lord by too frequent repetition of his holy name, this priesthood, in the days of the king of Salem, was "called the

Melchizedek Priesthood . . . because Melchizedek was such a great high priest" (D&C 107:2; see also v. 4).

But that is not the only time the Lord has called this order of the priesthood after a mortal high priest. Melchizedek "was ordained an high priest after the order of the covenant which God made with Enoch" (JST, Genesis 14:27). According to the Doctrine and Covenants, the high priesthood was called "after the order of Melchizedek, which was after the order of Enoch, which was after the order of the Only Begotten Son" (D&C 76:57). This high priesthood provides the means whereby the righteous may "commune with the general assembly and church of the Firstborn" (D&C 107:19). More specifically, those who receive and keep sacred covenants relating to the priesthood of Melchizedek become part of "the general assembly and church of Enoch, and of the Firstborn" (D&C 76:67). Thus, the king of Salem and the greater priesthood, which currently bears his name, have a very close connection with Enoch that may go unnoticed.

POWER FROM ON HIGH

The higher priesthood gave Melchizedek the power to perform many of the same types of miracles Enoch had performed. The Lord, in promising this power to Enoch, had said, "the mountains shall flee before you, and the rivers shall turn from their course" (Moses 6:34). Consequently, Enoch became a mighty man of miracles. According to the restored scriptural account, he "spake the word of the Lord, and the earth trembled, and the mountains fled, even according to his command; and the rivers of water were turned out of their course; and the roar of the lions was heard out of the wilderness; and all nations feared greatly, so powerful was the word of Enoch, and so great was the power of the language which God had given him" (Moses 7:13).

The Lord had previously made a covenant with Enoch that not only he but "every one" (JST, Genesis 14:30) who received the greater priesthood would have power—if he was faithful—to perform miracles; namely, "to break mountains, to divide the seas, to dry up waters, to turn them out of their course; to put at defiance the armies of nations, to divide the earth, to break every band, to stand in the presence of God; to do all things according to his will, according to his command, subdue principalities and powers; and this by the will of the Son of God which was from before the foundation of the world" (JST, Genesis 14:30–31).

When Melchizedek was but a child, he "stopped the mouths of lions, and quenched the violence of fire" (JST, Genesis 14:26). Moreover, because "Melchizedek was a priest of this order" (v. 33), meaning the order of Enoch, he had the ability to perform the same types of miraculous deeds Enoch had while Melchizedek and his people "sought for the city of Enoch" (v. 34).

Life and Ministry of Peace

The lives and ministries of Melchizedek and Enoch were very similar. Enoch's mortal father, Jared, taught him "in all the ways of God" (Moses 6:21; see also v. 41). The principle of faith was an important concept that Jared, a preacher of righteousness, taught his son (see Moses 6:23). The scriptures say that "so great was the faith of Enoch that he led the people of God" (Moses 7:13). As their leader, Enoch was able to establish peace among his people. First, he preached repentance. The Lord had specifically told Enoch to "prophesy unto this people, and say unto them—Repent" (Moses 6:27; see also 7:10). So Enoch did. He exhorted the people to change their ways and come unto the Lord (see Moses 6:37; 7:12). A few people hearkened, and they created a small righteous society under the peaceful leadership of Enoch. As President Ezra Taft Benson observed: "Small numbers do not insure peace; only righteousness does. . . . The whole city of Enoch was peaceful; and it was taken into heaven because it was made up of righteous people."[4]

The second means whereby Enoch established peace was righteous military defense. Because of Enoch's faithfulness:

> He led the people of God, and their enemies came to battle against them; and he spake the word of the Lord, . . . and all nations feared greatly, so powerful was the word of Enoch, and so great was the power of the language which God had given him.
>
> There also came up a land out of the depth of the sea, and so great was the fear of the enemies of the people of God, that they fled and stood afar off and went upon the land which came up out of the depth of the sea.

And the giants of the land, also, stood afar off; and there went forth a curse upon all people that fought against God;

And from that time forth there were wars and bloodshed among them; but the Lord came and dwelt with his people, and they dwelt in righteousness. (Moses 7:13–16)

Melchizedek's ministry was strikingly parallel to Enoch's. Alma said that Melchizedek, as king of Salem, "did reign under his father" (Alma 13:18). It is probable that Melchizedek's father also taught him to have faith in the Lord. This righteous parental instruction possibly assisted Melchizedek in gaining approval from God even as a young child (see JST, Genesis 14:26–27), because, like all of us, Melchizedek needed to learn obedience to the commandments of God. The author of Hebrews said that "though he were a Son, yet learned he obedience by the things which he suffered" (Hebrews 5:8). A note on the manuscript of Joseph Smith's translation of this verse makes clear that this is a reference to Melchizedek (see Hebrews 5:7a). Both the Book of Mormon and Joseph Smith's translation of Genesis state that Melchizedek was a man of great faith (see JST, Genesis 14:26; Alma 13:18). According to Alma, Melchizedek used this faith to bring about peace among his people and in his land.

Just as Enoch had done, Melchizedek established peace among his people in two ways. First, because the people of the land of Salem were terribly wicked, Melchizedek went on the spiritual offensive. "Melchizedek was a king over the land of Salem; and his people had waxed strong in iniquity and abomination; yea, they had all gone astray; they were full of all manner of wickedness; but Melchizedek having exercised mighty faith, and received the office of the high priesthood according to the holy order of God, did preach repentance unto his people" (Alma 13:17–18).

This preaching affected the people of Salem as it had the people of Enoch—they repented of their evil ways and humbled themselves before the Lord (see Alma 13:14, 18). Thus, in this way "Melchizedek did establish peace in the land in his days; therefore he was called the prince of peace" (Alma 13:18).

The other method by which Melchizedek established peace was defending his people, just as Enoch had done. The Lord's covenant with Enoch—that "every one" ordained after this order of the priesthood would be able "to put at defiance the armies of nations . . . [and to] subdue principalities and powers" (JST, Genesis 14:30–31)—applied to Melchizedek. The author of Hebrews spoke of biblical prophets "who through faith subdued kingdoms, wrought righteousness, obtained promises, stopped the mouths of lions, quenched the violence of fire, escaped the edge of the sword, out of weakness were made strong, waxed valiant in fight, [and] turned to flight the armies of the aliens" (Hebrews 11:33–34). Elder McConkie said of these verses, "This language is, of course, a paraphrase, a quotation, and a summary of what Genesis once contained relative to Melchizedek."[5] It seems evident that the life and ministry of Melchizedek were very similar to those of Enoch. Both of these prophets were able to establish peace by means of preaching repentance and by means of righteous military defense.

TEMPLE BLESSINGS IN ZION

The scriptures indicate that Melchizedek and Enoch received temple blessings during the process of establishing Zion. When Enoch climbed Mount Simeon, he was "clothed upon with glory" (Moses 7:3) and was privileged to see and converse with the Lord face to face (see Moses 7:4). Following that sacred experience in the presence of God, Enoch and the people of God "were blessed upon the mountains, and upon the high places, and did flourish" (Moses 7:17). In the ancient world, mountains were associated with sacred space, specifically with temple experiences.[6] President Brigham Young believed that there were temples in the city of Enoch. He said, "I will not say but what Enoch had Temples and officiated therein, but we have no account of it."[7] Similarly, concerning the possibility of temples in the city of Enoch, Elder Franklin D. Richards said, "I expect that in the city of Enoch there are temples; and when Enoch and his people come back, they will come back with their city, their temples, blessings and powers."[8] Initially, only Enoch walked before God, but eventually "Enoch and all his people walked with God, and he dwelt in the midst of Zion" (Moses 7:69). President Benson said of the temple experiences of Enoch and his people:

> Adam and his descendants entered into the priesthood order of God. Today we would say they went to the House of the Lord and received their blessings. The order of priesthood spoken of in the scriptures is sometimes referred to as the patriarchal

order because it came down from father to son. But this order is otherwise described in modern revelation as an order of family government where a man and woman enter into a covenant with God—just as did Adam and Eve—to be sealed for eternity, to have posterity, and to do the will and work of God throughout their mortality. If a couple are true to their covenants, they are entitled to the blessings of the highest degree of the celestial kingdom. These covenants today can only be entered into by going to the House of the Lord. Adam followed this order and brought his posterity into the presence of God. He is the greatest example for us to follow. Enoch followed this pattern and brought the Saints of his day into the presence of God.[9]

This evidence indicates that Enoch and his Zion society did indeed enjoy temple blessings, such that the Son of God revealed Himself and thereby dwelt with His people in Zion.

As Melchizedek and his people established their city of Zion, it seems that they, too, enjoyed temple blessings. Josephus, a Jewish historian who lived in the first century after Christ, knew of a tradition that Melchizedek, not Solomon, was the first person to build a temple of the Lord in Palestine. "Its [Salem's] original founder was a Canaanite chief, called in the native tongue 'Righteous King' [or Melchizedek]; for such indeed he was. In virtue thereof he was the first to officiate as priest of God and, being the first to build the temple, gave the city, previously called Solyma [or Salem], the name of Jerusalem."[10]

There are also modern references to Melchizedek and temple blessings. From Joseph Smith's translation of Genesis, it seems that Melchizedek received his priesthood blessings when he was "ordained an high priest after the order of the covenant which God made with Enoch, it being *after the order of the Son of God;* which order came, not by man, nor the will of man; neither by father nor mother; neither by beginning of days nor end of years; but of God" (JST, Genesis 14:27–28; emphasis added).

But what does entering into this order of the priesthood have to do with receiving temple blessings? President Benson explained what it means to enter into the order of the Son of God:

Adam and his posterity were commanded by God to be baptized, to receive the Holy Ghost, and to enter into the order of the Son of God. To enter into the order of the Son of God is the equivalent today of entering into the fullness of the Melchizedek Priesthood, which is only received in the house of the Lord. Because Adam and Eve had complied with these requirements, God said to them, "Thou art after the order of him who was without beginning of days or end of years, from all eternity to all eternity" (Moses 6:67).[11]

This order of the priesthood authorized Melchizedek "to stand in the presence of God" (JST, Genesis 14:31). According to the Doctrine and Covenants, that is the reason temples are built; namely, "that the Son of Man might have a place to manifest himself to his people" (D&C 109:5). Therefore, it seems that the society of Melchizedek, like the society of Enoch, enjoyed priesthood blessings associated with the temple of the Lord.

THE TRANSLATION OF ZION INTO HEAVEN

The last point of similarity between the lives of Melchizedek and Enoch is their establishment of their Zion community and eventual translation into heaven. One scriptural description of Zion is "the pure in heart" (D&C 97:21). Most of our information about Zion societies comes from the scriptures that describe the experience of Enoch and his people. The society of Enoch was called Zion "because they were of one heart and one mind, and dwelt in righteousness; and there was no poor among them" (Moses 7:18).

But Zion is not only righteous people; Zion is also a place. As Enoch and his people continued in righteousness, they "built a city that was called the City of Holiness, even Zion" (Moses 7:19). Stephen E. Robinson has commented on the use of the term *Zion* to designate a people and a place: "Zion is wherever the pure in heart dwell. . . . Zion is a spiritual category, which may in different contexts mean Salt Lake City, Far West, Jerusalem, or the city of Enoch."[12] After the Lord came and dwelt with His Zion people in the city of Zion, they, "in process of time, [were] taken up into heaven" (Moses 7:21), that is, they were translated (see Moses 7:23). Later, the scripture states, "Zion was not, for God received it up into his own bosom; and from thence went forth the saying, ZION IS FLED" (Moses 7:69).

Therefore, after Enoch established a community that was pure in heart and dwelt with the Lord on earth, the entire society, including the people and the city itself, was received up into heaven.

Enoch's people were not the only ones who were granted such a sacred privilege. The scriptures state that after Enoch was translated, "the Holy Ghost fell on many, and they were caught up by the powers of heaven into Zion" (Moses 7:27). In other words, those who achieved purity in their hearts were received into the city of Enoch to enjoy fellowship with those righteous people. Elder Bruce R. McConkie said that "righteous men, after the flood, not only sought an inheritance in Enoch's Zion, but also began the process of building their own City of Holiness in earth."[13] Melchizedek and his people were among those righteous people who actively "sought for the city of Enoch which God had before taken, separating it from the earth" (JST, Genesis 14:34). As Melchizedek did so, and because of priesthood power and mighty faith, he performed miracles, preached righteousness, and established Zion, as Enoch had done before him.

In the Zion society of Melchizedek, the storehouse was not to provide for him but "for the poor" (JST, Genesis 14:38). By that means they were able to live as had the people of Enoch, who had "no poor among them" (Moses 7:18). Melchizedek and his people were blessed greatly for their diligence and righteousness, for they "obtained heaven" (JST, Genesis 14:34). Elder McConkie declared:

> That this process of translating the righteous saints and taking them to heaven was still going on after the flood among the people of Melchizedek is apparent from the account in the Inspired Version of the Bible. . . . As far as we know, instances of translation since the day of Melchizedek and his people have been few and far between. After recording that Enoch was translated, Paul says that Abraham, Isaac, and Jacob, and their seed after them (they obviously knowing what had taken place as pertaining to the people of Melchizedek and others) "looked for a city which hath foundations, whose builder and maker is God" (Heb. 11:5–10), that is, they "sought for the city of Enoch which God had before taken." (*Inspired Version,* Genesis 14:34.)[14]

Elder John Taylor interpreted those verses in the same manner: "The fact of Enoch's translation was generally known by the people who lived immediately after the flood. It had occurred so short a time before, that it was almost a matter of personal recollection with the sons of Noah. They must also have been acquainted with the fact that others were caught up by the power of heaven into Zion, and it would appear strongly probable that Melchizedec and many of his people were also translated. Revelation does not state this in so many words, but the inference to be drawn from what is said, points clearly in that direction."[15]

The author of Hebrews said that Melchizedek "offered up prayers and supplications with strong crying and tears unto him [God] that was able to save him [Melchizedek] from death, and was heard" (Hebrews 5:7). A note on the manuscript of the Joseph Smith Translation indicates that this verse indeed refers to Melchizedek (see Hebrews 5:7*a*). The statement "to save him from death" could refer to salvation from spiritual death by means of the Atonement or to salvation from physical death by means of translation. The author of Hebrews may have had both interpretations in mind. Melchizedek and his people wanted to enjoy the same blessings Enoch's society had received. As a result, Melchizedek sought after the Zion of Enoch, and eventually Melchizedek and his society were also translated and received into the heavenly Zion.

Enoch and Melchizedek As Types of Christ

Melchizedek followed the pattern of righteous living set by his noble ancestor Enoch. The scriptures indicate that Melchizedek and his people sought after the Zion of Enoch and actually achieved it. It is possible that much of the information about the ministries of Melchizedek and Enoch was among the plain and precious parts taken from the Bible (see 1 Nephi 13:23–29) or lost before it was compiled.[16] Concerning these parts of the Bible, the Lord said to Moses, "And in a day when the children of men shall esteem my words as naught and take many of them from the book which thou shalt write, behold, I will raise up another like unto thee; and they shall be had again among the children of men—among as many as shall believe" (Moses 1:41). This man "like unto [Moses]" was the Prophet Joseph Smith,[17] who brought forth the restoration of these words through the Book of Mormon, the Doctrine and Covenants, the Pearl of Great Price, and his inspired revision of the Bible.

The Prophet Joseph Smith said, "The building up of Zion is a cause that has interested the people of God in every age; it is a theme upon which prophets, priests and kings have dwelt with peculiar delight."[18] Elder McConkie taught that establishing Zion is a goal for which many righteous people have sought: "Abraham, Isaac, and Jacob sought an inheritance in the City of Zion, as had all the righteous saints from Enoch to Melchizedek—an inheritance which would have been but prelude to gaining exaltation in the Celestial Zion where God and Christ are the judge of all. Since it is no longer the general order for the saints to be translated—their labors in the next sphere now being to preach the gospel to the spirits in prison, rather than to act as ministering servants in other fields—today's saints seek a heavenly country and a celestial city in the sense of striving for an inheritance in the Celestial City of exalted beings."[19]

The Prophet Joseph Smith also directly applied this principle to us when he taught that "we ought to have the building up of Zion as our greatest object."[20] Elder Orson Pratt summarized one of the reasons: "The Latter-Day Zion will resemble, in most particulars, the Zion of Enoch: it will be established upon the same celestial laws—be built upon the same gospel, and be guided by continued revelation. Its inhabitants, like those of the antediluvian Zion, will be the righteous gathered out from all nations: the glory of God will be seen upon it; and His power will be manifested there, even as in the Zion of old. All the blessings and grand characteristics which were exhibited in ancient Zion will be shown forth in the Latter-Day Zion."[21]

As the Prophet Joseph said, it is important for us to do as the ancient patriarchs did. Brigham Young taught the Saints: "If we obtain the glory that Abraham obtained, we must do so by the same means that he did. If we are ever prepared to enjoy the society of Enoch, Noah, Melchizedek, Abraham, Isaac, and Jacob, or of their faithful children, and of the faithful Prophets and Apostles, we must pass through the same experience, and gain the knowledge, intelligence, and endowments that will prepare us to enter into the celestial kingdom of our Father and God."[22]

We also must strive to build up Zion, as they did. Revelation through modern prophets teaches us how the ancient Saints sought after and obtained Zion. If we pattern our lives after theirs, just as Melchizedek did with Enoch's, we too can reach the same goals. If we are to go where the prophets are going, we must follow their righteous examples.

During one of his sermons of which we have record, Enoch wrote that the Lord said, "And behold, all things have their likeness, and all things are created and made to bear record of me, both things which are temporal, and things which are spiritual; . . . all things bear record of me" (Moses 6:63). Similarly, Nephi said that "all things which have been given of God from the beginning of the world, unto man, are the typifying of [Christ]" (2 Nephi 11:4). It seems that not only things but also people are types of the true Messiah. Elder McConkie taught that all prophets are types of Christ: "All the ancient prophets and all righteous men who preceded our Lord in birth were, in one sense or another, patterns for him. . . . Many of them lived in special situations or did particular things that singled them out as types and patterns and shadows of that which was to be in the life of him who is our Lord."[23]

Both of the great patriarchs Enoch and Melchizedek were thus types of the coming Savior. Elder John Taylor taught: "There is yet another source from which the ancients obtained their ideas of the life and mission of the Son of God. It is to be found in the translation of Enoch and his city."[24] In addition, the author of Hebrews referred to the Lord Himself as coming "after the similitude of Melchisedec" (Hebrews 7:15).

All of the similarities we have identified between Enoch and Melchizedek are important aspects of the mission of Jesus Christ. Enoch and Melchizedek were ordained after the same order of the priesthood, and they were types of the Savior, who, as Paul wrote, was the "High Priest of our profession" (Hebrews 3:1). As the patriarchs Enoch and Melchizedek were great miracle workers, so the true and living Miracle Worker was the One of whom King Benjamin prophesied: "For behold, the time cometh, and is not far distant, that with power, the Lord Omnipotent who reigneth, who was, and is from all eternity to all eternity, shall come down from heaven among the children of men, and shall dwell in a tabernacle of clay, and shall go forth amongst men, working mighty miracles, such as healing the sick, raising the dead, causing the lame to walk, the blind to receive their sight, and the deaf to hear, and curing all manner of diseases. And he shall cast out devils, or the evil spirits which dwell in the hearts of the children of men" (Mosiah 3:5–6). Those two patriarchs even established peace in their respective societies, but the real "Prince of Peace" (Isaiah 9:6) gave unto us the ultimate peace that we, through Him, might "overcome the world" (John 16:33; see also 14:27).

Lastly, Enoch and Melchizedek sought for and obtained Zion and were translated into heaven. But even they anticipated then, as we do now, that wonderful day when the Savior would come in power and glory and the righteous Saints would be "caught up in the cloud to meet [the Lord], that we may ever be with the Lord" (D&C 109:75).

It is even more fitting that we follow those ancient patriarchs because they were types of Jesus Christ. Elder McConkie summarized our duty when he explained that all righteous Saints "should be a type of Christ. Those who lived before he came were types and shadows and witnesses of his coming. Those who have lived since he came are witnesses of such coming and are types and shadows of what he was."[25] Truly there is no better example, for as our perfect Master said, "Therefore, what manner of men ought ye to be? Verily I say unto you, even as I am" (3 Nephi 27:27).

NOTES

1. For different views of Melchizedek, see Michael C. Astour, "Melchizedek," in *Anchor Bible Dictionary,* ed. David Noel Freedman (New York: Doubleday, 1992), 4:684–86.

2. Bruce R. McConkie, *The Mortal Messiah: From Bethlehem to Calvary* (Salt Lake City: Deseret Book, 1979), 1:86.

3. Bruce R. McConkie, *Doctrinal New Testament Commentary* (Salt Lake City: Bookcraft, 1973), 3:205.

4. Ezra Taft Benson, in Conference Report, April 1969, 12.

5. McConkie, *Mortal Messiah,* 1:271.

6. John M. Lundquist, "The Common Temple Ideology of the Ancient Near East," in *The Temple in Antiquity,* ed. Truman G. Madsen (Provo, UT: Religious Studies Center, Brigham Young University, 1984), 56, 59–60.

7. Brigham Young, in *Journal of Discourses* (London: Latter-day Saints' Book Depot, 1854–86), 18:303.

8. Franklin D. Richards, in *Journal of Discourses,* 25:237.

9. Ezra Taft Benson, "What I Hope You Will Teach Your Children about the Temple," *Ensign,* August 1985, 9.

10. Josephus, *The Jewish War* 6.10.1, trans. H. St. J. Thackeray (London: Cambridge University Press, 1928), 3:501, 503.

11. Benson, "What I Hope You Will Teach," 8.

12. Stephen E. Robinson, "Early Christianity and 1 Nephi 13–14," in *The Book of Mormon: First Nephi, the Doctrinal Foundation* (Provo, UT: Religious Studies Center, Brigham Young University, 1988), 183.

13. McConkie, *Mortal Messiah,* 1:85.

14. McConkie, *Doctrinal New Testament Commentary,* 3:202–3.

15. John Taylor, *The Mediation and Atonement* (Salt Lake City: Deseret News, 1882; reprint, 1975), 203.

16. Joseph Smith, *Teachings of the Prophet Joseph Smith,* comp. Joseph Fielding Smith (Salt Lake City: Deseret Book, 1938), 9–10.

17. Young, in *Journal of Discourses,* 7:289–90.

18. Smith, *Teachings,* 231.

19. McConkie, *Doctrinal New Testament Commentary,* 3:205.

20. Smith, *Teachings,* 160.

21. Orson Pratt, *The Seer,* May 1854, 265.

22. Brigham Young, in *Journal of Discourses,* 8:150.

23. Bruce R. McConkie, *The Promised Messiah: The First Coming of Christ* (Salt Lake City: Deseret Book, 1978), 448.

24. Taylor, *Mediation and Atonement,* 203.

25. McConkie, *Promised Messiah,* 451.

CHAPTER SIX

THE ABRAHAMIC TEST

LARRY E. DAHL

Everyone who achieves exaltation must successfully pass through an Abrahamic test. Let me repeat. Everyone who achieves exaltation must successfully pass through an Abrahamic test. The Prophet Joseph Smith, in speaking to the Twelve Apostles in Nauvoo, said: "You will have all kinds of trials to pass through. And it is quite as necessary for you to be tried as it was for Abraham and other men of God. . . . God will feel after you, and he will take hold of you and wrench your very heart strings, and if you cannot stand it you will not be fit for an inheritance in the Celestial Kingdom of God."[1] That is not a particularly comforting thought, but it is one that cannot be ignored if the scriptures are taken seriously. Why must there be an Abrahamic test? And how can we all be tested like Abraham was tested? Why use Abraham as the standard? What is there about the test Abraham experienced that is universally applicable? When our test comes, will we recognize it? How can we prepare?

MORTAL TESTING INTENDED AND PURPOSEFUL

It is interesting to review the Lord's own statements about His intent to test and try His people. In the very beginning, in the planning stages of this earth, the Lord said, "We will take of these materials, and we will make an earth whereon these may dwell; and we will prove them herewith, to see if they will do all things whatsoever the Lord their God shall command them" (Abraham 3:24–25). *All* things, not just *some* things! The angel taught King Benjamin this

---

Larry E. Dahl is professor emeritus of Church history and doctrine at Brigham Young University.

same truth: "For the natural man is an enemy to God, and has been from the fall of Adam, and will be forever and ever, unless he yields to the enticings of the Holy Spirit, and putteth off the natural man and becometh a saint through the atonement of Christ the Lord, and becometh as a child, submissive, meek, humble, patient, full of love, *willing to submit to all things which the Lord seeth fit to inflict upon him, even as a child doth submit to his father*" (Mosiah 3:19; emphasis added). To the beleaguered Saints being driven out of Jackson County, Missouri, the Lord affirmed that He would "give unto the faithful line upon line, precept upon precept; and I will try you and prove you herewith. And whoso layeth down his life in my cause, for my name's sake, shall find it again, even life eternal. Therefore, be not afraid of your enemies, for I have decreed in my heart, saith the Lord, that I will prove you in all things, whether you will abide in my covenant, even unto death, that you may be found worthy. For if ye will not abide in my covenant ye are not worthy of me" (D&C 98:12–15).

Five months later the Lord declared, "Therefore, they must needs be chastened and tried, even as Abraham, who was commanded to offer up his only son. For all those who will not endure chastening, but deny me, cannot be sanctified" (D&C 101:4–5). Notice the two words *chastened* and *tried.* Is there a difference in meaning between the two? A careful examination of the scriptural use of these two words shows that *chasten* is generally employed when people are being corrected or punished because of disobedience. *Tried,* on the other hand, is used to describe what happens to the righteous. In Doctrine and Covenants 98:12, the Lord specifies that the *faithful* were to be tried, even unto death. Both chastening and trying are needed in the process of becoming sanctified. Indeed, one of the meanings of *chasten* is "to make chaste or pure; purify; refine,"[2] and one of the meanings of *try* is "to make pure by melting or boiling."[3] The Saints needed to be chastened "in consequence of their transgressions" (D&C 101:2). In addition, they needed to be tried, even as Abraham, in consequence of their righteousness. In a revelation to President Brigham Young, the Lord explained, "My people must be tried in all things, that they might be prepared to receive the glory that I have for them, even the glory of Zion; and he that will not bear chastisement is not worthy of my kingdom" (D&C 136:31). The

Lord's intent is clear—those worthy of His kingdom will be tried and proven, even as Abraham.

ABRAHAM'S TEST

Even as Abraham! Concerning Abraham's test, the biblical record says simply: "God did tempt [the Joseph Smith Translation says "try" instead of "tempt"] Abraham, and said unto him, Abraham: and he said, Behold, here I am. And he said, Take now thy son, thine only son Isaac, whom thou lovest, and get thee into the land of Moriah; and offer him there for a burnt offering upon one of the mountains which I will tell thee of" (Genesis 22:1–2). What is not discussed at that point in the record is the seeming incongruities, even contradictions, that Abraham must have faced when he received that command.

First, consider the matter of human sacrifice. Abraham, as a young man, had been saved by the Lord from being offered as a sacrifice himself at the hands of an apostate priesthood who worshipped false gods. These idol worshippers offered to their gods "men, women, and children," specifically those who "would not bow down to worship gods of wood or of stone" (Abraham 1:8–11). The Lord had told Abraham to leave the area because of those evil practices (see Abraham 1:14) and go to a strange land that would eventually belong to his descendants (see Abraham 1:16–18; 2:6). Now he was being asked to offer a human sacrifice—a hard thing to reconcile. Further, God had made it clear to Abraham on several occasions that it was through Isaac the blessings of the covenant were to come to Abraham and to the whole world. Those blessings are the heart and soul of bringing salvation to the children of men, for the promise was that the seed of Abraham, through Isaac, would be scattered among and bless "all the families of the earth" (Abraham 2:8–11). How could that promise be fulfilled if Isaac were killed? Besides, Abraham loved Isaac dearly. After all, he had waited anxiously for Isaac to be born for at least twenty-five years from the time the Lord first promised him an heir.[4] That wait alone would be an Abrahamic test for many. And this long wait troubled Abraham. Several years after the promise of a son at Haran, after Abraham had traveled from Haran, through Canaan, to Egypt, and back to Canaan, and still no child, Abraham asked the Lord for an explanation. He even proposed that perhaps a child born "in my house," meaning a child of one of his servants, could become his heir. Without any details about how or when, the Lord simply reaffirmed the original promise of literal seed:

> Fear not, Abram: I am thy shield, and thy exceeding great reward.
>
> And Abram said, Lord God, what wilt thou give me, seeing I go childless, and the steward of my house is this Eliezer of Damascus?
>
> And Abram said, Behold, to me thou hast given no seed: and, lo, one born in my house is mine heir.
>
> And, behold, the word of the Lord came unto him, saying, This shall not be thine heir; but he that shall come forth out of thine own bowels shall be thine heir.
>
> And he brought him forth abroad, and said, Look now toward heaven, and tell the stars, if thou be able to number them: and he said unto him, So shall thy seed be. (Genesis 15:1–5)

To Abraham's credit, "he believed in the Lord; and he counted it to him for righteousness" (Genesis 15:6). More time passed. Sarai gave Hagar to Abraham, and Ishmael was born. Thirteen more years passed. Abraham was now ninety-nine years old, and Sarai was eighty-nine.

> And God said unto Abraham, As for Sarai thy wife, thou shalt not call her name Sarai, but Sarah shall her name be.
>
> And I will bless her, and give thee a son also of her: yea, I will bless her, and she shall be a mother of nations; kings of people shall be of her.
>
> Then Abraham fell upon his face, and laughed [the Joseph Smith Translation says "rejoiced"], and said in his heart, Shall a child be born unto him that is an hundred years old? and shall Sarah, that is ninety years old bear?
>
> And Abraham said unto God, O that Ishmael might live before thee!
>
> And God said, Sarah thy wife shall bear thee a son indeed; and thou shalt call his name Isaac: and I will establish my covenant with him for an everlasting covenant, and with his seed after him. (Genesis 17:15–19)

When Sarah heard the news, she "laughed within herself," realizing that both she and Abraham were "old and well stricken in age; and it ceased to be with [her] after the manner of women" (Genesis 18:11). I suspect most of us can empathize with Sarah's reaction. But the Lord's response was sobering—"Is anything too hard for the Lord? At the time appointed I will return unto thee, according to the time of life, and Sarah shall have a son" (Genesis 18:12–14). "At the set time of which God had spoken," Isaac was born (Genesis 21:2).

Can you imagine the joy that Abraham and Sarah must have felt—joy accompanied by deep gratitude and an undeniable realization of the power of God and the surety of His promises? They had waited for such a long time, yearning and praying and living righteously. The blessing had finally come. Surely now all would go smoothly. In their old age they could quietly witness the continued fulfillment of God's promises through Isaac. Or could they? First came family problems: Ishmael mocked Isaac and concern grew over who would be Abraham's heir. Hagar and Ishmael were sent away to be cared for by the Lord. Shortly thereafter came the unthinkable requirement: offer Isaac as a sacrifice!

Now, keeping in mind the historical events we have reviewed, try to put yourself in Abraham's place for a moment. How might you have reacted? I can feel myself wanting to say "No. It can't be. Human sacrifice is an abomination. All the blessings of the covenant are to come through Isaac. This doesn't make any sense to me. I have been obedient. I have been patient. And besides all that, I love him with all my heart. I don't want him to die. This is too painful. Why does it have to be this way?" For some reason it did have to be that way, with all its seeming incongruities and inconsistencies. And it was painful for Abraham. The Prophet Joseph Smith taught that "if God had known any other way whereby he could have touched Abraham's feelings more acutely and more keenly he would have done so."[5]

In spite of the hurt, Abraham passed his test. The Genesis account does not describe Abraham's thoughts or feelings or questions. It matter-of-factly says: "And Abraham rose up early in the morning . . . and went unto the place of which God had told him" (Genesis 22:3). But the Apostle Paul bears witness of Abraham's profound faith in

God: "By faith Abraham, when he was tried, offered up Isaac: and he that had received the promises offered up his only begotten son, of whom it was said, That in Isaac shall thy seed be called: accounting that God was able to raise him up, even from the dead; from whence also he received him in a figure" (Hebrews 11:17–19).

In spite of the mind-boggling contradictions of the situation, Abraham had faith to proceed. He had full confidence that *somehow* God could and would fulfill all His promises, even though the one through whom the promises were to come was bound on an altar and Abraham's knife was raised to slay him. It was not until the last, precarious moment that the Lord stopped Abraham, saying, "Abraham, Abraham: . . . Lay not thine hand upon the lad, neither do thou anything unto him; for I know that thou fearest God, seeing thou hast not withheld thy son, thine only son from me" (Genesis 22:11–12). What faith! What discipline! What a sterling example! No wonder Abraham is held up as the model!

OUR TESTS

What about us? How are we to be tested "even as Abraham"? Being asked to offer a child as a sacrifice just does not relate to our time and circumstance. But wrenching heartstrings does relate—to all times and circumstances. And there are many ways to wrench the heart in any age: being asked to choose God over other things we dearly love, even when those things are good and have been promised, and when we have worked for them, yearned for them, prayed for them, and have been obedient and patient; or being asked to persevere in righteousness and service (perhaps even Church service) in the face of terrible difficulty, uncertainty, inequities, ironies, and even contradictions; or watching helplessly as the innocent suffer from the brutal misuse of God-given agency in the hands of evil men.

We should remember that not all the difficulties that try the souls of men are specially designed Abrahamic tests from God. Most, in fact, are the inevitable consequences of living in a mortal, fallen world, where natural law and agency, for the most part, are allowed full sway. It is true that such conditions come from God in the sense that He created the earth and that the conditions here are allowed by Him, even designed by Him to be a universal, probationary testing ground for His children. Everyone experiences bumps in the road of life, which expose weaknesses and strengths, giving opportunity for self-understanding, growth, and refinement. We are not wise enough to sort out all the factors that contribute to our challenges in this life. The critical issue is not the source of the challenges, anyway. The critical issue is how we respond to them. We can lose our focus and our progress if we constantly examine every bump in the road to determine whose fault it is.

The same principle applies to anticipating tests. It is self-defeating to spoil the present by worrying incessantly about the "big test" that will someday come. And it just may be that the "big test" will be very different from what we expect. It is enough to know that God will try us—in His own time, and in His own way, and that the very best way to prepare for that eventuality is by faithfully dealing with present tasks.

It appears that in addition to the general trials of life that all people face, those who claim to be the people of the Lord are faced with special challenges both collectively and individually.

COLLECTIVE, OR GENERATIONAL, TESTS

The Prophet Joseph Smith, writing from Liberty Jail in March 1839 about the Saints being driven out of the state of Missouri, addressed the idea of different but equal generational Abrahamic trials:

> And now, beloved brethren, we say unto you that inasmuch as God hath said that He would have a tried people, that He would purge them as gold, now we think that this time He has chosen His own crucible, wherein we have been tried; and we think if we get through with any degree of safety, and shall have kept the faith, that it will be a sign to this generation, altogether sufficient to leave them without excuse; and we think also, it will be a trial of our faith equal to that of Abraham, and that the ancients will not have whereof to boast over us in the day of judgment, as being called to pass through heavier afflictions; that we may hold an even weight in the balance with them; but now, after having suffered so great sacrifice and having passed through so great a season of sorrow, we trust that a ram may be caught in the thicket speedily, to relieve the sons and daughters of Abraham from their great anxiety, and to light

up the lamp of salvation upon their countenances, that they may hold on now, after having gone so far unto everlasting life.[6]

The Saints in 1839 were being persecuted, hounded by mobs, and driven from their homes, which the Prophet said was a test equal to that of Abraham and "the ancients." What "ancients" might be included? Could the early Christians of nearly two thousand years ago qualify? Their generational trial involved a number of horrifying possibilities—being tortured, eaten by lions, dipped in oil and set afire, or being run through with a sword. Others of the ancients were stoned to death, scourged, forced to languish in vile prisons, burned at the stake. Knowing what the ancients suffered and what the early Saints of this dispensation went through leads naturally to the question of our own generation. What is our collective, generational trial? Consider the teachings of President Ezra Taft Benson, as he spoke to regional representatives of the Church in 1977, while he was President of the Quorum of the Twelve Apostles:

> Every generation has its tests and its chance to stand and prove itself. Would you like to know of one of our toughest tests? Hear the warning words of President Brigham Young, "The worst fear I have about this people is that they will get rich in this country, forget God and His people, wax fat, and kick themselves out of the Church and go to hell. This people will stand mobbing, robbing, poverty and all manner of persecution and be true. But my greatest fear is that they cannot stand wealth."
>
> Ours, then, seems to be the toughest test of all, for the evils are more subtle, more clever. It all seems less menacing and it is harder to detect. While every test of righteousness represents a struggle, this particular test seems like no test at all, no struggle and so could be the most deceiving of all tests.
>
> Do you know what peace and prosperity can do to a people—It can put them to sleep. The Book of Mormon warned us of how the devil, in the last days, would lead us away carefully down to hell.
>
> The Lord has on the earth some potential spiritual giants whom He saved for some six thousand years to help bear off

the Kingdom triumphantly, and the devil is trying to put them to sleep. The devil knows that he probably won't be too successful in getting them to commit many great and malignant sins of commission. So he puts them into a deep sleep, like Gulliver, while he strands them with little sins of omission. And what good is a sleepy, neutralized, lukewarm giant as a leader?

We have too many potential spiritual giants who should be more vigorously lifting their homes, the kingdom, and the country. We have many who feel they are good men, but they need to be good for something—stronger patriarchs, courageous missionaries, valiant genealogists and temple workers, dedicated patriots, devoted quorum members. In short, we must be shaken and awakened from a spiritual snooze.[7]

President Harold B. Lee adds his testimony about our current collective test:

We are tested and we are tried, we are going through some of the severest tests today and we don't realize perhaps the severity of the tests that we're going through. In those days, there were murderings, there were mobbings, there were drivings. They were driven out into the desert, they were starving and they were unclad, they were cold. They came here to this favored land. We are the inheritors of what they gave to us. But what are we doing with it? Today we are basking in the lap of luxury, the like of which we've never seen before in the history of the world. It would seem that probably this is the most severe test of any test that we've ever had in the history of this Church.[8]

That is a rather astonishing notion: ease and affluence can be an Abrahamic test equal, in the sense of proving one's faith, to the sufferings and deprivations of earlier generations. But that is the testimony of the prophets and the testimony of history. Given a choice (and maybe we were given such a choice long before we came to earth), who wouldn't choose ease and affluence rather than pain and suffering? It sounds so attractive, so generous of the Lord. And all we have to do is keep the commandments, using our affluence to build the kingdom of God and serve others. Why is that so difficult? Because ease and affluence tend toward self-indulgence and self-importance. We can become spiritually flabby and casual in our prayers because we seem to need nothing, indifferent to the needs of others because we do not know how it feels to go without. Not liking to be reminded that others have needs, we remove ourselves from the inner city of life to the "quiet hedonism of suburbia," both temporally and spiritually.[9]

We can gorge ourselves with temporal things to the point of spiritual death. Mormon's editorial comment about a deteriorating Nephite society adds another witness: "And thus we can behold how false, and also the unsteadiness of the hearts of the children of men. . . . Yea, and we may see at the very time when he doth prosper his people . . . then is the time that they do harden their hearts, and do forget the Lord their God, and do trample under their feet the Holy One—yea, and this because of their ease, and their exceedingly great prosperity" (Helaman 12:1–2).

The test of ease and affluence is real for much of the Church today. And it will become more a factor as the Church expands into third-world countries where there is poverty instead of abundance. It will take the best within us to meet the challenge. One more brief note about an additional collective trial we face today. It involves affluence but of a different kind. It is the affluence of knowledge. President Harold B. Lee called it sophistication. He said, "We are now going through another test—a period of what we might call sophistication. This is a time when there are many clever people who are not willing to listen to the humble prophets of the Lord. And we have suffered from that. It is rather a severe test."[10]

The prophet Jacob warned of that very challenge and told us how to successfully meet it: "O the vainness, and the frailties, and the foolishness of men! When they are learned they think they are wise, and they hearken not unto the counsel of God, for they set it aside, supposing they know of themselves, wherefore, their wisdom is foolishness and it profiteth them not. And they shall perish. But to be learned is good if they hearken unto the counsels of God" (2 Nephi 9:28–29).

It behooves us to take stock of ourselves and come to grips with our generational Abrahamic tests—tests of luxury and sophistication.

INDIVIDUAL TESTS

There are individual tests in addition to collective ones. Each person faces unique circumstances. Each person has a particular aggregation of strengths and weaknesses. What is a challenge for one may be simple for another, and vice versa. President Boyd K. Packer explained:

> The crucial test of life, I repeat, does not center in the choice between fame and obscurity, nor between wealth and poverty. The greatest decision of life is between good and evil.
>
> We may foolishly bring unhappiness and trouble, even suffering upon ourselves. These are not always to be regarded as penalties imposed by a displeased Creator. They are part of the lessons of life, part of the test.
>
> Some are tested by poor health, some by a body that is deformed or homely. Others are tested by handsome and healthy bodies; some by the passion of youth; others by the erosions of age.
>
> Some suffer disappointment in marriage, family problems; others live in poverty and obscurity. Some (perhaps this is the hardest test) find ease and luxury.
>
> All are part of the test, and there is more equality in this testing than sometimes we suspect.[11]

Our minds are almost paralyzed by the thought that these very different tests can be considered equal. Some of them seem so much more attractive than others. Would you rather be handsome, healthy, bright, and rich, or the opposite of those characteristics? And yet we are assured that all are being adequately tested with their particular circumstances and their unique combination of characteristics. Accepting and understanding that principle may be an Abrahamic test for some, maybe even for many. In our immaturity, we "see through a glass darkly" (1 Corinthians 13:12). We "cannot behold with [our] natural eyes, for the present time, the design of [our] God concerning those things which shall come hereafter, and the glory which shall follow after much tribulation" (D&C 58:3).

"In time," Elder Neal A. Maxwell observed, "each person will receive a 'customized challenge' to determine his dedication to God."[12] The Prophet Joseph Smith taught that before one can have his calling and election made sure he must be "thoroughly proved"; God must find "that the man is determined to serve Him at all hazards."[13] "All hazards" may at times mean there will be no ram in the thicket, no angel to stop the knife, as there were with Abraham. Paul faced that reality. He said, "And lest I should be exalted above measure through the abundance of the revelations, there was given to me a thorn in the flesh, the messenger of Satan to buffet me. . . . For this thing I besought the Lord thrice, that it might depart from me. And he said unto me, My grace is sufficient for thee: for my strength is made perfect in weakness" (2 Corinthians 12:7–9).

Paul's particular "thorn in the flesh" is reminiscent of the more general principle spoken by the Lord to Moroni: "I give unto men weakness that they may be humble; and my grace is sufficient for all men that humble themselves before me; for if they humble themselves before me, and have faith in me, then will I make weak things become strong unto them" (Ether 12:27). Not only Paul but many of us may suffer from a thorn in the flesh or a weakness that is painful but purposeful, and which God may see fit not to remove. All of us know people, faithful people, who are afflicted with some debilitating illness that lasts and lasts, maybe for a lifetime. Neither prayers nor tears nor blessings nor medicine relieves the condition. All that is left is to endure patiently. Truly that wrenches the heartstrings. Why is it necessary? What is gained?

The Purposes of Being Tested

There just have to be exalted purposes in all this testing. The scriptures help to identify some. Lehi explained that without opposition, neither righteousness nor happiness could be brought about (see 2 Nephi 2:11). In a revelation to the Prophet Joseph Smith, the Lord said, "If they never should have the bitter they could not know the sweet" (D&C 29:39; see also Moses 6:55). To President Brigham Young came the word that "my people must be tried in all things, that they may be prepared to receive the glory that I have for them, even the glory of Zion," though just how it prepares them is not said (D&C 136:31). The Lord indicates that being chastened and tried is a prerequisite to being sanctified (see D&C 101:4–5). James taught that the "trying of your faith worketh patience" (James 1:3). We learn from 2 Chronicles 32:31 that being tried exposes the heart: "God left him, to try him, that he might know all that was in his heart." Note what Christ's suffering did for Him, in addition to all that it did for us. Alma taught, "And he will take upon him their infirmities, that his bowels may be filled with mercy, according to the flesh, that he may know according to the flesh how to succor his people according to their infirmities" (Alma 7:12). Paul wrote, "For in that he himself hath suffered being tempted, he is able to succour them that are tempted" (Hebrews 2:18). In Abraham's case, his trial, being "a similitude of God and his Only Begotten Son" (Jacob 4:5), brought to him a piercing understanding of Another's feelings.[14] The same is true for all of us—experiencing trials can bring deep empathy. Perhaps all these purposes just mentioned are encompassed in the following explanation given in the Lectures on Faith:

> An actual knowledge to any person, that the course of life which he pursues is according to the will of God, is essentially necessary to enable him to have that confidence in God without which no person can obtain eternal life. . . .
>
> Such was, as always will be, the situation of the saints of God, that unless they have an actual knowledge that the course they are pursuing is according to the will of God they will grow weary in their minds, and faint. . . .
>
> Let us here observe, that a religion that does not require the sacrifice of all things never has power sufficient to produce the faith necessary unto life and salvation; for from the first existence of man, the faith necessary unto the enjoyment of life and salvation never could be obtained without the sacrifice of all earthly things. It was through this sacrifice, and this only, that God has ordained that men should enjoy eternal life; and it is through the medium of the sacrifice of all earthly things that men do actually know that they are doing the things that are well pleasing in the sight of God.[15]

Simply put, choosing to do the will of God at all hazards brings a righteous and necessary self-awareness and self-confidence, a perfect faith in God and in our ability to do His will. We then know something about ourselves that God has known all along. President Hugh B. Brown, in answer to the question of why Abraham was asked to "offer as a sacrifice his only hope for the promised posterity," said, "Abraham needed to learn something about Abraham."[16] Knowledge about ourselves thus gained puts our relationship to God on a higher plane. We truly become heir to "all that my Father hath" (D&C 84:38), and our "confidence" will "wax strong in the presence of God" (D&C 121:45). That confidence is not arrogance or self-righteousness; it is not a feeling we have simply received that which we have earned. It is, rather, being at ease or comfortable in the presence of Goodness, having complete faith and trust in One who has been gracious—who has *given* us that which we could never, on our own, achieve, once we have proven what the deepest yearnings of our heart and soul really are. Note the confidence with which Job, as he successfully dealt with his own Abrahamic trials, withstood those who accused him of unrighteousness:

> Hold your peace, let me alone, that I may speak, and let come on me what will. . . . Though he slay me, yet will I trust in him. . . . He also shall be my salvation: for an hypocrite shall not come before him. Hear diligently my speech, and my declaration with your ears. Behold now, I have ordered my cause; I know that I shall be justified. (Job 13:13–18)
>
> But he knoweth the way that I take; when he hath tried me, I shall come forth as gold. (Job 23:10)
>
> For I know that my redeemer liveth, and that he shall stand at the latter day upon the earth: and though after my skin worms destroy this body, yet in my flesh shall I see God: whom I shall see for myself, and mine eyes shall behold, and not another; though my reins be consumed within me. (Job 19:25–27)

There is a profound difference between submitting to God by choosing to serve Him at all hazards, and submitting to God by simply giving up, crumbling as it were under the load of suffering. The first brings power and confidence; the other results in impotence and despair. President John Taylor described the spirit of that difference: "I was not born a slave! I cannot, will not be a slave. I would not be a slave to God! I'd be His servant, friend, His son. I'd go at His behest; but would not be His slave. I'd rather be extinct than a slave. His friend I feel I am, and He is mine. A slave! The manacles would pierce my very bones—the clanking chains would grate against my soul—a poor, lost, servile, crawling wretch, to lick the dust and fawn and smile upon the thing who gave the lash! . . . But stop! I am God's free man; I will not, cannot be a slave!"[17]

The object of Abrahamic tests is to make us God's free men and women, not slaves. There is no eternal life in slavery. Eternal life comes with freely choosing to become an heir, at all hazards.

ABOUT PERSPECTIVES

The stark reality is that understanding the need for Abrahamic tests and the nature of such tests does not take away the pain that comes with them. It helps, however, to realize that we are not alone. Others have traveled similarly and endured it well. And so can we. It is at the same time both comforting and somewhat disquieting to read the exchange between the Lord and Joseph Smith as the Prophet cried out in frustration from his cell in Liberty Jail:

> O God, where art thou? And where is the pavilion that covereth thy hiding place?
> How long shall thy hand be stayed? . . .
> My son, peace be unto thy soul; thine adversity and thine afflictions shall be but a small moment;
> And then, if thou endure it well, God shall exalt thee on high; thou shalt triumph over all thy foes. . . .
> Thou art not yet as Job. (D&C 121:1–2, 7–8, 10)
> Know thou, my son, that all these things shall give thee experience, and shall be for thy good.
> The Son of Man hath descended below them all. Art thou greater than he?
> Therefore, hold on thy way. . . . Thy days are known, and thy years shall not be numbered less; . . . God shall be with you forever and ever. (D&C 122:7–9)

That promise applies to us. Few of us are as Job, and none of us suffers as did the Son of Man. To be sure, God will try us—to see if we are determined to serve Him at all hazards. Just as surely, He will be with us and sustain us in our faithful strivings to meet those trials successfully.

NOTES

1. Joseph Smith, as reported by John Taylor in *Journal of Discourses* (Liverpool: F. D. Richards & Sons, 1851–86), 24:197.

2. *World Book Dictionary* (Chicago: Doubleday, 1986), s.v. "chasten."

3. *World Book Dictionary*, s.v. "try."

4. The promise of a great nation coming from Abraham came while he resided in Haran (see Genesis 12:1–3; Abraham 2:1–11). According to Genesis 12:4, Abraham was seventy-five years old when he left Haran. Isaac was born when Abraham was one hundred years old (see Genesis 21:5). Hence the twenty-five-year wait. If, however, Abraham 2:14 gives Abraham's correct age at leaving Haran (sixty-two years old), then the wait was thirty-eight years.

5. John Taylor, in *Journal of Discourses*, 24:264.

6. Joseph Smith, *Teachings of the Prophet Joseph Smith,* comp. Joseph Fielding Smith (Salt Lake City: Deseret Book, 1938), 135–36.

7. Ezra Taft Benson, "Our Obligation and Challenge," Regional Representatives Seminar, September 30, 1977, 2–3; unpublished typescript in author's possession.

8. Harold B. Lee, address to Church employees, Salt Lake City, December 13, 1973; unpublished typescript in author's possession.

9. Neal A. Maxwell, "The Gospel Gives Answers to Life's Problems," address to seminary and institute personnel, Provo, Utah, Brigham Young University, Summer 1970, 2.

10. Harold B. Lee, "Sweet Are the Uses of Adversity," *Instructor,* June 1965, 217.

11. Boyd K. Packer, in Conference Report, October 1980, 29.

12. Neal A. Maxwell, as quoted in *Daily Universe,* Brigham Young University, Provo, Utah, October 7, 1983.

13. Smith, *Teachings,* 150.

14. Rabbinic traditions and apocryphal writings contain the notion that Isaac was a grown man and fully subscribed to his being offered as a sacrifice. Such an idea, though not affirmed in the scriptures, makes the comparison with the Atonement of Christ more poignant and meaningful (see Louis Ginzberg, *The Legends of the Jews* [Philadelphia: Jewish Publication Society of America, 1968], 271–83; and *The Book of Jasher* (Salt Lake City: J. H. Parry & Co., 1887), 59–63.

15. Joseph Smith, "Lecture Sixth," *Lectures on Faith* (Salt Lake City: Deseret Book, 1985), paragraphs 2, 4, 7.

16. Hugh B. Brown, as reported by Truman G. Madsen in *Joseph Smith the Prophet* (Salt Lake City: Bookcraft, 1989), 93.

17. *Oil for Their Lamps,* comp. M. Lynn Bennion (Salt Lake City: LDS Department of Education, 1943), 73; see also Boyd K. Packer in "Follow the Brethren," address to Brigham Young University students, Provo, Utah, March 23, 1965.

CHAPTER SEVEN

THE WIFE/SISTER EXPERIENCE: PHARAOH'S INTRODUCTION TO JEHOVAH

GAYE STRATHEARN

A most important aspect of the ministry of Abraham was his concept of the nature of deity. Throughout the ancient world, nations worshiped a pantheon of gods that were responsible for particular geographical areas. The ancient Babylonians, Assyrians, and Egyptians were henotheistic, that is, they were quite willing to allow that other gods existed outside their pantheon. Nevertheless, each nation believed that the power of its gods was superior to that of the gods of the other nations, and this belief was determined, to a large extent, on the battlefields. If the Egyptians won a battle against the Assyrians, then that showed the Egyptian gods were more powerful than the Assyrian gods. In contrast, the book of Abraham makes it clear that as Abraham traveled throughout the Levant; he did not shift his divine allegiance as he crossed a new political border. Instead, he worshipped a god who knew no geographical boundaries, and Abraham taught those he encountered about that god. Abraham's God, Jehovah, was the same whether Abraham was in Ur of the Chaldees (see Abraham 1:1–16), Haran (see Abraham 2:5–14), Bethel (see Abraham 2:20), or Egypt. But that was not all: not only was Jehovah unencumbered by geographical boundaries but His power knew no equal. Although the power of Jehovah was

---

Gaye Strathearn is an assistant professor of ancient scripture at Brigham Young University.

manifested dramatically in Egypt and in the various Israelite battles, during the life of Abraham, Jehovah's power was manifested in more subtle ways. One important manifestation of Jehovah's influence and power occurred in the confrontation between Abraham and Pharaoh in Egypt in which Pharaoh took Sarah into his harem. That event ultimately led to Pharaoh's seeking a blessing at the hands of Abraham—an interesting demonstration of humility for someone of Pharaoh's power and prestige.

THE WIFE/SISTER MOTIF

The book of Genesis contains a trilogy of incidents in which the wife/sister motif was used by either Abraham or Isaac. The first account describes Abraham's journey into Egypt after a famine enveloped the land of Canaan (see Genesis 12:10–13:4). Similar situations arose later when both Abraham and Isaac dwelt in the city of Gerar (see Genesis 20:1–2; 26:7–8). Although in each instance the patriarch identified his wife as his sister to avert a potentially dangerous situation, these accounts have puzzled many readers and scholars because of the apparent deception involved. Why did the patriarchs resort to such action? That is a difficult theological issue. In attempting to justify the patriarchs' actions, writers have proposed a number of different explanations that offer some significant insights into the three episodes; however, we can gain a still greater understanding, especially of the episode of Abraham's sojourn in Egypt, if we take into account the insights provided by the book of Abraham and the Genesis Apocryphon (1QapGen), one of the scrolls from the Dead Sea corpus. By doing so, we see the hand of God in Abraham's request of Sarah, for Abraham's actions initiated a confrontation between himself and Pharaoh. Because of Abraham's obedience, God was able to introduce Himself to the Egyptian Pharaoh in power and glory. Even though it was only the first of a series of such encounters, it is clear that the God of Abraham was announcing His jurisdiction over all the families of the earth and not just over Abraham and his descendants. That concept is fundamental to our understanding of all of Jehovah's subsequent dealings with humankind throughout the Old Testament.

The biblical account introduces the episode in the following manner: "And there was a famine in the land: and Abram went down into Egypt to sojourn there; for the famine *was* grievous in the land. And it came to pass, when he was come near to enter into Egypt, that he said unto Sarai his wife, Behold now, I know that thou *art* a fair woman to look upon: Therefore it shall come to pass, when the Egyptians shall see thee, that they shall say, This *is* his wife: and they will kill me, but they will save thee alive. Say, I pray thee, thou *art* my sister: that it may be well with me for thy sake; and my soul shall live because of thee" (Genesis 12:10–13).

From these verses it appears that Abraham's major motivation for asking Sarah to say she was his sister was the beauty of Sarah, which would put his life in danger. Certainly that situation was not unique to Abraham and Sarah. Israel's great king David was willing to kill Uriah for his wife Bathsheba (see 2 Samuel 11:14–17), and we see similar incidents in the Egyptian literature. One example, which is found in the Pyramid Texts, records a king boasting of his virility by declaring, "I am the owner of seed who takes women from their husbands whenever he wishes, according to his desire."[1] Similarly, the Papyrus D'Orbiney recounts the "Tale of Two Brothers," in which the Pharaoh, on the advice of his wise men, sent envoys in search of the daughter of Ra-Harmachis. The text describes her as "more beautiful . . . than any woman in the whole land." Unfortunately for the Pharaoh, she was married to Bata, who was willing to slay anyone who tried to take her from him. When Bata killed his envoys, the Pharaoh sent soldiers and a woman who lured the daughter of Ra-Harmachis away from her husband with "all kinds of beautiful ladies' jewelry." The story then explains that, having been given the "rank of Great Lady,"[2] the woman advised the Pharaoh to dispose of Bata, which he promptly did. Although in this instance the Pharaoh acted at the behest of the wife, it is clear that he had no compunction in terminating Bata's life so that he could have an uncontested claim to a beautiful woman.

HISTORICAL INTERPRETATIONS

Though these records seem to validate Abraham's concern for his life, both ancient and modern authors have been concerned about the method Abraham used. Did Abraham ask Sarah to lie just to protect himself? The question of whether there was indeed any blood relationship between Abraham and Sarah has been a constant source of dispute. The ancient Jewish historian Josephus approached the incident by merely saying that Abraham "pretended to be her [Sarah's] brother."[3] A number of scholars believe that there is at least some basis for the identification and thus have attempted to justify the action. Appealing to the Bible, we find only two passages that address this issue. In Genesis 11:27–29 we read: "Now these are the generations of Terah: Terah begat Abram, Nahor, and Haran; and Haran begat Lot. And Haran died before his father Terah in the land of his nativity, in Ur of the Chaldees. And Abram and Nahor took them wives: the name of Abram's wife was Sarai; and the name of Nahor's wife, Milcah, the daughter of Haran, the father of Milcah, and the father of Iscah."

In the past, some have argued that the Iscah mentioned in verse 29 is Sarah.[4] Unfortunately, the book of Abraham does not shed any light on the matter. In Abraham 2:2, in the Pearl of Great Price, we read merely that Abraham's brother, Nehor, married his niece, Milcah, but the author says nothing about Sarah's family line. Since the turn of the century, scholars have dismissed the attempt to equate Iscah with Sarah,[5] but it is clear that Jewish and Muslim writings in antiquity assumed that Sarah was Abraham's niece through Haran.[6] In discussing this problem, it is important to realize that in the ancient Near East the nuclear family, as we now know it, did not exist. Rather, a family unit encompassed grandparents, aunts, uncles, and cousins. This state is reflected in ancient Semitic languages, including biblical Hebrew, in which there is no definite linguistic separation between siblings and their offspring. We find one example of this in the passage that tells of the five Canaanite kings capturing Sodom and Gomorrah. When Abraham is advised of Lot's capture, twice he refers to Lot as his brother (see Genesis 14:14, 16) even though, by western standards, he is clearly Abraham's "nephew" (see Genesis 11:27). So it is at least possible that Sarah belonged to Abraham's extended family and was thus considered to be his "sister" in the sense of a near blood relative. Even allowing for that possibility, however, those who write about this biblical incident generally feel uncomfortable relying solely on such an explanation.[7] Therefore, the search for understanding continues.

The second biblical passage relating to Sarah's and Abraham's nonmarital relationship is found in Genesis 20:12. Here Abraham justified identifying Sarah as his sister to Abimelech by saying that "indeed *she* is my sister; she *is* the daughter of my father, but not the daughter of my mother" (Genesis 20:12). In other words, Abraham claimed that Sarah was his half-sister. Two later Christian documents clearly based their understanding of the wife/sister motif by appealing to that claim. The author of *The Book of the Cave of Treasures*, dating from the sixth century A.D., indicated that Sarah was Terah's daughter by another wife. Hence we read, "Now Sârâ was the sister of Abraham on the father's side, because Terah took two women to wife. When Yâwnû, the mother of Abraham, died, Terah took to wife a woman whose name was "Naharyath" (or Shalmath, or Tona, or Taḥdif), and of her Sârâ was born."[8] Similarly, the *Book of the Bee*, another Syriac text (thirteenth century A.D.), states that Terah's two wives were Yônâ and Shelmath.[9] There are obvious similarities between these two names and the ones in the *Cave of Treasures*.

Those interpretations were the prevailing arguments up until the late 1960s. In 1963, E. A. Speiser proposed another theory. By a legal process found in the Nuzi documents, artifacts of a Near Eastern Bronze Age city-state, Speiser asserted that under Hurrian law a woman could legally be adopted by her husband to give her greater privileges and social status.[10] Speiser's argument initially received wide support in the academic arena, but in recent years a number of scholars have questioned his conclusions. Van Seters acknowledges that the documents do describe an adoptive process, but he argues that this practice was for commercial purposes. By adopting the woman, a man would become her legal guardian and could then benefit from a marriage dowry; however, Van Seters argues, "this did not necessarily create a variety of different marriage types or place women on varying levels of social status."[11] Therefore, it is difficult to understand Abraham's request by an appeal to a linguistic or cultural understanding of the term *sister*.

ANOTHER LOOK AT A COMPLEX SITUATION

So where does that leave us? Although these hypotheses have some merit in adding to our understanding of a difficult passage of scripture, they fail to take into account the insights provided by the book of Abraham and the Genesis Apocryphon. Both of these texts demonstrate that Abraham acted not merely out of an interest in self-preservation but in obedience to a divine command. Thus we read in Abraham 2:22–25: "And it came to pass when I was come near to enter into Egypt, the Lord said unto me: Behold, Sarai, thy wife, is a very fair woman to look upon; Therefore it shall come to pass, when the Egyptians shall see her, they will say—She is his wife; and they will kill you, but they will save her alive; therefore see that ye do on this wise: Let her say unto the Egyptians, she is thy sister, and thy soul shall live. And it came to pass that I, Abraham, told Sarai, my wife, all that the Lord had said unto me—Therefore say unto them, I pray thee, thou art my sister, that it may be well with me for thy sake, and my soul shall live because of thee."

Similarly, the author of the Genesis Apocryphon, which differs slightly in detail from the book of Abraham, explains the nature of Abraham's request at great length. When Abraham traveled to Egypt, he was given instructions in a dream. It is not explicitly stated, but the implication is that the dream came from God. "And I, Abram, had a dream in the night of my entering into the land of Egypt and I saw in my dream [that there wa]s a cedar, and a date-palm (which was) [very beautif]ul; and some men came intending to cut down and uproot the cedar, but leave the date-palm by itself. Now the date-palm cried out and said, 'Do not cut down the cedar, for cursed (?) is he who fells (?) the [cedar].' So the cedar was spared with the help of the date-palm, and [it was] not [cut down]" (1QapGen XIX:14–17).[12]

When Abraham awoke, he described the dream to Sarah. Although the text is somewhat damaged at this point, it is clear that Abraham identified himself with the cedar and Sarah with the date-palm. Therefore, he asked Sarah to identify herself as his sister.

But why did God require Abraham to make such a request? In discussing this question, Stephen Ricks shows that though this commandment might seem strange, obedience is the primary concern.[13] There are numerous passages throughout the scriptures in which God commands people to perform "strange" acts. God's commandment to Nephi to slay Laban was obviously difficult for Nephi, who wrote: "I was constrained by the Spirit that I should kill Laban; but I said in my heart: Never at any time have I shed the blood of a man. And I shrunk and would that I might not slay him" (1 Nephi 4:10).[14] Also, when Abraham returned to the land of Canaan he was given another difficult commandment—to sacrifice his son Isaac (see Genesis

22:1–2). Given the circumstances in Abraham's own life, in which Abraham faced a sacrificial death himself (see Abraham 1:12–15), this commandment must certainly have appeared contradictory to him. On another occasion, God commanded the Apostle Peter in a dream to eat meat that was unclean under the law of Moses (see Acts 10:9–18). Each of those commandments seems to violate one of God's laws. Each one placed the individual in a position where he had either to follow a preexisting law or follow God's current command. The Prophet Joseph Smith taught us: "That which is wrong under one circumstance, may be, and often is, right under another. God said, 'Thou shalt not kill;' at another time He said, 'Thou shalt utterly destroy.' This is the principle on which the government of heaven is conducted by revelation adapted to the circumstances in which the children of the kingdom are placed. Whatever God requires is right, no matter what it is, although we may not see the reason thereof till long after the events transpire."[15]

As we read of the commandments given to Nephi, Abraham, and Peter, in each case the scriptures go on to show us the reason for God's actions. For Nephi, it was so that his people would have the scriptures to remind them of their covenants (in contrast to the people of Zarahemla, who had no records). The scriptures also tell us that Abraham was asked to sacrifice Isaac as a test of his obedience and as a foreshadowing of the eventual sacrifice of God's Only Begotten Son. And the commandment given to Peter was to let him know that God was opening the way for the Gentiles to hear the gospel. But the scriptural account is silent about God's instruction concerning Sarah. We must turn instead to the Genesis Apocryphon to provide us with some insight concerning God's possible motivation.

THE INTERCHANGE BETWEEN ABRAHAM AND PHARAOH

The very fact that Abraham went down into Egypt sets up an important contrast between himself and Pharaoh. Bowie observes: "How insignificant Abraham and all he represented appeared to be as compared with Egypt! On the one hand, an unimportant wanderer; on the other hand, a proud civilization, ancient and deep-rooted. At the time when Abraham . . . came within its borders the history of its life already went back more than two thousand years. From the rich valley of the Nile and from their conquests beyond it the Pharaohs drew the wealth to build the magnificence of Memphis and Thebes and the colossal temples at Karnak; and the pyramids were even then centuries old. What did it matter to Egypt or to history that this Hebrew should exist? To Egypt, nothing: to history, more than Egypt itself would ultimately mean. Egypt represented material pride and power and possessions, and all these would crumble. Abraham represented a new spiritual impulse, and this would be creative long after Egypt should have ceased to count."[16]

Why did Abraham, even though he was insignificant in comparison to the mightiest man of his time, have such a profound influence on the history of the world? It seems that Jehovah was setting the scene to make a statement not only to Pharaoh but also to all of Egypt and to all who read of this event that He wanted them to understand His power and sphere of influence. Therefore, He orchestrated the circumstances around Abraham's introduction to the Egyptian Pharaoh. As Abraham's sister, Sarah provided that introduction, but that was only the first step in a powerful set of events. To appreciate the whole saga, we must delve deeper into the social and religious implications of the confrontation between the apparently insignificant Abraham and the mighty Egyptian Pharaoh.

As a result of the Pharaoh's reaction to Sarah's beauty, the Genesis account tells us that "the Lord plagued Pharaoh and his house with great plagues" (Genesis 12:17). As we turn again to the Genesis Apocryphon we find a similar reaction: "In that night the Most High God sent a pestilential spirit to afflict him and every man of his house, an evil spirit that kept afflicting him and every man in his house" (1QapGen. XX:16b–17a). As a result of these plagues, the Pharaoh called in all his wise men, both the religious advisers (ʿspy) and the physicians (aśy). This division of the wise men into religious and medical groups reflects the dualistic approach the ancient Egyptians had to the healing of sickness. They acknowledged the limitations of their considerable scientific knowledge and recognized the need for divine intervention from deity. To fully appreciate the significance of these divisions in the Egyptians' attitudes toward healing and their effect on the Genesis account, we must first explore the nature of ancient Egyptian medical practices. We can only appreciate the nature of the contest if we understand the power of the Pharaoh.

EGYPTIAN MEDICAL PRACTICES

In antiquity, other nations considered Egypt the center of medical science. The fame of Egyptian physicians commanded international respect. Homer wrote in the *Odyssey* that "there [in Egypt] every man is a physician, wise above human kind."[17] There are similar statements in other ancient writings. Herodotus commented that the Persian emperors Cyrus and Darius were impressed by their Egyptian physicians and that "each physician is a healer of one disease and no more. All the country is full of physicians, some of the eye, some of the teeth, some of what pertains to the belly, and some of the hidden diseases."[18] Stead explains that "by trial and error the Egyptians learnt the use of many natural drugs and realised the importance of rest and care of the patient, as well as basic hygiene as a means of preventing the onset of certain problems."[19]

Two important medical documents dating from the sixteenth century B.C. are the Edwin Smith Papyrus and the Ebers Papyrus. The Edwin Smith Papyrus is a surgical textbook, which "differentiates with utter strictness between the examination method, diagnosis, therapy or prescription, and prognosis."[20] Even today those aspects are an integral part of modern medical practice. Indeed, Wiseman comments that the "level of knowledge" the Edwin Smith Papyrus demonstrates "was not otherwise attained until later classical Greek times or in England in the sixteenth century A.D."[21] The inclusion in the Ebers Papyrus of religious formulas, along with the medical discussions, indicates that the art of healing during this time was not a pure science but was used in conjunction with religious rituals. It began with an appeal for the gods *Rê* and *Thot* to aid the physicians in their healings.[22]

Thus we find two types of physicians mentioned in the ancient writings of Egypt: the *ḥry-ḥᵉb,* "carrier of the ritual book," a religious adviser, and the *synw,* "physician."[23] Wiseman believes that "both probably underwent a formal training based on traditions passed down from father to son."[24] It was the *synw* who held the governmental positions, however. In the account in the Genesis Apocryphon, it appears that Pharaoh summoned both groups to his aid, yet both of them failed. Egypt, with all of its medical knowledge and religious powers, was not able to provide any relief for its Pharaoh. With no other recourse available to them, Pharaoh's servant

Hirqanos came and "begged . . . [Abraham] to pray over the king" and to "lay *(sămak)* . . . [his] hands upon him that he might live" (1QapGen. XX:22). Fitzmyer notes that this line is the first time in a Jewish source that the rite of the laying on of hands is used for healing.[25] The author's word choice and its significance in this instance is important in helping us understand the nature of Abraham's action. Why did the author choose the verb *sămak* to describe the nature of laying on of hands? In the Old Testament the word *sămak* has some very specific connotations that are important for an understanding of our passage.

THE OLD TESTAMENT PRACTICE OF LAYING ON OF HANDS

In the King James Version of the Bible, the translators consistently use the verb *lay* to describe the action of placing hands upon something during priesthood activities. That is true regardless of the ritual being performed. But in the Hebrew text two different verbs are used: *šît* and *sămak*.[26] To distinguish between these two verbs is important because the author of the Genesis Apocryphon specifically used the latter to describe Abraham's blessing of Pharaoh. Generally *šît* was the verb of preference when the laying on of hands was associated with a blessing. That was certainly the case when Jacob blessed each of his sons: "and Israel [Jacob] stretched out his right hand, and laid *(šît)* it upon Ephraim's head, who was the younger, and his left hand upon Manasseh's head, guiding his hands wittingly; for Manasseh was the firstborn" (Genesis 48:14). This usage contrasts with the specialized usage of *sămak*. Daube argues that the difference between *šît* and *sămak* can be distinguished by the amount of pressure used by the officiator. He prefers to translate *šît* as "place," and *sămak* as "lean." The difference was that when a person "leans" *(sămak)* during the rite of the laying on of hands, there was a symbolic transference of something from the officiator to the recipient.[27]

The matter can be clarified further when we examine the occasions when *sămak* was the verb of choice in describing the rituals of the laying on of hands. As Réne Péter demonstrates, its use is categorized in one of two ways—it is used in either sacrificial or nonsacrificial occasions.[28] The sacrificial use is not relevant to our discussion, but the nonsacrificial use is very enlightening because Abraham's blessing of Pharaoh clearly falls into that category. Thus it is grouped with such incidents as the scapegoat ritual on the Day of Atonement (see Leviticus 16:5–10, 21–22), the case of the blasphemer (see Leviticus 24), and Joshua's ordination by Moses (see Numbers 27:18–23). In each of these occasions *sămak* is used to indicate not a blessing but the transference of something from the officiator to the recipient. In the case of the scapegoat, Aaron symbolically transferred the iniquities of Israel to the goat. In the story of a man who blasphemed during an altercation, Moses was instructed to have those who heard the offense "lay *[sămak]* their hands upon his head, and let all the congregation stone him" (Leviticus 24:14). Although there is considerable scholarly debate concerning the nature of the laying on of hands in this instance,[29] it appears that the laying on of hands represents a retransference of the impurity back to the offender. The third example occurred when Moses set Joshua apart as the next Israelite leader (see Numbers 27:23). In that instance, Moses symbolically transferred his honor, or authority, to Joshua (see Numbers 27:20).[30]

In all three of these cases, the verb *sămak* was chosen instead of *sît*. It is clear that it had a specialized meaning in association with nonsacrificial rituals. Unfortunately, though, there is no Old Testament instance where the ritual of the laying on of hands was associated with healing. As Mackay points out, that lack is "understandable since the O. T. is almost entirely the record of the House of Israel under the Law of Moses, that is, without the Melchizedek Priesthood."[31] It was not until the dawning of the Christian era, and hence the return of the Melchizedek Priesthood through the Savior, that the practice was generally associated with the healing of the sick. But Latter-day Saints know that Abraham did hold the Melchizedek Priesthood. The Doctrine and Covenants tells us that he received it from Melchizedek (see D&C 84:14). Therefore, it is certainly not out of place to find in the Genesis Apocryphon that Abraham lays *(sămak)* his hands upon the head of Pharaoh to heal him from the plagues sent by the Lord.

THE LAYING ON OF HANDS AND THE GENESIS APOCRYPHON

As mentioned previously, the discovery and translation of the Genesis Apocryphon provided scholars with the first Jewish source where healing was achieved by the laying on of hands. In response to Hirqanos's plea for help, Abraham's nephew, Lot, responded that Abraham could not pray for the Pharaoh until he returned Sarah (1QapGen. XX:22–23). When Pharaoh acted accordingly, the author recorded Pharaoh's plea and Abraham's response as follows: "But now pray for me and for my house that this evil spirit will be rebuked from us. So I [Abraham] prayed [. . .] and I laid *[sămak]* my hands upon his head and the plague fell from him and the evil spirit was rebuked and he lived" (1QapGen. XX:28–29). It is significant that Abraham did not initiate this scene with Pharaoh. Instead, he waited for Pharaoh to approach him. In fact, this whole episode appears to have been orchestrated so that Pharaoh would seek out Abraham's assistance.

Although the biblical account of this incident does not mention Abraham's praying for the Pharaoh, it is mentioned in the similar account with the king of Gerar, Abimelech. Here we are informed that "Abraham prayed unto God: and God healed Abimelech, and his wife, and his maidservants; and they bare children" (Genesis 20:17). Then the plague which Jehovah had sent upon them is explained: "for the Lord had fast closed up all the wombs of the house of Abimelech, because of Sarah Abraham's wife" (Genesis 20:18). The Genesis Apocryphon gives no indication of the nature of the plague against Pharaoh, and although scholars have suggested numerous hypotheses,[32] it is at least possible, given the corresponding circumstances, that Pharaoh experienced problems similar to those of Abimelech.

Noteworthy in both the passages from the Genesis Apocryphon is the use of *sămak* rather than *šît* to indicate the laying on of hands. From the parallel passages in the Old Testament, it appears that the author chose the word *sămak* to indicate a transference of something to Pharaoh. In both instances in the Genesis Apocryphon, *sămak* is found in connection with *ṣᵉlā*, the verb for praying. The two words seems to be integrally connected. It was not Abraham's power that cured Pharaoh; it was the power of Jehovah, with Abraham as a conduit, that effected the cure. The concept of having a priesthood holder act as a conduit for divine purposes is certainly not unfamiliar to Latter-day Saints. In the Doctrine and Covenants, we read of Jehovah's telling Edward Partridge that "I will lay my hand upon you by the hand of my servant Sidney Rigdon, and you shall receive my

Spirit, the Holy Ghost, even the Comforter, which shall teach you the peaceable things of the kingdom" (D&C 36:2). In a similar way, priesthood holders lay their hands upon the sick to invoke the power of God. Brigham Young once declared: "When I lay hands on the sick, I expect the healing power and influence of God to pass through me to the patient, and the disease to give way. . . . When we are prepared, when we are holy vessels before the Lord, a stream of power from the Almighty can pass through the tabernacle of the administrator to the system of the patient, and the sick are made whole."[33] Abraham performed in a similar manner as he approached Pharaoh.

But was the actual healing of Pharaoh the principal reason behind Abraham's actions? I believe that Abraham's actions have a much more significant purpose than the mere healing of Pharaoh. Abraham brought about something that the Egyptians could not do for themselves, even though they were the leading authorities in ancient medical practices and even though they possessed their own pantheon of gods. Those gods failed to cure Pharaoh, but Abraham and his God were successful. This was a contest between man's knowledge—man's gods—and Jehovah, the God of Abraham. Therefore, in recording that Abraham laid his hands upon Pharaoh, the author of the Genesis Apocryphon used the verb *sămak* to convey a message to his readers—one that is not readily evident in the English translation but that was very significant to a Hebrew audience. In using the language of the Torah, the author conveyed the idea of a transference of power from Jehovah (through Abraham) to Pharaoh. Could there now be any doubt in Pharaoh's mind concerning the jurisdiction and strength of Jehovah's power? This incident was only the first of a number of contacts between Egypt and Abraham and his descendants. The contest between Pharaoh's wise men and Abraham's God to secure a cure parallels the events some centuries later when Abraham's successor, Moses, also confronted an Egyptian Pharaoh. Once again, Jehovah orchestrated the events so that His power was manifested both to the Pharaoh and to the children of Israel.[34]

CONCLUSION

The prophet Abraham stands uncontested in history as the father of three monotheistic religions: Judaism, Christianity, and Islam.

While the people in the world around him worshipped a plethora of deities, Abraham stood firm in his commitment to Jehovah. Whenever Abraham journeyed throughout Chaldea, Canaan, or Egypt, he proclaimed the power of Jehovah. His allegiance did not shift from one country to another. In examining the controversial incident in Egypt, the book of Abraham and the Genesis Apocryphon help us to see Abraham continuing his missionary activities. When Abraham responded to God's commandment to call Sarah his sister, he acted with immediacy and unquestioned obedience. One of the great characteristics of such individuals as Abraham, Nephi, and Peter was their commitment to God's current commandments, not just his previous ones. As we go through life, we also encounter times when we are given commandments that seem strange or that are difficult to understand. We may not always see their immediate purpose, but if we respond as Abraham did, then we can also experience the power of God in our lives and in the lives of those around us. Surely that is one of the great lessons to learn from our mighty ancestor, Abraham.

NOTES

1. Utterance 317, in *The Ancient Egyptian Pyramid Texts,* trans. R. O. Faulkner (Oxford: Clarendon Press, 1969), 99.

2. "Tale of Two Brothers," in Miriam Lichtheim, *Ancient Egyptian Literature: A Book of Readings* (Berkeley: University of California Press, 1976), 2:207–8.

3. Josephus, *Jewish Antiquities* 1.8.1, trans. H. St. J. Thackeray, in *Loeb Classical Library,* ed. E. H. Warmington (Cambridge, MA: Harvard University Press, 1967), 81.

4. For example, Josephus substitutes the name of Sarah for that of Iscah by saying that Sarai and Milcah were Haran's daughters (*Jewish Antiquities* 1.6.5 [Thackeray, 75]). A footnote to this episode notes that in making the connection between Sarai and Iscah, Josephus is following rabbinical tradition. Later Augustine also equates the two women. See *City of God* 16.12, in *A Select Library of the Nicene and Post-Nicene Fathers of the Christian Church,* First Series, ed. Philip Schaff (Grand Rapids, Mich.: Eerdmans Publishing, 1956), 2:318. Similarly, the *Targum Jonathan* Genesis 11:29 qualifies the name of Iscah by adding the phrase "who is Sarai" (*Targum du Pentateuque,* trans. Roger Le Déaut, *Sources Chrétiennes 245* [Paris: Les Éditions du Cerf, 1978], 147).

5. See Adam Clarke, *The Holy Bible: Containing the Old and New Testaments* (New York: Eaton and Mains, 1883), 1:93–94; and

J. Skinner, *Genesis,* in *International Critical Commentary,* ed. Samuel R. Driver, Alfred Plummer, and Charles A. Briggs (New York: Scribner's Sons, 1910), 1:238. Since that time scholars have insisted on a distinction between Sarah and Iscah. See Claus Westermann, *Genesis 12–36: A Commentary,* trans. John J. Scullion (Minneapolis: Augsburg Publishing, 1984), 137–38; and Victor P. Hamilton, *The Book of Genesis Chapters 1–17,* in *The New International Commentary on the Old Testament,* ed. R. K. Harrison (Grand Rapids, MI: Eerdmans, 1990), 362.

6. Josephus, *Jewish Antiquities* 1.6.5 (Thackeray, 75); and G. Weil, *The Bible, the Koran, and the Talmud; or, Biblical Legends of the Mussulmans* (New York: Harper, 1855), 79.

7. For example, see Thomas Whitelaw, "Genesis and Exodus," in *The Pulpit Commentary,* ed. H. D. M. Spence and Joseph S. Exell (New York: Funk and Wagnalls, 1950), 1:187–88.

8. *The Book of the Cave of Treasures,* trans. E. A. Wallis Budge (London: The Religious Tract Society, 1927), 149.

9. *The Book of the Bee,* trans. E. A. Wallis Budge (Oxford: Clarendon Press, 1886), 42.

10. Ephraim A. Speiser, "The Wife-Sister Motif in the Patriarchal Narratives," in *Biblical and Other Studies,* ed. Alexander H. Altmann (Cambridge, MA: Harvard University Press, 1963), 15–28.

11. John Van Seters, *Abraham in History and Tradition* (New Haven: Yale University Press, 1975), 74. For further arguments, see S. Greengus, "Sisterhood Adoption at Nuzi and the 'Wife-Sister' in Genesis," *HUCA* 46 (1975): 5–31; and Thomas L. Thompson, *The Historicity of the Patriarchal Narratives: The Quest for the Historical Abraham* (New York: de Gruyter, 1974), 234–48.

12. Translation from Joseph A. Fitzmyer, *The Genesis Apocryphon of Qumran Cave 1: A Commentary* (Rome: Biblical Institute Press, 1966), 51, 53.

13. Stephen D. Ricks, "The Early Ministry of Abraham," *Studies in Scripture, Volume 2: The Pearl of Great Price,* ed. Robert L. Millet and Kent P. Jackson (Salt Lake City: Randall Book, 1985), 221–22.

14. For a discussion of some of the legal implications of Nephi's action, see John W. Welch, "Legal Perspectives on the Slaying of Laban," *Journal of Book of Mormon Studies* 1 (Fall 1992): 119–41.

15. Joseph Smith, *Teachings of the Prophet Joseph Smith,* sel. Joseph Fielding Smith (Salt Lake City: Deseret Book, 1938), 256.

16. Walter Russell Bowie, "Genesis," in *The Interpreter's Bible,* ed. George Arthur Buttrick, et al. (New York: Abingdon Press, 1952), 1:579–80.

17. Homer, *Odyssey* 4.231–32, trans. A. T. Murray, in *Loeb Classical*

Library, ed. E. H. Warmington (Cambridge, Mass: Harvard University Press, 1974), 1:123.

18. Herodotus 2.84, trans. A. D. Godley, in *Loeb Classical Library* (Cambridge, MA: Harvard University Press, 1966), 1:369.

19. Miriam Stead, *Egyptian Life* (London: British Museum, 1986), 70.

20. E. Brunner-Traut, as cited in Klaus Seybold and Ulrich B. Mueller, *Sickness and Healing,* trans. Douglas W. Stott (Nashville: Abingdon, 1978), 33.

21. Donald J. Wiseman, "Medicine in the Old Testament World," *Medicine and the Bible,* ed. Bernard Palmer (Exeter: Paternoster Press, 1986), 14.

22. Ebers 1, as cited in P. Ghalioungui, *The House of Life,* Per Ankh: *Magic and Medical Science in Ancient Egypt* (Amsterdam: B. M. Israël, 1973), 1.

23. J. V. K. Wilson, "Medicine in the Land and Times of the Old Testament," in *Studies in the Period of David and Solomon and Other Essays,* ed. T. Ishada (Tokyo: Yamakawa-Shuppansha, 1982), 338.

24. Wiseman, "Medicine in the Old Testament World," 16.

25. Joseph A. Fitzmyer, "Some Observations on the *Genesis Apocryphon,*" *The Catholic Biblical Quarterly* 22 (1960): 283–84.

26. This difference between the two Hebrew verbs is also found in the Septuagint, where *šît* is translated as *epiballo* and *sǎmak* is translated as *epitithēmi.*

27. David Daube, *The New Testament and Rabbinic Judaism* (London: Athlone Press, 1956), pp. 225–26.

28. Réne Péter, "L'imposition des mains dans l'Ancien Testament," *Vetus Testamentum* 27 (1977): 48–55.

29. Jacob Milgrom, after reviewing the arguments, cogently argues in favor of a transferral ritual in this passage. He believes that "those who heard the blasphemy were contaminated by it and, via the hand-leaning, they effectively transferred the pollution back to the blasphemer and eliminated it by executing him outside the camp." See *Leviticus 1–16,* in *The Anchor Bible,* ed. William Fox Albright and David Noel Freedman (New York: Doubleday, 1991), 3:1041. This is in contrast to David P. Wright, "The Gesture of Hand Placement in the Hebrew Bible and in Hittite Literature," *Journal of the American Oriental Society,* 106, no. 3 (1986): 435. This author argues against the "transferral theory" and instead supports a legal inter-pretation whereby the witnesses proclaim the guilt of the accused.

30. See Péter, "L'imposition," 54.

31. Thomas W. Mackay, "Abraham in Egypt: A Collection of Evidence for the Case of the Missing Wife," *Brigham Young University Studies* 10 (Summer 1970): 436.

32. Two midrashic traditions identify the plague as leprosy. See Lech Lecha 41.2 and Vayera 52.13 in *Midrash Rabba: Genesis,* 3rd ed., trans. Rabbi Dr. H. Freedman (New York: Soncino Press, 1939), 1:334, 460. Hugh Nibley, in *Abraham in Egypt,* argues that Pharaoh was afflicted with impotence. That both these incidents should be associated with the creation of offspring is important, given the nature of the Abrahamic covenant that should pass through Abraham's lineage. During these accounts Abraham and Sarah were still awaiting the time when they would be given a son to carry on the covenant. It should also be noted that although many scholars believe that the incidents with Pharaoh and Abimelech are two versions of the same story (see W. W. Sloan, *A Survey of the Old Testament* [New York: Abingdon Press, 1957], 43–44; and Robert Davidson, *Genesis 12–50, Cambridge Bible Commentary,* ed. P. R. Ackroy, A. R. C. Leaney, and J. W. Packer [New York: Cambridge University Press, 1979], 2:4), it is clear from the Joseph Smith Translation of the Bible that the Prophet Joseph Smith considered them to be two separate events: "and when Abraham said *again* of Sarah his wife, She is my sister" (Joseph Smith Translation, Genesis 20:2; emphasis added).

33. Brigham Young, in *Journal of Discourses* (London: Latter-day Saints Book Depot, 1854–86), 14:72.

34. See John S. Kselman, "Genesis," *Harper's Bible Commentary,* ed. James L. Mays (San Francisco: Harper and Row, 1988), 95; and Meredith G. Kline, "Genesis," in *Eerdmans Bible Commentary,* ed. D. Guthrie and J. A. Motyer (Grand Rapids, MI: Eerdmans, 1987), 93.

CHAPTER EIGHT

JACOB IN THE PRESENCE OF GOD

ANDREW C. SKINNER

Few prophets in the Old Testament teach us more about covenant making and personal revelation than Jacob, the father of the twelve tribes. Jacob was a son of promise and of *the* promise. His own father was the meek and obedient Isaac, whose willingness to be offered as a sacrifice in the presence of God forever stands as a similitude of the Atonement of God's Only Begotten Son (see Genesis 22; Jacob 4:5). Indeed, the Apostle Paul refers to Isaac as Abraham's "only begotten son" (Hebrews 11:17). As a consequence of obedience, the promises God had established with Abraham were handed down to the patriarch's posterity—from Abraham to Isaac, from Isaac to Jacob (see Genesis 22:16–18; 26:1–5), and so on.

It is not difficult to imagine that as children Jacob and his twin brother, Esau, were taught or, at the very least, heard about their father's and grandfather's supreme faithfulness. As the brothers matured, however, they took different paths. Esau became a cunning hunter, while Jacob is described in the Hebrew text as an *'ish tam,* a man "whole, complete, perfect" (Genesis 25:27*b*). The implication is that Esau was concerned about one pursuit to the exclusion of other important considerations.

As a younger man, Esau seems to have possessed little sensitivity to spiritual matters. Certainly, he thought more about immediate physical concerns than either the covenants of God or those turning

Andrew C. Skinner is dean of Religious Education at Brigham Young University.

117

points in life which go on to determine the future. Thus, Esau sold the birthright (see Genesis 25:29–34). And, like some of us, he valued what was lost only after it was gone (see Genesis 27:38).

Esau added to his own misery and that of his parents by vowing to kill Jacob because of the lost birthright and blessing, even though he himself was responsible for the loss and Isaac did give him a blessing in the end (see Genesis 27:39–42). Moreover, Esau married outside the covenant, which caused great grief to Isaac and Rebekah (see Genesis 26:34–35). Without doubt, Esau's behavior was on his mother's mind when she exclaimed: "I am weary of my life because of the daughters of Heth: if Jacob [also] take a wife of the daughters of Heth . . . what good shall my life do me?" (Genesis 27:46). In other words, Rebekah saw all her life's work, all her planning and teaching about the importance of the Abrahamic covenant, all her care in guarding and guiding its perpetuation according to divine desires, as worthless and wasted if Jacob were to follow in Esau's footsteps.

Here we see the Old Testament at its best, for the recurring problems of the ages are laid bare in an ancient context. Is there anything so heart-wrenching for a parent as a child of hope choosing to devalue covenants of the eternal family bond or anything so depressing as a loved one who esteems lightly matters of the Spirit? Do faithful parents of any gospel dispensation ever *not* worry about their Esaus?

After Esau saw "that the daughters of Canaan pleased not Isaac his father," he took another wife from the lineage of Ishmael, Abraham's posterity (Genesis 28:8–9). But again he missed the point. It was not simply a matter of marrying someone from a proper family; it was a matter of understanding and appreciating the significance of the covenant, of one's whole attitude toward sacred things.

By contrast, Jacob trifled not with sacred things (see D&C 6:12). He chose to obey his mother and father in many things and ultimately set out on a journey to seek a wife from among a known and acceptable branch of the covenant family. That was of paramount importance to his mother, for she was ever conscious of God's promises regarding her twin boys, especially the promise of Jacob's ascendancy over nations, though he was the younger (see Genesis 25:23). Perhaps Jacob's foretold soberness and obedience were qualities that had been developed, nurtured, and proven over and over throughout the long eons of a premortal existence and thus lay at the heart of Jehovah's promise to Rebekah of Jacob's future greatness (see Genesis 25:23–26).

Before Jacob left his home to go to Padan-aram, his father, Isaac, blessed him in accordance with patriarchal privileges and recon-firmed to him the opportunity of receiving the blessings and covenant of Abraham: "Arise, go to Padan-aram, to the house of Bethuel thy mother's father; and take thee a wife from thence of the daughters of Laban thy mother's brother. And God Almighty bless thee, and make thee fruitful, and multiply thee, that thou mayest be a multitude of people; and give thee the blessings of Abraham, to thee, and to thy seed with thee; that thou mayest inherit the land wherein thou art a stranger, which God gave unto Abraham. And Isaac sent away Jacob" (Genesis 28:2–5).

With this blessing fresh on his mind, Jacob left Beer-sheba on what would prove to be a journey of many years. What Jacob thought about on this first leg of his travels we do not know, but one supposes it was about the covenants of the Lord and promises of obe-dience. For when he got to the place he would later name Bethel, he settled down to spend the night and, while asleep, a marvelous vision was opened to him (see Genesis 28:11–15).

Jacob saw a ladder on the earth, which reached to heaven. Ascending and descending on the ladder were the angels of God, sen-tinels to the portals of heaven. Above the ladder was the Lord Himself, whom Jacob heard and with whom he would make the very same covenant that his grandfather Abraham had made—the same covenant his father, Isaac, had prepared him to receive. "And, behold, the Lord stood above it, and said, I am the Lord God of Abraham thy father, and the God of Isaac: the land whereon thou liest, to thee will I give it, and to thy seed; and thy seed shall be as the dust of the earth, and thou shalt spread abroad to the west, and to the east, and to the north, and to the south: and in thee and in thy seed shall all the families of the earth be blessed. And, behold, I am with thee, and will keep thee in all places whither thou goest, and will bring thee again into this land; for I will not leave thee, until I have done that which I have spoken to thee of" (Genesis 28:13–15).

When Jacob arose in the morning, he sanctified the site of his vision with anointing oil and vowed, or covenanted, to live in complete harmony with God's will. He concluded his affirmation with a promise to tithe all that he would come to possess (see Genesis 28:18–22).

The significance of Jacob's first vision was at least sixfold. First, as the Prophet Joseph Smith indicated, this vision was Jacob's opportunity to begin to comprehend for himself "the mysteries of Godliness."[1] From this comment we also know that Jacob was a righteous Melchizedek Priesthood holder, because the Doctrine and Covenants teaches that "this greater priesthood administereth the gospel and holdeth the key of the mysteries of the kingdom, even the key of the knowledge of God" (D&C 84:19). Jacob would later use that key to unlock a spiritual door.

Second, Jacob's status as a prophet was confirmed. He heard the voice of the Lord Jehovah, the premortal Christ, and, as the Apostle John later taught, "the testimony of Jesus is the spirit of prophecy" (Revelation 19:10).

Third, Jacob learned that in his seed, or through his own lineage, all the other families of the earth would be blessed (see Genesis 28:14). That promise was literally fulfilled in the mortal advent of the Savior, Jesus Christ (see Galatians 3:16), and it is not impossible that Jacob glimpsed that fulfillment. Moreover, this promise has also been fulfilled as Jacob's seed have become Melchizedek Priesthood ministers and missionaries of the name and gospel of God, which gospel will ultimately bring salvation, even eternal life, to everyone who receives it (see Abraham 2:10–11).

Fourth, Jacob learned that if he kept the covenant, God would be with him everywhere he went, that God would fulfill everything He promised to do for Jacob, and that God would bring him back to the land of his inheritance.

Fifth, Jacob learned that sanctity and place can be, and often are, linked together. "Surely, the Lord is in this place; and I knew it not; . . . this is none other but the house of God," said Jacob (Genesis 28:16–17).

Sixth—and this point ties the other five points together—Jacob received his endowment at Bethel on the occasion of his first vision. President Marion G. Romney said:

> When Jacob traveled from Beersheba toward Haran, he had a
> dream in which he saw himself on the earth at the foot of a

ladder that reached to heaven where the Lord stood above it. He beheld angels ascending and descending thereon, and Jacob realized that the covenants he made with the Lord there were the rungs on the ladder that he himself would have to climb in order to obtain the promised blessings—blessings that would entitle him to enter heaven and associate with the Lord. . . . Temples are to us all what Bethel was to Jacob. Even more, they are also the gates to heaven for all of our unendowed kindred dead. We should all do our duty in bringing our loved ones through them.[2]

The great promises and blessings proffered to Jacob on this occasion were conditional rather than absolute. Nowhere does the text say that they were sealed or ratified with surety at this point, as is sometimes supposed. Jacob would have a long time to prove his loyalty and secure for himself the unconditional guarantee of all the terms of the covenant. Neither does the text say that Jacob's dealings with the Lord constituted the ultimate theophany, or revelation of God, which the scriptures promise to the faithful. Such would come later, after years of righteousness. From Bethel, Jacob undoubtedly came away understanding the order of heaven, the possibilities for exaltation, and the promises of the Abrahamic covenant if he proved faithful.

Other great prophets have left us accounts of their Jacob-like experiences, especially the Apostle Paul and the Prophet Joseph Smith. Joseph Smith said, apparently to help us understand his own visions: "Paul ascended into the third heavens, and he could understand the three principal rounds of Jacob's ladder—the telestial, the terrestrial, and the celestial glories or kingdoms, where Paul saw and heard things which were not lawful for him to utter. I could explain a hundred fold more than I ever have of the glories of the kingdoms manifested to me in the vision, were I permitted, and were the people prepared to receive them."[3]

Jacob's life after the vision at Bethel (see Genesis 29–31) is one of the best-known biblical love stories, set as it is against the background of a manipulative uncle turned father-in-law. It need not concern us here, except as it points out Jacob's patience and loyalty to God in the face of frustrations, challenges, and manipulations. After more than twenty years of labor under the household rule of the scheming and jealous Laban (see Genesis 31:1–15, 38), Jacob finally left Padan-aram to return to the land of his covenantal inheritance. But his departure was not without a final confrontation with the father of his two wives, who hotly pursued Jacob's caravan. Ultimately, Jacob and Laban came to a respectful parting of the ways and established a boundary covenant, which would long divide the territory of the Israelites from the northern Aramaeans (see Genesis 31:44–45). But, the point is, Jacob's life was never one of ease or devoid of challenges and conflicts. Indeed, Jacob says in effect to Laban at a moment of intense frustration during their last confrontation: "Why are you chasing me? Why won't you let me go home in peace? What is my sin against you? I have served you in the day when drought consumed me and at night in frost and sleep departed from my eyes . . . You have changed my wages ten times . . . and except the fear of God had been with me, surely you would have sent me away destitute" (see Genesis 31:36–42).

Perhaps that last statement is one we should focus on when we think of Jacob. God was with him as had been promised. In the face of every trial, Jacob remained faithful and retained the companionship of the Lord who watched over him. It was, after all, the Lord who commanded Jacob to leave Laban's land and return to the land of Canaan. The vision of God's instruction to leave Padan-aram bears a significant similarity to one given to Abraham, in which he also was told to leave a country and go to Canaan (see Genesis 1:11–13; see also Abraham 1:16–18).

Jacob's journey home was remarkable for its continuing theophany. En route, the patriarch was met by "God's host," angels of the Lord, who undoubtedly blessed him. It is also likely these angels reminded Jacob of his powerful and life-changing vision of the ascending ladder at Bethel when he was leaving the promised land twenty years before. Now, Jacob was returning and carrying with him those troubles incident to the brotherly conflict with Esau, which had been partially responsible for his flight from Canaan in the first place. The angelic ministration during Jacob's return trip appears to have been a sign and a reminder of divine protection and assistance in what surely must have seemed to Jacob an inevitable and intense confrontation with Esau.

That the looming conflict weighed heavily on Jacob's mind seems beyond question, because immediately after his encounter with the angels, Jacob sent messengers to Esau's territory in hopes of laying the groundwork for a peaceful reunion with his brother (see Genesis 32:3–5). The messengers returned with gravely distressing news: Esau was coming to meet him with four hundred men. Jacob became exceedingly fearful and divided his entourage into two groups intending to preserve at least part of his covenantal family should Esau attack. The threat of a vengeful brother probably cannot be overestimated, for it was a life crisis of staggering proportion. In Jacob's mind, his family, as well as the covenant itself, faced annihilation. Just as important, the promises of God were on trial. Perhaps for a moment or two they looked like empty words and hollow phrases. But this life crisis set the stage for two events that would confirm forever the course of Jacob's future. First, Jacob yearningly prayed to God for safety; second, he wrestled that night for a desperately needed blessing at the hand of Deity (see Genesis 32:9–13, 24–30).

We do not know how long Jacob prayed that day at the river Jabbok, but surely his prayer was intense. In it, Jacob acknowledged the Lord's goodness as well as his own sincerely felt unworthiness before God. He pleaded for deliverance from the impending catastrophe, reminding God that He had told Jacob to leave Padan-aram and that He had also promised Jacob that his posterity would be as innumerable as the sands of the sea. How could this promise come to pass if Jacob and his family were annihilated? (see Genesis 32:9–12).

That night, as Jacob was settling down, inspiration came. He selected a large herd of animals as a gift to be given to Esau and instructed his servants how to offer the present when Esau approached (see Genesis 32:13–21). Jacob's gift of 580 animals indicates how much wealth he had accumulated while in the land of Laban and how much he had prospered through the Lord's guidance.

Next, Jacob sent his wives and eleven sons away from the main camp, across the Jabbok River on the east side of the Jordan, so they could have an extra measure of protection. Then, with the provisions set in order, Jacob was left alone—alone in terms of mortal company—to ponder, pray, and prepare.

Night is a horrible time for those who face trials. How much more difficult the night must be in the face of a test of a lifetime, an Abrahamic test of complexity and contradiction. Nighttime seems to magnify challenges; at night problems seem to weigh particularly heavy on the mind. Night is the time when the prince of darkness does his best work.

At some point, Jacob was joined by a being who would wrestle with him for the rest of the night. The details of Jacob's wrestle are not made clear in the biblical record, but we have enough information that we can see profound truths and patterns in this episode of the patriarch's life.

It seems reasonable to conclude that Jacob's wrestle was physical as well as spiritual, because the text is emphatic in its description of Jacob's dislocated hip (see Genesis 32:25, 31–32). Perhaps that detail is mentioned precisely to show that his wrestle was a literal as well as a metaphoric occurrence. It is also reasonable to suppose that Jacob's opponent that night was a being from the unseen world of heavenly messengers, a divine minister possessing a tangible but translated body, because he was able to wrestle all night and throw Jacob's hip out of joint (see Genesis 32:24–25).

That the personage was merely a mortal seems unlikely, first of all, because the text takes care to point out that Jacob was left completely alone, with no other humans close by (see Genesis 32:22–24). Second, the nature of Jacob's encounter was of special and profound consequence. The Hebrew word used to describe Jacob's visitor is simply *'ish,* meaning "man," with no overt reference to divine status.[4] Nevertheless, the same word is used elsewhere to denote divine messengers in several Old Testament passages that deal with angels or heavenly beings who are sent to convey revelation. When used in this way, the word also often connotes the operation of the principle of divine investiture of authority—the authorization that God grants to others to speak in His name, even sometimes as though they were God Himself. "Thus, the angel of Yahweh ([Hebrew] *mal'akh*) often appears in the form of an *'ish,* 'a man.' Either both terms are used interchangeably for an angel . . . or angels who appear at first only as men [but] afterwards speak with divine authority (Gen. 19:12ff.; Jgs. 13:3ff.; Josh. 5:15) or even as God Himself (Gen. 18:9ff.), or they act in the place of God (19:10f.; Jgs. 13:20) . . . Also in the prophets, the angel of God appears in the form of an *'ish.*"[5]

As implied in Doctrine and Covenants 129:4–7, divine messengers of Jacob's day (or any dispensation, for that matter) who had physical contact with earthly beings had to possess physical bodies themselves. The Prophet Joseph Smith "explained the difference between an angel and a ministering spirit; the one a resurrected or translated body, with its spirit ministering to embodied spirits—the other a disembodied spirit, visiting and ministering to disembodied spirits."[6] Furthermore, Elder Joseph Fielding Smith indicated that whenever divine messengers had a mission to perform among mortals, those messengers "had to have tangible bodies" and thus were translated beings.[7]

The Prophet Joseph Smith taught that translated beings are coworkers with God to bring to pass His great plan of salvation. "Their place of habitation is that of the terrestrial order, and a place prepared for such characters He held in reserve to be ministering angels unto many planets."[8] Of Enoch, the preeminent translated personage, the Prophet said: "He is a ministering Angel to minister to those who shall be heirs of Salvation."[9]

It seems very unlikely that the being involved with Jacob was Jehovah Himself, because the Lord did not yet possess a physical body. And the being could not have been a one-time mortal who was now a resurrected being because Christ was the "firstfruits" of the Resurrection (1 Corinthians 15:20), the first of our Heavenly Father's children on this earth to be resurrected. Therefore, one of two possibilities regarding the identity of Jacob's night visitor is that he was a translated being who had been an inhabitant of this earth, since "there are no angels who minister to this earth but those who do belong or have belonged to it" (D&C 130:5).

Though encounters with translated beings in Jacob's day are not explicitly recorded, those beings certainly existed. Enoch and his entire city had been translated and taken up into heaven as a result of their righteousness (see Moses 7:18–24). Melchizedek possessed that same kind of great faith. He "and his people wrought righteousness, and obtained heaven, and sought for the city of Enoch which God had before taken" (JST Genesis 14:34). In fact, other men with that same faith and possessing the same priesthood as Melchizedek and Enoch had also been translated and taken up into heaven (see Joseph Smith Translation, Genesis 14:32).

At Jabbok, Jacob faced a crossroads. He was brought to the brink of his faith and understanding. He stood in the place his grandfather Abraham had stood when God asked for the life of Isaac, and Abraham could not see how the promises of the covenant (specifically the promise of a great posterity) would be fulfilled. But Abraham was obedient in the face of a test that shook him to his very core. The Prophet Joseph Smith said, "The sacrifice required of Abraham in the offering up of Isaac, shows that if a man would attain to the keys of the kingdom of an endless life; he must sacrifice all things."[10] Furthermore, in an 1833 revelation, the Prophet wrote, "Therefore, [the Saints] must needs be chastened and tried, even as Abraham" (D&C 101:4).

Jacob likewise was obedient in the face of his ordeal and desired a blessing to strengthen his resolve and faith. He wanted and needed greater light, knowledge, and power. Despite his intimate contact with Deity and his temple experience twenty years earlier, the threatening situation with Esau was more than he could comprehend. How could the covenant continue if the bearers of the covenant were destroyed? In faith he wrestled for a blessing with a divine visitor, one appointed to guard the portals of heaven and also sent to test Jacob's resolve and his request. They wrestled all night, and Jacob would not let the celestial sentinel go until he gave Jacob the requested blessing. Jacob's resolve was great, and his fortitude enduring.

Other men and women in every dispensation have had to wrestle at some point in their lives for blessings, greater truth, and light from God. Sometimes, those spiritual wrestles or struggles of tremendous magnitude have become intensely physical even though they have not encountered a tangible being as Jacob did. Enos said at the beginning of his record that he wanted to tell us "of the wrestle which [he] had before God" (Enos 1:2). The story of his wrestle has become a classic account of persistent, powerful faith exercised in order to receive a blessing at the hand of God.

Likewise, Alma "labored much in the Spirit, *wrestling* with God in mighty prayer" that others would be blessed (Alma 8:10; emphasis added). Though it was to no avail, for the people hardened their hearts and rejected the Spirit, the wrestle was a great blessing in

Alma's own life as the Lord revealed Himself to the prophet (see Alma 8:15).

The Prophet Joseph Smith applied the concept of "wrestling for a blessing" to Zacharias, whose situation, at least in principle, parallels that of Jacob. Zacharias had no children. He "knew that the promise of God must fail, consequently he went into the temple to *wrestle* with God according to the order of the priesthood to obtain a promise of a son."[11]

President Brigham Young said that all of us are situated "upon the same ground," in that we must "struggle, *wrestle,* and strive, until the Lord bursts the veil and suffers us to behold His glory, or a portion of it."[12] And so it was with Jacob on that lonely night near the River Jabbok, when he began to wrestle with a divine visitor for a blessing—a blessing that would, in President Young's words, "burst the veil" and shower down on him greater light and glory from God.

The biblical text at this point is most instructive:

> And he [the visitor] said, Let me go, for the day breaketh. And he [Jacob] said, I will not let thee go, except thou bless me. And he [the visitor] said unto him, What is thy name? And he said, Jacob. And he [the visitor] said, Thy name shall be called no more Jacob, but Israel: for as a prince hast thou power with God and with men, and hast prevailed. And Jacob asked him, and said, Tell me, I pray thee, thy name. And he [the visitor] said, Wherefore is it that thou dost ask after my name? And he [the messenger] blessed him there. And Jacob called the name of the place Peniel: for I have seen God face to face, and my life is preserved (Genesis 32:26–30).

This passage discloses some specific concepts that illuminate Jacob's experience and ultimately suggests the other possible identity of Jacob's visitor. First we see that Jacob's spiritual tenacity, aided by his great physical strength, achieved for him his desired result. After intense persistence and endurance, Jacob was rewarded with an endowment of power as the divine minister said, "for as a prince hast thou power with God and with men" (Genesis 32:28). This great endowment came in accordance with the principle described in Ether 12:6: "For ye receive no witness until after the trial of your faith." As

President Young might have said, after the wrestle comes the bursting of the veil.

Second we discern that the bestowal upon Jacob of the rich gift, or endowment, of power followed a familiar pattern. Jacob was asked first to disclose his given name, and then he was given a new name, Israel, which symbolized his struggle before God and men for a blessing. Jacob's blessing that night seems to have been bestowed in two stages. After the divine visitor announced that Jacob had been given a new name and great power, which was the first stage of the blessing, Jacob then turned the tables and asked the name of the visitor: "Tell me, I pray thee, thy name" (Genesis 32:29). Perhaps he was really asking what name or personage the visitor represented and by whose authority he, the visitor, bestowed the new name and new power. Numerous passages of scripture show that the Hebrews attached great importance to the meaning and possession of names. A name of power was a symbol of authority. In some respects, even to know a name was regarded as giving one power or control over the object or being in question.

The visitor answered Jacob's question with another question: "Wherefore is it that thou dost ask after my name?" (Genesis 32:29). The messenger wanted to know why Jacob was asking. But the biblical text at this juncture records no response from Jacob, and yet some exchange must have taken place, for the visitor was satisfied enough that he gave Jacob something more, something beyond a new name and new power. "He blessed him there" (Genesis 32:29).

The sequence of events up to this point is clear:

1. Jacob wrestled all night for a blessing in the face of great trial, in which he, his family, and the fulfillment of the covenant all faced annihilation.

2. Jacob was asked for his name, and he disclosed his own given name to a divine being or minister.

3. Jacob was then presented with a new name.

4. Jacob was next given an endowment of power, which would be recognized in the eyes of both God and men.

5. Jacob was finally given an additional blessing, and the divine being was not heard from again.

The text is silent about the nature of the additional blessing. We get only Jacob's response to the blessing bestowed upon him at that moment. But what an arresting response it was, for it tells us what we may read into the narrative. The text says, "And he [the divine being] blessed him there. . . . And Jacob called the name of the place Peniel: for I have seen God face to face, and my life is preserved" (Genesis 32:29–30). Let there be no misunderstanding; the text says Jacob was blessed, and then the very next words out of his mouth which are (or, perhaps, can be) reported to us are, "I have seen God face to face, and my life is preserved" (Genesis 32:30). Thus, the great blessing Jacob received that night was no less than the ultimate theophany of his (or anyone's) life—his being privileged to enjoy the literal presence of God and to have every promise of past years sealed and confirmed upon him.

Thus, the other, and likely, possibility regarding the identity of Jacob's visitor is that it was God Himself. Not Jehovah—for He did not yet possess a physical body. Rather, it would have been God the Father or Elohim. As we have already seen, the term "man" (Hebrew, *'ish*) used in Genesis 32:24 to describe Jacob's visitor, was a word sometimes used anciently to refer to God. In fact, the ancient rabbis believed that "man" was one of the many titles of God. In addition, the phrase "face to face" (Hebrew, *panim 'el panim*) occurs several times in the Hebrew Bible, each referring to a heavenly vision, and only once does God not perform the visitation.

In the end, one supposes it could be argued that the identity of Jacob's visitor is not so important as the fact that the result of the visit was that the patriarch ultimately saw God and came to know that he had seen Him. In terms of the physical wrestle Jacob experienced, Hugh Nibley states, "The word conventionally translated by 'wrestled' can just as well mean 'embrace' and . . . this [was a] ritual embrace that Jacob received."[13]

CONCLUSION

The events described in chapter 32 of Genesis may be seen as the culmination of a process begun twenty years before at Bethel, when Jacob first encountered God and became a candidate for exaltation by vowing to live according to the Abrahamic covenant. At Bethel, Jacob had his first temple experience, according to President Romney. For twenty years thereafter, Jacob proved himself at every hazard and under every circumstance.

In describing circumstances like Jacob's, the Prophet Joseph Smith said: "When the Lord has thoroughly proved [someone], and finds that the man is determined to serve Him at all hazards, then the man will find his calling and his election made sure, then it will be his privilege to receive the other Comforter. . . . Now what is this other Comforter? It is no more nor less than the Lord Jesus Christ Himself, . . . that when any man obtains this last Comforter, he will have the personage of Jesus Christ to attend him, or appear unto him from time to time, and even He will manifest the Father unto him, and they will take up their abode with him, . . . and the Lord will teach him face to face, and he may have a perfect knowledge of the mysteries of the Kingdom of God; and this is the state and place the ancient Saints arrived at."[14]

That describes Jacob. The crisis of Jacob's life at the River Jabbok pushed him to the brink of his understanding—it pushed him to the limits of his faith. Life seemed to hang in the balance. Perhaps just as important to Jacob was the possibility that God's promises to fulfill the Abrahamic covenant through him were all empty words, that God was not omnipotent and omniscient, that He was, after all, just like the gods of the Canaanites.

Events on the eve of that life crisis caused Jacob to wrestle for a blessing, just as Enos and Alma would do. His wrestle resulted in, to use President Brigham Young's poignant words, "the Lord burst[ing] the veil . . . to behold [reveal] His glory."[15] Indeed, the story of Jacob's wrestle discloses tokens and promises with which all his posterity, literal or adopted, may become familiar. At the River Jabbok, Jacob was given the ultimate blessing and guarantee that can be given in mortality—the guarantee of eternal life sometimes referred to as calling and election made sure. Years later, as he was blessing the sons of Joseph, the aged patriarch referred to events on the night of his wrestle when he mentioned "the Angel which redeemed me from all evil" (Genesis 48:16).

Thus we see a pattern and are able to recognize consistency in the great plan of happiness given to all people by a loving Heavenly Father. Joseph Smith taught that "all that were ever saved, were saved through the power of this great plan of redemption, as much so before the coming of Christ as since; if not, God has had different plans in operation, (if we may so express it,) to bring men back to dwell with himself; and this we cannot believe."[16]

Abraham, Isaac, and Jacob desired, sought for, wrestled for, and craved the literal presence of God. They prayed for it, worked for it, and lived for it. Abraham, Isaac, and Jacob were successful in their quest, and the Old Testament is a powerful, personal record of their success. The Doctrine and Covenants tells us that these patriarchs "have entered into their exaltation, according to the promises, and sit upon thrones, and are not angels but are gods" (D&C 132:37).

We are the seed of Abraham, Isaac, and Jacob and the inheritors of the Abrahamic covenant. What is the Abrahamic covenant to us? Is it not candidacy for exaltation? As with Jacob, the task of turning candidacy into reality is up to us. Let us wrestle for this blessing as we continue to worship in the temples of our God.

NOTES

1. Joseph Smith, *History of The Church of Jesus Christ of Latter-day Saints,* ed. B. H. Roberts, 2nd ed. rev. (Salt Lake City: The Church of Jesus Christ of Latter-day Saints, 1932–51), 1:283.

2. Marion G. Romney, "Temples—The Gates to Heaven," *Ensign,* March 1971, 16.

3. Joseph Smith, *Teachings of the Prophet Joseph Smith,* comp. Joseph Fielding Smith (Salt Lake City: Deseret Book, 1938), 304–5.

4. Joseph Fielding Smith thought it "more than likely" that the visitor was a messenger but not an angel. Joseph Fielding Smith, *Doctrines of Salvation,* comp. Bruce R. McConkie (Salt Lake City: Bookcraft, 1970), 1:17.

5. G. Johannes Botterweck and Helmer Ringgren, eds., *Theological Dictionary of the Old Testament,* rev. ed. (Grand Rapids, MI.: Eerdmans, 1983), 1:233.

6. Smith, *Teachings,* 191.

7. Smith, *Doctrines of Salvation,* 2:110–11.

8. Smith, *Teachings,* 170.

9. Joseph Smith, *The Words of Joseph Smith,* comp. and ed. Andrew F. Ehat and Lyndon W. Cook (Orem, UT: Grandin Book, 1991), 41.

10. Smith, *Teachings,* 322.

11. Smith, *Words,* 235; emphasis added.

12. Brigham Young, in *Journal of Discourses* (London: Latter-day Saints' Book Depot, 1856), 3:192; emphasis added.

13. Hugh Nibley, *The Message of the Joseph Smith Papyri: An Egyptian Endowment* (Salt Lake City: Deseret Book, 1975), 243.

14. Smith, *Teachings,* 150–51.

15. Young, in *Journal of Discourses,* 3:192.

16. Joseph Smith, *The Evening and the Morning Star,* March 1834, 143.

CHAPTER NINE

THE LAW OF MOSES AND THE LAW OF CHRIST

EDWARD J. BRANDT

When many people hear the words "the law of Moses," they tend to associate that law with something very undesirable—a program or a system that is all outward and temporal and so far removed from what they would hope or expect to be associated with the gospel of Christ that some might wonder if there were any worth in it at all. Such a view of the law of Moses is false.

The law of Moses could not influence a person's life unless that person had some measure and portion of the Spirit of the Lord in his or her life. The lack of that spiritual influence caused great difficulties in ancient Israel. They lost the spirit of the law, which is why the law turned into such a burden, as is illustrated later in the scriptural record. All of the standard works, not just the Old and the New Testament, teach of this law. A proper perspective on this law provides a meaningful dimension to gospel understanding.

The most important text to help us fully appreciate the spirit and purpose of the law of Moses is the Book of Mormon. The Book of Mormon people maintained the spirit of the law of Moses, and it served them well. Their faithful observance finally helped prepare a responsive group to receive the Messiah in their day.

In a great revelation on priesthood, Doctrine and Covenants 84, the Lord established an important foundation for understanding the relationship between the law of Moses and the law of Christ. After

---

Edward J. Brandt is the director of the Evaluation Division of the Correlation Department of The Church of Jesus Christ of Latter-day Saints.

reviewing the line of authority in conferring the priesthood in ancient times, we read:

> And the Lord confirmed a priesthood also upon Aaron and his seed, throughout all their generations, which priesthood also continueth and abideth forever with the priesthood which is after the holiest order of God.
>
> And this greater priesthood administereth the gospel and holdeth the key of the mysteries of the kingdom, even the key of the knowledge of God.
>
> Therefore, in the ordinances thereof, the power of godliness is manifest. [That is to say, in the ordinances of the Melchizedek, or the higher, priesthood is the power of godliness manifest.]
>
> And without the ordinances thereof [or the ordinances of the higher priesthood], and the authority of the priesthood, the power of godliness is not manifest unto men in the flesh;
>
> For without this [that is, the temple ordinances] no man can see the face of God, even the Father, and live. (D&C 84:18–22)

This passage is often used and misused by anti-Mormons against the claims of the First Vision. They are fond of quoting verse 22 out of context, contending that if you have to have priesthood to see the face of God and live, then, they ask, how was it possible for Joseph Smith to see the claimed vision because he had not yet received priesthood. Such an interpretation is a wresting of the context of the passage. The proper context of this revelation is that without the ordinances of the higher priesthood [the temple ordinances], no man can see the face of God and *live in His presence.*[1] These verses provide a true perspective of purpose and power of the priesthood ordinances. Then follows the scriptural explanations of the law of Moses:

> Now this Moses plainly taught to the children of Israel in the wilderness, and sought diligently to sanctify his people that they might behold the face of God;
>
> But they hardened their hearts and could not endure his presence; therefore the Lord in his wrath, for his anger was kindled against them, swore that they should not enter into his rest while in the wilderness, which rest is the fulness of his

glory. [To enter into the rest of the Lord is to enter into His presence—into His glory.]

Therefore, [as a consequence of this rebellion] he took Moses out of their midst, and the Holy Priesthood also;

And the lesser priesthood continued [now ask yourselves, what did the lesser priesthood minister?], which priesthood holdeth the key of the ministering of angels and the preparatory gospel;

Which gospel is the gospel of repentance and of baptism, and the remission of sins, and the law of carnal commandments, which the Lord in his wrath caused to continue with the house of Aaron among the children of Israel until John, whom God raised up, being filled with the Holy Ghost from his mother's womb. (D&C 84:23–27)

The Doctrine and Covenants says that the law of Moses consists of the preparatory gospel and the law of carnal commandments. The preparatory gospel includes the elements of faith in Jesus Christ, repentance, and baptism. We are counseled to "come unto Christ," which ultimately means to become Christlike. The Lord has established a path to help us achieve that end. There are many significant steps along the way, all centered in the gospel of Jesus Christ. Some fundamentals open the door and set one on the path. These fundamentals are called the first principles of the gospel: faith in Jesus Christ, repentance, baptism. They are a part of the preparatory gospel, which is part of the law of Moses. Other scriptures include the law of sacrifice or the burnt offering as an integral part of the preparatory gospel.[2] Doctrine and Covenants 84 indicates that the Lord added something to these fundamental things. He described it in verse 27 as the "law of carnal commandments." The purpose of the law of carnal commandments was to help the children of Israel focus on the basic fundamentals of the gospel. These two elements, then—the preparatory gospel and the law of carnal commandments—are what we commonly call the law of Moses.[3]

LAW OF MOSES

1. Preparatory Gospel
   a. Burnt offering
   b. Faith in Jesus Christ, repentance, and baptism

     c. The Ten Commandments
     d. The law of the covenant
  2. Law of Carnal Commandments
     a. Ordinances—offerings
     b. Performances—including dietary and purification laws

To accurately describe the law of Moses, we would have to say that it contained the basic part of the gospel of Jesus Christ. It was never intended to be something apart, separated, or even lower than the gospel of Christ. It was simply to help the people in their focus and understanding.

An instructive perspective about this law is found in Mosiah 13 in the Book of Mormon. This is the great discourse given by the prophet Abinadi as he labored with the wicked priests of King Noah. They had questioned the prophet, asking the meaning of a verse in Isaiah 52: "How beautiful upon the mountains are the feet of him that bringeth good tidings" (Mosiah 12:21; see also Isaiah 52:8). The prophet answered and in the process revealed something of the nature of the law of Moses that the people of Noah were practicing:

"And now I say unto you that it was expedient that there should be a law given to the children of Israel, yea, even a very strict law; for they were a stiffnecked people, quick to do iniquity, and slow to remember the Lord their God; Therefore, there was a law given them, yea, a law of performances and of ordinances, a law which they were to observe strictly from day to day, to keep them in remembrance of God and their duty towards him" (Mosiah 13:29–30).

Verse 30 states that this law, which included the law of carnal commandments, consisted of a law of ordinances and performances. The ordinances and performances were teaching instruments of the law of carnal commandments. A synonym for the word *carnal* is *flesh*. The law of carnal commandments was, therefore, commandments intended to help the children of Israel to control the flesh—to develop self-control and self-discipline in their lives. It was to help them to get a handle on their lives so they could begin to focus on the basic fundamentals that would lead them to Christ. That was its primary purpose and the spirit and the intent of the law of carnal commandments.

Perhaps a brief explanation of the two systems—ordinances and performances—might be helpful. Ordinances had to do with the law of offerings. In ancient Israel a number of offerings were offered by the children of Israel, some of them with special intent: the peace offering, the sin offering, and the trespass offering.[4] The first ten chapters of Leviticus provide the scriptural instruction for these offerings.

The peace offering[5] was intended to help individuals express that they had made peace with God, that they had come to grips with their problems in life. It was offered at one of those moments in life when an individual was at peace, ready to take the next step in personal development and growth. The children of Israel were asked to acknowledge being blessed with that peace in their lives through the peace offering.[6]

The peace offering was also called a vow offering and a thank offering. Done periodically, the vow offering[7] was one of recommitment to the covenants the Israelites had made. It had a similar value for ancient Israel as partaking of the sacrament has in the Church today. The thank offering was to offer thanks[8] to God for the great blessings that had been extended to the Israelites, His grace and His goodness in their lives. In Luke 2:22–23, we discover that Joseph and Mary went to the temple to offer an offering. It was a thank offering because they had received a blessing of peace in the gift of this Son who had come to their family and, more importantly, to Israel, to the whole world.

All these offerings were free-will offerings, not by command or upon demand. These offerings were to help the Israelites to focus on God and their relationship to Him, and for them to acknowledge who it was that gave them great blessings in their lives.

The sin offering and the trespass offering were the most important offerings under the law of carnal commandments. A sin offering[9] was given in recognition that a person had come to grips with the sins in his life that were not generally well known by others. There were sins of omission, or sins in one's heart and thoughts, not so much outwardly manifest as inwardly manifest. The trespass offering,[10] on the other hand, was a direct result of outward transgressions. An integral part of the trespass offering was the requirement upon the participant to have repented of the sin and made some sort of restitution. The law was very specific about the kinds of restitutions that were to be offered. For example, if one had stolen five of another man's finest sheep, the law required that he restore to him double, or ten. If people were really sincere in honoring the law, they thought twice about borrowing their neighbor's sheep. In some instances, the law required a recompense or restitution of only 20 percent, but in other instances, it was as much as 100 percent.[11]

Now, what was the purpose of the sin offering and the trespass offering? To teach the people to repent and to obtain the power of repentance in their personal lives so that they could develop self-control and get their feet on the path that leads to salvation. That was the simple purpose of it. Could a person go through the outward practice of the law and never do it with full intent? Yes. Does that ever happen when an individual partakes of the sacrament thoughtlessly? They also had to struggle with their intent in their religious practice. These offerings were the chief ordinances that were a part of the law of carnal commandments.

There was also the heave offering, or the wave offering,[12] which was a very specialized offering given by the priests only. It was possible, for example, if you chose the right kind of an animal, to offer one offering for all of the offerings. Some have the misconception that the Israelites were running in every day burning up sheep or goats. That was not the purpose of the offering. Usually a family presented an offering once or twice a year on a special occasion, such as at a feast or conference time, the birth of a child, or other special events, or when they had come to grips with their problems and really wanted a renewal and a refreshment. If they had sufficient resources, they provided the sheep or the goat. If not, the law in some instances permitted lesser substitutions.[13] They took the offering to the tabernacle or, later in their history, to the temple, where the priest would receive them at the gate. The family was not allowed to go past the precincts for the congregation into the area for offerings and sacrifices. The priests took the animal and ceremonially slaughtered it. The priest was allowed to receive or keep the hide as part of the payment for his service.[14] Some of the inner parts were burnt, and some were disposed of in other ways.[15] The animals that were slaughtered were prepared in a special way so as to teach the people of the Atonement. Then the family took the animal of the offerings home, roasted it, and had a special religious meal in commemoration of the things they were trying to accomplish, or it was taken to the priest's family, depending on which type of offering was given.[16]

The priest did not have time to keep flocks as others did, so he was allowed to keep one quarter of an animal as payment for his service. He usually took one of the front quarters of the animal. Again one brought the animal to the priest, and he took it into the precincts. One could watch him as he prepared the animal for the family. He took the hide and probably gave it to one of his sons who attended him there, and then he removed the quarter that was to be payment for his family. He then took that quarter and lifted it up, pointing towards the area where the individual was waiting, and the priest heaved it or waved it above his head, indicating, "This is my payment." Then the individual acknowledged, "Yes, that is your payment." That was the heave or the wave offering—payment for his service.[17]

The priest was required to tithe his portion. He took a small amount of the meat to the altar and acknowledged that this was a gift from God for the service that he had rendered as a priesthood bearer in behalf of one of the children of Israel.[18] Then he could take that roast home for his family and they would be cared for. It was a very practical system, and it all had significance to enable people to have focus in their personal lives and to help them develop self-control.

The performances of the law of carnal commandments are enumerated in numerous places in the Old Testament—such as, do not mix crops in the field.[19] The Israelites were not to sow oats and barley together. They could not have three rows of corn and four rows of peas. They were not to mix the fabric of garments—no wool with linen, for example. The fibers had to be separate. What was the purpose of such performances? To remind them of their covenants. When they sowed a field, they were always reminded that Israel was a part of the covenant people, and they were not to intermingle with nations outside the covenant. That simple reminder was intended to remind them of their covenants. These are only a sample of a multitude of examples, all of which had a practical purpose.

The Book of Mormon teaches of the full spirit of all of these laws that were revealed. In 2 Nephi 11:4 we read, "Behold, my soul delighteth in proving unto my people the truth of the coming of

Christ; for, for this end hath the law of Moses been given; and all things which have been given of God from the beginning of the world, unto man, are the typifying of him."

Notice how Nephi reminds them that everything involved in the practices of the law of Moses, as he identified it, was associated with Christ; and it was done with the intent to bring them to Christ.

In 2 Nephi is recorded:

> And, notwithstanding we believe in Christ, we keep the law of Moses, and look forward with steadfastness unto Christ, until the law shall be fulfilled.
>
> For, for this end was the law given; wherefore the law hath become dead unto us, and we are made alive in Christ because of our faith; yet we keep the law because of the commandments.
>
> And we talk of Christ, we rejoice in Christ, we preach of Christ, we prophesy of Christ, and we write according to our prophecies, that our children may know to what source they may look for a remission of their sins.
>
> Wherefore, we speak concerning the law that our children may know the deadness of the law; and they, by knowing the deadness of the law, may look forward unto that life which is in Christ, and know for what end the law was given [that they may look for what end the law was given, all to focus on Christ]. And after the law is fulfilled in Christ, that they need not harden their hearts against him when the law ought to be done away. (2 Nephi 25:24–27)

The Spirit of the Lord was essential to the full significance of this system of performances and ordinances.

Additional examples of performances can be cited from the great Passover feast established in Exodus 11 and 12 in the Old Testament. Many symbols in this feast are associated with the Atonement. Some of them are very obvious; for example, the firstborn animal—the lamb without blemish.[20] Study the book of Leviticus in detail to see how the priests were to slaughter the lamb. They were careful never to break the bones. The throat was to be cut in just a special way so that the blood would be let out totally. What was the significance of all of that? To teach and remind of the Atonement of Christ.[21]

There were other, more subtle types of performances. First, the animal chosen was to be sufficient to feed the group that one was hosting at the home. It was to be, however, just enough to feed all who were present because the law required that it was to be totally consumed.[22] In other words, the sacrifice of the animal had to be complete or total. To use Book of Mormon language, it was to be an infinite sacrifice like unto the "infinite" Atonement.[23] There was to be none left. If some was left, it was to be burned. Why did they put the blood on the doorpost? Because only under the covenant of Christ, or under the blood of the Lamb, could Israel be saved. That is to say, unless we fall under the effects of the blood of the Atonement of Jesus Christ, there is no salvation in Israel.[24]

There are many ramifications in the symbolism and the practices of the feasts in ancient Israel. As Nephi said, "We are made alive in Christ because of our faith" (2 Nephi 25:25). This statement is indeed true, but only if one has the Spirit of the Lord. The Book of Mormon prophets saw this system of laws with that perspective, and it had great power in their lives. In 2 Nephi 5:10, Nephi reports on this observation and practice, "And we did observe to keep the judgments, and the statutes, and the commandments of the Lord in all things according to the law of Moses."

In Jacob 4:5, the brother of Nephi testified of the effect of the law of Moses through all the ages:

> Behold, they believed in Christ and worshipped the Father in his name, and also we worship the Father in his name. And for this intent we keep the law of Moses, it pointing our souls to him [not just by way of remembrance, you see; even the practices were to help them in their personal lives to start down the road and to find edification from it]; and for this cause it is sanctified unto us for righteousness, even as it was accounted unto Abraham in the wilderness to be obedient unto the commands of God in offering up his son Isaac, which is a similitude of God and his Only Begotten Son.

The prophet Alma likewise taught:

> Yea, and they did keep the law of Moses; for it was expedient that they should keep the law of Moses as yet, for it was not all fulfilled. But notwithstanding the law of Moses, they did

look forward to the coming of Christ, considering that the law of Moses was a type of his coming, and believing that they must keep those outward performances until the time that he should be revealed unto them. Now they did not suppose that salvation came by the law of Moses; but the law of Moses did serve to strengthen their faith in Christ; and thus they did retain a hope through faith, unto eternal salvation, relying upon the spirit of prophecy, which spake of those things to come. (Alma 25:15–16)

Therefore, it is expedient that there should be a great and last sacrifice; and then shall there be, or it is expedient there should be, a stop to the shedding of blood; then shall the law of Moses be fulfilled; yea, it shall be all fulfilled, every jot and tittle, and none shall have passed away. And behold, this is the whole meaning of the law, every whit pointing to that great and last sacrifice; and that great and last sacrifice will be the Son of God, yea, infinite and eternal. (Alma 34:13–14)

What of New Testament times? How understood was the true spirit of the law in the days of the Savior and His Apostles? In Luke 24:44 is a significant statement. Jesus reminded the disciples what had happened when He was with them and then said that "all things must be fulfilled, which were written *in* the law of Moses [what is the focus of the law of Moses? Christ is the focus; He is the purpose], and in the prophets [their testimonies were of the Messiah], and in the psalms, concerning me" (emphasis added).

What book of the Old Testament was the most frequently quoted scripture by Jesus and the Apostles in the New Testament?[25] The book of Psalms. What was the second most quoted scripture in the New Testament by Jesus and the Apostles? The book of Isaiah, of which about 80 percent is written in poetic form. Why would they choose these two books instead of others? Because the people were best acquainted with these particular books. For the common folk (the Bedouin) in the desert, the Semitic tradition of the Middle East was for the people to sit around the campfires and sing the songs of their religious heritage. The poetic writings (songs) were chiefly the Psalms and Isaiah. They memorized them, or at least parts of them, through the long established tribal system of oral transmission. They learned to sing from the books of Psalms and Isaiah, for these books were the most readily accessible to them. The third most quoted book in the New Testament is the book of Deuteronomy and then other books of the Pentateuch. In comparison to the Psalms and Isaiah, however, they are almost insignificant, because most people had little familiarity with, or at best a limited access to, the rest of the scriptural record. In view of the teachings of the Savior and His reminder of what the scriptural sources taught of Him, His testimony was that if one had the spirit of those scriptures, they all pointed to Him.

At a special time when some were permitted to go to the Apostle Paul in his place of residence in Rome, he taught them about his great ministry and testimony and witness as an Apostle. "And when they had appointed him a day, there came many to him into *his* lodging; to whom he expounded and testified the kingdom of God, *persuading them concerning Jesus, both out of the law of Moses, and out of the prophets*" (Acts 28:23; emphasis added).

When the spirit of the law of Moses is really understood, can one teach of Christ? Paul did, and he used it in power while teaching.

In the first chapter of the Gospel of John, the Apostle reports of the power of the proper spirit of the law with great power and testimony: "The day following Jesus would go forth into Galilee, and findeth Philip, and saith unto him, Follow me. Now Philip was of Bethsaida, the city of Andrew and Peter. Philip findeth Nathanael, and saith unto him, We have found him, *of whom Moses in the law, and the prophets, did write, Jesus of Nazareth,* the son of Joseph" (John 1:43; emphasis added). They had found the Messiah. It is this Messiah, this Christ, of whom the law of Moses taught, as well as other prophets. Those who had the true spirit of the law in New Testament times or in Book of Mormon times recognized the efficacy and power of the law of Moses in helping them to focus on what would bring them to Christ.

What caused many of God's people to detour from the purpose of the law? Again, the Book of Mormon provides the answer:

> Behold, my brethren, he that prophesieth, let him prophesy to the understanding of men; for the Spirit speaketh the truth and lieth not. Wherefore, it speaketh of things as they really are, and of things as they really will be; wherefore, these things are manifested unto us plainly, for the salvation of our souls. [If you are able to maintain the spirit of the law of Moses, it gives

you focus and foundation to lead you to salvation.] But behold, we are not witnesses alone in these things; for God also spake them unto prophets of old.

But behold, the Jews were a stiffnecked people; and they despised the words of plainness, and killed the prophets, and sought for things that they could not understand. Wherefore, because of their blindness, which blindness came by looking beyond the mark [when they lost the spirit of it, they could not keep the focus; they didn't know the direction they were heading; and problems developed], they must needs fall; for God hath taken away his plainness from them, and delivered unto them many things which they cannot understand, because they desired it. And because they desired it God hath done it, that they may stumble. (Jacob 4:13–14)

The New Testament record provides an excellent illustration of this problem. Matthew 9:16 and 17 discusses a metaphor that new cloth is not put on or sewn with old cloth and new wine is not put in old bottles.[26] These verses certainly illustrate a principle that seems to be out of context with the law of Moses. In the Joseph Smith Translation (JST), we find the Prophet Joseph Smith added four verses, which suggests that something was lost from the text. This restored text gives a perspective to the problem that had come to the Israelites because of their looking beyond the mark.

Then said the Pharisees unto him, Why will ye not receive us with our baptism, seeing we keep the whole law?

But Jesus said unto them, Ye keep not the law. If ye had kept the law, ye would have received me [if you had the spirit of the law, you would have known what I was trying to teach you], for I am he who gave the law.

I receive not you with your baptism, because it profiteth you nothing.

For when that which is new is come, the old is ready to be put away. (JST, Matthew 9:18–21)

What had happened? Why did the Jews use the phrase "our baptism," as opposed to "his baptism"? Baptism was a part of the preparatory gospel of the law of Moses.[27] The Apostle Paul, in 1 Corinthians 10, bears testimony that Israel was baptized in the Red

Sea with Moses.[28] Doctrine and Covenants 84 is a confirming testimony that this principle was inherent in the law that the ancients practiced. The Book of Mormon bears testimony that baptism was a part of the law of Moses, which they brought with them, for the practice of it is found in the record from the very beginning to the end.[29] But the Jews had lost the spirit and power of it and had confused and eventually combined it with, or in some cases, substituted it for, something else. Some of the performances given under the law of carnal commandments were a series of washings and cleansings that were to be performed at different times in people's lives. There were many washings of purification.[30] Some of them had very practical purposes, but everything that was done under the law of carnal commandments was spiritually based. The performances were intended to teach a principle or to give focus and perspective. Therefore, there was no separation, so to speak, of church and state, of the temporal and the spiritual.

But when Judah (the Jews) fell into apostasy and lost the priesthood, they took the principle of baptism and some of these washings and mixed them together, forming a new interpretation and initiating the tradition that is still practiced today. They call it the *mikveh*, meaning "gathering of water." It is a ritual bath, an immersion, of cleansing or washing.[31] Jews of varying religious interpretations use it in a variety of different ways. Some do it only once or twice in their lifetime, whereas others do it frequently. In Qumran near the Dead Sea are numerous of these washing pools. They look like baptismal fonts, but they are the *mikveh* (bath) of the Jews who lived there.[32] The ancient fortress of Masada likewise has these pools.[33] The excavations south of the Temple Mount in Jerusalem also reveal many *mikveh*.[34]

The reintroduction of gospel principles in Jesus' day came with John, who was to prepare the way. Was there great concern over John the Baptist's immersing or cleansing people? No. They never raised a question about that. Why? Because the *mikveh* bath of purification was a common practice and part of their religious worship. It was not a strange thing. In fact, Jewish law says that the purest form of washing in the *mikveh* is with a running stream.[35] When John chose to baptize in the Jordan River, he chose the purest pool of washing that their tradition allowed. Why, then, all the contention about John the

Baptist? Because of his message! He announced himself as one sent to prepare the way for the Messiah.[36] It was the directness of this theological assertion that threatened the Jewish leaders. He also came with priesthood authority and power to baptize and restored the ordinance of baptism to its proper order. The great lavern basin in the temple of Solomon was a baptismal font for the living.[37] That knowledge was lost from the Old Testament record as we have it. That is why this restored text in the Matthew account of the Savior's teaching to the Pharisees who had developed another tradition is so important.

The full history of the *mikveh* bath is very difficult to trace. By the time the recorded oral tradition of the Jews was established, which is called the Mishnah, the tradition and practice of the *mikveh* was firmly in place. It obviously had Old Testament roots. The Mishnah is usually dated as early as 200 B.C. The *mikveh* bath is an apostate form of baptism that came down from the Old Testament times with this modified purpose. The full significance of the baptismal ordinance had been lost to them. The Mishnaic tradition specified that the convert to Judaism must fulfill three requirements.[38] First, male converts had to be circumcised. Second, all converts were to wash themselves clean by immersion in a *mikveh* bath.[39] Third, they were to offer sacrifice in the temple. Many Jews were never able to make such a pilgrimage during the time of the temple. How then did they fulfill the requirement of sacrifice? They commissioned another person to offer a proxy sacrifice for them. After the temple was destroyed, how was the requirement of sacrifice satisfied? The traditional rabbinical substitute for the law of sacrifice and offerings was prayer and the study of the Torah.[40]

In Matthew 23 is a great discourse by Jesus that reveals some additional principles that were stumbling blocks to wayward Israel:

> Then spake Jesus to the multitude, and to his disciples,
> Saying, The scribes and the Pharisees sit in Moses' seat:
> All therefore whatsoever they bid you observe, *that* observe and do; but do not ye after their works: for they say, and do not.
> For they bind heavy burdens and grievous to be borne, and lay *them* on men's shoulders; but they *themselves* will not move them with one of their fingers.

But all their works they do for to be seen of men: they make broad their phylacteries, and enlarge the borders of their garments. (Matthew 23:1–5; emphasis added)

Christ openly condemned some of the religious paraphernalia and tradition that had already long been used among the Jews of His day. He mentioned specifically the phylactery boxes that were used for their prayers and their prayer shawls.[41] He condemned these practices as not being in the spirit of the law. He described them as "heavy burdens to be borne." These and other added practices are often confused with the law of Moses. Also from some of the performances of the law of carnal commandments developed a whole system of traditions that are misinterpretations and distortions of the law of Moses. These traditions deprived the children of Israel of the spirit of the law of Moses and robbed them of the power and direction that that law could give them. The Savior's condemnation continues:

"But woe unto you, scribes and Pharisees, hypocrites! for ye shut up the kingdom of heaven against men; for ye neither go in yourselves, neither suffer ye them that are entering to go in. Woe unto you, scribes and Pharisees, hypocrites! for ye devour widows' houses, and for a pretence make long prayer: therefore ye shall receive the greater damnation" (Matthew 23:13–14).

"Woe unto you, scribes and Pharisees, hypocrites! for ye compass sea and land to make one proselyte, and when he is made, ye make him twofold more the child of hell than he was before like unto yourselves" (JST, Matthew 23:12; see also Matthew 23:15).

Christ is very condemnatory in this setting. Why? Because they surfeited even the proselyte (the convert) with these false traditions. Later in the same chapter He taught another great principle: "Woe unto you, scribes and Pharisees, hypocrites! for ye pay tithe of mint and anise and cumin, and have omitted the weightier matters of the law [you've lost the whole spirit and direction of it, and what it means in a person's life, such as], judgment, mercy, and faith: these ought ye to have done, and not to leave the other undone" (Matthew 23:23).

Another familiar New Testament scriptural passage, Luke 14:34, seems to have little to do with the law of Moses. "Salt is good: but if the salt have lost his savour, wherewith shall it be seasoned?"

The Joseph Smith Translation provides the proper context for this passage as an example of the Pharisaic traditions: "Then certain of them came to him, saying, Good Master, we have Moses and the prophets, and whosoever shall live by them, shall he not have life? And Jesus answered, saying, Ye know not Moses, neither the prophets; for if ye had known them, ye would have believed on me; for to this intent they were written. For I am sent that ye might have life. Therefore I will liken it unto salt which is good; but if the salt has lost its savor, wherewith shall it be seasoned?" (JST, Luke 14:35–37).

They had corrupted the law—the salt—to the extent that the salt had lost its savor. Their traditions had contaminated the law, and it had lost its purpose and power to bring people to Christ.

The net effect of these traditions on the adherents of the law of Moses in the Apostles' day is described in modern revelation: "And it came to pass that the children, being brought up in subjection to the law of Moses, gave heed to the traditions of their fathers and believed not the gospel of Christ, wherein they became unholy" (D&C 74:4).

Remember what the Apostle Paul said of the law in Galatians 3:17–25:

> And this I say, that the covenant, that was confirmed before of God in Christ, the law, which was four hundred and thirty years after, cannot disannul, that it should make the promise of none effect.
>
> For if the inheritance be of the law, it is no more of promise: but God gave it to Abraham by promise.
>
> Wherefore then serveth the law? It was added because of transgressions, till the seed should come to whom the promise was made; and it was ordained by angels in the hand of a mediator.
>
> Now a mediator is not a mediator of one, but God is one.
>
> Is the law then against the promises of God? God forbid: for if there had been a law given which could have given life, verily righteousness should have been by the law.
>
> But the scripture hath concluded all under sin, that the promise by faith of Jesus Christ might be given to them that believe.

But before faith came, we were kept under the law, shut up unto the faith which should afterwards be revealed.

Wherefore the law was our schoolmaster to bring us unto Christ, that we might be justified by faith.

But after that faith is come, we are no longer under a schoolmaster.

Why was the law of carnal commandments given? "It was added because of transgressions." To what was it added? The preparatory gospel. And what was the purpose of the added law of carnal commandments? To teach the children of Israel how to repent, so they could increase the Spirit in their lives to become more focused and come unto Christ. In Galatians 3:24, Paul makes a great statement in which he described the law as a "schoolmaster to bring us unto Christ." The Joseph Smith Translation adds a very significant change: "The law was our schoolmaster until Christ" (JST, Galatians 3:24). The law was not just to bring us to Christ but a schoolmaster till Christ came, and then it was fulfilled.

The law and its purposes, particularly the law of carnal commandments, were fulfilled at Christ's first advent, both to the Church established in the holy land[42] and also to the peoples of the Americas. Jesus declared that this law was fulfilled in Him and that it therefore had an end:

> And it came to pass that when Jesus had said these words he perceived that there were some among them who marveled, and wondered what he would concerning the law of Moses; for they understood not the saying that old things had passed away, and that all things had become new.
>
> And he said unto them: Marvel not that I said unto you that old things had passed away, and that all things had become new.
>
> Behold, I say unto you that the law is fulfilled that was given unto Moses.
>
> Behold, I am he that gave the law, and I am he who covenanted with my people Israel; therefore, the law in me is fulfilled, for I have come to fulfill the law; therefore it hath an end.
>
> Behold, I do not destroy the prophets, for as many as have

not been fulfilled in me, verily I say unto you, shall all be fulfilled.

And because I said unto you that old things have passed away, I do not destroy that which hath been spoken concerning things which are to come.

For behold, the covenant which I have made with my people is not all fulfilled; but the law which was given unto Moses hath an end in me.

Behold, I am the law, and the light. Look unto me, and endure to the end, and ye shall live; for unto him that endureth to the end will I give eternal life. (3 Nephi 15:2–9)

In 2 Corinthians 3 the Apostle Paul wrote to the Saints at Corinth who were, for the most part, converts from Judaism:

Forasmuch as ye are manifestly declared to be the epistle of Christ ministered by us, written not with ink, but with the Spirit of the living God; not in tables of stone, but in fleshy tables of the heart.

And such trust have we through Christ to God-ward:

Not that we are sufficient of ourselves to think any thing as of ourselves; but our sufficiency is of God;

Who also hath made us able ministers of the new testament [or the new covenant]; not of the letter, but of the spirit: for the letter killeth, but the spirit giveth life. (2 Corinthians 3:3–6)

The key that made the law of Moses operative in their lives was the Israelites' ability to obtain and keep the spirit of it. If they followed only the letter of the law, it became dead to them. Many, today, tend to interpret the law of Moses with "the letter" alone. That is an error. The law of Moses viewed in the proper perspective had the Spirit and power and made it possible for individuals to obtain the Spirit in their own lives.

The scripture continues: "But their minds were blinded: for until this day remaineth the same vail untaken away in the reading of the old testament; which vail is done away in Christ" (2 Corinthians 3:14). When Christ is recognized in the Old Testament, then comes understanding and a love of it! But even to this day when Moses (or the Old Testament) is read, "the vail is upon their heart" (2 Corinthians 3:15). Paul gave us the key that removes the veil from one's mind: "Nevertheless when it shall turn to the Lord, the vail shall be taken away" (2 Corinthians 3:16). The Joseph Smith Translation adds two words that give a clearer focus: *their heart.* Nevertheless, "when their heart shall turn to the Lord, the vail shall be taken away" (JST, 2 Corinthians 3:16). In other words, there must be humility, teachableness, meekness, and obedience. To have the veil removed makes it possible for the individual to repent and come unto Christ. That was the true spirit of the law of Moses.

Do we ever wander in a "wilderness" as a people? Do we have a "law of Moses" added because of transgressions? Are we really ready to build Zion? What then is the true purpose of the law of tithing and the Welfare Services program? Do we have "schoolmasters" to bring us to consecration, to Zion, to prepare for the Millennium? President Joseph F. Smith prophetically declared:

> We expect to see the day, if we live long enough (and if some of us do not live long enough to see it, there are others who will), when every council of the Priesthood in the Church of Jesus Christ of Latter-day Saints will understand its duty; will assume its responsibility, will magnify its calling, and fill its place in the Church. . . . When that day shall come, there will not be so much necessity for work that is now being done by the auxiliary organizations, because it will be done by the regular quorums of the Priesthood. The Lord designed and comprehended it from the beginning, and he has made provision in the Church whereby every need may be met and satisfied through the regular organizations of the Priesthood.[43]

Are not the auxiliaries and various programs "schoolmasters" to us? Are we really so different from ancient Israel?

May the Lord bless us and help us that we might capture the spirit of the law of Moses, for I testify that it was an integral part of the gospel of Jesus Christ and its intent was to lead that people to Christ and help them become Christlike. We should hope that abiding by our "laws and performances" might also have a similar effect in leading us to a more Christlike character.

NOTES

1. Joseph Fielding Smith, *Answers to Gospel Questions,* 5 vols. (Salt Lake City: Deseret Book, 1979), 3:115–17; 5:84–86.

2. See Moses 5:5–8.

3. Smith, *Answers to Gospel Questions,* 4:155–60. See also 1:116–18; 3:154–57.

4. Edward J. Brandt, "The Priesthood Ordinances of Sacrifice," *Ensign,* December 1973, 49–53.

5. See Leviticus 3; 7:11–38.

6. See Leviticus 7:16; 22:18, 21, 23; Numbers 15:3; 29:39; Deuteronomy 12:6, 13; 16:10; 23:23.

7. See Leviticus 7:16; 22:18, 21, 23; Numbers 15:3, 8; 29:39; Deuteronomy 12:6.

8. See Leviticus 7:12–13, 15; 22:29.

9. See Leviticus 4; 5:1–13; 6:25–30; JST, Matthew 26:24.

10. See Leviticus 5:15–19; 6:1–7; 7:1–10.

11. See Leviticus 5:16; 6:5–17; 27:13, 15, 19, 27, 31; Numbers 5:6–10.

12. See Exodus 29:26–27; Leviticus 7:14, 32–34; Numbers 18.

13. See Leviticus 5:7, 11.

14. See Leviticus 6:25–30; 7:7–8, 16; 14:13.

15. See Leviticus 3:3–5.

16. See Leviticus 7:16.

17. See Leviticus 7:35–36; Deuteronomy 18:1–8.

18. See Leviticus 2:2, 9, 16; 5:12; 6:15; Numbers 5:26; 18:26–29.

19. See Leviticus 19:19; Deuteronomy 22:9–11.

20. See Exodus 12:5; 13:6.

21. See Leviticus 16.

22. See Exodus 12:4.

23. See 2 Nephi 9:7; 25:16; Alma 34:10, 12, 14.

24. See Exodus 12:7.

25. See Bible Dictionary, s.v. "Quotations," 756–59.

26. See Matthew 9:16–17; Mark 2:21–22; Luke 5:36–37.

27. See D&C 84:27.

28. See 1 Corinthians 10:1–4. See also Louis Ginzberg, *The Legends of the Jews* (Philadelphia: Jewish Publication Society of America, 1968), 3:88; 6:34.

29. See 2 Nephi 31:5; Mosiah 18:10; 21:35; Alma 7:14; 3 Nephi 1:27; Moroni 8:25.

30. See notes to Exodus 30:19–21; 40:31; Leviticus 11, 15.

31. Philip Birnbaum, *A Book of Jewish Concepts* (New York: Hebrew, 1964), 239, 391.

32. Frank Moore Cross Jr., *The Ancient Library of Qumran*, rev. ed. (Garden City, NY: Anchor Books, 1961), 67–68; see also William Sanford LaSor, *The Dead Sea Scrolls and the New Testament* (Grand Rapids, MI: William B. Eerdmans, 1972), 40, 134, 149–51.

33. Yigael Yadin, *Masada* (London: Sphere Books Ltd., 1973), 164–67. See also Hershel Shanks, *Judaism in Stone* (New York: Harper & Row, 1979), 18–19, 26–30.

34. Nahman Avigad, *Discovering Jerusalem* (Nashville: Thomas Nelson Publishers, 1983), 139–43. See also Benjamin Mazar, *The Mountain of the Lord* (Garden City, NY: Doubleday, 1975), 128–29, 145–47.

35. Herbert Danby, *The Mishnah* (Oxford: Oxford University Press, 1967), 732–33.

36. See John 1:19–28.

37. See 1 Kings 7:23–26; 2 Chronicles 4:2–5.

38. Ginzberg, *Legends of the Jews,* 3:88.

39. Birnbaum, *Book of Jewish Concepts,* 239.

40. Birnbaum, *Book of Jewish Concepts,* 551.

41. See Deuteronomy 6:8*b*.

42. See Hebrews 8:13; see also 2 Corinthians 5:17.

43. Joseph F. Smith, *Gospel Doctrine* (Salt Lake City: Deseret Book, 1977), 159.

CHAPTER TEN

TRUST IN THE LORD: EXODUS AND FAITH

S. KENT BROWN

Everyone knows that the experience of the Israelites both before and during the Exodus formed a major focus for their faith in God from the age of Moses until our own day. For it was in this series of events that God revealed His mighty arm—and profound mercy—on behalf of an obscure, enslaved people whom He chose and then freed in order to bear His covenant of life and salvation to the nations of the earth. To illustrate, one needs to recall only a few events of the Exodus that serve to underscore this point.

Initially, it is worthwhile observing that, among the recitative formulae which constitute some of the earliest Israelite devotional celebrations, we find a clear, ringing reference to God's many acts in Egypt standing at the center of the expression of faith.[1] We turn first to an injunction in Deuteronomy chapter 6. Here not only were parents to teach God's law to their children but, when children asked about the origin of the statutes and judgments given by God, the reply was to run as follows:

> We were Pharaoh's bondmen in Egypt; and the Lord brought us out of Egypt with a mighty hand:
> And the Lord shewed signs and wonders, great and sore, upon Egypt, upon Pharaoh, and upon all his household, before our eyes:

S. Kent Brown is a professor of ancient scripture and director of ancient studies at Brigham Young University.

And he brought us out from thence, that he might bring us in, to give us the land which he sware unto our fathers.

And the Lord commanded us to do all these statutes, to fear the Lord our God, for our good always, that he might preserve us alive. (Deuteronomy 6:21–24)

One next recalls a second recitation, found in Deuteronomy chapter 26, which each Israelite was to utter at the altar when bringing the first fruits of the land as an offering to the Lord.[2]

A Syrian ready to perish was my father, and he went down into Egypt, and sojourned there with a few, and became there a nation, great, mighty, and populous:

And the Egyptians evil entreated us, and afflicted us, and laid upon us hard bondage:

And when we cried unto the Lord God of our fathers, the Lord heard our voice, and looked on our affliction, and our labour, and our oppression:

And the Lord brought us forth out of Egypt with a mighty hand, and with an outstretched arm, and with great terribleness, and with signs, and with wonders:

And he hath brought us into this place, and hath given us this land, even a land that floweth with milk and honey. (Deuteronomy 26:5–9)

The last example that I shall cite from a biblical celebration occurred at the important covenant ceremony conducted by Joshua at Shechem shortly before his death. It is recorded that when all the people had "presented themselves before God" (Joshua 24:1), Joshua spoke in the name of the Lord, saying:

Thus saith the Lord God of Israel, Your fathers dwelt on the other side of the flood [Euphrates River] in old time, even Terah, the father of Abraham, and the father of Nachor: and they served other gods.

And I took your father Abraham from the other side of the flood, and led him throughout all the land of Canaan, and multiplied his seed, and gave him Isaac. . . .

But Jacob and his children went down into Egypt.

I sent Moses also and Aaron, and I plagued Egypt, according

to that which I did among them: and afterward I brought you out.

And I brought your fathers out of Egypt: and ye came unto the sea; and the Egyptians pursued after your fathers with chariots and horsemen unto the Red sea. . . .

The Lord . . . brought the sea upon them, and covered them; and your eyes have seen what I have done in Egypt: and ye dwelt in the wilderness a long season. . . .

And ye went over Jordan. . . .

And I have given you a land for which ye did not labour, and cities which ye built not, and ye dwell in them; of the vineyards and oliveyards which ye planted not do ye eat.

Now therefore fear the Lord, and serve him in sincerity and in truth: and put away the gods which your fathers served on the other side of the flood, and in Egypt; and serve ye the Lord. (Joshua 24:2–7, 11, 13–14)

When we combine these notices of ancient celebration, along with that of the Passover commemoration, we see that Israelite worship was founded on a vivid memory of God's mighty acts, an inspiration for faith among Israelites that the God of their fathers would continue His merciful care of His people.

It is worth noting further that, by the time of Jeremiah, the Lord was frequently referred to as the Lord "which brought up the children of Israel out of the land of Egypt" (Jeremiah 23:7; compare 1 Samuel 14:39; 2 Nephi 25:20). This honorific epithet, applied to Jehovah, serves to highlight His redemptive act of freeing Israel from suffocating bondage. It is thus made plain that, in terms of Jehovah's dealings with His people, the one act that characterized Him in the minds of ancient Israelites was His engineering their Exodus from Egypt. In fact, so strong was this memory that it became frozen in speech in the form of a most solemn oath: "The Lord liveth, which brought up the children of Israel out of the land of Egypt." Interestingly, it is Jeremiah who, quoting the Lord Himself, tells us that the grandeur of the Exodus would be eclipsed only by one other majestic divine act, that of gathering Israel a second time: "Therefore, behold, the days come, saith the Lord, that it shall no more be said, The Lord liveth, that brought up the children of Israel out of the land of Egypt; But, The Lord liveth, that brought up the children of Israel from the land of the north, and from all the lands whither he had driven them: and *I will bring them again* into their land that I gave unto their fathers" (Jeremiah 16:14–15; emphasis added).[3]

It is of more than passing importance to observe that when the Old Testament prophets spoke of the future return of Israel from exile, they frequently cast their description as of a second exodus.

One has only to recollect the words of the prophet, Hosea, who says of the returning exiles: "They shall walk after the Lord: he shall roar like a lion: when he shall roar, then the children shall tremble from the west. They shall tremble as a bird out of Egypt, and as a dove out of the land of Assyria: and I will place them in their houses, saith the Lord" (Hosea 11:10–11).

Furthermore, not long afterward, Isaiah foretold an event centuries removed from himself when he declared: "The voice of him that crieth in the wilderness, Prepare ye the way of the Lord, make straight in the desert a highway for our God. Every valley shall be exalted, and every mountain and hill shall be made low: and the crooked shall be made straight, and the rough places plain: And the glory of the Lord shall be revealed, and all flesh shall see it together: for the mouth of the Lord hath spoken it" (Isaiah 40:3–5).

The mention of the highway into the desert finds a compatible parallel to the path by which the Israelites first escaped to the wilderness from Egypt and then passed to the promised land, crossing both the sea and Jordan River on dry ground (see Jeremiah 44:26–28).

It is important for Latter-day Saints to observe that the Exodus, standing as the primal evidence for faith in God's kind intentions towards His people, also appears in the Book of Mormon. In a classic passage detailing Nephi's struggle to bring his unbelieving brothers back to faith and obedience, Nephi quickly and naturally recalled God's concern and power manifested in the events of the Exodus:

> I, Nephi, spake unto them, saying: Do ye believe that our fathers, who were the children of Israel, would have been led away out of the hands of the Egyptians if they had not hearkened unto the words of the Lord?
>
> Yea, do ye suppose that they would have been led out of bondage, if the Lord had not commanded Moses that he should lead them out of bondage?

Now ye know that the children of Israel were in bondage; and ye know that they were laden with tasks, which were grievous to be borne. . . .

Now ye know that Moses was commanded of the Lord to do that great work; and ye know that by his word the waters of the Red Sea were divided hither and thither, and they passed through on dry ground.

But ye know that the Egyptians were drowned in the Red Sea, who were the armies of Pharaoh.

And ye also know that they were fed with manna in the wilderness. . . .

And after they had crossed the river Jordan he did make them mighty unto the driving out of the children of the land. (1 Nephi 17:23–28, 32)

According to his own record, then, Nephi appealed to the Exodus as the most profound evidence that his brothers needed to recall in order to come to trust and obey the Lord, as well as their divinely led father, while the Lord guided them during their own exodus to a promised land apart.

Notwithstanding the enormous emphasis and wide thematic treatment of the Exodus in scripture as a foremost focus of faith, it should also be recognized that the book of Exodus itself reveals an effort made by God to engender within the Israelites an absolutely firm trust in Himself.[4] Let me sketch some essential features of this process.

The idea of Israel's inclination to doubt was already present in Moses' interview with Jehovah during his call (see Exodus 3–4). This notion first appeared in Moses' question about God's name, for Moses was certain that the Israelites would not believe his announced purpose to deliver them from bondage if he could not repeat a name which the Israelite elders would recognize (see Exodus 3:13). Further, the signs which Moses was to perform—changing his rod to a serpent, making his hand leprous, and changing water to blood (see Exodus 4:1–9)—constituted a second indication of natural Israelite skepticism. And it was this tendency to doubt which the Lord set about to reverse by a series of unusual but orchestrated circumstances.

The book of Exodus, one must understand, makes it clear at the outset that God was in charge of events and that nothing could stay His hand. This becomes plainly visible in the fact that the Pharaoh who "knew not Joseph" (Exodus 1:8) was unable to stem the tide of Israelite male births, no matter how he tried. In the long view, in fact, it did not matter much what Moses or the Israelites or the Egyptians thought or did. The story of this book forms an account of God taking charge of events and bringing them to a conclusion that satisfied Him, even when the costs were high.[5] Let us now turn to the evidence for this observation.

After his return to Egypt, Moses' first encounter with disbelief did not come in his initial meeting with the Israelite leaders but, remarkably, in his opening clash with Pharaoh. In that scene, narrated in chapter 5, we read that Pharaoh asked, "Who is the Lord [i.e., Jehovah], that I should obey his voice to let Israel go? I know not the Lord, neither will I let Israel go" (Exodus 5:2).

Pharaoh believed, it is clear, that he knew all the gods who mattered as far as Egyptian affairs were concerned. And then turning despotic, he decided to crush the Israelite's unrest by requiring them to gather their own straw.[6] We all remember the response of the Israelites when the proclaimed deliverers, Moses and Aaron, were returning to the Israelite villages after that first disappointing meeting with Pharaoh: "The Lord look upon you, and judge; because ye have made our savour to be abhorred in the eyes of Pharaoh, and in the eyes of his servants, to put a sword in their hand to slay us" (Exodus 5:21).

The upshot of this scenario with Pharaoh and its resulting difficulties for the children of Israel was that even slaves, to obtain freedom, would have to suffer, in the language of Paul, "the loss of all things" (Philippians 3:8). Unbeknownst to the Israelites, they were beginning to be forced by God to rely neither on the now capricious Pharaoh and his foremen nor on their own abilities and resources. Said another way, the mainstays of their secure world, such as it was, had begun to collapse. Instead, God had begun to propel Israel toward a situation in which they would have to rely on Him alone, not upon anything or anyone else.

In answering the now grief-stricken Moses (see Exodus 5:22–23), God quietly assured him and his fellow Israelites that He would surely bring events to their proper end. We notice the series of statements in the first verses of Exodus 6, which all appear in the first person singular:

> Now shalt thou see what I will do to Pharaoh. . . .
>
> I am the Lord. . . . I appeared unto Abraham. . . .
>
> I have also established my covenant with them. . . .
>
> I have also heard the groaning of the children of Israel . . . I have remembered my covenant. . . .
>
> I am the Lord, and I will bring you out from under the burdens of the Egyptians, . . . and I will redeem you with a stretched out arm. . . .
>
> I will take you to me for a people, and I will be to you a God. . . .
>
> I will bring you in unto the land, concerning the which I did swear to give it to Abraham, to Isaac, and to Jacob; and I will give it you for an heritage: I am the Lord. (Exodus 6:1–8)

This unusually heavy stress by the Lord on His own actions, both past and future, must have begun to open Moses' eyes to the important concept that he and his fellow Israelites were to rely totally on God, He being in control of the destiny of succeeding events. As a matter of fact, by means of two signs God soon made it plain to the Israelites that He could effectively differentiate them from the Egyptians and was thus to be trusted fully. First, beginning with the fourth plague, that of the flies (see Exodus 8:20–32), God kept the Israelites safe from the plagues and their deepening consequences by making Goshen into something of an island of safety (see Exodus 8:22; compare 11:7). Second, the plague of death, obviated for Israelites in the Passover, not only was to remind them in a somber manner where their trust was to lie, but was additionally to be commemorated perpetually as a memorial not of death but of their deliverance by God from a circumstance from which He alone had power and mercy to deliver (see Exodus 11–12).

With the passing of the plagues, the Israelites doubtlessly departed Egypt in a spirit of joy and euphoria, happy to be free of Pharaoh's chains. And at their departure, they hastily prepared provisions for their journey into the desert (see Exodus 12:39). But they could neither have carried much nor did they apparently take many weapons for defense. These two situations, taken in reverse order, led to the next two crises of faith. In the first scene, we see the Israelites encamped at the edge of the sea when suddenly the chariot army of Pharaoh appeared at their rear. Quite rightly, the Israelites feared for their lives and said so in these words: "Is not this the word that we did tell thee in Egypt, saying, Let us alone, that we may serve the Egyptians? For it had been better for us to serve the Egyptians, than that we should die in the wilderness" (Exodus 14:12).

But again God delivered His people by leading them to safety while destroying the Egyptian hosts, thus negating their fearful distrust that He had led them out of bondage only to stand aside while they were slaughtered. When the Israelites miraculously survived this rather difficult circumstance, it should have been signal enough to them that, if they would only ask and have faith, God would succor them.

In the second scene, we find the children of Israel in the wilderness of Shur at a place called Marah, a name which means bitterness (see Exodus 15:22–26). We all know that when people travel in the desert, the most critical necessity for life is water. It is moreover the most burdensome to transport. In the case of the Israelites, by the time they reached Marah, they had spent their water, both for themselves and for their animals, and found themselves in dire need. But the water at Marah was unpotable, and this led to a questioning complaint: "What shall we drink?" (Exodus 15:24). Once again, the Lord, through Moses His prophet, mercifully demonstrated to the Israelites that He could be trusted. And when the bitter waters were wonderfully healed, the children of Israel would have learned that God would and could also heal them.

It was diminished provisions which brought a further crisis, this time in the wilderness of Sin. In chapter 16 we are told that six weeks after their departure from Egypt, the Israelites had run out of food: "the whole congregation of the children of Israel murmured against Moses and Aaron in the wilderness: And the children of Israel said unto them, Would to God we had died by the hand of the Lord in the land of Egypt, when we sat by the flesh pots, and when we did eat bread to the full; for ye have brought us forth into this wilderness, to kill this whole assembly with hunger" (Exodus 16:2–3).

At this point, of course, there was no turning back out of the desert. God had led them into a place where they would have to depend wholly on Him for their daily needs. And once more the Lord did not abandon them, proving to be trustworthy. Compassionately, the Lord came to their aid and provided them with manna, not for that day only but for the entire period of their stay in the desert (see Exodus 16:1–35).

What I have been leading to is this. Part of the Lord's program for the Israelites was to force them to come to trust and rely upon Him for all of their needs. This process took place over time, beginning with the first interview of Moses and Aaron with Pharaoh and ending several weeks after they had left Egypt. The point of the growing lesson was that the Lord could be trusted and, indeed, had to be trusted. In effect, He left the Israelites without any resource upon which to call except Himself. It is my own view that the Israelites had to be brought to this state of mind and heart to become fully free. Without being able to trust in the Egyptians and now having only the Lord to rely upon, whether in Egypt or in the desert, the Israelites had to bring themselves to trust God more than man. The book of Exodus carries the profound message, then, that the Lord can in fact be trusted; for He alone is perfectly reliable.

NOTES

1. Gerhard von Rad, in *The Problem of the Hexateuch, and Other Essays* (New York: McGraw-Hill, 1966), 1–78, argues in an interesting vein that it was these recitations, all spoken on ritual occasions, which formed the skeletal frame of Israelite history. Moreover, this history was written only later by employing this general outline, which highlights events from Genesis to Joshua. Thus, von Rad urged an original hexateuch, a primal history of six books, rather than an initial pentateuch. Though his hypothesis has not received wide support, I am intrigued by his suggestion that it was ceremony—more precisely, what was said during certain important rites—that shaped Israel's view of its past.

2. This occasion is also known as Shavuoth, or the Feast of Weeks.

3. Also Jeremiah 23:7–8, a passage which the Septuagint version places at the end of chapter 23, an observation made by both Wilhelm Rudolph (*Jeremia,* 3rd ed. [Tubingen: J. C. B. Mohr, 1968], 148) and by John Bright (*Jeremiah* [Garden City, NY: Doubleday, 1965], 144). Bright also believes that the passage originally belongs in chapter 23, and not in 16 (see also Monte S. Nyman, *The Words of Jeremiah* [Salt Lake City, Utah: Bookcraft, 1982], 53–54).

4. I am indebted in much of what follows to the observations of

J. Coert Rylaarsdam, "The Book of Exodus: Introduction and Exegesis," *The Interpreter's Bible,* vol. 1 (Nashville: Abingdon Press, 1952).

5. Rylaarsdam, "Book of Exodus," 857: "Despite Israel's troubles, the God who is its redeemer always has the initiative." Compare 853–57, 869; also Karl Friedrich Keil and Franz Julius Delitzsch, *Biblical Commentary on the Old Testament,* vol. 1 (Edinburgh: T. & T. Clark, 1865), 424–26.

6. Properly, the Hebrew *teven* is leavings from threshing (see F. H. Wilhelm Gesenius, *Hebrew-Chaldee Lexicon to the Old Testament* [Grand Rapids, MI: Eerdmans, 1949], 856; and Francis Brown, Samuel Rolles Driver, and Charles A. Briggs, *A Hebrew and English Lexicon of the Old Testament* [Oxford: Oxford University Press, 1968], 1061–62).

CHAPTER ELEVEN

THE PROVOCATION IN THE WILDERNESS AND THE REJECTION OF GRACE

M. CATHERINE THOMAS

Camped in the hot, waterless wilderness of southern Palestine, the Israelites challenged Moses, saying, "Wherefore is this that thou hast brought us up out of Egypt, to kill us and our children and our cattle with thirst?" (Exodus 17:3). This complaint might have been understandable had these people never seen the hand of God in their lives, but this incident occurred after the miraculous Passover, after their passage through the Red Sea dry shod, and after the outpouring of manna and quail from heaven. In response to the Israelites' faithlessness, an exasperated Moses cried out to the Lord, "What shall I do unto this people? they be almost ready to stone me" (Exodus 17:4). The Lord answered: "Behold, I will stand before thee there upon the rock in Horeb; and thou shalt smite the rock, and there shall come water out of it, that the people may drink. And Moses did so in the sight of the elders of Israel. And he called the name of the place Massah, and Meribah" (Exodus 17:6–7).

Psalm 95 provides the linguistic link that identifies this incident as the Provocation: "To day if ye will hear his voice, Harden not your heart, as in the *provocation* [Hebrew *meribah*], and as in the day of temptation [Hebrew *massah*] in the wilderness: When your fathers tempted me, proved me, and saw my work. Forty years long was I

M. Catherine Thomas is assistant professor emeritus of ancient scripture at Brigham Young University.

grieved with this generation, and said, It is a people that do err in their heart, and they have not known my ways: Unto whom I sware in my wrath that they should not enter into my rest" (Psalm 95:7–11; emphasis added; see also Hebrews 3:8–11, 15).

The event at Meribah is the Provocation mentioned throughout the Bible. In that incident, the Lord tested the faith of the children of Israel and their willingness to accept His love and grace. Grace is the Lord's divine enabling power, given to humankind to help them with all the challenges of their lives; grace ultimately empowers them to lay hold on heaven itself. But the Israelites' response to the Lord's abundant generosity illustrates a religious paradox: God offers His children grace, but the children will not seek it; God offers His children heaven, but the children will not enter in.

We shall see that the Provocation refers not only to the specific incident at Meribah but to a persistent behavior of the children of Israel that greatly reduced their spiritual knowledge (see Psalm 95:10: "they have not *known* my ways"; emphasis added) and thus removed them from sublime privileges. After a succession of provocations, the Israelites in time rejected and lost the knowledge of the anthropomorphic nature of the Gods, the divine relationship of the Father and the Son, and the great plan of grace inherent in the doctrine of the Father and the Son.

The Israelites sought to be self-prospering and became angry when the God of Israel tested or tried them. The Provocation constitutes a recurring theme in the Old Testament, and indeed, in every extant scripture since. The pages of Exodus and Deuteronomy, which narrate the history of the Israelites in the wilderness, describe three additional incidents of provocation. First, at the foot of Sinai, where the Lord tried to sanctify His people and to cause them to come up the mountain, enter His presence, and behold His face, the Israelites refused to exercise sufficient faith to overcome their fear and enter into the fire, smoke, and earthquake that lay between them and the face of God. They said to Moses, "Speak thou with us, and we will hear: *but let not God speak with us,* lest we die" (Exodus 20:19; emphasis added). Moses responded, "Fear not" (Exodus 20:20). Nevertheless, "the people stood afar off, and Moses drew [alone] near unto the thick darkness where God was" (Exodus 20:21).

Second, when the Israelites were camped at Kadesh Barnea in the wilderness, the Lord tried to bring them into the promised land, but they were so frightened by the report of giants in the land that neither Moses nor Caleb and Joshua could get them to exercise enough faith to enter and conquer the land (see Deuteronomy 9:22–23). Again, as at Massah and Meribah, they refused the grace of the Lord.

Third, again at Sinai, when Moses went up to receive the fulness of the gospel from the Lord on the first set of plates, the Israelites made and set up the golden calf. Their rejection of the Lord in the very moment that Moses was receiving the fulness of the gospel for them was a most serious provocation. When he discovered what they had done, Moses broke the tables before the children of Israel. A second, lesser set of plates was made, but they were missing "the words of the everlasting covenant of the holy priesthood" (Joseph Smith Translation, Deuteronomy 10:2), meaning the higher, sanctifying ordinances of the Melchizedek Priesthood. Those were the very ordinances that gave access to the presence of the Lord (see Joseph Smith Translation, Exodus 34:1–2).

With their rejection of the higher priesthood, Israel began to lose the true doctrine of the Father and the Son.[1] The Lord gives the reason: "This greater priesthood administereth the gospel and *holdeth the key* of the mysteries of the kingdom, *even the key of the knowledge of God*. Therefore, in the ordinances thereof, the power of godliness is manifest. And *without the ordinances thereof,* and the authority of the priesthood, the power of godliness is not manifest unto men in the flesh; For without this no man can see the face of God, even the Father, and live. Now this Moses plainly taught to the children of Israel in the wilderness, and sought diligently to sanctify his people that they might behold the face of God; But they hardened their hearts and could not endure his presence; therefore, the Lord . . . swore that they should not enter into his rest while in the wilderness, which rest is the fulness of his glory. Therefore, he took Moses out of their midst, and the Holy Priesthood also" (D&C 84:19–25; emphasis added).

The Prophet Joseph Smith observed: "God cursed the children of Israel because they would not receive the *last law* from Moses. . . . When God offers a blessing or knowledge to a man and he refuses to receive it he will be damned. . . . The Israelites [prayed] that God would speak to Moses [and] not to them in consequence of which he cursed them with a carnal law. . . . [The] law revealed to Moses in Horeb . . . never was revealed to the [children] of Israel."[2] Thus, the children of Israel wandered an unnecessary forty years in the wilderness as God tried to teach them to rely on Him.

We really begin to appreciate the Old Testament when we realize that Israel's experiences in the wilderness are both literal and allegorical of our own experiences. Moses, speaking of manna as a symbolic teaching device, said, "[God] humbled thee, and suffered thee to hunger, and fed thee with manna . . . *that he might make thee know* that man doth not live by bread only, but by every word that proceedeth out of the mouth of the Lord" (Deuteronomy 8:3; emphasis added).

The Apostle Paul spoke similarly of the manna and the water and the rock: "Brethren, I would not that ye should be ignorant, how that all our fathers were under the cloud, and all passed through the sea; And were all baptized unto Moses in the cloud and in the sea; And did all eat the same *spiritual meat* [manna]; And did all drink the same *spiritual drink* [water at Meribah]: for they drank of that *spiritual Rock* that followed them: and that Rock was Christ" (1 Corinthians 10:1–4; emphasis added). The Savior called Himself manna, or the Bread of Life (see John 6:51, 54), indicating mankind's persisting need for divine nourishment.

Exploring scriptural symbols further, in both the Old Testament and the Book of Mormon a *wilderness* symbolizes any place in which the people are tested, tried, proven, refined by trials, taught grace, and prepared to meet the Lord (see Alma 17:9; see also Christ's preparations in the wilderness in Matthew 4:1–2). Scriptural *journeys* often symbolize man's earthly walk from birth through the spiritual wildernesses of a fallen world (see Ether 6:4–7 for the ocean allegory of man's journey; see also 1 Nephi 8 for the *path* leading to the tree of life). God seeks to teach that His children cannot be self-prospering and thereby fulfill the purposes of their earthly lives. They must learn to seek and accept His grace to reach their destinations, which are *promised lands* or places of deliverance and spiritual peace where Zion can be established. The Lord speaks to modern Israel: "Zion cannot be built up unless it is by the principles of the law of the celestial kingdom; otherwise I cannot receive her unto myself. And my people must needs be chastened until they learn obedience, if it must needs be, by the things which they suffer" (D&C 105:5–6). Therefore, the Lord provides in our lives wildernesses and waterlessness and overwhelming challenges to entice His children to involve Him as they struggle through life.

The Book of Mormon supplies further insight into what the Provocation actually refers to. Jacob referred to Psalm 95 (on the plates of brass) when he wrote: "Wherefore we labored diligently among our people, that we might persuade them *to come unto Christ, and partake* of the goodness of God, that they might *enter into his rest,* lest by any means he should swear in his wrath they should not enter in, as in the *provocation* in the days of temptation while the children of Israel were in the wilderness" (Jacob 1:7; emphasis added).

Alma enlarged the implications still further in speaking of the first provocation, or man's first spiritual death at Adam's fall, and the second provocation, or man's continuing spiritual death that comes through rejecting the Lord: "If ye will harden your hearts ye shall not enter into the rest of the Lord . . . as in the *first provocation,* yea, according to his word in the *last provocation.* . . . Let us repent, and harden not our hearts, that we provoke not the Lord our God . . . but *let us enter into the rest of God,* which is prepared according to his word" (Alma 12:36–37; emphasis added).

The Provocation, then, seems to encompass a preference for spiritual death—a preference for a return to Egypt—rather than the demanding trek through repentance to sanctification. The Provocation, in all its manifestations, implies a refusal to come to Christ to exercise faith in the face of such a daunting call, a refusal to partake of the goodness of God, a refusal to accept the restoration to God's presence or rest, a refusal to allow the Savior to work His mighty power in one's life, a refusal to enter into the at-one-ment for which He suffered and died, a refusal to be "clasped in the arms of Jesus" (Mormon 5:11). The Provocation is anti-Atonement and anti-Christ. Abinadi laments over men and women who have "gone according to their own carnal wills and desires; having never called upon the Lord while the arms of mercy were extended towards them; for the arms of mercy were extended towards them, and they would not" (Mosiah 16:12).

But who, indeed, was the God who had stood before Moses upon the rock at Meribah? (see Exodus 17:6–7). That God had revealed

Himself to our fathers Abraham, Isaac, and Jacob as a glorified, exalted man, that is, as an anthropomorphic (in the form of man) God who had created male and female in the image of heavenly parents.[3] This God sought a constant interaction with and a response from His children. He spoke of Himself as father and Israel as His children (see Malachi 2:10). He spoke of the covenant people as bride and Himself as bridegroom (see Hosea 2:19–20). The scriptures ring with manlike descriptions of an interactive God: "The eyes of the Lord" (Psalm 34:15), the ears of the Lord, and the mouth of the Lord; the heavens as the works of His fingers (see Psalm 8:3); the tablets of the covenant "written by the finger of God" (Exodus 31:18). We read of "his countenance" (Numbers 6:26), which He causes to shine or which He hides. We read of His "right hand" (Psalm 118:16), His arm stretched out in mercy and invitation. In Genesis He walks about in the garden (see Genesis 3:8), He goes down to Sinai or to His temple (see Genesis 11:5; 18:21) to reveal Himself (see Exodus 19:18, 34:5) and to dwell in the midst of the children of Israel, and He goes up again (see Genesis 17:22; 35:13). He sits on a throne (see Isaiah 6:1) and causes His voice to be heard among the cherubim (see Numbers 7:89). Moses not only sees the Lord's back (see Exodus 33:23) but speaks to Him face to face and mouth to mouth (see Numbers 12:8). Among several emotions, the Lord expresses tenderness, mercy, love, joy, delight, and pity, as well as sadness, frustration, and anger.

With the loss of the Melchizedek Priesthood, however, and the Jews' resulting vulnerability to Greek and other cultural and philosophical influences, there arose among the Jews a resistance to the idea of an anthropomorphic God. At least by the intertestamental period (the period following Malachi, between the Old Testament and the New), the scribes and rabbis found the anthropomorphisms in the Hebrew Bible offensive and made small textual changes, which they described as "biblical modifications of expression"[4] (see Jacob 4:14 for Jacob's acknowledgment of Israel's deliberate mystification of God). For example, in place of "I [God] will dwell in your midst," they substituted "I shall cause you to dwell," avoiding the idea that God would dwell with men. The text of Exodus 34:24 was subtly altered from "to see the face of the Lord" *(lir'ot 'et-pene yhwh)* to the phrase "to appear before the Lord" *(lera'ot 'et-pene yhwh)*. Again, the effect is to distance and dematerialize God.

It appears that the Jewish translators of the Septuagint Bible (from Hebrew to Greek; abbreviated LXX) also attempted to dematerialize God.[5] An example is Exodus 29:45 (KJV): "I will dwell among the children of Israel, and will be their God." Instead of "I will dwell," the Septuagint reads, "And I shall be called upon [or named] among the children of Israel and will be their God" (Exodus 29:45).[6] The effect of the change from *to dwell* to the phrase *to be called upon* is to distance God from His children.[7]

This attempt to dematerialize God is also found among the Israelite apostates in the Book of Mormon. Ammon and Aaron had to teach that God, the Great Spirit, would not always be spirit, but would tabernacle Himself in the flesh (see Alma 18:34–35; 22:8–14; see also Mosiah 3:5). Abinadi, in fact, was martyred for his very declaration that this spirit God would take on the form of man in order to perform the great Atonement (see Mosiah 13:32–35). The apostate Zoramites' belief that God is a spirit and never would be anything else really meant they believed there would be no Christ, no incarnation of God on earth, and thus, no Atonement (see Alma 31:15–16).

A Jewish scholar named Philo lived in the period just prior to Jesus' advent. His writings, which influenced Judaism as well as Christianity, taught that the physical and emotional references in the scriptures to God were allegorical, not literal. He wrote that when Moses described God with human emotions, the reader needed to know that "neither the . . . passions of the soul, nor the parts and members of the body in general, have any relation to God."[8] Philo explained that Moses used these expressions as an elementary way to teach those who could not otherwise understand. Thus, when the Savior came to the Jews in the meridian of time, He found many of them obsessed with religion, with purity, and with scrupulous observance of law, but He found few who knew God.

Removing the body, parts, and passions from God also removes His ability to suffer and thus obscures the real meanings behind the Atonement. The Book of Mormon, however, teaches that one of the reasons the Savior came to earth was His desire to "take upon him [mankind's] infirmities, that his bowels may be filled with mercy, according to the flesh, that he may know according to the flesh how to succor his people according to their infirmities" (Alma 7:12). Alma quotes Zenos on the accessibility of the Father's grace through the Atonement of the Son: "And thou didst hear me because of mine afflictions and my sincerity; and it is because of thy Son that thou hast been thus merciful unto me, therefore I will cry unto thee in all mine afflictions, for in thee is my joy; for thou has turned thy judgments away from me, because of thy Son" (Alma 33:11). Alma then quotes Zenock on the nature of Israel's Provocation: "Thou art angry, O Lord, with this people, because they will not understand thy mercies which thou hast bestowed upon them because of thy Son" (Alma 33:16).

Related to God's nature is God's name. The reluctance to offend God by anthropomorphic references grew stronger with time so that even the use of the name *YHWH* (Yahweh or Jehovah) was avoided. At least by the third century B.C., *adonai,* meaning "lord," was substituted for the divine name[9] and it ultimately became both illegal and blasphemous to speak the name aloud among the Jews, even in the temple or synagogue. One scholar notes: "The divine name, once the 'distinguishing mark' of divine presence and immanence, had become the essence of God's unapproachable holiness so that in the Jewish tradition 'the Name' (*ha shem*) could be synonymous with 'God.'"[10] A moment's reflection leads us to see that since God had ordained His name as a keyword by which a covenant person could gain access to Him (see Moses 5:8; 1 Kings 8:28–29; Mormon 9:21), to forbid the divine name was to forbid access, through holy ordinances, to God Himself.

With the dematerializing of God came the obscuring of the Father-Son relationship. Religious history reveals that one major apostate objective has been to merge the members of the Godhead into one nebulous being. That merging clouds several significant truths, among which I mention two in passing and a third for discussion:

1. The doctrine of a divine Father and Son begins to reveal that there must be family relationships, parents, husbands, and wives, all of which continue in the eternities.

2. Eternal families being possible, there is need for temple ordinances that seal these relationships for eternity.

3. The Son models for humankind the relationship of grace by which one gains exaltation and which men and women must model in order to be like the Gods.

It is particularly that last truth that I would like to explore here, but first a word about merging the Gods into one amorphous being. That which set the Israelites apart from all others in the polytheistic Greco-Roman and Near Eastern cultures was their steadfast declaration of one omnipotent God, that is, their belief in monotheism. It was perhaps because they had interpreted Deuteronomy 6:4, "Hear, O Israel: The Lord our God is one Lord" to mean that there was only one God, that the later Jews rejected Christ (see John 8:41, 58–59). After all, Christ taught that He is the Son of God, and so, they said, He made Himself equal with God and seemed, in fact, to be multiplying Gods (see John 5:18).[11] Nevertheless, although it is true that there is one omnipotent God, that truth is not the whole truth. When the Savior came to the earth in the meridian of time, one of His tasks was to restore the Melchizedek Priesthood and thus restore the *knowledge of the Father.* Jesus taught that He, the Son, is the only avenue to exaltation or reunion with the Father.

But one of the most important revelations from the divine Father-Son relationship is the model it provides of the *nature of a saving relationship* with God. The Savior showed us how to live in total submission; He drew continually on His Father's grace. He says, "The Son can do *nothing* of himself, but what he seeth the Father do: for *what things soever* he doeth, these also doeth the Son. . . . For the Father loveth the Son, and sheweth him all things that himself doeth" (John 5:19–20; emphasis added). And again, "As the living Father hath sent me, and *I live by the Father:* so he that eateth me [reference to the sacrament], even *he shall live by me*" (John 6:57; emphasis added). And again, "I do *nothing* of myself; but as my Father hath taught me, I speak these things. And he that sent me is with me: the Father hath not left me alone; for I do always those things that please him" (John 8:28–29; emphasis added). Further, He said, "Believest thou not that I am in the Father, and the Father in me? the words that I speak unto you I speak not of myself: but the Father that dwelleth in me, *he doeth the works*" (John 14:10; emphasis added). Ultimately, Christ will even deliver up the kingdom, for which He died, to His Father (see D&C 76:107). This relationship of the at-one-ment of the Father and the Son is the divine model for the Saints of God and was revealed that we might emulate it.

The Savior taught this at-one-ment relationship to His disciples and, indeed, to all who become His disciples. The means of at-one-ment with the Son and the Father is the Holy Ghost. It is through cultivating the Holy Ghost that we enter into at-one-ment with the Son and the Father. Jesus told His disciples: "I will pray the Father, and he shall give you another Comforter, that *he may abide with you for ever;* Even the Spirit of truth . . . for *he dwelleth with you,* and *shall be in you*" (John 14:16–17; emphasis added; see also John 17:20–23).[12]

The Apostle Paul experienced this relationship of oneness with the Savior; he wrote to the Galatians: "I am crucified with Christ: nevertheless I live; yet not I, but Christ liveth in me: and the life which I now live in the flesh I live by the faith of the Son of God, who loved me, and gave himself for me" (Galatians 2:20).

In scenes recorded in 3 Nephi, the resurrected, perfected Christ gave abundant evidence of His continuing dependence on His Father. He makes frequent reference to the commandments and will of His Father. He seems very eager to return to the full presence of His Father (3 Nephi 17:4); we see Him kneel and bow Himself to the earth, pouring out both His troubled heart (3 Nephi 17:14) as well as His joy (3 Nephi 17:20–21), His thanks (3 Nephi 19:20, 28), and His needs (3 Nephi 19:21, 29). Perhaps this relationship of divine dependence and atonement continues far into the eternities. It is revealed to us in this life so we can learn to live in that relationship and thus gain admission to that community of grace-linked Gods.

The relationship of grace helps us understand more fully this passage in Doctrine and Covenants: "[Christ] received not of the fulness at the first, but received grace *for* grace; And he received not of the fulness at first, but continued from grace *to* grace, until he received a fulness. . . . I give unto you these sayings that you may understand and know how to worship, and know what you worship, that *you* may come unto the Father in my name, and in due time receive of his fulness. For if you keep my commandments you shall receive of his fulness, and be glorified in me as I am in the Father; therefore, I say unto you, you shall receive grace *for* grace" (D&C 93:12–13, 19–20; emphasis added).

By this scripture we understand that as Christ gave grace to those around Him, He received from His Father increasingly more grace to give. Thus, receiving grace *for* grace, Jesus grew from grace *to* grace: a model for us. "Freely ye have received, freely give," the Savior told

His disciples (Matthew 10:8). The Lord has blessed each of us individually many times over with many more forms of grace than we now know or could count. Perhaps all of the Lord's grace to us—His many kindnesses to each of us, our talents, our gifts of spirit and personality, our bodies, our material resources—is given to us so that we will have something to give one another. As we give of this grace in countless ways to those around us, especially where it may not seem to be merited, the Lord increases His gifts of grace to us; in this process of our receiving grace *for* the grace we give, we grow from grace *to* grace, as Christ did, until we obtain a fulness.

Living in such a relationship as the Father and the Son's, either on earth or in heaven, requires a total willingness to dethrone oneself as the regent in one's own kingdom and to enthrone Christ as He enthroned the Father. President Ezra Taft Benson observed that "Christ removed self as the force in His perfect life. It was not *my* will, but *thine* be done."[13]

How privileged we are to know about the relationship of grace and to know of the divine possibilities for ourselves through connection with the Father and the Son, to experience the exquisitely loving and personal nature of the Gods in their great chains of light and grace.

In various forms, the Provocation continues with us today. We recognize in ourselves the rejection of grace as we keep trying to struggle through life on our own judgment and power, keeping our own personal agenda on the throne. Mormon described the philosophy of the anti-Christ Korihor as the belief that man prospers and conquers by his own strength and genius, not through dependence on a greater divine being (see Alma 30:17). Thus, struggling alone without calling on God reflects the doctrine of the anti-Christ. It is apparent that even the Son of God could not have prospered without His Father's grace.

Moroni also emphasizes grace: "And now, I would commend you to *seek this Jesus* of whom the prophets and apostles have written, that the *grace of God the Father,* and also *the Lord Jesus Christ,* and the Holy Ghost . . . abide in you forever" (Ether 12:41; emphasis added; see also Moroni 10:32).

We see in Israel's provocations a key to understanding nearly every interaction between God and Israel recorded in the pages of the Bible. On the one hand, God's whole efforts are bent toward helping the covenant people to prosper through His grace; on the other hand, Israel strives to be self-prospering. In the midst of abundant miracles and divine gifts, the persistent rejection of God's grace is Israel's Provocation.

NOTES

1. Of course, all the prophets had the Melchizedek Priesthood, but their right to confer it or teach its mysteries was restricted. See Joseph Smith, *Teachings of the Prophet Joseph Smith,* comp. Joseph Fielding Smith (Salt Lake City: Deseret Book, 1938), 181.

2. Andrew F. Ehat and Lyndon W. Cook, eds., *The Words of Joseph Smith* (Provo, UT: Religious Studies Center, Brigham Young University, 1980), 244, 247; emphasis added.

3. Because God created man in His own image, it is more accurate to speak of man as *theomorphic* (in the form or image of God) than to speak of God as anthropomorphic.

4. Cecil Roth and Geoffrey Wigoder, eds. *Encyclopedia Judaica,* (Jerusalem: Keter, 1982), 3:54, s.v. "anthropomorphism."

5. Perhaps it is helpful to note here, with respect to apostate movements, that in any apostasy there are the deliberate initiators and perpetrators of lies (see 1 Nephi 13:27; Jacob 4:14; Moses 1:41), but there is usually also a larger group of innocent and well-intentioned victims (see 1 Nephi 13:29; D&C 123:12). Not all promoters of false ideas have malignant intent; most are to some extent the victims of those who have gone before.

6. Another example is found in Numbers 12:8. The Hebrew version reads: "With [Moses] will I speak mouth to mouth, even apparently, and not in dark speeches; and the image [or *form*] of the Lord shall he behold." The Greek version reads: "Mouth to mouth will I speak to him, in his sight and not in riddles, and he shall see the glory of the Lord." The change from *image* to *glory* is from the specific to a more nebulous description of God.

7. For a fuller discussion of the Apostasy of the doctrine of God during the intertestamental period, see the author's chapter entitled "From Malachi to John the Baptist: The Dynamics of Apostasy," *Studies in Scripture,* Vol. 4: *1 Kings to Malachi,* ed. Kent P. Jackson (Salt Lake City: Deseret Book, 1993), 471–83. See also an in-depth study of the dematerializing of God in the author's "The Influence of Asceticism on the Rise of Christian Text, Doctrine, and Practice in the First Two Centuries," (PhD diss., Brigham Young University, n.d.).

8. Philo, "The Unchangeableness of God," *Loeb Classical Library* (Cambridge, MA: Harvard University Press, 1930), 3:37.

9. Roth and Wigoder, *Encyclopedia Judaica,* 7:680, s.v. "God, Name of."

10. Another scholar suggests that, with ascendancy of the law in Israel and the need to buffer the law against violations, *any* use of the divine name had to be denied. The prohibition was motivated by a desire to ensure that the name would not be used "in vain" (Exodus 20:7) either by Jews or non-Jews. The name used in the temple or the synagogue was eventually affected by this fear. In the Septuagint the name of Yahweh was rendered throughout with *kyrios* ("Lord"), following the Jewish preference for *adonai*. Martin Rose, "Names of God in the OT," *The Anchor Bible Dictionary* (New York: Doubleday, 1992), 1010.

11. An extension of this merging of Gods occurred in the early period of the Christian Church at the Council of Nicea (AD 325) when the decision to fabricate a trinity of three beings into one made it possible to make Christianity securely monotheistic, again in a threateningly pagan environment. Both of these beliefs, monotheism and trinitarianism, did violence to the full truth about the true nature of the Godhead and of godliness itself (see my article, "The Conspiracy Begins," in *From the Last Supper through the Resurrection: The Savior's Final Hours,* ed. Richard Neitzel Holzapfel and Thomas A. Wayment [Salt Lake City: Deseret Book, 2003], 474–75).

12. Joseph Smith, *Lectures on Faith,* comp. N. B. Lundwall (Salt Lake City: Bookcraft, n.d.), Lecture 5, 48–49, explains how the Father and the Son are one through the medium of the Spirit and how all the Saints may in the same manner come into at-one-ment with them: "The Only Begotten of the Father, full of grace and truth, and having overcome, received a *fullness* of the glory of the Father, *possessing the same mind* with the Father, which *mind is the Holy Spirit,* that bears record of the Father and the Son, and these three are one; or, in other words, these three constitute the great, matchless, governing, and supreme power over all things . . . the Father and the Son possessing the same mind, the same wisdom, glory, power, and fullness—filling all in all; the Son being filled with the fullness of the mind, glory, and power; or, in other words, the *spirit,* glory, and power, of the Father . . . which Spirit is shed forth upon all who believe on his name and keep his commandments. . . . all those who keep his commandments shall grow up from grace to grace, and become heirs of the heavenly kingdom, and joint heirs with Jesus Christ; possessing the same mind, being transformed *into the same image* or likeness, even *the express image* of him who fills all in all; being filled with the fullness of his glory, and become one in him, even as the Father, Son and Holy Spirit are one" (emphasis added).

13. Ezra Taft Benson, in Conference Report, April 1986, 6.

CHAPTER TWELVE

"GREAT ARE THE WORDS OF ISAIAH"

HUGH W. NIBLEY

I have reached the stage where I have nothing more to say. As far as I am concerned, the scriptures say it all. "Behold, I say unto you, that ye ought to search these things. Yea, a commandment I give unto you that ye search these things diligently; for great are the words of Isaiah. For surely he spake as touching all things concerning my people which are of the house of Israel; therefore it must needs be that he must speak also to the Gentiles. And all things that he spake have been and shall be, even according to the words which he spake" (3 Nephi 23:1–3). That quotation alone spares us the trouble of an apology for Isaiah. The book of Isaiah is a tract for our own times; our very aversion to it testifies to its relevance. It is necessary to remind us of its importance, however, because Isaiah's message has not been popular, and he tells us why. The wicked do not like to be told about their faults. Every society, no matter how corrupt, has some good things about it—otherwise it would not survive from year to year. Isn't it much pleasanter to talk about the good things than the bad things? The people of Zarahemla, said Samuel the Lamanite, wanted prophets that would tell them what was right with Zarahemla, not what was wrong. There is a great danger in that: the many things that are right with any society can hardly damage it, but one serious flaw can destroy it. One goes to the physician not to be

Hugh W. Nibley (1910–2005) was professor emeritus of ancient scripture at Brigham Young University.

told what parts are functioning well but what is making him ill or threatening him with the worst.

But, says Isaiah, the people of Israel want to hear smooth things: "Prophesy not unto us right things, speak unto us smooth things" (Isaiah 30:10). And ever since, the process of interpreting Isaiah has been one of smoothing him out. Consider some conspicuous examples of this.

1. The idea that Isaiah is moralizing, not talking about doctrine. Yet he starts out calling Israel God's children (Isaiah 1:2); he insists on this all along—God is their Father. It is the first article of faith. But they won't see it (Isaiah 1:3); they want nothing of the doctrine (Isaiah 1:4). They don't see anything that they don't want to see, says Isaiah. They are functionally blind. They have deliberately cut the wires, and then they complain that they get no message. Isaiah is full of obvious things that nobody else sees, especially for Latter-day Saints. The rabbis have always made fun of the suggestion that he is actually referring to Christ. But we go further than that. We see in the Book of Mormon even the particular calling of the Prophet Joseph Smith. And who is to say that we are wrong?

2. The idea that the God of Isaiah is the savage, vengeful Old Testament God of wrath, the tribal God. This means we do not have to take Him too seriously. It lets us off the hook. But Isaiah's God is kindness itself. "Come now, and let us reason together," he says, "though your sins be as scarlet, they shall be as white as snow" (Isaiah 1:18). There is nothing authoritarian about him; he is constantly willing to discuss and explain. His most threatening statements are instantly followed by what seems a reversal of mood and judgment. He is always willing, ready, waiting, urging, patiently pleading; it is Israel that will not hear, it is they who break off the discussion and walk away, turning their back upon Him and asking Him to please be quiet.

3. The idea that Isaiah is addressing special groups. Indeed he talks about good people and bad people—but they are the same! Woe to Israel! Good tidings to Israel! One and the same Israel. And not just to Israel but to all mankind; he addresses the nations and their leaders by name. And not only to his generation does he speak, but to all. Nephi applied the words of Isaiah to his own people in the desert "that it might be for our profit and learning" (1 Nephi 19:23). Six

hundred years later, Jesus Christ called upon the Nephites to do the same thing, and the angel Moroni handed the same message over to our generation. Isaiah has just one audience because he has but one message. He is addressing whatever mortals upon the face of the earth happen to be in need of repentance. This takes us to our next point.

4. The idea that there is more than one Isaiah and that they all tell different things. Since there is only one message and one audience, this is a mere quibble. The message is a happy one: "Repent—and all will be well—better than you can ever imagine!" Only to those who do not intend to repent is the message grim. Isaiah does not distinguish between the good and the bad but only between those who repent and those who do not. He does not ask where we are—he knows that—but only the direction in which we are moving. Of course, only those can repent who need to, and that means everybody—equally. Does not one person need repentance more than another? Ezra and Baruch protested to God that while Israel had sinned, the Gentiles had acted much worse, and asked why they should be let off so much more easily. But God was not buying that argument. You can always find somebody who is worse than you are to make you feel virtuous. It's a cheap shot: those awful terrorists, perverts, communists—*they* are the ones who need to repent! Yes, indeed they do, and for them repentance will be a full-time job, exactly as it is for all the rest of us.

5. The doctors, Jewish and Christian alike, love to labor the idea that for Isaiah, the supreme and unforgivable sin was the worship of idols. Well, he says that idolatry is foolish and irrational but never that it is the unforgivable sin. The darling illusion of the schoolmen is that as modern, enlightened, rational thinkers they have made a wonderful discovery: that wood or metal dolls or images cannot really see or hear, and so on. They labor the point to death. But the ancients knew that as well as we do. That is exactly *why* they patronized the idols. There is the famous story of the Eloquent Peasant from the Middle Kingdom in Egypt that tells how the rascally manager of an estate, when he saw a peasant passing by on his way to the market with a load of goods, cried out, "Would that I had some idol that would permit me to rob this man's goods." A dumb image would offer no opposition to any course he chose to take. That was the beauty of

idols: they are as impersonal and amoral as money in the bank—the present-day as well as the ancient equivalent of a useful idol.

6. This is matched by the idea that the greatest of moral and intellectual virtues was the acknowledgment of the one and only God. Again, that was another ancient commonplace. Isaiah does not denounce polytheism as the greatest of sins. Indeed, a number of researchers have shown that polytheism as such is nowhere condemned in the Bible. But Isaiah does lay heavy emphasis on oneness. There is to be no compromise. There is only *one* way for a person to go, *one* God for Israel or the *one* human race to serve. To defuse this uncomfortable teaching, the doctors have converted it into a theological exercise for the schools.

7. The idea that Isaiah is denouncing pagan practices before all else. But it is the rites and ordinances that God gave to Moses and that the people were faithfully observing that Isaiah describes as an exercise in desperate futility.

ISAIAH CHAPTER 1

The quickest way to get an overview of the immense book of Isaiah is simply to read the first chapter. Scholars have long held that this is not part of the original book but a summary by a disciple. If so, that makes it nonetheless valuable, and indeed it is remarkable that this, the most famous chapter of Isaiah, is never quoted in the Book of Mormon. Let's take it verse by verse.

1:2. The people of Israel are God's children—He is their Father. This is the doctrine they have forgotten, and they will be in no condition to receive it again until they have undergone the moral regeneration that is the burden of Isaiah's preaching.

1:3. That doctrine they have rejected. They refuse to hear it.

1:4. Because they can't live with the doctrine in their sinful state, they have run away from it. This is inexcusable; God does not look upon it with forbearance. He knows that they are quite capable of understanding and living by the gospel. Accordingly, He is more than displeased; He is angry.

1:5. Yet it is not He who has been giving them a hard time. They decided to go their own way, openly revolting against Him. And their system is simply not working. They are not able to cope with the situation mentally, nor do they have the spirit to carry it through. Men on their own are pitiful objects.

1:6. The whole thing is sick, sick, sick. Every attempt to correct the situation fails miserably. Nothing works.

1:7. The result is internal depression and international disaster.

1:8. God's chosen people are holed up, trusting in their miserable defense, trapped by their own walls.

1:9. The reason they survive at all so far is that there are still a few righteous, a small remnant of honest people among them.

1:10. So it is time they were considering the alternative, which Isaiah herewith offers them.

1:11. You are not going to appease God by trying to buy Him off, by going through the pious motions of religious observances, your meetings and temple sessions.

1:12. It is not for you to decide what to do to please God—it is for Him to decide, and He has not required all this display of piety from you.

1:13. Your most dedicated observances, even following God's ancient prescriptions, if done in the wrong spirit are actually iniquity—not to your credit but to your loss.

1:14. God is not impressed but disgusted by it.

1:15. Even when you pray, God will not hear you. Why not? Answer: Because there is blood on your upraised hands.

1:16. The blood and sins of this generation are on you in the temple. What blood and sins? Your evil ways.

1:17. What evil ways? What should we be doing? Answer: Dealing justly, relieving those oppressed by debt instead of collecting from them, giving a fair deal to the orphans and assistance to the widow; in other words, showing some thought for people without money.

1:18. God is not being capricious or arbitrary. He is eminently reasonable. Is His way the only way? Let Him tell you why, and then see if you do not agree: "Come now, and let us reason together, saith the Lord." Then a surprising statement: "Though your sins be as scarlet, they shall be as white as snow." Plainly God does not take pleasure in these rebukes; He does not gloat as men would (for example, Thomas Aquinas) over the punishment in store for the wicked. He loves them all and holds forth the most wonderful promises for them. There is a way out, and that is why Isaiah is speaking, not because he is a puritanical scold.

1:19. Have they had enough? They need only to listen and to follow advice and all will be well.

1:20. But you cannot go on as you have been. You will be wiped out by war if you do. "For the mouth of the Lord hath spoken it." The "consumption decreed" (D&C 87:6) is another quotation from Isaiah.

1:21. You can do it—because you once did. And then you lost it all—went over to unbridled sex and murder.

1:22. And for what? Property and pleasure, for silver that is now as worthless as garbage and wine that is flat.

1:23. The leaders set the worst example. They work with crooks; everybody is on the take: "Every one loveth gifts, and followeth after rewards," while the poor don't get a break in court and a widow can't even get a hearing.

1:24. God wants nothing to do with such rascals; He is going to get rid of them. They have made themselves His enemies.

1:25. This calls for a thorough housecleaning. All that dross must be purged away.

1:26. To bring back the old order, to "restore thy judges as at the first" (as quoted in the well-known hymn). It is still possible, and God is going to bring it about. There will yet be "the city of righteousness, the faithful city."

1:27. Zion is going to be redeemed with many of these same sinful people living in it, along with a lot of converts from the outside.

1:28. All the rest will have to go, but not because God chooses to throw them out. They will walk away from safety right into destruction; with eyes wide open they will forsake the Lord and be consumed.

1:29–31. These verses are the only references to paganism—popular cults that will wither and be burned up—not be destroyed, however, because they follow pagan manners or forms, as the doctors, ministers, and commentators love to tell us, but because they were part of the cover-up for avaricious, hard, and immoral practices.

THE WORST VICES

For the rest of the time I want to talk about those human qualities Isaiah describes as pleasing to God and those qualities He despises. They both come as a surprise. As to the second, the traits and the behavior Isaiah denounces as the worst of vices are without exception those of *successful* people. The wickedness and folly of Israel do not consist of indolence, sloppy dressing, long hair, nonconformity (even the reading of books), radical and liberal unrealistic ideas and programs, irreverence toward custom and property, contempt for established idols, and so on. The wickedest people in the Book of Mormon are the Zoramites, a proud, independent, courageous, industrious, enterprising, patriotic, prosperous people who attended strictly to their weekly religious duties with the proper observance of dress standards. Thanking God for all He had given them, they bore testimony to His goodness. They were sustained in all their doings by a perfectly beautiful self-image. Well, what is wrong with any of that? There is just one thing that spoils it all, and that is the very thing that puts Israel in bad with the Lord, according to Isaiah. The Jews observed with strictest regularity all the rules that Moses gave them—"and yet . . . they cry unto thee" *and yet* they are really thinking of something else. "Behold, O my God, their costly apparel, . . . all their precious things . . . their hearts are set upon them, *and yet* they cry unto thee and say—We thank thee, O God, for we are a chosen people unto thee, while others shall perish" (Alma 31:27–28; emphasis added).

God sums up the cause of anger against Israel in one word: "For the iniquity of his covetousness was I wroth, and smote him: I hid me, and was wroth." With what effect? It didn't faze the guilty, but "he went on frowardly in the way of his heart" (Isaiah 57:17). Like the Zoramites, covetous Israel was quite pleased with itself, just as in these last days. Modern Israel was put under "a very sore and grievous curse" because of "covetousness, and . . . feigned words"; that is, greed and hypocrisy (D&C 104:4). By far the commonest charge Isaiah brings against the wicked is "oppression," *'ashaq*. The word means to choke; to grab by the neck and squeeze, grasp, or press; to take the fullest advantage of someone in your power; in short, to maximize profits. It is all centralized in "Babylon, . . . the golden city,"—"the oppressor" (Isaiah 14:4), which gives us instant insight into the social and economic structure of Isaiah's world. It is a competitive and predatory society, "Yea, they are greedy dogs which can never have enough, and they are shepherds that cannot understand [they do not know what is going on, because everyone is looking out for himself]: they all look to their own way, every one for his gain, from his quarter" (Isaiah 56:11).

The charge applies to our own day, when "every man walketh in his own way, and after the image of his own god, whose image is in the likeness of the world, and whose substance is that of an idol, which waxeth old and shall perish in Babylon, even Babylon the great, which shall fall" (D&C 1:16). Babylon had flourished long before Isaiah's day, and it was to flourish long after. At that particular time it was on the way up again, but the word is used throughout the scriptures as the type and model of a world that lived by the economy. Its philosophy is nowhere better expressed than in the words of Korihor: "Every man fared in this life according to the management of the creature; therefore every man prospered according to his genius, and . . . every man conquered according to his strength, and whatsoever a man did was no crime" (Alma 30:17).

In Isaiah, the successful people are living it up. It is as if they said, "Come ye, . . . I will fetch wine, and we will fill ourselves with strong drink" (Isaiah 56:12). We'll have drinks and a party at my place. And tomorrow more of the same, but even better, even richer. The economy looks bright; all is well.

Isaiah has a good deal to say about the beautiful people in words that come uncomfortably close to home:

28:1. "Woe to the crown of pride, to the drunkards of Ephraim, whose glorious beauty is a fading flower, which are on the head of the fat valleys of them that are overcome with wine!"

28:2. "Behold, the Lord hath a mighty and strong [wind], which . . . shall cast down to the earth with the hand."

28:3. "The crown of pride, the drunkards of Ephraim, shall be trodden under feet."

28:7. "But they also have erred through wine . . . ; they stumble in judgment."

He describes the party people, the fast set: "Woe unto them that rise up early in the morning, that they may follow strong drink; that continue until night, till wine inflame them!" (Isaiah 5:11). They are stupefied by the endless beat of the Oriental music that has become part of our scene: "And the harp, and the viol, the tabret, and pipe, and wine, are in their feasts: but they regard not the work of the Lord, neither consider the operation of his hands" (Isaiah 5:12). And of course there is the total subservience to fashion: "Because the daughters of Zion are haughty, and walk with stretched forth necks and wanton eyes, walking and mincing as they go" (Isaiah 3:16)—in the immemorial manner of fashion models. An instructive list of words from the boutiques that only the fashion-wise will know tells us that "the Lord will take away . . . their cauls, and their round tires like the moon, the chains, and the bracelets, and the mufflers, the bonnets, and the ornaments of the legs, and the headbands, and the tablets, and the earrings, the rings, and nose jewels" (Isaiah 3:18–21), and of course clothes, "the changeable suits of apparel, and the mantles, and the wimples, and the crisping pins" (Isaiah 3:22). Their beauty aids will defeat their purpose as their hair falls out and their perfumes are overpowered (see Isaiah 3:24).

Naturally there is the more lurid side of sex, the more reprehensible: "Hear the word of the Lord, ye rulers of Sodom; . . . ye people of Gomorrah. . . . How is the faithful city become an harlot!" (Isaiah 1:10, 21). Just as Nephi "did liken all scriptures unto us, that it might be for our profit and learning" (1 Nephi 19:23), so right at the outset Isaiah here not only likens Jerusalem to the long vanished cities of Sodom and Gomorrah but addresses them directly by name as actually *being* Sodom and Gomorrah—showing us that we may not pass these charges off as not applying to us because we live in another time and culture. Is the scene so different?

The costly fashions reflect a world in which people are out to impress and impose themselves on others. Everyone is after a career, everyone is aspiring to be a VIP: "The mighty man, and the man of war, the judge, and the prophet, and the prudent, and the ancient. The captain . . . , and the honourable man, and the counsellor, and the cunning artificer, and the eloquent orator" (Isaiah 3:2–3). What about them? "I will give children to be their princes, and babes shall rule over them" (Isaiah 3:4). So much for their authority—and why? Because everyone is out for himself in this game of one-upmanship: "And the people shall be oppressed, every one by another, and every one by his neighbour [there's competition for you!]: the child shall behave himself proudly against the ancient [what else can you expect?], and the base against the honourable" (Isaiah 3:5). Everything will get out of control. A man will take hold of his brother, saying, "You have clothes, so you be our ruler; you be responsible for this mess!" But he will refuse the great honor, saying, "Don't try to make me a ruler—I'm flat broke!" (see Isaiah 3:6–7). Because everybody will be broke, Isaiah continues: "For Jerusalem is ruined" (Isaiah 3:8)—all because they stubbornly think they can go it alone: "Woe to the rebellious children, saith the Lord, that take counsel, but not of me: and that cover with a covering, but not of my spirit, that they may add sin to sin" by justifying themselves at every step (Isaiah 30:1). The rebellious people, the lying children will not hear the law of the Lord. The law of God have they rejected; they reject the law of sacrifice. Oh yes, they sacrifice, but they do not do it the way the Lord wants them to—"Have I required this thing at your hands?" (see Isaiah 1:12). They have violated the law of chastity, for Israel is a harlot. They have violated the law of consecration, for they are idolators—coveting for themselves is now their consecration. They have rejected the law of God, for they will not do things His way, as they covenanted (see Isaiah 30).

The one who sets the supreme example for the people is that most inspiring and ambitious of all spirits. "How art thou fallen from heaven, O Lucifer, son of the morning! how art thou cut down to the ground, which didst weaken the nations! For thou hast said in thine heart, . . . I will exalt my throne . . . : I will sit also upon the mount of the congregation" (Isaiah 14:12–13). He is out to rule the world, which he does, with disastrous effect; the result is depression and ruin: "Behold, the Lord maketh the earth empty, and maketh it waste, and turneth it upside down, and scattereth abroad the inhabitants thereof. And it shall be, as with the people, so with the priest; as with the servant, so with his master; . . . as with the buyer, so with the seller; as with the lender, so with the borrower; as with the taker of usury, so with the giver of usury to him. The land shall be utterly emptied, and utterly spoiled: for the Lord hath spoken this word" (Isaiah 24:1–3).

Isaiah knows how to describe a world in total collapse, and we have a rich and very ancient lamentation literature, both of the Egyptians and the Babylonians, appearing periodically over a span of thousands of years, along with abundant business documents, letters, and ritual texts to confirm that such conditions actually did prevail in the world from time to time exactly as Isaiah tells them, always with the same combination of social, economic, and political hysteria. Notice the strong emphasis on economy and finance in the passage just cited. "Ye do always remember your riches," says Samuel the Lamanite, and for that very reason you will lose them (see Helaman 13:22, 31). They are cursed and will "become slippery" is the way he puts it, and Isaiah has a comparable expression: "The land shall be utterly . . . spoiled. . . . [It] fadeth away . . . because they [the people] have transgressed the laws, changed the ordinance, broken the everlasting covenant" to suit themselves (Isaiah 24:3–5). "Therefore hath the curse devoured the earth" (Isaiah 24:6); few men are left, everything is desolate; there are no crops, it doesn't rain; therefore, many people are gone into captivity because they have no knowledge, and their honorable men are famished; the multitude is dried up with thirst. "For it is a people of no understanding: therefore he that made them will not have mercy on them, and he that formed them will shew them no favour" (Isaiah 27:11).

Societal Woes

Plainly, men are held responsible by God to show some sense. Self-deception costs dearly; the Lord "frustrateth the tokens of the liars, and maketh diviners mad; . . . turneth wise men backward, and maketh their knowledge foolish" (Isaiah 44:25). They have despised His word and trust oppression and perverseness and persist in it. These are tough-minded people. They hold out to the end, like the breaking of "a high wall." They will hold out in their ways with great tenacity. Nothing will move them. Like a high dam when it breaks, it breaks all at once. (This is the principle of "the 29th day.") First the wall begins to bulge, and then everything goes: the "breaking cometh suddenly at an instant" (Isaiah 30:12–13). He will not spare even a shard. The smashup is quick and complete.

All this because everything is out of line. No one can trust anyone else in this freely competitive society. "None calleth for justice, nor any pleadeth for truth: they trust in vanity, and speak lies" (Isaiah 59:4). "The act of violence is in their hands. They shed innocent blood. Their thoughts are the thoughts of iniquity" (see Isaiah

59:6–7). This reads like a prospectus of TV fare. Such a course can only leave a trail of distrust: "The way of peace they know not; . . . they have made them crooked paths" (Isaiah 59:8); "speaking oppression and revolt, conceiving and uttering from the heart words of falsehood. . . . Yea, truth faileth; and he that departeth from evil maketh himself a prey" (Isaiah 59:13, 15). It is profitable to break the rules only as long as there are people simple and gullible enough to keep them. And if you don't play the game, you can expect to become a victim. Isaiah does not applaud such realism: "Woe to thee that spoilest, and thou wast not spoiled; and dealest treacherously, and they dealt not treacherously with thee!" (Isaiah 33:1). The Lord goes even further in our dispensation, telling us that we have no right to cheat even those clever people who are trying to cheat us: "Wo be unto him that lieth to deceive because he supposeth that another lieth to deceive" (D&C 10:28).

Naturally Isaiah takes us into the law courts: "Woe unto them that call evil good, and good evil" (Isaiah 5:20)—that being the rhetorical art, the art, as Plato tells us, "of making good seem bad and bad seem good by the use of words," which in the ancient world came to its own in the law courts. "Woe unto them that are wise in their own eyes, and prudent in their own sight! . . . which justify the wicked for reward, and take away the righteousness of the righteous from him!" (Isaiah 5:21, 23). This recalls how the Gadianton robbers, when they finally got control of the government and the law courts, when "they did obtain the sole management of the government," at once turned "their backs upon the poor and the meek" (Helaman 6:39), "filling the judgment-seats" with their own people (Helaman 7:4), "letting the guilty and the wicked go unpunished because of their money" (Helaman 7:5). They "justify the wicked for reward," says Isaiah (5:23), and he warns them in their own legal language that God will bring charges against the elders of Israel and "the princes thereof: for ye have eaten up the vineyard; the spoil of the poor is in *your* houses!" (Isaiah 3:14; emphasis added). The stuff that is in your houses really belongs to them. "What mean ye that ye beat my people to pieces, and grind the faces of the poor?" (Isaiah 3:15). "Woe unto them that decree unrighteous decrees [in their untouchable authority], and that write grievousness which they have prescribed" (Isaiah 10:1)—serving their own interests by the laws and regulations they make, "to turn aside the needy from judgment, and to take away the right from the poor of my people, that widows may be their prey, and that they may rob the fatherless!" (Isaiah 10:2).

Everything is rigged; everybody is on the take; the harlot city is full of murderers; the princes are rebellious, companions of thieves; "every one loveth gifts, and followeth after rewards: they judge not the fatherless, neither doth the cause of the widow come unto them" (Isaiah 1:23). Even when right is plainly on his side, the poor man doesn't stand a chance, for "the churl . . . deviseth wicked devices to destroy the poor with lying words, even when the needy speaketh right" (Isaiah 32:7). "For the vile person will . . . practise hypocrisy, and . . . utter error . . . to make empty the soul of the hungry, and he will cause the drink of the thirsty to fail" (Isaiah 32:6). Real estate is a special province for such people, and the ancient record is full of the slick and tricky deals by which they acquired their great estates, from the earliest of Greek preachers, Hesiod and Solon, to the last of the Roman satirists, including the terribly modern Petronius. "Woe unto them that join house to house, that lay field to field, till there be no place, that they may be placed alone in the midst of the earth!" (Isaiah 5:8).

Isaiah has a lot to say about trade and commerce, "The burden of Tyre," the crowning city, "whose merchants are princes, whose traffickers are the honourable of the earth." The Lord intends "to stain the pride of all glory, and to bring into contempt all the honourable of the earth" (Isaiah 23:1, 8–9). They are a restless lot, these enterprising people: "Peace, peace to him that is far off, and to him that is near, saith the Lord. . . . But the wicked are like the troubled sea, when it cannot rest, whose waters cast up mire and dirt" (remember Lehi's "filthy waters") (Isaiah 57:19–20). "There is no peace, saith the Lord, unto the wicked" (Isaiah 48:22; 57:21). Babylon is at once restless and busy, selfish and carefree; "None seeth me," she says; there is "none else beside me" (Isaiah 47:10). She has all the technical and commercial know-how at her command. All the experts are working for her—the charmers, the astrologers, the expert analysts, the skillful accountants—and all will be burned as stubble. In the thirteenth chapter of Isaiah, we see the burden of Babylon, the vast activity, the noise, the bustle, the self-importance, the consuming hunger for profits in this great world center that is also another Sodom, a sink of moral depravity.

PRIDE OF NATIONS

By a great miracle King Hezekiah of Judah was snatched from death and given fifteen more years of life. In an outburst of joy and gratitude, he voiced his thanks and his infinite relief at knowing that God was able to give whatever one asked of Him, even life itself; what is the security of all the world's wealth in comparison to that? And then a significant thing happened. Ambassadors arrived from Babylon, and Hezekiah simply could not resist showing them through his treasury, displaying his wealth and power. "Then came Isaiah the prophet unto King Hezekiah, and said unto him, What said these men? and from whence came they unto thee? And Hezekiah said, They are come from . . . Babylon. Then said he, What have they seen in thine house? And Hezekiah answered, All that is in mine house have they seen. Then said Isaiah to Hezekiah, Hear the word of the Lord of hosts: Behold, the days come, that all that is in thine house . . . shall be carried to Babylon" (Isaiah 39:3–6). The man couldn't resist showing off, and by his vanity he only whetted their greed. They liked what they saw and came back later to fetch it. He had played right into their hands.

Isaiah is very much into the international picture in which the fatal flaw is the assumption that things are in the hands of the great men of the earth, while in fact there are no great men but just ordinary guys with disastrous delusions of grandeur. *Haughty* is a favorite word with Isaiah.

"And I will punish the world for their evil, and the wicked for their iniquity; and I will cause the arrogancy of the proud to cease, and will lay low the haughtiness of the terrible" (Isaiah 13:11).

"I will make a man more precious than fine gold; even a man than the golden wedge of Ophir" (Isaiah 13:12).

"The lofty looks of man shall be humbled, and the haughtiness of men shall be bowed down, and the Lord alone shall be exalted in that day" (Isaiah 2:11).

"Behold, the Lord, the Lord of hosts, shall lop the bough with terror: and the high ones of stature shall be hewn down, and the haughty shall be humbled" (Isaiah 10:33).

"The earth mourneth and fadeth away, the world languisheth and fadeth away, the haughty people of the earth do languish. The earth also is defiled. . . . Therefore hath the curse devoured the earth, and they that dwell therein are desolate: therefore the inhabitants of the earth are burned, and few men left" (Isaiah 24:4–6).

What makes a nation great? Power and gain is the answer we give today; the thing is to be number one in military and economic clout. They thought so in Isaiah's day too: Woe unto them that rely on horses and chariots because they are powerful, but "look not unto the Holy One of Israel"; "The Egyptians are men, and not God; and their horses flesh, and not spirit" (Isaiah 31:1, 3). No real security is to be gained by alliances, no sword either of the strong or of the weak power shall overcome Assyria; the Lord had His own plans for Assyria, and no one could have guessed what they were. Where does security lie? In digging the defenses of Jerusalem you are merely digging your graves! The only true defense is the calling of the priesthood in the temple. If you play the game of realistic power politics, you can't expect any but the usual reward.

The Assyrians guaranteed security. They were the top nation militarily. "Go along with us," they said to Jerusalem (and Isaiah has preserved their letters), "and you will be safe. You are fools. How can God deliver you if you have no army? You need us. God is on the side of the big battalions." This is what is called Realpolitik, which has repeatedly destroyed its practitioners in modern times. When Isaiah tells the people to trust God and not Egypt, the people say that that is not realistic! So here come the Assyrians, those super-realists, with their irresistible might—and they were wiped out in their camp as they were sleeping. The great nations? "Behold, the nations are as a drop of a bucket, and are counted as the small dust of the balance" (Isaiah 40:15). All the nations before Him are as nothing, and they are counted to Him as less than nothing and vanity because they pretend to be something (see Isaiah 10:33). "For Tophet is ordained of old" and is waiting for them right now—("a prison have I prepared for them," the Lord tells Enoch [Moses 7:38]). "Yea for the king it is prepared"—for *Assyria*. "He hath made it deep and large: the pile thereof is fire and much wood; the breath of the Lord, like a stream of brimstone, doth kindle it" (Isaiah 30:33). Don't be impressed by "the mighty man, and the man of war, the judge, and the prophet, and the prudent, and the ancient" (Isaiah 3:2). There is only one in whom you can put your trust. Assyria vanished overnight and was never heard of again, while lesser nations as ancient as Assyria who could not afford to gamble for supremacy on the winning of battles are still with us.

"CLEAN HANDS, AND A PURE HEART"

As surprising as the traits Isaiah despises are those he prizes—not drive, initiative, industry, enterprise, hard work, thrift, piety—none of the Zoramite virtues, though they are truly virtues when they are not vitiated by selfish motives or a morbid obsession with routine. And let me observe in passing that work is, after all, not a busy running back and forth in established grooves, though that is the essence of our modern business and academic life, but the supreme energy and disciplined curiosity required to cut *new* grooves. In Isaiah's book, the qualities that God demands of men are such as our society looks down on with mildly patronizing contempt. Isaiah promises the greatest blessings and glory to the meek, the lowly, the poor, the oppressed, the afflicted, and the needy. What! Is being poor and oppressed an achievement? Are we encouraged to join the ranks of the down-and-outers? What possible merit can there be in such a negative and submissive stance? Well, there *is* virtue in it, and it is the presence of Satan in the world that is the deciding factor. We are promised there will be no poor in Zion. That is because Satan will not be present there with his clever arrangement of things. But he is the prince of this world, freely permitted for a time to try men and to tempt them. Here he calls the tune.

And how does he try and tempt us? In the worldwide mythology of the human race, the devil is the lord of the underworld who sits on the treasure of the earth in his dark kingdom; he is Pluto, the god of wealth, who by his control of the earth's resources dictates the affairs of men. Aristophanes' last play, the *Plutus,* is one long, bitter commentary on the kind of people who succeed in this world. Indeed, "the spurns that patient merit of the unworthy takes" is a stock theme of the world's literature from the Egyptian story of the two brothers through Lazarus and Dives to the vicissitudes of the Joad family in the *Grapes of Wrath.* If we believe Isaiah, the Son of Man Himself was "despised and rejected" (Isaiah 53:3), from which one concludes that to be highly successful in this life is hardly the ultimate stamp of virtue. For Satan's golden question, "Have you any money?" has a paralyzing and intriguing effect that enlists all but the noblest spirits in the great conspiracy: "And judgment is turned away backward," says Isaiah, "and justice standeth afar off: for truth is fallen in the street, and equity cannot enter. Yea, truth faileth; and he that departeth from evil maketh himself a prey" (Isaiah 59:14–15). Whoever refuses to put up with this sort of thing, in their words, must expect to take a beating. "The Lord saw it," continues Isaiah, "and it displeased him that there was no judgment" (Isaiah 59:15). Everybody is cheating, and God does not like it at all. "Behold the world lieth in sin at this time, and none doeth good, no not one, . . . and mine anger is kindling against the inhabitants of the earth to visit them according to this ungodliness."[1] Such were the opening words of the Lord in this dispensation spoken to the Prophet Joseph in the grove. The words "the world lieth in sin" call for a more particular statement in the manner of Isaiah, and we find the same expression explained in D&C 49:20: "It is not given that one man should possess that which is above another, *wherefore* the world lieth in sin" (emphasis added). Mammon is a jealous god; you cannot serve him and any other master. To escape the powerful appeal of the things of this world and the deadly threat that hangs over all who do not possess them takes a meek and humble soul indeed—and a courageous one.

What does Isaiah say that God demands of those who would be justified? First of all, they must be clean of all defilement: "Wash you, make you clean," he says in the first chapter (Isaiah 1:16). Don't make your prayers when your hands are covered with blood. And the person with clean hands and a pure heart, says the Psalmist, is one "who hath not lifted up his soul unto vanity, nor sworn deceitfully" (Psalm 24:4). Isaiah agrees: it is "he that despiseth the gain of oppressions, that shaketh his hands from holding of bribes, that stoppeth his ears from hearing of blood, and shutteth his eyes from seeing evil" (Isaiah 33:15). The people fasted as God had commanded and asked Isaiah in perplexity why God had not heard them. In reply he told them, "Is not this the fast that I have chosen? to loose the bands of wickedness . . . and that ye break every yoke? Is it not to deal thy bread to the hungry, . . . [to] bring the poor that are cast out to thy house? When thou seest the naked, that thou cover him . . . ?" (Isaiah 58:6–7). This is a reminder that our own fasts require an offering for the poor. God is not impressed by the magnificent temples people build for Him—He owns it all anyway, "but to *this* man will I look, even to him that is poor and of a contrite spirit, and trembleth at my word" (Isaiah 66:2; emphasis added). If they go on justifying themselves—"yea, they have chosen their own ways, and their soul delighteth in their abominations" (Isaiah 66:3)—God will not curtail their agency; He will give them all the rope they want: "I also will choose their delusions, . . . because when I called, none did answer; . . . they . . . chose that in which I delighted not" (Isaiah 66:4).

After describing the way of Israel, the burden of Damascus, the burden of Egypt, the burden of Babylon and of Assyria—in short, the world as it is and as it should not be—Isaiah in glowing terms depicts the world as it should be—as it was meant to be and as it was created to be. "He created it not in vain, he formed it to be inhabited" (Isaiah 45:18). Under His rule, He is the Lord and there is none else. Unto Him every knee shall bow and every tongue confess. "In that day . . . the fruit of the earth shall be excellent" (Isaiah 4:2). All that remain are Zion and Jerusalem. "The Lord shall have washed away the filth of the daughters of Zion, and shall have purged the blood of Jerusalem" (Isaiah 4:4).

With Babylon gone from the scene, a huge sigh of relief goes up; at last the world is quiet and at rest. The golden city, the oppressor, is no more (see Isaiah 14:4). The whole earth is at rest. "Good tidings unto the meek; he hath sent me to bind up the brokenhearted, to proclaim liberty to the captives, and the opening of the prison to them that are bound" (Isaiah 61:1). "Violence shall no more be heard in thy land, wasting nor destruction within thy borders" (Isaiah 60:18). On the contrary, "with righteousness shall he judge the poor, and reprove with equity for the meek of the earth" (Isaiah 11:4). "Where is the fury of the oppressor?" (Isaiah 51:13). "Ho, . . . he that hath no money; come ye, buy, and eat; yea, come, buy wine and milk without money and without price. Wherefore do ye spend money for that which is not bread? . . . Come unto me: hear, and your soul shall live" (Isaiah 55:1–3). Wonder of wonders, in that day a man will be worth more than gold—a complete reversal of values. At the same time the forests return and the trees rejoice: "No feller is come up against us" (Isaiah 14:8). Isaiah often equates the growing wickedness of the world with the brutal and wasteful exploitation of nature, which has reached an all-time climax in the present generation. We all know his most poetic lines: "The leopard shall lie down with the kid; and the calf and the young lion and the fatling together; and a little child shall lead them. And the cow and the bear shall feed; their young ones lie down together: and the lion shall eat straw like the ox" (Isaiah 11:6–7). In my school days this was the prize illustration of the unrealistic Isaiah, zoological nonsense. It was not the "nature red in tooth and claw" of our own neo-Darwinian world. Since then a lot has been learned about the true nature of certain savage beasts. "They shall not hurt nor destroy in all my holy mountain: for the earth shall be full of the knowledge of the Lord, as the waters cover the sea" (Isaiah 11:9). "The wilderness and the solitary places shall be glad for them; and the desert shall rejoice, and blossom as the rose. It shall blossom abundantly, . . . In the wilderness shall waters break out, and streams in the desert. And the parched ground shall become a pool, and the thirsty land springs of water" (Isaiah 35:1–2, 6–7); "that they may see, and know, and consider, and understand together, that the hand of the Lord hath done this" (Isaiah 41:20).

And this happy world is for everybody, even as Isaiah's message of warning and promise of forgiving is for everyone. The sons of the stranger, taking hold of the covenant, "even them will I bring to my holy mountain." They will come to the temple, which will "be called an house of prayer for all people" (Isaiah 56:7). The Lord God, who gathers the "outcasts of Israel" and all the "beasts of the field," says there won't be any watchdogs to frighten them off anymore; it will be a happy time of man and beast (see Isaiah 56:8–10). "Great are the words of Isaiah" (3 Nephi 23:1). We have been commanded to search them, study them, ponder them, take them to heart, and understand that the calamities and the blessings therein are meant for our own generation. May the words of this great prophet prepare us for these calamities and blessings is my prayer.

NOTE

1. Milton V. Backman, *Joseph Smith's First Vision: Confirming Evidences and Contemporary Accounts*, 2nd ed. rev. (Salt Lake City: Bookcraft, 1980), 159.

CHAPTER THIRTEEN

ISAIAH AND THE GREAT ARRAIGNMENT

TERRY B. BALL

The resurrected Christ gave special recognition to the writings of Isaiah. As He spoke to the Book of Mormon people gathered at the temple in Bountiful, the Savior proclaimed, "And now, behold, I say unto you, that ye ought to search these things. Yea, a commandment I give unto you that ye search these things diligently; for great are the words of Isaiah" (3 Nephi 23:1). Considering how difficult it is for many people to understand Isaiah's words, we may wish the Savior had picked an easier book to command us to study! We might be more comfortable if He had said, "Master the writings of Ruth," or perhaps, "Ponder the doctrine of Omni." But there is a reason why Isaiah's writings are worthy of the distinction afforded them by the Lord. As He explained to the Nephites: "For surely he spake as touching all things concerning my people which are of the house of Israel; therefore it must needs be that he must speak also to the Gentiles. And all things that he spake have been and shall be, even according to the words which he spake" (3 Nephi 23:2–3). Thus we can be assured that Isaiah spoke not only to ancient covenant Israel but also to the latter-day covenant people. Moreover, we have the Savior's personal witness that everything Isaiah foretold has been or will be fulfilled.

Not only are Isaiah's writings distinctive, but the man himself seems to stand out as an anomaly when compared with other

Terry B. Ball is department chair of ancient scripture at Brigham Young University.

prophets of his dispensation. When we think of an Old Testament prophet, we may picture a humble, simple man, one living in the wilderness and being fed by ravens like Elijah the Tishbite (see 1 Kings 17:3–4), or perhaps a gatherer of sycamore fruit and a herdsman like Amos (see Amos 7:14). Isaiah, however, seems to have been a man of relatively high social station who could find audience with kings (see, for example, Isaiah 37; 38:1). Josephus proposes that King Hezekiah was actually Isaiah's son-in-law.[1] Moreover, the complexity and beauty of his writings, complete with all the poetic elements of metaphor, parallelism, and elevated language, reflect his station as a well-educated man.[2] Furthermore, Isaiah enjoyed exceptional longevity as an Old Testament prophet, serving half a century from about 740 B.C. to about 690 B.C. under four different kings of Judah: Uzziah, Jotham, Ahaz, and Hezekiah (see Isaiah 1:1).[3]

While Isaiah may have differed from other Old Testament prophets in social station, education, and longevity, he was very much the same in how he fulfilled his calling as a prophet to a covenant people. As part of their calling, Old Testament prophets provided many "services" for those to whom they ministered. They taught of the coming of both the mortal and millennial Messiah. They provided instruction concerning the stewardship associated with being a covenant people. Some led their people to battle, and others controlled the elements to accomplish God's will. One of the most important roles of Old Testament prophets was to act as "spiritual physicians" for the people. As such they offered diagnoses of the spiritual maladies afflicting the people, suggested prescriptions whereby they might be healed, and gave them prophetic prognoses of what they could expect if they did or did not choose to follow the prescriptions.

The first five chapters of Isaiah are an excellent example of a prophet acting as a spiritual physician. These opening chapters of Isaiah can be called the Great Arraignment, for in them the prophet lays out the charges the Lord wishes to bring against His people. One approach that can help us understand Isaiah's teachings in the Great Arraignment is to classify, analyze, and consider the counsel contained therein as diagnoses, prescriptions, or prognoses given by the Lord's designated spiritual practitioner. Doing so not only makes the prophet's message to ancient Israel[4] clear and poignant but also reveals important counsel for a latter-day covenant people.

THE DIAGNOSIS

Despite some moments of righteousness and repentance during Isaiah's tenure as prophet, the house of Israel habitually chose to be afflicted with a number of spiritual maladies.[5] Isaiah identified ignorance, apathy, greed, worldliness, idolatry, and failure to thrive as some of the infirmities prevalent among the people of this day.

Ignorance and apathy. Isaiah begins the diagnosis of the spiritual maladies that afflicted ancient Israel with a telling poetic verse found in the opening chapter of the Great Arraignment:

> The ox knoweth his owner,
> and the ass his master's crib:
> but Israel doth not know,
> my people doth not consider.
>   (Isaiah 1:3)

Isaiah seems to be suggesting a hierarchy of intelligence and obedience among these creatures.[6] First is the ox, smart enough and obedient enough to know its master, whom it should obey and to whom it should look for guidance. Next is the ass, which may not know its master but at least knows where to look for the food its master provides. Last is Israel; these people know comparatively nothing concerning their master or where to receive sustenance. To make matters worse, not only do they not know these things but apparently they do not even care: "my people doth not consider." The message to Israel is vivid. They are so spiritually bankrupt that God considers them less responsive than even domesticated animals.

Isaiah uses a medicinal metaphor to reaffirm this diagnosis and explain the extent of spiritual ignorance and apathy afflicting the covenant people: "Why should ye be stricken any more? ye will revolt more and more: the whole head is sick, and the whole heart faint. From the sole of the foot even unto the head there is no soundness in it; but wounds, and bruises, and putrifying sores: they have not been closed, neither bound up, neither mollified with ointment" (Isaiah 1:5–6). Herein he questions why the people would choose to continue in their apathy when it causes illness to their entire beings, to their "whole head," or thoughts, and to their "whole heart," or desires. He marvels that in spite of the sickness filling their entire society from their "head" right down to the "sole of the foot," with "wounds, and bruises, and putrifying sores," the people could care so little that they refused to seek treatment for the malady. Rather, their wounds had "not been closed, neither bound up, neither mollified with ointment." Apparently oblivious to their condition, they had become "wise in their own eyes" (Isaiah 5:21) and sought counsel from peoples outside the covenant (Isaiah 2:6) rather than looking to the Lord for healing. Ignorance and apathy were destroying the covenant people.

Greed and worldliness. Isaiah lamented over the city of Jerusalem: "How is the faithful city become an harlot! it was full of judgment; righteousness lodged in it; but now murderers. Thy silver is become dross, thy wine mixed with water: Thy princes are rebellious, and companions of thieves: every one loveth gifts, and followeth after rewards: they judge not the fatherless, neither doth the cause of the widow come unto them" (Isaiah 1:21–23). He marveled that this great city, which was once a seat of justice and righteousness, had become the abode of harlots and murderers. He placed much of the blame for the corruption upon the leaders of the people, who had allowed greed and worldliness to dictate their actions. Consequently they had become the friends of thieves and acceptors of gifts or bribes, who cared little for the plight of the poor and helpless. Isaiah makes it clear, however, that the disease of avarice was not confined to the leaders only. He suggests that greedy vendors were practicing deception by cutting their wine with water and adulterating their precious metals with worthless alloys: "thy silver is become dross" (Isaiah 1:22).[7] Misers were hoarding wealth (Isaiah 2:7), land mongers were monopolizing real estate (Isaiah 5:8),[8] and drunkenness, gluttony, and riotous living were becoming round-the-clock activities for many, especially the men of renown and strength (Isaiah 5:11, 22).[9] Moreover, some were challenging values, calling good evil and evil good (Isaiah 5:20). Indeed, so intent were the people on satisfying carnal desires that they went out of their way to bring themselves opportunities to sin. Isaiah pronounced woe upon such people "that draw iniquity with cords of vanity, and sin as it were with a cart rope" (Isaiah 5:18).

The prophet referred to the covenant people of this time as the "daughters of Zion." Like all good daughters of his day, they should have been keeping themselves pure and virtuous, awaiting the day when they would meet their bridegroom, or Christ.[10] Instead, these worldly people were doing just the contrary: "The daughters of Zion are haughty, and walk with stretched forth necks and wanton eyes, walking and mincing as they go, and making a tinkling with their feet" (Isaiah 3:16). Rather than virtuously preparing for marriage, they were prostituting themselves. Rather than seeking beauty in purity and devotion, they had decked themselves in all manner of worldly adornments to attract other lovers (see Isaiah 3:16–23). Rather than maintaining the faith and fidelity requisite to finding everlasting joy through the Lord's covenant, they were wantonly seeking for pleasure in promiscuity and indulgence. Greed and worldliness were destroying the covenant people.

Idolatry. Historically, the Lord had blessed ancient Israel in spectacular fashion. He parted the Red Sea and the Jordan River for them, fed them manna for forty years, brought down the walls of Jericho, and rained down stones from heaven upon their enemies (see Exodus 14:21–22; 16:35; Joshua 6:16–20; 10:8). Yet, all of these remarkable events failed to prevent Israel from turning to other gods during Isaiah's time. The prophet lamented that "their land also is full of idols; they worship the work of their own hands, that which their own fingers have made" (Isaiah 2:8). Isaiah noted that the idolatry was widespread, as both "mean" or ordinary men and great men were bowing down and humbling themselves before idols (Isaiah 2:9).[11] In groves of trees and gardens, they had established places of idol worship (see Isaiah 1:29).[12] Idolatry was destroying the covenant people.

Failure to thrive syndrome. Some infants do not grow and develop normally or respond to the treatment that would help them do so. For some reason they refuse to eat, or if they do, their bodies do not assimilate the nourishment. These infants are clinically diagnosed as having "failure to thrive syndrome." In the fifth chapter of Isaiah, the prophet uses a botanical metaphor to warn the house of Israel that they have chosen to afflict themselves with what could be called a spiritual version of failure to thrive syndrome. In this metaphor, known as the song of the vineyard (see Isaiah 5:1–7), he likens the

Lord to a "wellbeloved" husbandman who plants a vineyard in an exceptionally choice location and does everything requisite for producing a wonderful harvest of grapes. "And he fenced it, and gathered out the stones thereof, and planted it with the choicest vine" (Isaiah 5:2). He built a tower in the vineyard to protect it, and in anticipation of the abundant harvest, he hewed out a winepress within the vineyard itself. Imagine the husbandman's disappointment when, in spite of all his efforts, the vineyard refused to produce good grapes. Rather it brought forth "wild grapes," or in the Hebrew, *be'ushim,* literally meaning stinking, worthless things.[13] When the house of Israel should have thrived in righteousness, it floundered in sin. Such failure to thrive was destroying the covenant people.

THE PRESCRIPTION

Isaiah was anxious to see the house of Israel healed from its afflictions. Accordingly, in the Great Arraignment, he prescribed the course of action the people should follow to regain their spiritual health. He counseled them to put an end to their sins and become clean: "Wash you, make you clean; put away the evil of your doings from before mine eyes; cease to do evil" (Isaiah 1:16). He further instructed them to develop charity in their lives, to care for the poor and helpless, and to "learn to do well; seek judgment, relieve the oppressed, judge the fatherless, plead for the widow" (Isaiah 1:17). He commanded them to cease relying on the arm of flesh and things temporal, reminding them of the insignificance of such things: "Cease ye from man, whose breath is in his nostrils: for wherein is he to be accounted of?" (Isaiah 2:22). He pled with them to return to their God. "O house of Jacob, come ye, and let us walk in the light of the Lord" (Isaiah 2:5).

Although this prescription constitutes only a small portion of the Great Arraignment, adherence to it would have brought about a remarkable recovery in the spiritual well-being of the people of Isaiah's day. Such medicine is beneficial to a covenant people in any dispensation.

THE PROGNOSIS

In the Great Arraignment, Isaiah gave clear prophecies of what the members of the house of Israel could expect if they chose not to follow the Lord's prescription for health for a covenant people. He also made it clear what the prognosis would be if they repented and followed the prescription.

The prognosis for continued rebellion. The prophet warned Israel that the prognosis for continued rebellion would include abandonment, captivity, desolation, and humiliation. Perhaps the greatest portion of the Great Arraignment is devoted to emphasizing this point.

Abandonment. In the song of the vineyard, once the wellbeloved husbandman realized that all his nurturing and efforts to produce grapes were in vain, he described how he would respond to the vineyard's refusal to thrive: "And now go to; I will tell you what I will do to my vineyard: I will take away the hedge thereof, and it shall be eaten up; and break down the wall thereof, and it shall be trodden down: and I will lay it waste: it shall not be pruned, nor digged; but there shall come up briers and thorns: I will also command the clouds that they rain no rain upon it" (Isaiah 5:5–6). In this response, the Lord does not personally go about tearing out and destroying the vines. Rather, He abandons the vineyard. He ceases His nurturing and withdraws His protection from the vineyard, leaving the rebellious vines on their own. Consequently, they are trampled, ravaged, and eventually displaced by other vegetation or peoples. Such was indeed the eventual lot of ancient Israel.

Captivity. Isaiah cautioned Israel that once they were abandoned by the Lord, they would be easy prey for the empire builders of the ancient Near East, who sought to conquer and enslave the weaker nations around them. He warned the southern kingdom of Judah that Jerusalem would be ruined and would fall (see Isaiah 3:8), a prophecy fulfilled in 587 B.C. when the Babylonian Empire conquered the people of Judah and carried them away into captivity in Babylon. Likewise, he warned the northern kingdom of Israel that they too could expect to be overrun by a terrifying army. He described the army's attack as one that would be so swift that none would escape and declared that it would leave darkness and sorrow in its wake (Isaiah 5:26–30).[14] This prophecy was fulfilled in 721 B.C. when the Assyrians conquered and deported many of the ten tribes of the kingdom of Israel.

Desolation. Isaiah prophesied that life would be desolate and difficult for the remnant of Israel who were not carried away into captivity: "Your country is desolate, your cities are burned with fire: your land, strangers devour it in your presence, and it is desolate, as overthrown by strangers" (Isaiah 1:7). The prophet likened the desolation to a cottage or harvest shack and to a lodge or a watchman's hut, both left dilapidated and forsaken after the harvest is over (see Isaiah 1:8).[15] He warned that as a result of the deportations there would be a shortage of food, leaders, teachers, and craftsmen in the land. Only the poor, ignorant, and unskilled would be left. In their desperation, children would rule over them, and one who merely had clothing would be considered qualified to be king (Isaiah 3:1–8).[16] Moreover, the land would become unproductive, so that five acres[17] of a vineyard would produce only one bath (eight gallons) of wine, and a homer (six bushels) of seed would yield only an ephah (four gallons) of grain. Isaiah's prognosis in these passages accurately describes the pitiful circumstances the remnant of Israel faced after the Babylonian and Assyrian deportations.

Humiliation. The prophet also warned that in the "day of the Lord"[18] the proud, the worldly, the uncharitable, and any others who trusted or looked for happiness in something outside the Lord's plan for joy would be humbled: "The lofty looks of man shall be humbled, and the haughtiness of men shall be bowed down, and the Lord alone shall be exalted in that day. For the day of the Lord of hosts shall be upon every one that is proud and lofty, and upon every one that is lifted up; and he shall be brought low" (Isaiah 2:11–12). Isaiah likened the proud and worldly to tall cedars and oaks, to high hills and mountains, to formidable towers and walls, and to luxurious ships and other desirable objects, all of which would be abased and banished (Isaiah 2:13–16; see also Isaiah 5:13–17). He described the embarrassment of the worldly in that day of the Lord's coming, as they would frantically try to hide their hoarded wealth and useless idols in "holes of the rocks" and "caves of the earth" with the moles and the bats in hopes that the Lord would not notice them. Isaiah assured them that all such attempts would be in vain as the Lord rises in "the glory of his majesty" to "shake terribly the earth" (Isaiah 2:17–21). Isaiah described further how all the temporal, vain, and worldly adornments with which the promiscuous "daughters of Zion" had hoped to beautify themselves in an effort to attract adulterous (idolatrous) lovers would be taken away, leaving them disgusting and repulsive rather than tempting and alluring (Isaiah 3:18–24): "And it shall come to pass, that instead of sweet smell there shall be stink; and instead of a girdle a rent; and instead of well set hair baldness; and instead of a stomacher a girding of sackcloth; and burning instead of beauty" (Isaiah 3:24). In their humbled and contemptible state, they would sit at the gates of the city and wail, but to no avail, for the lovers they sought would have fallen "by the sword," and those remaining would not take these foul and filthy daughters regardless of what they offered (Isaiah 3:25–4:1). Every evil thing in which they trusted and hoped to find pleasure would be lost or turned against them. Instead of finding happiness, they could expect to find abandonment, captivity, desolation, and humiliation.

The prognosis for the righteous and repentant. While the abominable apostate daughters of Zion would be weeping, bald-headed, stinking, and repulsive, Isaiah promised that the righteous, the "branch of the Lord," would be lovely: "In that day shall the branch of the Lord be beautiful and glorious, and the fruit of the earth shall be excellent and comely for them that are escaped of Israel. And it shall come to pass, that he that is left in Zion, and he that remaineth in Jerusalem, shall be called holy, even every one that is written among the living in Jerusalem: When the Lord shall have washed away the filth of the daughters of Zion, and shall have purged the blood of Jerusalem from the midst thereof by the spirit of judgment, and by the spirit of burning" (Isaiah 4:2–4). The prophet further promised the obedient that the Lord would dwell with and protect them (Isaiah 4:5–6). Moreover, they could expect to enjoy the "good of the land" (Isaiah 1:19), to have righteous leaders rule over them, and to be known as "the city of righteousness" (Isaiah 1:25–27). Ancient Israel did not see these prophecies fulfilled.

For those who had strayed but were willing to repent, the prognosis was especially encouraging. Using beautiful imagery, Isaiah recorded the tender invitation of the Lord: "Come now, and let us reason together, saith the Lord: though your sins be as scarlet, they shall be as white as snow; though they be red like crimson, they shall be as wool" (Isaiah 1:18). The imagery of the scarlet and the wool points to the Atonement, the means whereby the penitent could find forgiveness. As they repented and returned to the Lord, they could expect their stained souls to be "washed white through the blood of the Lamb" (Alma 13:11).

CONCLUSION

The Great Arraignment offers a compelling message for any covenant people. As Isaiah diagnoses the spiritual maladies that afflicted the house of Israel in his day, a modern covenant people should learn to avoid similar sicknesses, particularly ignorance, apathy, rebellion, greed, worldliness, idolatry, and failure to thrive. Moreover, a covenant people in the dispensation of the fullness of times can learn from the Great Arraignment that repentance, charity, humility, faith, and obedience constitute proper prescriptions or medicine for a return to spiritual health. Finally, all who have entered the covenant should learn from the Great Arraignment that the prognosis for refusing to repent is abandonment, captivity, desolation, and humiliation, while those who repent and remain faithful can be assured forgiveness, prosperity, and eternal joy.

In the Great Arraignment, Isaiah foresaw that "in the last days" there will indeed be a righteous and repentant covenant people. He promised that they will enjoy the blessings of having temples, "the Lord's house shall be established in the top of the mountains" (Isaiah 2:2).[19] People from all nations will be drawn to such temples to learn of God's ways and to covenant to "walk in his paths" (Isaiah 2:2–3). He prophesied that there will be holy cities for the righteous, one in Zion in the Western Hemisphere, and another in Jerusalem in the Eastern Hemisphere (see Isaiah 2:3).[20] He promised that the faithful will flock to the gospel, the "ensign to the nations," as it beckons to them (Isaiah 5:26). He foretells that though they will come from "the end of the earth," their gathering will be swift and employ rapid means of transportation (Isaiah 5:26–30).[21] He acknowledges that in that day the Lord personally will "judge among the nations" and that peace will reign. Instruments of destruction will be converted to tools of production as men "beat their swords into plowshares, and their spears into pruninghooks" (Isaiah 2:4). Not only will men no longer practice war but they will cease even to learn about it (see Isaiah 2:4). It will be a world in which no one finds a use for violence. It will be the millennial day for which Isaiah yearned, and for which we prepare.

NOTES

1. Louis Ginsberg, *Legends of the Jews* (Philadelphia: Jewish Publication Society, 1941), 4:279. In this text Josephus claims that Isaiah was killed by his own grandchild, Manasseh. Manasseh's father was King Hezekiah.

2. For an introduction to biblical poetry, see James L. Kugel, *The Idea of Biblical Poetry* (New Haven, CT: Yale University Press, 1981).

3. A pseudepigraphic work known as the Martyrdom and Ascension of Isaiah records that Isaiah's life ended when he was sawn in half by King Hezekiah's wicked son Manasseh, a claim supported by Josephus (see "Martyrdom and Ascension of Isaiah," in *The Old Testament Pseudepigrapha,* ed. James H. Charlesworth [Garden City, NY: Doubleday, 1985], 16; see also Ginsberg, *Legends of the Jews,* 4:279). The circumstances surrounding the martyrdom are different in the Josephus account, but both accounts identify Manasseh as the one responsible for Isaiah's tragic death.

4. Isaiah was a prophet to both the kingdom of Israel and the kingdom of Judah. Because both kingdoms were a covenant people, I will use the term *Israel* to refer to either one or both.

5. One of the few periods of relative righteousness during Isaiah's ministry was King Hezekiah's reign (see Isaiah 37–38).

6. Kugel, *Idea of Biblical Poetry,* 9.

7. Ludlow suggests this interpretation for Isaiah 1:22 (see Victor L. Ludlow, *Isaiah: Prophet, Seer, and Poet* [Salt Lake City: Deseret Book, 1982], 79).

8. For a clear interpretation of this verse, see footnote *c* to Isaiah 5:8 in the Latter-day Saint edition of the King James Version of the Bible.

9. Nyman suggests that a modern parallel can be seen in the lives of current celebrities. See Monte S. Nyman, *Great Are the Words of Isaiah* (Salt Lake City: Bookcraft, 1980), 45.

10. The metaphor of Jehovah as the bridegroom and the covenant people as those espoused or married to Him is found throughout the prophetic writings of the Old Testament. The imagery is powerful. The love, devotion, faith, and trust that should exist between God and His covenant people should be as great as, or greater than, that which should exist between a husband and wife.

11. The Book of Mormon account of this verse in 2 Nephi 12:9 reads, "the mean man boweth not down, and the great man humbleth himself not," suggesting that these men were not worshipping Jehovah.

12. For a discussion of the relationship between vegetation and idol worship, see Terry B. Ball, "Isaiah's Imagery of Plants and Planting," in *Thy People Shall Be My People and Thy God My God: The 22nd*

Annual Sperry Symposium (Salt Lake City: Deseret Book, 1994), 24–25.

13. Francis Brown, *The New Brown-Driver-Briggs-Gesenius Hebrew and English Lexicon* (New York: Houghton Mifflin, 1906; reprint, n.p.: Christian Copyrights, 1983), 93. For a more thorough discussion of this botanical metaphor, see Ball, "Isaiah's Imagery," 18–20.

14. Isaiah 5:26–30 is a dualistic prophecy, meaning it applies to more than one time period and may have more than one interpretation. Latter-day Saints have traditionally placed the fulfillment of this prophecy in the last days and given it another interpretation, which will be discussed in the conclusion of this paper. Most commentators, however, see this as a prophecy that was fulfilled in Isaiah's day and interpret it as discussed above.

15. Ball, "Isaiah's Imagery," 27–28.

16. Ludlow offers a fascinating discussion of the chiasmus in these verses and suggests that the chiastic structure of the passage indicates that the people's oppression of one another is the major cause of their difficulties (see Ludlow, *Isaiah*, 104–5).

17. The King James Version here states ten acres, but the Hebrew reads ten yoke or the amount ten yoke of oxen could plow in a day, which is equivalent to about five acres.

18. The phrase "day of the Lord" is used frequently by Isaiah and seems to refer to any day of retribution or reward. For example, the day when Judah fell to the Babylonians was a day of the Lord, as will be the day of His Second Coming. It is both a great and dreadful day, great for the righteous and dreadful for the wicked (see Malachi 4:5).

19. Isaiah's use of a mountain as a metaphor for the temple is appropriate, for there is much about a mountain that is similar to a temple. For example:

Both mountains and temples are high places where we can go to get nearer to God. Ancient prophets, such as Moses, Elijah, and Enos, and later the Savior frequently went to the mountains to communicate with God and seek answers to questions. Today, we can go to the temple to draw nearer to our Father in Heaven and receive direction from Him.

Mountains are impressive, firm, and enduring. So are the doctrines taught and the ordinances performed in the temple.

It takes effort for us to reach the top of a mountain. To do so we must maintain good physical health and be willing to expend the energy required to make the climb. It is not a task for the feeble or lazy. Likewise, to enter the temple we must be in good spiritual health and be willing to live a life in harmony with the will of our Father in Heaven. It is not a task for the spiritually flabby or the unrepentant soul. As the psalmist put it, "Who shall ascend into the hill of the Lord? or who shall stand in his holy place? He that hath clean hands, and a pure heart; who hath not lifted up his soul unto vanity, nor sworn deceitfully" (Psalm 25:3–4).

The view from the top of a mountain is both spectacular and beautiful. We gain a new perspective of our surroundings from the high elevation. From a mountaintop we can see where we have come from and all the potential destinations to which we may travel. The view from the temple is equally spectacular and beautiful. There we gain an eternal perspective. We learn where we came from and where we may go if we are willing to be true and faithful to the covenants we make in the house of the Lord.

20. In view of the Hebrew poetic device of parallelism, some would argue that Zion and Jerusalem in this passage are not two different cities, but one and the same, the Old World Jerusalem. LDS theology traditionally interprets the passage as I have. For a further discussion of the two religious capitals interpretation, see Bruce R. McConkie, *The Mortal Messiah* (Salt Lake City: Deseret Book, 1979–81), 1:95.

21. Elder LeGrand Richards interpreted Isaiah 5:28–30 as being a metaphorical reference to modern means of transportation. For example, he understood the phrase "their horses' hoofs be counted like flint, and their wheel like a whirlwind" to be referring to trains, while the phrase "their roaring . . . be like a lion" was a reference to airplanes. He gives the entire passage a latter-day context and convincingly illustrates Isaiah's prophetic vision (see LeGrand Richards, *A Marvelous Work and a Wonder* [Salt Lake City: Deseret Book, 1976], 229).

CHAPTER FOURTEEN

A Latter-day Saint Reading of Isaiah: The Example of Isaiah 6

Paul Y. Hoskisson

Because Isaiah remains imposing and obscure, a few more words of help for the Latter-day Saint student of Isaiah might be justified.

At least six factors contribute to the difficulties modern readers encounter in understanding Isaiah.[1] First, Isaiah wrote to a great extent in poetry,[2] and poetry is by nature obscure, if not cryptic, even to the native speaker of the poetic language.

Second, Isaiah, when not writing in poetry, often wrote in elevated Hebrew literary style. As with all literatures, Hebrew is endowed with its own esoteric peculiarities that could escape even Isaiah's contemporary readers. These same peculiarities often baffle the modern reader also.

Third, Isaiah is removed culturally from our day. Isaiah's contemporaries wore different clothes, ate different foods, read from right to left, lived between the superpowers of Egypt and Assyria, and were deeply embroiled in petty squabbles with neighbors. References to Isaiah's culture in his writings leave most modern readers out of the picture.

Fourth, Isaiah is removed in time from our day. Though this may seem similar to cultural distance, it is actually a different dimension. For instance, contemporary Western readers of Japanese poetry,

---

Paul Y. Hoskisson is professor of ancient scripture at Brigham Young University.

however removed in culture and literature from Japan, still may have contact with and access to living informants both here in the United States and on the isles of native Japanese culture in Asia. Though this does not alleviate all problems, it does eliminate many. With Isaiah, however, we must content ourselves with a few scraps of Hebrew literature, some contemporary documents,[3] and no living informants.

Fifth, Isaiah draws heavily on scripture and doctrine outside his time and place. To understand and appreciate these embedded allusions, it is necessary to be familiar with more than the times and culture of Isaiah. In this respect, Latter-day Saints have a distinct advantage because of our extended scriptural database.

And sixth, Isaiah was above all else a prophet. Though eloquent, well versed and culturally astute,[4] this would supply only the medium, not the content of his book. To understand the content it is necessary to realize that he spoke from the higher ground of his prophetic insights and visions. This does not mean that the book of Isaiah must remain enigmatic to those of us who do not stand on the same ground. On the contrary, in some cases history has recorded the fulfillment of Isaiah's prophetic statements and one need not, therefore, be a prophet to understand the visions given to Isaiah. In addition, and more important, the same prophetic insights and visions given to Isaiah are available to Latter-day Saints.[5]

These six potential impediments to an understanding of Isaiah can be turned around and employed as tools in the hands of the serious student of Isaiah. Equipped with some knowledge of the poetry, literature, culture, and history of Isaiah's time, and with an awareness of the scriptures, doctrine, prophetic insights and vision available to Isaiah, we can study and enjoy Isaiah and glean from his writings wisdom for our day.

Using Isaiah 6 as an example, these six points will be employed, though not in any particular order or frequency, to help elucidate the text.[6] In the conclusion, an example of a specific application of each of these six points will be given.

Isaiah 6:1 "In the year that king Uzziah died."

It was the usual practice in Isaiah's time to date events by the regnal year of a king. Here, Isaiah dates the theophany recorded in the verses that follow to the year in which King Uzziah died, about

742 B.C.[7] Isaiah's contemporaries would have been able to relate this date to events in their lives and thus perhaps been able to relate to the setting in time of this vision. However, Isaiah's dating of his theophany was not intended solely for his contemporaries. He also wrote for those who were to follow, and the dating of this vision was intended to help the subsequent readers place it in the times in which it was given.

By 742 B.C. Israel and Judah had already had contact with the Assyrians. At least as early as 853 B.C., Israel had been involved with other Syro-Palestinian states in a coalition that had opposed an Assyrian campaign led by Shalmaneser III into the area of the Levant. Several times in the latter half of the ninth century, the Assyrians ventured close to Palestine, but it was not until Tiglath-pilezer III seized the Assyrian throne in 744 B.C. that the Judean kingdom was brought into the orb of Assyrian might. 2 Kings 15:19–20 records the rendering of tribute by Menahem of Israel and Azariah (Uzziah) of Judah to Tiglath-pilezer.[8]

Because Isaiah saw beyond his day, we must not stop examining the history of his day when we reach the supposed year of the composition of chapter 6. About ten years after ascending the Assyrian throne (734–732 B.C.), Tiglath-pilezer returned in force to Syria-Palestine, laid waste the Syrians with their capital in Damascus, and humbled Israel, capturing all of the Northern Kingdom except the city of Samaria and taking into exile the northernmost tribes. Tiglath-pilezer's successors, first Shalmaneser V, then Sargon II, and finally Sennacherib, destroyed Samaria and exacted tribute from Judah (by 720 B.C.), forced the remainder of the Northern Kingdom into exile, moved non-Israelites into the vacuum (by about 716 B.C.), laid waste all of Judea except Jerusalem (701 B.C.), and carried thousands of Judeans into Assyrian exile (701 B.C.).

Isaiah lived to see all of this and more. Israel as a political entity ceased to exist. Judah was reduced to servility and would remain so until the reign of Josiah, long after the death of Isaiah. Assyria would totally dominate Palestine and beyond into Egypt, and would continue to do so until well into the last quarter of the seventh century. Such is the historical milieu connoted by the introductory line of this chapter.

ISAIAH 6:1 "I SAW ALSO THE LORD SITTING UPON A THRONE, HIGH AND LIFTED UP, AND HIS TRAIN FILLED THE TEMPLE."

In the introduction (verses 1–8) to what has traditionally been labeled the call to the ministry (verses 9–13), Isaiah related features of the theophany he experienced. Here, as throughout most of the Bible, the translators of the King James Version have made a partial and helpful interpretation of the Hebrew text.[9] Thus, the Lord he sees is not a worldly master but his heavenly master, God, who was seen in His earthly palace, the temple. These phrases pose no problem for most students of literature: God's throne is exalted and His train, not to be taken as a literal extension of His robe but rather as a symbol of His glory and majesty, fills His earthly palace.[10]

ISAIAH 6:2 "ABOVE IT STOOD THE SERAPHIM."[11]

Hebrew dictionaries define a seraph in the Old Testament as a mythological being with six wings.[12] The fact, however, that the word "seraphim" is not attested elsewhere in the Old Testament may suggest that Isaiah employed the word here in a unique meaning. As Isaiah and his schooled contemporaries knew, the meaning of the root from which this noun is formed denotes in its verbal aspect to burn or be fiery.[13] Knowing this, Latter-day Saints should have no trouble recognizing that seraphim represent celestial beings who attend God at His throne.[14] (See the explanation of Revelation 4:6 in D&C 77:2.)

ISAIAH 6:2 "EACH ONE HAD SIX WINGS; WITH TWAIN HE COVERED HIS FACE, AND WITH TWAIN HE COVERED HIS FEET, AND WITH TWAIN HE DID FLY."

Based on the explanation in Doctrine and Covenants 77:4 of the three sets of wings of the beasts in Revelation 4:6,[15] Latter-day Saints should recognize that the wings of the seraphim symbolize power. The latter set of wings signify the ability to move. The connotation of the former two sets of wings requires a certain amount of speculation. The word used here for feet in Hebrew, *regel,* is employed, though infrequently, in the Old Testament as a euphemism for genitalia in particular and their functions in general.[16] Therefore, it would not be amiss to suggest that the second set of wings covered the nakedness of the seraphim. It has been suggested that the first set of wings covered the faces of the seraphim to hide them from the majesty of the Lord[17] and therefore had the power to protect the seraphim from the glory of God.

Even without the help of the Doctrine and Covenants but with a little knowledge of the ancient Near East, it is possible to come to the same conclusions; namely, that wings in the ancient Near East stood for power. For instance, in Malachi 4:2 the sun of righteousness shall "arise with healing in his wings"; i.e., the Son of righteousness will come with the power of healing. There are also numerous examples of winged, supernatural creatures in the ancient Near East, not the least of which is the uraeus. From Tell Halaf there is also an example of a six-winged creature.[18]

ISAIAH 6:3 "AND ONE CRIED UNTO ANOTHER, AND SAID, HOLY, HOLY, HOLY, IS THE LORD OF HOSTS: THE WHOLE EARTH IS FULL OF HIS GLORY."

This straightforward praise expresses the sanctity and majesty of God and needs no further comment.

ISAIAH 6:4 "AND THE POSTS OF THE DOOR MOVED AT THE VOICE OF HIM THAT CRIED."

To understand what is intended by these words, it is necessary to know a few things about the construction of buildings in the ancient Near East. Large doors, such as the doors to a temple, did not have hinges as we know them; the leaves of the door were attached to a large post which itself pivoted in a socket (usually stone) top and bottom.[19] Thus, if the post was to bear the weight of the large doors, often covered with metal,[20] it had to be one of the more massive and solidly anchored wooden pieces in the structure. If this post moved at all, it could be caused only by a powerful force. In other words, the voice of the seraph, "the one who cried," was strong enough to cause the door post to move. The equivalent metaphorical statement in English would be that the roof was raised by the sound of his voice.

ISAIAH 6:4 "AND THE HOUSE[21] WAS FILLED WITH SMOKE."

While it could mean that the Lord, after initially showing Himself to Isaiah, hid His face from him, it is more likely that this wonderfully obtuse poetic metaphor indicates the Lord's presence, as it clearly does in Exodus 19:18 and 2 Samuel 22:9.[22]

ISAIAH 6:5 "THEN SAID I, WOE IS ME! FOR I AM UNDONE; BECAUSE I AM[23] A MAN OF UNCLEAN LIPS, AND I DWELL IN THE MIDST OF A PEOPLE OF UNCLEAN LIPS: FOR MINE EYES HAVE SEEN THE KING, THE LORD OF HOSTS."

It was a fairly common belief in the ancient Near East that one could not look upon the countenance of a god and still live.[24] In addition, Isaiah added a new dimension for his audience to this theme, the fear that being a person of unclean lips—i.e., personal unworthiness to receive this theophany (not just because of the things that came out of his mouth but a general unworthiness)— would worsen the matter and that somehow his association with a ritually unclean people would taint him even more. Even though Isaiah, at this point, stood perhaps at the incipient stage of his calling, it must have been this latter fear that would have concerned Isaiah more than the former fear.

ISAIAH 6:6–7 "THEN FLEW ONE OF THE SERAPHIM UNTO ME, HAVING A LIVE COAL IN HIS HAND, WHICH HE HAD TAKEN WITH THE TONGS FROM OFF THE ALTAR: AND HE LAID IT UPON MY MOUTH AND SAID, LO, THIS HATH TOUCHED THY LIPS; AND THINE INIQUITY IS TAKEN AWAY, AND THY SIN PURGED."

To remove Isaiah's unworthiness, to make him fit to stand in the presence of the Lord, one of the seraphim touched his lips with a live coal from the altar. The realization of the significance of this symbolic act derives from an understanding of the altar and its use under the law of Moses. The purpose of the sacrifices under the law of Moses was to look forward through this similitude to the cleansing sacrifice of Jesus Christ and the Atonement that would purge all sins from the lips of those who stand before God.[25] The live coal from the sacrificial altar represents the element that makes the burnt offering possible, the element that cleanses our soul, fire. With this cleansing Isaiah is able to stand with confidence in the presence of the Lord.

ISAIAH 6:8 "AND[26] I HEARD THE VOICE OF THE LORD,[27] SAYING, WHOM SHALL I SEND, AND WHO WILL GO FOR US? THEN SAID I, HERE AM[28] I; SEND ME."

The surface meaning is clear, Isaiah has answered the call of the Lord to serve as His messenger to the house of Israel. However, without the aid of other scripture it would be nearly impossible to understand fully the Lord's question and Isaiah's response. Students of the scriptures will immediately be reminded of the exchange recorded in Abraham 3:27, in which God asked in the council in the premortal life, "Whom shall I send?" to save His people. In answering, "Here am I, send me," Christ indicated His willingness to carry the message of salvation to God's children and accomplish the Atonement. By using similar language in this exchange, Isaiah is indicating to those who have ears to hear not only acceptance of his calling to be the bearer of God's message but also the nature of that message, namely, salvation for his generation.[29]

ISAIAH 6:9–10 "AND HE SAID, GO, AND TELL THIS PEOPLE, HEAR YE INDEED, BUT UNDERSTAND NOT; AND SEE YE INDEED, BUT PERCEIVE NOT. MAKE THE HEART OF THIS PEOPLE FAT, AND MAKE THEIR EARS HEAVY, AND SHUT THEIR EYES; LEST THEY SEE WITH THEIR EYES, AND HEAR WITH THEIR EARS, AND UNDERSTAND WITH THEIR HEART, AND CONVERT, AND BE HEALED."[30]

The message of the Lord to Isaiah for the people is at best enigmatic but not totally opaque. However, before the message can be examined for its intent, the plain meaning of the words must be established; that is, what do the ears, eyes, and heart symbolize? In Hebrew literature the ear was the organ of understanding, the eye was the organ of perception, and the heart was the organ of thought.[31] Normally these are the organs that would have been utilized to make the people aware of the Lord's word to them (for example, see 1 Nephi 12:17). Thus, Isaiah is told to tell the people that they have the physical capacity to understand and perceive God's message but that they do not. If they had the ability to comprehend the message and they did not, it must mean that the people chose not to comprehend.

Isaiah is further told, according to the King James Version, to make the people's organs of thought dull, to cause their organs of understanding to be clumsy, and to close their organs of perception so that the people would not use them and be cured by the divine message.

The reading of these verses, however, is not difficult because of the literary devices used by Isaiah but rather by the theological hurdles it poses. How can a loving God commission His prophet to prevent the people from being cleansed from their uncleanness by causing their organs of comprehension to be ineffective? Because of this theological improbability, exegetes have proposed various solutions, most of which are improbable or implausible.[32]

The best solution to this theological difficulty derives from a knowledge of the Hebrew grammatical forms used in this passage. The King James Version rests on the usual reading of the Hebrew *hiph'il* form of the three verbs involved. Normally the *hiph'il* conjugation has a causative meaning, and thus the translation "make the heart . . . fat." However, one of the modes of the *hiph'il* connotes a declarative,[33] and would yield the translation "declare the heart of this people to be fat." Thus, the *New English Bible* for this passage reads, "This people's wits are dulled, their ears are deafened and their eyes blinded, so that they cannot see with their eyes nor listen with their ears nor understand with their wits, so that they may turn and be healed." This rendering would eliminate the theological difficulties imposed on the passage by reading a causative, because it would no longer be God through His prophet who makes the people incapable of realizing their moral turpitude. Isaiah becomes rather God's appointed accuser of the people.

ISAIAH 6:11 "THEN SAID I, LORD, HOW LONG?"

Is it possible that Isaiah was not only asking for more details of his mission, but that he was allowing his humanness to show? Well might one ask the Lord, if one had the necessary chutzpah, for how many years he was to deliver this message.

ISAIAH 6:11–12 "AND HE ANSWERED,[34] UNTIL THE CITIES BE
WASTED WITHOUT INHABITANT, AND THE HOUSES WITHOUT MAN,
AND THE LAND BE UTTERLY DESOLATE, AND THE LORD HAVE
REMOVED MEN FAR AWAY, AND THERE BE A GREAT FORSAKING IN
THE MIDST OF THE LAND."[35]

The Lord's answer that Isaiah must continue his message until the
land be devastated and empty can only mean that for as long as
Isaiah was alive he was to deliver that message.[36] During Isaiah's lifetime, the land was never totally devastated or emptied. If this theophany took place in 742 B.C., it would be several years before
Tiglath-pileser would devastate the Northern Kingdom. Between 725
and 705 B.C., Shalmaneser V and Sargon II would finish what Tiglath-
pileser had started in the Northern Kingdom and also attack Judea.
In 701 B.C. Sennacherib would devastate all of the walled cities of
Judea except Jerusalem. Jerusalem never fell to the Assyrians and the
Assyrians did not empty the land but left the poorest social strata to
occupy it. If the land was ever emptied, it would have been under
Nebuchadnezzar (see 2 Chronicles 36:20) around 586 B.C., at least
eighty years[37] after Isaiah's death. But even then it would seem that
not all the local population was deported, as 2 Kings 25:12 and 22
report. If a total depopulation of the land is to be sought for, it might
be during the Bar Kokhba rebellion against Rome beginning about in
AD 132. However, even this brutal suppression of Judah did not completely empty the land.[38]

ISAIAH 6:13 "BUT YET IN IT SHALL BE A TENTH, AND IT[39] SHALL
RETURN, AND SHALL BE EATEN: AS A TEIL TREE, AND AS AN OAK
WHOSE SUBSTANCE IS IN THEM, WHEN THEY CAST THEIR LEAVES:
SO THE HOLY SEED SHALL BE THE SUBSTANCE THEREOF."

Well did Jacob in the Book of Mormon declare "that none of the
prophets have written, nor prophesied, save they have spoken concerning Christ" (Jacob 7:11). In this verse Isaiah recorded one of the
more clear prophecies concerning the Messiah. The Lord declared to
Isaiah that after he had given his message of accusation all the days
of his life and after the land had been devastated and Isaiah was
dead, there would be a tenth[40] of the people who would return to the
land of Palestine.

This remnant is symbolized in the King James Version by dormant trees,[41] signifying that this rest of the house of Israel will be spiritually fallow. The key to understanding that this verse also refers to Christ lies in the words "the holy seed." As Paul states in Galatians 3:16, the "seed" referred to in the Old Testament is Christ.[42] And it is that "seed" that comprised the substance, that is, the life of Israel, here symbolized by trees. In other words, the Messiah of Israel would be born of the spiritually dormant remnant of Israel living in the land of Palestine, and He is the life substance of Israel.[43]

As depressing as Isaiah's message for the people could have seemed to him, the Lord did not leave him reason for despair. Isaiah was told that after his death, a remnant of the house of Israel would be in Palestine, and out of this rest would come the promised Messiah, the life and light of God's chosen people in Israel and on the isles of the sea.[44]

CONCLUSION

Each of the stumbling blocks to an understanding of Isaiah has been utilized as a stepping-stone to a greater comprehension of his message.

First, poetry. The poetic imagery of the ears, eyes, and heart in verses 9 and 10 as used in the Bible, when comprehended, contribute to our appreciation and understanding of the passage. These organs are seen as representing the potential for understanding, perceiving and comprehending.

Second, literary style. The use of the word "seraphim," otherwise unattested in the Bible or elsewhere in Semitic literature, would have been immediately understood by his audience as a figure of fire or light. This ability to coin new words (if indeed Isaiah was the first to employ seraphim) from the basal forms by using existing patterns is characteristic of Semitic literature.

Third, cultural distance. Today doors are not usually constructed using a heavy beam which pivots top and bottom and from which the leaves of the door are hung. Normally we make the hinging mechanism as unobtrusive as possible. (Witness the glass doors today seemingly without hinges but which pivot top and bottom.) Without knowing that the posts of the doors were among the most sturdy beams in any edifice, the significance of the door posts moving would probably not occur to us.

Fourth, time differential. With the simple statement, "In the year that King Uzziah died," Isaiah is able to convey to his contemporary readers and those in the future the political, military, religious and cultural setting of his theophany. By learning of the times involved we can approximate in our own minds the milieu in which Isaiah composed his beautiful verses.

Fifth, scripture and doctrine. The poetic imagery of "the house was filled with smoke" can more easily be understood in combination with other Old Testament scriptures recording the presence of the Lord on earth. A knowledge of the doctrine of the Atonement and how it is shadowed in the law of Moses and the law of sacrifice make it possible to comprehend the significance of the live coal and its effect on Isaiah's uncleanness.

And sixth, prophetic vision. Because Isaiah had the vision to see what his calling meant for his generation, based on his knowledge of the calling of the Messiah in the premortal life, he was able to reply, "Here am I, send me." The Lord gave Isaiah further insight when He told him that the Messiah would arise from among the rest that remained after the great destructions following Isaiah's death. When one realizes that Isaiah could speak from the higher ground of prophetic vision, then one can begin to comprehend the gospel message in Isaiah.

Each potential stumbling block to an appreciation of Isaiah can become the stepping-stone to a comprehension and love of one of the greatest prophets and poets who ever lived on this earth.

NOTES

1. See a similar discussion in Victor L. Ludlow, *Isaiah: Prophet, Seer, and Poet* (Salt Lake City: Deseret Book, 1982), 135–37.

2. See the New English Bible attempt to indicate this by putting the sections its editors deemed poetic in verse form.

3. All extant Hebrew inscriptions contemporary with any section of the Old Testament, let alone with Isaiah, would require much less space than this article.

4. The poetry of Isaiah is to be compared with Shakespeare's, Goethe's, Dante's, and Pushkin's in its beauty and use of the language.

5. This is one of the main points made by Elder Bruce R. McConkie, "Ten Keys to Understanding Isaiah," *Ensign,* October 1973, 78–83.

6. How this chapter fits in with the other words of Isaiah will not be discussed here. The reader is referred to the standard commentaries on the Bible for this information.

   I acknowledge my debt to R. B. Y. Scott, "The Book of Isaiah, Chapters 1–39," in G. A. Buttrick, et al., eds., *The Interpreter's Bible* (New York and Nashville: Abingdon, 1956), 5: 204–12. I referred in the preparation of this paper quite often to this source. However, if I have relied only on this source for a particular point, I have given due credit.

7. The date is, of course, only approximate. King Uzziah also bore the name Azariah (see 2 Kings 15, for instance).

8. In these verses Tiglath-pilezer III is referred to by his Babylonian name, Pul. The Assyrian form of his name reads Tukulti-apil-ussur.

9. The Hebrew text reads literally, "I saw my Lord sitting on a chair, high and lifted up, and his trains filled the palace/temple." The Hebrew word *hekal* is used both for temple and for palace. It is a borrowed word into Hebrew, originally from a Sumerian word chain meaning, "large house." The denotation of "my lord" is clearly God, and more specifically Jehovah. However, since the Old Testament does not usually distinguish between God the Father and God the Son (Elohim and Jehovah respectively in current Latter-day Saint usage), I will not delineate between the Father and the Son in this paper. The reader is well advised to turn to James E. Talmage, "The Antemortal Godship of Christ," in *Jesus the Christ* (Salt Lake City: Deseret Book, 1975), 32–41, for a discussion of the titles used for Jehovah and His relationship to the Father.

   Throughout this paper, I will use the King James Version (hereafter cited as KJV) as a base text and will make divergences from it based on (unless otherwise noted) the Masoretic text of *Biblia Hebraica Stuttgartensia,* 2nd ed. (Stuttgart: Deutsche Bibelgesellschaft, 1984).

10. For the most complete discussion of the images in Isaiah 6, see Othmar Keel, *Jahwe-Visionen und Seigelkunst,* Stuttgarter Bibelstudien 84/85 (Stuttgart: Katholisches Bibelwerk, 1977), 46–124, with many ancient Near Eastern pictures and much literature.

11. The "s" of the KJV is redundant. The "-im" on "seraph" is the Hebrew plural ending. The 1920 and 1981 editions of the Book of Mormon, 2 Nephi 16:2 correctly read "seraphim" in place of previous Book of Mormon readings, including the Printer's Manuscript (see *Book of Mormon Critical Text I: I Nephi–Words of Mormon* [Provo, Utah: Foundation for Ancient Research and Mormon Studies, 1984], 183–86 [hereafter cited as *Critical Text* plus page number],

for the Book of Mormon variants to Isaiah 6), and the KJV. I have omitted the spurious "s."

12. E.g., F. Brown, S. R. Driver and C. Briggs, *A Hebrew and English Lexicon of the Old Testament* (Oxford: Clarendon, 1968), 977a (hereafter cited as BDB); and L. Koehler and W. Baumgartner, *Lexicon in veteris testamenti libros* (Leiden: Brill, 1958), 932b (hereafter cited as KB). Note that the former lists the singular as "[*saraph*]," meaning that the singular does not occur in the Old Testament; while the latter regards *sariph* as the singular and thus connects the plural here in Isaiah 6:2 and 6 with a singular in Isaiah 14:29 and 30:6, with the brass serpent in Numbers 21:8, and with the serpent in Deuteronomy 8:15 and Numbers 21:6.

    The definition of *seraph* is therefore based mostly on the context here in Isaiah 6.

13. From this basic meaning, no doubt, the related noun forms of this root in Deuteronomy 8:15, Numbers 21:6 and 8, and even in Isaiah 14:29 and 30:6 denote probably a serpent in the literal sense in the former passages and also as symbol in the latter two references. It would be easy to postulate that the name for a serpent would therefore be derived from a form of the root "to burn," because the bite of a serpent is "fiery." (Note, however, that this is a form of circular logic, not an uncommon but nevertheless faulty scholarly practice applied to poorly attested words, usually hapax legomenon, in dead languages.) The seraphim, in Isaiah 6:2, however, are not serpents, nor are they mythological beings.

14. That they attend God at His throne rather than hover above the throne, as the KJV reads, becomes evident from two considerations. First, the pronoun "it" in the KJV is the translation for the Hebrew "him." Therefore, the antecedent in the Masoretic text could be either God or the throne. ("Throne" in Hebrew is masculine. Because the word for throne is simply the word for seat, the context dictates whether throne or chair is the proper translation.)

    Second, the use of the syntagm "stand above" to connote attending (as in Genesis 18:8, where Abraham ministers to three visitors; the King James Bible translates "stood by them" but the Hebrew reads literally "stood above them") would indicate that the reading "Him" is preferred.

    Thus, the seraphim are celestial beings who attend God at His throne. This has been properly recorded under "seraphim" in the Bible Dictionary.

15. Note that the "beasts" of Revelation 4:6–9 is the KJV translation of the Greek word *zoon,* meaning not necessarily an animal, as "beast" would indicate, but rather any being that has life. (Latin *vita,* Greek *zoe,* and English *quick* are related words having to do with being

alive. See "gwei—" in *The American Heritage Dictionary,* ed. William Morris [Boston: Houghton Mifflin, 1981], 1519).

16. Perhaps one of the better examples is in Judges 3:24. The KJV slavishly translates "feet," but the intent of the passage is that Eglon was relieving himself, literally, "pouring out his feet" (see the New English Bible for a translation reflecting this reading of the Hebrew text; see also Exodus 4:25).

17. *Interpreter's Bible,* 208.

18. For this see Keel, figure 28. For numerous other examples of winged creatures in the ancient Near East, see Keel, *passim.*

19. For a picture of two of these ancient Near Eastern door socket stones, see J. B. Pritchard, ed., *The Ancient Near East in Pictures Relating to the Old Testament* (Princeton: Princeton, 1954), nos. 750 and 751.

20. For a picture of the remains of the massive, bronze-covered door of Shalmaneser III from Balawat (now located in the British Museum), see Eva Strommenger, *Fünf Jahrtausende Mesopotamien* (Munich: Hirmer, 1962), figures 209–214. Note that the doors of Solomon's temple were covered with gold (see 1 Kings 6:31–35).

21. The house here, of course, designates the house of God.

22. Note that "cloud," which filled the temple of Solomon at its dedication and which also signifies the presence of the Lord (see 1 Kings 7:10), is connected with smoke in Exodus 14:19–25. In this latter account, the Israelites are guided and protected by a pillar of fire at night and a cloud by day; that is, the cloud by day is the smoke of the fire which is visible at night.

23. In most Book of Mormon editions (including the 1981), the account of Isaiah 6 (2 Nephi 16) reads as in the King James Version. However, the Printer's Manuscript, the Printer's Manuscript Corrected and the 1830 edition all read, "I a man," leaving out the copula "am." This reflects the absence of a copula in the Hebrew Text (Masoretic) and speaks against a slavish copying of the King James Version by the Prophet Joseph Smith during the process of translation from the Gold Plates. See also note 28.

24. See the story concerning Samson's parents in Judges 13:21–23. The incident in the Book of Mormon involving the brother of Jared being struck with fear because he had seen the finger of the Lord (see Ether 3:6) illustrates this same concept.

25. This is also operative under the law of sacrifice given to Adam and his posterity.

26. The KJV, probably to avoid repetitions that grate on the ears of native English speakers (see the incipit of verses 3, 4, 7, and 9), translates the Hebrew conjunction *waw* with "also." This word used

as a conjunction in English could easily convey the idea that hearing the word of the Lord that follows is incidental to the cleansing. An accurate translation, as I have rendered it here, though grating on the sensitivities of English speakers, should convey the sequential nature (expressed by the use of the *waw*-consecutive) of the events Isaiah reported.

27. The Hebrew here is the plural form of "lord" plus the first person singular pronominal suffix and should be translated as "my lord." Since the denotation of "my lord" and the KJV "the Lord" is identical and the differences in the connotations of these terms are insignificant, I have let the KJV stand.

28. The Printer's Manuscript and the 1830 edition of the Book of Mormon read, "here I." This speaks against a slavish copying of the King James text in the translation process of the Book of Mormon. See also note 23.

29. If this interpretation is correct, this would also indicate that Isaiah had access to an account of the council in the premortal life not presently extant from Bible times. Perhaps this was one of the plain and precious things taken away from the Old Testament, as explained in 1 Nephi 13:26, 28, and 40.

30. Compare the New Testament quotations and paraphrases of this part of Isaiah with Matthew 13:14–15; Mark 4:12; Luke 8:10; John 12:40; Acts 28:26–27; and Romans 11:8. Note that the post-1830 editions of the Book of Mormon read for this verse in 2 Nephi 16:10 (see Isaiah 6:10) "be converted." The Printer's Manuscript and the 1830 editions read as the KJV (see the *Critical Text,* 184–5).

31. It should be clear from this passage alone, though there are enough other examples in the Old Testament to put this question beyond dispute (despite the fact that the Old Testament is not always consistent in this usage).

32. Perhaps the best of these solutions for Latter-day Saints has been pointed out by Victor Ludlow in his book, *Isaiah: Prophet, Seer, and Poet.* Quoting from the *New Jewish Version,* which he accepts as a correct rendering of the Hebrew (Masoretic text and 1QIs[a] of Qumran), he explains that the reflexive inserted in the last phrase by the New Jewish Version means that the people would attempt "to heal themselves, which is impossible, especially in a spiritual context, since healing and forgiveness come only through Christ."

Other exegetes have proposed, for example, that "the imperative ['make the heart fat'] is used here idiomatically to express a future certainty," and "the prophet is commanded to declare the will of the Lord, even though the result will be that men's unwillingness to respond will develop into stubborn opposition, eventually making their response impossible" *(The Interpreter's Bible,* 211–12). This, however, does not remove the theological stumbling block.

33. See *Gesenius' Hebrew Grammar,* edited and enlarged by E. Kautzsch, second English edition by A. E. Cowley (Oxford: Clarendon, 1970), §53c. This declarative mode of the Hebrew *hiph'il* is no doubt related to the factitive use of the š-Stamm in Akkadian, on which see Wolfram von Soden, *Grundriss der akkadischen Grammatik,* Analecta Orientalia 33/47 (Rome: Pontificium Institutum Biblicum, 1969), §89c.

34. Note that the Masoretic text, the Septuagint, the Syriac, the Targum, and 1QIs[a] all read with the Book of Mormon, 2 Nephi 16:11, "said," instead of the KJV "answered" (see *Critical Text* I, 185). This again speaks against a slavish copying of the KJV during the Book of Mormon translation process.

35. Here again the Book of Mormon, 2 Nephi 16:12, varies somewhat from the KJV. Whereas the latter reads (with the Masoretic text and the Septuagint), "and there be a great forsaking in the midst of the land" the former reads, "for there shall be a great forsaking in the midst of the land" (see *Critical Text* I, 185).

36. This manner of dealing with men who trouble the Lord with questions should be familiar to Latter-day Saints from the story of the Prophet Joseph Smith. The Prophet importuned with the Lord in 1843 "to know the time for the coming of the Son of Man" and received as answer that if he lived until he was eighty-five years old he would "see the face of the Son of Man; therefore let this suffice and trouble me no more on this matter" (D&C 130:14–15). In other words, the Lord put Joseph off because He knew that Joseph would not live to be eighty-five years old and therefore could safely say that if the Prophet would live to be that age he would see the Second Coming.

37. This is based on the estimate that Isaiah could have lived until 672 B.C. If he started his prophetic career in 742 and was twenty years old at the time and lived until he was ninety years old, he would have died in 672.

38. See H. H. Ben-Sasson, ed., *A History of the Jewish People* (Cambridge: Harvard, 1976), 330–35.

39. Against the Masoretic text, the Septuagint, and the Syriac, and hence the King James Version "it," 2 Nephi 16:13 and the Targum read "they" (see *Critical Text* I, 185).

40. The figure "a tenth" here need not be taken in a strictly literal sense. In Isaiah's day, a tenth could also have been a figure of speech for a small percentage of the population.

41. "And as an oak whose substance is in them, when they cast their leaves" points to a tree that is still alive—i.e., has its substance in

it—but bears no leaves and thus is in a dormant stage. For the tree as a symbol of Israel, see Joseph F. McConkie, *Gospel Symbolism* (Salt Lake City: Bookcraft, 1985), 10–11. See also the parable of the olive tree in Jacob 5 and the olive tree in Romans 11:16–24.

42. See also Abraham 1:4.

43. With this verse the Lord informs Isaiah that the remnant in Israel, after the Assyrian and Babylonian depredations, would be as barren trees, yet in this remnant the Holy Seed, the Lord, would be the eternal memorial of Israel.

44. See Isaiah 61:3 for the tree becoming alive spiritually in latter days.

CHAPTER FIFTEEN

OBADIAH'S VISION OF SAVIORS ON MOUNT ZION

GARY P. GILLUM

The prophet Obadiah's claim to fame among Latter-day Saints is the final verse of his twenty-one-verse prophecy against Edom: "And saviours shall come up on mount Zion to judge the mount of Esau; and the kingdom shall be the Lord's." Joseph Smith and succeeding latter-day prophets and other Church leaders are nearly unanimous in their interpretation of this scripture: Obadiah was referring to temple work for our kindred dead.[1] The purpose of this discussion is to explore a broader interpretation of Obadiah's prophecy and enlarge upon the definition of *saviors* to include work for the living as well as for the dead. I believe that the great truths contained in Obadiah's vision relate not only to the ongoing restoration of the Church but to individual restoration and progression as well.[2]

The book of Obadiah was probably written sometime after 587 B.C., when Jerusalem was destroyed by the Babylonians with the help of the Edomites. (While Edomite participation in the destruction of Jerusalem is not specifically described in the Old Testament, it is mentioned in the apocryphal 1 Esdras 4:45 and alluded to in Lamentations 4:21–22.) Nothing is known of the prophet for whom the book is named, although Obadiah most likely lived in Judah about the time of Jeremiah, Lehi, and their contemporaries. The Edom against which he prophesied is now known as Petra, the mountainous region southeast of the Dead Sea.

Gary P. Gillum is religion and ancient studies librarian at Brigham Young University.

Christian scholars recognize that the name *Obadiah* is attributed to at least twelve different men in the Old Testament, none of whom fits the time and place of the author of the book. *Obadiah,* a Hebrew name, translates as "servant of Yahweh" or "worshiper of Yahweh."[3] Thus *Obadiah* could be an appellation such as *Malachi* ("messenger") or *Theophilus* ("friend of God") instead of a personal name. If *Obadiah* is just an appellation, then almost any righteous servant of God could have been inspired to write this prophecy. This is possible, but it is more likely that a prophet named Obadiah wrote the text.

The twenty-one verses of Obadiah fall neatly into three main parts. In verses 1 through 9, Obadiah prophesies of Edom's judgment and destruction. The following five verses, 10 through 14, give the reasons for this judgment and the fate of both Edom and Jerusalem. The final verses, 15 through 21, speak of the day of the Lord, which brings both judgment and salvation as well as the restoration of Israel. Although Obadiah's prophecy represents the smallest book in the Old Testament, interpretation raises some difficult questions. Various Judeo-Christian commentaries on Obadiah present a microcosm of the many ways in which commentators of various denominations interpret Old Testament prophecies: fundamentalist versus mainstream, conservative versus liberal, higher criticism versus literary style. Many journal articles, as well as two recent book-length commentaries about the vision of Obadiah,[4] contain a rich store of theological, historical, and literary[5] studies; however, a spiritual assessment of the text is missing from all commentaries. This is a significant part of the message; the economy of scripture insists that it be so. Why else would Obadiah be included as part of the Old Testament, particularly when so much of the first portion of it is repeated almost word for word in Jeremiah 49:7–22? As the Reverend Ray C. Stedman noted, "The Scriptures have that beautiful faculty of appearing to be one thing on the surface, but on a deeper level, yielding rich and mighty treasures. That is certainly true of this amazing book of Obadiah."[6]

CHRISTIAN PERSPECTIVES

Obadiah's use of the term *savior* has interested Christian scholars. Methodist reformer John Wesley identified the saviors-deliverers with Jesus Christ, His Apostles, and other preachers of the gospel, both past and present.[7] Etymologically, the Hebrew word *yâsha* is the root word from which the words *Jesus* and *salvation* are derived. They denote the saving power of God, which brings to the world salvation that "properly belongs to the divine sphere."[8] Saviors are those who preserve or deliver from danger and destruction. In Nehemiah 9:27, saviors are probably judges. But saviors can also be wise men and women of spiritual insight and faith. The definition—along with work for the dead—that is closest to Latter-day Saint doctrine is that saviors are "the chosen instruments [of God] which go forth to teach all nations and make known the glory of the King in their midst."[9] Raabe's 1996 translation of Obadiah renders *saviors* as *deliverers,* giving a little more of the sense of "rescuer" or "liberator," very similar to the deliverers raised up by the Lord in Judges 3:9. The meaning of Obadiah is related to a message of "faith in God's moral government and hope in the eventual triumph of His just will"—a pastoral message to aching hearts that God is on the throne and cares for His own.[10]

Reverend Stedman discussed a spiritual teaching of Obadiah by examining the description of pride among the descendants of Esau, the Edomites. Stedman's perspective parallels remarkably President Ezra Taft Benson's oft-quoted talk on pride.[11] The proud look, self-sufficiency (to a fault), violence, indifference, gloating, and exploitation are all mentioned. Adding to that impressive list, Stedman further explains how this "pride of their heart" has deceived the Edomites and kept them from knowing the truth.[12]

Another perspective from Christian scholars relates to Obadiah's themes of "judgment and salvation, of justice and restoration with a vision of history's consummation."[13] In this context, "the 'holiness' of Mount Zion . . . [v. 17] means its freedom from the violation of heathen invaders and from any 'abomination of desolation.'"[14] Reformer John Calvin interprets this to mean that God would be mindful of His covenants. Concerning verse 17, Calvin states, "Obadiah clearly promises that there would be a restoration of the Church."[15] A temple will once again be consecrated. Others interpret this verse as signifying "the conversion and restoration of the Jews, and that under Jesus Christ the original *theocracy* shall be restored."[16]

JEWISH PERSPECTIVES

Many Jews consider Obadiah one of the important "minor" prophets. The Babylonian Talmud insists that the prophet Obadiah was the same versatile man who somehow served both King Ahab and Elijah in the mid-800s B.C. and who hid one hundred righteous prophets (or believers in God) from Ahab[17] (see 1 Kings 18). Louis Ginzberg comments on Ahab's Obadiah and the connection all of this has to a savior or deliverer on Mount Zion: "By birth an Edomite, Obadiah had been inspired by God to utter the prophecy against Edom. In his own person he embodied the accusation against Esau, who had lived with his pious parents without following their example, while Obadiah, on the contrary, lived in constant intercourse with the iniquitous King Ahab and his still more iniquitous spouse Jezebel without yielding to the baneful influence they exercised."[18]

According to *The Legends of the Jews,* the Aggadat Bereshit 14, 32, relates that Isaiah and Obadiah "uttered their prophecies in seventy-one languages."[19] This number is interesting, for the same source says that Obadiah was forced to prophesy against Edom "by the seventy-one members of the 'heavenly Synedrion' [sanhedrin]."[20] From this legend one may even imply that saviors on Mount Zion are not alone in doing their saving work: they are assisted by angelic messengers.

Although members of The Church of Jesus Christ of Latter-day Saints and many other Christians look at the broader perspective of Esau and the Edomites, one Jewish perspective accepts Obadiah's narrow nationalism as he condemned Israel's enemy, Edom, and the other pagan nations and looked forward to the exaltation of his own people, Israel. This anti-Edom sentiment is part of a continuum that runs all the way from the womb where Esau and Jacob wrestled (see Genesis 25:21–23), to the refusal of the Edomites to allow the Israelites of the Exodus to pass through their land (see Numbers 20:14–21), to the present-day political and religious difficulties. A Jewish apocryphal work, 1 Esdras 4:45, even insists that the Edomites not only helped the Babylonians conquer the Israelites but specifically destroyed the temple in Jerusalem.[21]

LATTER-DAY SAINT PERSPECTIVES

Like the prophetic messages of other minor prophets, Obadiah's message becomes for Latter-day Saints both a literal scripture as well as an allegory of good versus evil—Mount Esau versus Mount Zion. Because of its wickedness and lasting hatred for Israel, Edom, like Babylon, becomes a symbol for the world and worldliness (see D&C 1:36). Latter-day Saints typically ignore the first twenty verses of Obadiah and his harangues against the Edomites, perhaps because other prophets, namely Jeremiah, wrote in like manner, or most likely because the exciting prospects in verse 21 outshine the negativity of the preceding verses. Latter-day Saint prophets and other General Authorities almost unanimously interpret verse 21 in a completely different manner from that of any other church. Saviors on Mount Zion are those who perform work for our kindred dead. The Lord counseled Joseph Smith on this matter in these words: "The keys are to be delivered, the spirit of Elijah is to come, the Gospel to be established, the Saints of God gathered, Zion built up, and the Saints to come up as saviors on Mount Zion. But how are they to become saviors on Mount Zion? By building their temples, erecting their baptismal fonts, and going forth and receiving all the ordinances, baptisms, confirmations, washings, anointings, ordinations and sealing powers upon their heads, *in behalf of all their progenitors who are dead,* and redeem them that they may come forth in the first resurrection and be exalted to thrones of glory with them; and herein is the chain that binds the hearts of the fathers to the children, and the children to the fathers, which fulfills the mission of Elijah."[22] Joseph Smith elaborated further: "A view of these things reconciles the Scriptures of truth, justifies the ways of God to man, places the human family upon an equal footing, and harmonizes with every principle of righteousness, justice and truth."[23]

Elder Matthias Cowley gave another definition of saviors that was a direct result of missionary work: "The man who forsakes his father and mother for the Gospel's sake has accepted something in the Gospel that will bring his father and mother, his sister and brother to him, and they will fulfill the words of the prophet Obadiah that 'saviors shall come up on mount Zion.'"[24]

Finally, President Charles W. Penrose talked about saviors from the perspective of individual families: "Now, brethren, what I am after is this: Let us Latter-day Saints, called to be saviors of men, called to be saviors of this world, called to be saviors to introduce that which will save mankind and bring them up from their lowest state into a condition where they will be fit to hold converse with Deity, let us be careful that we plant in the minds of our children the truth and nothing but the truth so far as we can understand it. . . . The boundless universe is before us all to learn and to live and to come up to the standard occupied by our Eternal Father and to be fit for his society."[25]

A PERSONAL PERSPECTIVE

Early in the morning on Wednesday, February 19, 1997, I had an extraordinarily vivid dream of a dilapidated truck full of eight abused and sad children, pleading with their eyes that I could rescue them from their pain and sorrow. The haunting details were seared in my memory deeply enough that I can still remember one teenager with a torn, checkered blouse, muddy skirt, and stringy, matted hair. I did not know the significance of this dream until I was in my office a couple of hours later, wondering whether I should work on this article or turn to more pressing needs in the library. It was then that I noticed a new title from the book cart, *My Parents Married on a Dare* by Carlfred Broderick. I thumbed through the book, and my eyes stopped on page 119, where the words "Saviors on Mount Zion" fairly leaped out at me. I quote from his chapter "Children Being Born into Abusive Families": "In suffering innocently that others might not suffer, such persons, in some degree, become as 'saviors on Mount Zion' by helping to bring salvation to a lineage."[26]

I immediately realized one of the chief reasons for my own passion for the gospel. Again, in the words of Dr. Broderick: "God actively intervenes in some destructive lineages, assigning a valiant spirit to break the chain of destructiveness in such families. Although these children may suffer innocently as victims of violence, neglect, and exploitation, through the grace of God some find the strength to 'metabolize' the poison within themselves, refusing to pass it on to future generations."[27]

I also realized that I had fulfilled this mission four times: once by leaving my own abusive and alcoholic family; twice more by marrying first one and then another abused woman, both of whom died of cancer nine years apart; and most recently by marrying a widow who had, along with some of her eleven children, been abused before her husband died. Together, my wife and I could consider ourselves saviors on Mount Zion who have the opportunity to stop the cycle of abuse in both of our lineages.

From this perspective, I am interested in broadening the definition of saviors on Mount Zion to include that of Dr. Broderick. I discovered that compared to the perspectives of other religions, the Latter-day Saint interpretation of the word *saviors* is unique. This may be related to our distinctive belief that we are children of God, created in the image of our Father in Heaven, and that we are "joint-heirs with Christ" (Romans 8:17). The non-LDS perspective that is most similar to Dr. Broderick's comes from the well-known *Interpreter's Bible:* "Herein lies the painfulness of man's relationship to man. One stands aside and lets another suffer. One takes pleasure in another's distress. One capitalizes on another's misfortunes. Despite all that can be said about the amiability of human nature, this is what happens again and again all down the line of human social life. It is not always so. But we need to be asking ourselves continually about our neutralities, our inward cruelties, our ruthlessness."[28]

CONCLUSION

Several observations can be made concerning the book of Obadiah, its vision of the Edomites, and the saviors on Mount Zion.

In likening the scriptures to ourselves, Latter-day Saints can be saviors on Mount Zion not only for the dead but also for the living. At the very least, Latter-day Saints should spend a great deal of time repenting, forgiving, and enduring.

According to many Judeo-Christian scholars, the family of Abraham will become the saviors on Mount Zion when the Messiah finally comes. Like the tribe of Judah, we Latter-day Saints are a covenant people. Being saviors is a daunting task that we cannot do without help from above, even a pillar of fire by night and a cloud by day. Whether Latter-day Saints look at the vision of Obadiah as history, as prophecy fulfilled, or as an allegory for the victory of good over evil, the message is clear that "only the Day of the Lord, which will establish once and for all the reign of God in history, will *break this cycle of violence* and insure Judah a future of self-determination and security."[29] How remarkable it is that after twenty verses of condemnation, Obadiah concludes his prophecy with a clear message of hope for all men and women: that we can not only be saviors but will be judged by saviors as well and not by tyrants of the soul.

Latter-day Saints know from the Bible as well as the Book of Mormon that the Lord sometimes intervenes in human lives to set us straight (Alma the Younger), redirect our purposes for a greater good (the Apostle Paul), change the course of our lives (President Gordon B. Hinckley), or rescue a lineage (those who have been converted to the gospel). In discovering Obadiah's message, I thus found another reason not only for my own conversion but for my wife's as well: to deliver our families from the cycle of abuse and to save our lineages. Saviors on Mount Zion, among others, are those "who refuse to pass on the destructive, toxic parenting they received. . . . It gives meaning to the sacrifice and recognition to the courage of those who have committed their lives to purifying a lineage."[30]

More than one hundred years ago, President Wilford Woodruff said that "saviors upon Mount Zion have been raised up, while the kingdom is the Lord's, as the prophet Obadiah said they would be."[31] These saviors are not only ordained missionaries but are also the many Saints who labor to help break the cycle of spiritual, emotional, or physical abuse and restore Zion and the purity of the gospel to individuals and families. Every Latter-day Saint, man or woman, young or old, should feel alive and awake to a duty to teach and live correct principles that prevent the miniholocausts that can and do exist at the family level.

Finally, by using and magnifying our spiritual gifts, Latter-day Saints can act as saviors on Mount Zion by helping the world overcome and eliminate the barbarisms of abuse, war, torture, force, genocide, poverty, ignorance, exclusion, bigotry, and hatred. That is the larger legacy of Latter-day Saints and children of Abraham: saviors on Mount Zion.

NOTES

1. Joseph Smith, *Teachings of the Prophet Joseph Smith*, comp. Joseph Fielding Smith (Salt Lake City: Deseret Book, 1972), 330. Other Latter-day Saint comments on Obadiah: Ellis T. Rasmussen, "Zephaniah, Obadiah, and Micah: Prophets during Times of Crises," *Instructor*, July 1963, 248–49; *Church News*, July 14, 1973, 15. The Scripture Citation Index on the Gospel Infobases *Collector's Edition 1997 CD-ROM* lists Obadiah as quoted by four General Authorities in general conferences: F. Arthur Kay, April 1985;

LeGrand Richards, October 1975; Theodore M. Burton, October 1970 and October 1972; and Russell M. Nelson, October 1994. Many additional uses are listed, including citations in the *Times and Seasons* and in Bruce R. McConkie, *Mormon Doctrine,* 2nd ed. (Salt Lake City: Bookcraft, 1962), 678.

2. The Restoration of the gospel is not just an event called the First Vision but an ongoing process in the dispensation of the fullness of times, both in the Church generally and for its members individually.

3. James P. Boyd, *The Self-Pronouncing Bible Dictionary* (Philadelphia: A. J. Holman, 1924), 209.

4. Paul R. Raabe, *Obadiah,* vol. 24D of *The Anchor Bible,* ed. William Foxwell Albright and David Noel Freedman (New York: Doubleday, 1996). This Missouri Synod Lutheran theologian has written a very understandable and perceptive commentary of 310 pages. Original Hebrew words are transliterated. Ehud Ben Zvi, *A Historical-Critical Study of the Book of Obadiah* (Berlin: Walter de Gruyter, 1996) is a more scholarly treatment in which the author, presumably Jewish in background, uses Hebrew characters rather than Roman transliterations. Both commentaries have extensive bibliographies and scripture indexes.

5. Robert B. Robinson, "Levels of Naturalization in Obadiah," *Journal for the Study of the Old Testament* 40 (1988): 88, mentions anaphorae, chiasms, assonance, parallelism, and alliteration.

6. Ray C. Stedman, "Obadiah: Death to Edom!" in *World Wide Study Bible* on Web site http://ccel.wheaton.edu/wwsb/obadiah/.

7. John Wesley, "Notes on the Book of Obadiah," on Web site http://wesley.nnc.edu/wesley/notes/031obad.txt.

8. G. Johannes Botterweck and Helmer Ringgren, eds., *Theological Dictionary of the Old Testament* (Grand Rapids, MI: Eerdmans, 1990), 6:462–63.

9. Arno C. Gaebelein, *Gaebelein's Concise Commentary on the Whole Bible* (Neptune, NJ: Loizeaux Brothers, 1985), 692.

10. Leslie C. Allen, "Obadiah," in *Holman Bible Dictionary* (Nashville: Holman Bible Publishers, 1991), 1035.

11. Ezra Taft Benson, "Beware of Pride," *Ensign,* May 1989, 4–7.

12. Stedman, "Obadiah."

13. William P. Brown, *Obadiah through Malachi* (Louisville, KY: Westminster John Knox Press, 1996), 7.

14. Carl F. Henry, ed., *The Biblical Expositor* (Grand Rapids, MI: Baker Book House, 1985), 2:316.

15. John Calvin, *Commentaries on the Twelve Minor Prophets* (Grand Rapids, MI: Eerdmans, 1950). Printed from the Internet:

http://www.iclnet.org/pub/resources/text/ipb-e/epl-04/
cvobd-04.txt.

16. Adam Clarke, *The Holy Bible . . . with a Commentary and Critical Notes* (Nashville, TN: Abingdon, 1977), 696.

17. Rabbi Dr I. Epstein, *The Babylonian Talmud: Seder Nezikin* III (London: Soncino Press, 1935), 253.

18. Louis Ginzberg, *The Legends of the Jews* (Philadelphia: Jewish Publication Society of America, 1937), 4:240, 241. Epstein, *Babylonian Talmud,* reports the following on page 253: "Let Obadiah, who has lived with two wicked persons [Ahab and Jezebel] and yet has not taken example by their deeds, come and prophesy against the wicked Esau, who lived with two righteous persons [Isaac and Rebekah] and yet did not learn from their good deeds."

19. Ginzberg, *Legends of the Jews,* 5:195.

20. Ginzberg, *Legends of the Jews,* 6:344.

21. David W. Baker, *Obadiah* (London: Inter-Varsity Press, 1988), 22.

22. Smith, *Teachings,* 330; emphasis added.

23. Joseph Smith, *History of The Church of Jesus Christ of Latter-day Saints,* ed. B. H. Roberts, 2nd ed. rev., (Salt Lake City: Deseret Book, 1973), 4:599.

24. Matthias Cowley, in Conference Report, October 1903, 55.

25. Charles W. Penrose, in Conference Report, April 1918, 22.

26. Carlfred Broderick, *My Parents Married on a Dare* (Salt Lake City: Deseret Book, 1996), 119; chapter originally published in "I Have a Question," *Ensign,* August 1986.

27. Broderick, *My Parents Married on a Dare,* 119.

28. *The Interpreter's Bible,* ed. George A. Buttrick (New York: Abingdon Press, 1953), 6:863–64.

29. Kathleen Nash, "Obadiah: Past Promises, Future Hope," *Bible Today,* 25 (January 1987): 281; emphasis added.

30. Broderick, *My Parents Married on a Dare,* 117.

31. Wilford Woodruff, in *Collected Discourses, 1894–1896,* comp. and ed. Brian H. Stuy (B. H. S. Publishing, 1991), 4:10.

CHAPTER SIXTEEN

CONSIDER YOUR WAYS: THE BOOK OF HAGGAI AND THE RESPONSIBILITIES AND BLESSINGS OF TEMPLE WORK

RAY L. HUNTINGTON

Even though the prophet Haggai is mentioned in the books of Ezra and Haggai, we know little about his birthplace, family background, personal life, or the events surrounding his prophetic calling. But then, the aim of the Old Testament is to record prophetic messages and not to provide minute details about the prophets' lives.

DATING HAGGAI

The name *Haggai* probably means "festal" or "feast" and may indicate Haggai was born during one of three important Jewish feasts: Unleavened Bread, Pentecost (or Weeks), or Tabernacles.[1] Textual information from the book of Haggai reveals that Haggai began his Jerusalem ministry during the second year of Darius, king of Persia, in 520 B.C. This date is eighteen years after the Jews returned from Babylonian captivity in 538 B.C. to rebuild the temple in Jerusalem (see Haggai 1:1). Dating from the book of Haggai also shows that Haggai prophesied in Jerusalem for only three and one-half months—beginning in late August and ending in early December of

Ray L. Huntington is an associate professor of ancient scripture at Brigham Young University.

520 B.C. It is reasonable to assume, however, that his ministry continued well beyond this short time period.

Jewish tradition suggests that Haggai saw the temple of Solomon before its destruction in 586 B.C. and was among the captives taken to Babylon. Others, such as Augustine, suggest that both Haggai and Zechariah prophesied in Babylon before the return of the Jewish exiles in 538 B.C.[2] If either of these traditions are true, it suggests that Haggai was fairly old when he began his ministry.

HISTORICAL SETTING OF THE BOOK OF HAGGAI

After Judah's ill-fated rebellion against Babylon in 586 B.C., the city of Jerusalem, together with the magnificent temple of Solomon, was burned and leveled to the ground. Unlike any other event in Judah's history, the destruction of the temple symbolized her complete spiritual demise and the withdrawal of God's blessings and divine protection.[3]

After the Medes and Persians captured Babylon in 538 B.C., Cyrus, king of Persia, issued a decree authorizing the Jews to return to Jerusalem and rebuild their temple (see Ezra 1:2–4; 6:3). According to the Book of Ezra, under the leadership of Zerubbabel (see Ezra 2), close to fifty thousand exiles made the long journey home to Jerusalem. What they saw when they approached the ruined city of Jerusalem must have been disheartening. The city's walls and buildings lay in waste. Worse, Solomon's magnificent temple—the jewel of Jerusalem—was now a pile of cold ash and stone.

For the next two years, the returnees labored on the temple, and by 536 B.C. had rebuilt the altar of sacrifice and parts of the foundation (see Ezra 3:3–11). Their work would have been impressive, had they continued to rebuild the temple. But in the face of Samaritan opposition and a good deal of apathy on their part, they chose to discontinue their labors for the next sixteen years (see Ezra 4:1–5, 24). And, it was not until the inspired ministry of Haggai in 520 B.C. that work on the Lord's house resumed.

HAGGAI'S PROPHETIC MESSAGE

The central focus of Haggai's message is certainly clear: Now is the time to build God's holy temple! Haggai began his prophetic message by declaring: "Thus speaketh the Lord of hosts, saying, This people say, The time is not come, the time that the Lord's house should be built" (Haggai 1:2). Yes, the altar and parts of the foundation had been rebuilt, but the work had been set aside for sixteen years. More importantly, the people didn't seem bothered by their inattentiveness to the Lord's work. In fact, they rationalized it was not the time to rebuild the temple. Clearly, they had other work they felt was more important.

But what could be more important than rebuilding God's temple? Evidently, the people felt that beautifying their own homes was of greater value than rebuilding God's house. The Lord addressed this when he declared through Haggai, "Is it time for you, O ye, to dwell in your cieled houses, and this house lie waste?" (Haggai 1:4). The phrase "cieled houses" may refer to the costly cedar paneling many of the wealthy were using to decorate the interior of their homes. It is certainly understandable why the Lord would be displeased with their efforts to beautify their homes while neglecting His house.

The Jews' neglect in rebuilding God's temple reflected their lack of understanding and appreciation for temple work. They either didn't know, or didn't care that one of the central purposes for the gathering of God's covenant children is to "build unto the Lord a house whereby He could reveal unto His people the ordinances of His house and the glories of His kingdom, and teach the people the way of salvation: for there are certain ordinances and principles that, when they are taught and practiced, must be done in a place or house built for that purpose."[4]

Without temple ordinances, the Jews of Haggai's day were lacking a vital ingredient to their spiritual welfare. Moreover, their efforts to beautify their homes while failing to rebuild the Lord's house clearly demonstrated that they preferred the profane over the sacred—a choice that is always costly to God's covenant people in any age or time.

The book of Haggai is especially relevant for our day, since many of our worldly endeavors, such as work, civic involvement, schooling, or recreation, may influence us to procrastinate or even abandon the important work done within the walls of the temple.

Regarding this issue, President Spencer W. Kimball stated, "Many people spend most of their time working in the service of a self-image that includes sufficient money, stocks, bonds, investment portfolios, property, credit cards, furnishings, automobiles, and the like to *guarantee* carnal security throughout, it is hoped, a long and happy life. Forgotten is the fact that our assignment is to use these many resources in our families and quorums to build up the kingdom of God—to further the missionary effort and the genealogical and temple work. . . . Instead, we expend these blessings on our own desires."[5]

In contrast, those who are burdened with life's demands and challenges will find the temple to be a place of peace and joy and a refuge from life's daunting challenges. In support of this idea, Elder John A. Widtsoe wrote: "I believe that the busy person on the farm, in the shop, in the office, or in the household, who has his worries and troubles, can solve his problems better and more quickly in the house of the Lord than anywhere else. If he will . . . [do] the temple work for himself and for his dead, he will confer a mighty blessing upon those who have gone before, and . . . a blessing will come to him, for at the most unexpected moments, in or out of the temple will come to him, as a revelation, the solution of the problems that vex his life. That is the gift that comes to those who enter the temple properly."[6]

CONSIDER YOUR WAYS

Haggai continued the Lord's message by asking the Jews to consider their ways (see Haggai 1:5). The word *consider* is translated from the Hebrew word *soom,* which means "to attend to" and is used five times in the book of Haggai.[7] In this case the prophet was asking the Jews to carefully "attend to," or carefully "assess," their neglect of the temple, since the Lord was not obligated to bless their lives. Haggai wrote:

> Ye have sown much, and bring in little; ye eat, but ye have not enough; ye drink, but ye are not filled with drink; ye clothe you, but there is none warm; and he that earneth wages earneth wages to put it into a bag with holes.
>
> Thus saith the Lord of hosts; Consider your ways. . . .
>
> Ye looked for much, and, lo, it came to little; and when ye brought it home, I did blow upon it. Why? saith the Lord of hosts. Because of mine house that is waste, and ye run every man unto his own house.

Therefore the heaven over you is stayed from dew, and the earth is stayed from her fruit.

And I called for a drought upon the land, and upon the mountains, and upon the corn, and upon the new wine, and upon the oil, and upon that which the ground bringeth forth, and upon men, and upon cattle, and upon all the labour of the hands. (Haggai 1:6–11)

The writings of Haggai leave little doubt that both temporal and spiritual blessings are withheld from the Saints when they neglect their temple work. In contrast, if the Jews resumed their labors to rebuild the temple, the Lord declared, "I am with you" (Haggai 1:13; 2:4).

The Lord's promise, "I am with you," can be understood in two equally important ways. The first is the Lord's promise to render divine help and strength to those involved in rebuilding the temple in Haggai's day. The second, and the broader of the two meanings, is the Lord's promise that He will be with us through the bestowal of profound blessings that come from faithful temple attendance (see Haggai 2:18–19).

The following statements from the Brethren are clear evidence of the positive linkage between God's blessings and temple work:

Many parents, in and out of the Church, are concerned about protection against a cascading avalanche of wickedness which threatens to engulf [the world]. . . . There is a power associated with ordinances of heaven—even the power of godliness—which can and will thwart the forces of evil if we will but be worthy of those sacred [covenants made in the temple of the Lord]. . . . Our families will be protected, our children will be safeguarded as we live the gospel, visit the temple, and live close to the Lord.[8]

The Lord will bless us as we attend to the sacred ordinance work of the temples. Blessings there will not be limited to our temple service. We will be blessed in all of our affairs. We will be eligible to have the Lord take an interest in our affairs both spiritual and temporal.[9]

I am satisfied that if our people would attend the temple more, there would be less of selfishness in their lives. There would be less of absence of love in their relationships. There would be more of fidelity on the part of husbands and wives. There would be more of love and peace and happiness in the homes of our people.[10]

The people of Haggai's day undoubtedly received similar blessings as they participated in the temple ordinances available to them. It is also clear they began to appreciate the value of temple work and the promised blessings, since they readily harkened to Haggai's call to renew their labors on the temple: "And the Lord stirred up the spirit of Zerubbabel the son of Shealtiel, governor of Judah, and the spirit of Joshua the son of Josedech, the high priest, and the spirit of all the remnant of the people; and they came and did work in the house of the Lord of hosts, their God" (Haggai 1:14).

Once work on the temple resumed, Haggai asked those who had seen the temple of Solomon to compare it with the temple they were currently building. It is apparent from the Lord's question, "Is it not in your eyes in comparison of it as nothing?" that the second temple was not as beautiful and ornate as Solomon's temple (Haggai 2:3).

Nevertheless, the Lord counseled the Jews to "be strong" and "work," with the assurance that He would be with them in their labors, as He was with the Israelites in their exodus from Egypt (see Haggai 2:4–5). Moreover, the Lord made it clear why their efforts to beautify the temple were important, by declaring that the "desire of all nations" would soon come to the temple in Jerusalem. Haggai recorded, "For thus saith the Lord of hosts; Yet once, it is a little while, and I will shake the heavens, and the earth, and the sea, and the dry land; and I will shake all nations, and the desire of all nations shall come: and I will fill this house with glory, saith the Lord of hosts" (Haggai 2:6–7).

THE DESIRE OF ALL NATIONS

Who is the "desire of all nations"? The "desire of all nations" is the Holy One of Israel—even Jesus Christ. The Messiah would eventually come to His holy temple in Jerusalem. Haggai's prophecy in verses 6 and 7 is probably dualistic; it may refer to the Savior's numerous visits to the temple in Jerusalem during His mortal ministry, and His visitation to the temple at the time of His Second Coming. During this visit, the Lord will shake the heavens, earth, sea, and dry land, and the desire of all nations (Christ) shall come.[11] Thus, Haggai reminded the Jews that their continued efforts to build and beautify the temple would not be in vain because Jehovah Himself would personally visit the temple and fill it with His glory. In this context it is easy to understand what Haggai meant when he prophesied that the "glory of this latter house shall be greater than of the former" because the Lord's anticipated personal visits to the temple would glorify the current edifice beyond that of Solomon's temple (Haggai 2:9).

In a broader sense, all dedicated temples of the Lord are sacred edifices in which God's Spirit and glory reside. Joseph Smith taught this doctrine to the Saints during the dedicatory prayer of the Kirtland Temple: "That thy glory may rest down upon thy people, and upon this thy house, . . . that it may be sanctified and consecrated to be holy, and that thy holy presence may be continually in this house; and that all people who shall enter upon the threshold of the Lord's house may feel thy power, and feel constrained to acknowledge that thou hast sanctified it, and that it is thy house, a place of holiness" (D&C 109:12–13).

As we continually visit the house of the Lord, we can also partake of the Lord's Spirit and feel His glory manifest within the sacred structure. We will also partake of God's peace found abundantly in His holy temples (see Haggai 2:9). In referring to the sacred environs of the temple, Elder David B. Haight declared, "The moment we step into the house of the Lord, the atmosphere changes from the worldly to the heavenly, where respite from the normal activities of life is found, and where peace of mind and spirit is received. It is a refuge from the ills of life and a protection from the temptations that are contrary to our spiritual well-being."[12]

TEMPLE WORK AND HOLINESS

In Haggai 2:11–14, the prophet reminded the Jews that the consecrated meat of the animal sacrifices used in the temple made the priests' clothing holy because it was in direct contact with the garment (see Leviticus 6:27); however, the garment itself could not transmit that holiness to a third or fourth object. Moreover, anything touched by an unclean individual would become unclean (see Numbers 19:11–13, 22). Thus, uncleanness is much more easily transmitted than holiness.[13] Through references to the Mosaic law regarding holiness and uncleanness, Haggai may have been alluding to the fact that the Jews' sacrifices and offerings on the rebuilt altar of the temple could not transmit holiness to them nor absolve them of their failure to continue rebuilding the temple. Furthermore, even though the Jews had returned to a promised land consecrated by the Lord, that fact alone could not make them a holy people. The only way for them to become a holy people was to rebuild the temple and worthily participate in the temple service.

The Lord also asked the Jews to "consider from this day and upward" the consequences of failing to rebuild the temple (Haggai 2:15). Haggai lists the consequences as poor harvests (2:16); blasting, or intense heat, from the eastern winds; mildew; and hail (2:17), which would have had disastrous effects upon their crops. Conversely, Haggai promised the Jews that their obedience in rebuilding the temple would result in "seed in the barn" as well as abundant harvests from the vine, fig tree, pomegranate, and the olive tree (2:19). Indeed, the Lord would bless them.

Although many of the Old Testament prophets' messages and exhortations went unheeded by the ancient house of Israel, Haggai's ministry appears to be an exception. As a result of his work, the faithful Jews in Jerusalem resumed their work on the temple and continued until its completion in 515 B.C. Because of their obedience to a prophet's message, the temple once again stood in Jerusalem as a blessing in the lives of God's faithful Saints.

Latter-day Israel must remind itself of Haggai's important message. Temple work is just as important in this day as it was in Haggai's. God has reserved many temporal and spiritual blessings for those who faithfully attend the temple. As we set aside our "cieled houses" and devote time to the temple, the Lord will pour out His blessings collectively upon the Church and individually upon our homes and families.

NOTES

1. Kenneth Barker ed., *The NIV Study Bible* (Grand Rapids, MI: Zondervan, 1985), 1400.
2. Sidney B. Sperry, *Old Testament Prophets* (Salt Lake City: Deseret Sunday School Union, 1965), 71.

3. "Temples through the Ages," in *Encyclopedia of Mormonism,* ed. Daniel H. Ludlow (New York: Macmillan, 1992), 4:1463.

4. Joseph Smith, *Teachings of the Prophet Joseph Smith,* comp. Joseph Fielding Smith (Salt Lake City: Deseret Book, 1938), 308.

5. Spencer W. Kimball, as quoted by Marion G. Romney, in Conference Report, April 1977, 121; emphasis in original.

6. John A. Widtsoe, "Temple Worship," *Utah Genealogical and Historical Magazine,* 7 (April 1921): 63–64.

7. William Gesenius, *Gesenius' Hebrew and Chaldee Lexicon to the Old Testament Scriptures,* trans. Samuel P. Tregelles (Grand Rapids, MI: Eerdmans, 1949), 787.

8. Ezra Taft Benson, "Atlanta Georgia Temple Cornerstone Laying," June 1, 1983, as quoted by Dean L. Larsen, "The Importance of the Temple for Living Members," *Ensign,* April 1993, 12.

9. Boyd K. Packer, *The Holy Temple* (Salt Lake City: Bookcraft, 1980), 182.

10. Gordon B. Hinckley, as quoted by Larsen, "Importance of the Temple," 12.

11. Bruce R. McConkie, *The Millennial Messiah* (Salt Lake City: Deseret Book, 1982), 272–73.

12. David B. Haight, "The Temple: A Place of Refuge," *Ensign,* November 1990, 61.

13. Barker, *NIV Study Bible,* 1403.

CHAPTER SEVENTEEN

THE PROPHETS OF THE EXILE: SAVIORS OF A PEOPLE

RICHARD D. DRAPER

The thunder of Nebuchadnezzar's battering rams should have sounded the death knell of the Jews as a people, but it did not. To say it another way, Jerusalem's destruction, followed by the Babylonian captivity, marks a major break in the course of Jewish history but not its end. Those battering rams were instrumental in ending both Judah's institutional and corporate life but not that of the people or their religion. Some things, however, did come to an end. Never again would the old social and religious pattern be constructed in exactly the same way. The destruction of the Jewish capital with its temple successfully demolished the Jewish state and ended its priestly activities. In 580 B.C. the Jewish people, beaten and scattered, were but an agglomeration of individual refugees living under foreign rule.[1] The threat posed by the exile must not be minimized or trivialized.[2] Loss of identity threatened the Jewish people more fully than at any other time in their existence with the possible exception of the Egyptian bondage. The possibility is underscored by the fact that a number of Jewish communities that took root outside Palestine eventually lost their Jewish character and eroded into the cultures of the area.[3] That Judah's history did not end with the Babylonian captivity is nothing short of a miracle, but Judah not only survived the calamity but also formed a new and viable society built on the ruins of the old.[4] In the process, she refined, disciplined, and strengthened

---

Richard D. Draper is associate dean of Religious Education at Brigham Young University.

her faith, giving it a vigor and direction that would carry it into and beyond New Testament times.[5]

One aspect of that miracle central to the success of all the others is prophecy. Judah's prophets kept her faith from extinction and her culture from decay. They did this, in part, by reminding her of her unique relation to her God and the mission He had assigned her. The prophets also fueled the Jews' desire to return to their own land, rebuild God's temple, and once more become His people. Further, these inspired men facilitated the miracle by satisfactorily answering the exile's most urgent questions and, in the process, giving the Jews both hope and direction.[6]

It is noteworthy that the impetus of the miracle did not come, as one might suppose, from those Jews still living in and around Judea. The Babylonians left quite a nucleus of Jews in the land. Though the disruption of their life was extreme, it was by no means complete.[7] Many were able to eke out a living in various parts of Judea.[8] Evidence suggests that most of these Jews continued to practice an impure form of Jehovah worship.[9] Still, some, if not many, would have been loyal to their religion. These godly souls would have mourned for Zion and wished for her return. But for seventy years, all they did was wish. There was no spark, no energy, no attempt at restoration from this source.[10]

To the north, the Jewish communities experienced little disruption of life compared to their southern neighbors. Many hundreds of Jews continued to exist in Samaria and Galilee. Nebuchadnezzar destroyed few buildings and no cities in these areas. Few of these Jews, if any, were taken hostage by the king. They were the dominant population throughout the Jezreel and Galilee. Their worship, like that of the unfaithful Jews around Judea, would have contained many pagan elements.[11] But even here an orthodox strain would have yearned for the temple and prayed to their God. But pray was all they did. No restoration pressure existed here,[12] no fires of nationalistic zeal burned in the area. At best, it smoldered well beneath the surface, unable to produce the energy necessary to renew and rebuild what was lost.

The same is true of those Jews living in lands outside of Palestine. Even before the Babylonians marched, Jews had established a few communities and bolstered the population of others as they attempted to escape to more secure climes.[13] As chapters 42 through 44 of Jeremiah show, Egypt became very attractive for many of these. Quite a number of Jews settled in Daphnae, a city in the Nile delta; others moved farther south. Some were hired as mercenaries and developed a colony at Elephantine, near the first cataract of the Nile.[14] The successful Jewish communities in Egypt acted as magnets, and more Jews flowed into that country. But Egyptian favoritism did not act to stir into flame the coals of Judah's desire to return. Rather, Egyptian wiles seem to have acted more to cool what little heat there was.

Both Transjordan and Syria received an influx of Jewish refugees. Jewish villages grew up here and there on the eastern end of the Mediterranean area,[15] but no pressure for restoration came from these Jews, either. Though they were much closer to Jerusalem and had influence with local leaders and sufficient resources to reenter the land of Judea and at least lay the foundation for further growth, none are known to have stirred. Indeed, the embers of gathering lay cold in these lands.

The scattered circumstance of the Jews underscores one point: prophecy was being fulfilled. Though Judah was not yet scattered the world over, the process was beginning in earnest. Never again would all, or even most, of her sons and daughters reside in Palestine. Never again would there be a full return before her Messiah came in glory.[16] But, considering the magnitude of the calamity that overtook her, the wonder is that she did not disappear into the vortex of history forever, as had so many nations before and after her. Many of these, like Judah's northern sister, Ephraim, and her great enemy, the Philistines, lost their identity as a people during this time.[17] That Judah did not stems in large measure from the Jews in Babylon and the work going on among them.

It was in Babylon, in a land far away from Judah, that the desire for return actually burned. It is to these Jews, those who were actually taken into captivity by Nebuchadnezzar, that one must give the largest credit for the survival of the people. Three major factors contributed. First, the policy of deportation carried out by the Babylonians meant that the Jews in Babylon were the top of Judah's intellectual, political, and ecclesiastical leadership. Jeremiah gives the total number of those deported (in 597, 587, and 582 B.C.) as forty-six hundred (see Jeremiah 52:28–30). This figure most likely represents only adult males, suggesting that the actual number was closer to twenty thousand.[18] That is not very many Jews, certainly far fewer than those living in either Palestine, Syria, or Egypt.

On the surface it seems surprising that the force that would preserve the nation would come from so few people, even if they were the more elite, but here the second factor came into play. Conditions in Babylon contributed markedly to their success. Though the Jews did suffer some discomfort and instability (especially during the first few years of exile) and were not free to return to their homeland, they were not prisoners, either. Theirs was a kind of modified, somewhat benevolent, internment that allowed them to buy land, open shops, move into civil service, and attend to their many chores. Eventually many of them settled into a comfortable, if unconnected, lifestyle.[19] The historical writings of the Bible suggest that they developed communities of their own and prospered in peace.[20] The Babylonians allowed them to assemble and to carry out certain civil and religious duties among themselves.[21] Many Jews entered trade, and some became quite wealthy.[22] Facilitating that favorable internment would have been the Jewish administrators, such as Daniel, Shadrach, Meshach, and Abednego, who were moving up in the ranks of Babylonian government. By the year 531 B.C., Zerubbabel had risen to the position of cup bearer, second in command among the palace bureaucrats. Some of the Jewish leaders were in an excellent position both to assist the captives and to enhance their desire to return and restore their homeland and temple.

In all, the Jews in Babylon produced the capital and manpower necessary to do the work essential for the return. But other areas of Jewish settlement had all these things as well. What they lacked was the one thing the Babylonian Jews had uniquely: the prophets. The Jews taken captive to Babylon included not only the socially elite but the spiritually elite as well. This brings us to the third factor that helped these Jews keep alive the spirit of restoration. It was here—not in Palestine, Syria, Jordan, or Egypt—where God placed His prophets. From them came the explanation, the direction, and the impetus for the restoration of the whole community and the religion.[23]

Nevertheless, Judah's restoration, even with the prophetic push, did not transpire easily or automatically. It took a lot of soul-searching and a profound readjustment in her theological understanding to get things moving.[24] Yet the role played by the prophets must not be underestimated. Hindsight makes it easy for the modern reader to understand why Judah fell. But to many of the Jews living at the time, it was anything but clear. They questioned Jehovah's dealings with His people, and some felt betrayed.

Because of that, Judah's danger of apostatizing in Babylon was real and immediate. It may have been more acute here than anywhere else. Though the state and the religion of Judah emphasized the worship of Jehovah alone, insisting that all other gods were "no gods," Judah was never more than a step away from polytheism. Archaeological evidence seems quite convincing that the common people practiced a symbiotic religion, mixing elements of Jehovah worship with worship of the gods of the land.[25] The writings of the prophets show that the people felt justified in doing this and were sure they should receive Jehovah's blessings (see, for example, Hosea 9:9–10; Jeremiah 11:12–13).

The fall of Jerusalem did not immediately shatter those beliefs. Some felt that somehow Jehovah had failed them. When many of the Jews looked at what they considered Jehovah's broken promise, evidenced in the victory of Babylon, they might have wondered if Babylon's gods were not more real or at least more mighty than theirs.[26] To some it might have appeared that Jehovah was a petty god unable to protect even His petty state.

Others were not so willing to give credit to foreign gods. They felt Jehovah was responsible, but they questioned if He was really just. Many whined that their lot was unfounded and unfair.[27] Their attitude is perfectly reflected in the Book of Mormon, in the insistence of Laman and Lemuel that "we know that the people who were in the land of Jerusalem were a righteous people; for they kept the statutes and judgments of the Lord, and all his commandments, according to the law of Moses; wherefore, we know that they are a righteous people" (1 Nephi 17:22). Nothing could have been further from the truth, but the attitude displayed by these two ruthless brothers was popular in Judah as well. The prophet Habakkuk's willingness to question God's justness in using Babylon as His tool to chastise Judah underscores how pervasive the feeling was (see Habakkuk 1:1–17).

A third group, those who believed in the words of the prophets, feared that Judah had committed a mortal sin for which she could never be forgiven. As a result of this sin, she had lost her place as the covenant people as well as her homeland.[28] The Jews cried to their God for mercy but seemingly without hope. They knew that Jerusalem's "gates are sunk into the ground; he [God] hath destroyed and broken her bars: her king and her princes are among the Gentiles: the law is no more; her prophets also find no vision [of hope] from the Lord" (Lamentations 2:9). Even for the faithful, the future appeared hopeless.

As a result, wholesale abandonment of Jehovah and His word threatened the Jews; the seductive power of Babylon compounded the problem. Jerusalem, seen through the eyes of parochialism, had seemed strong, beautiful, and mighty. Now, more cosmopolitan eyes, having looked upon the strength and splendor of Babylon and all she had to offer, saw Jerusalem as small, dingy, weak, and unsophisticated. Judah could neither ignore nor forget what had happened. She was forced to clarify her position in relation to the national tragedy and Babylon and its gods. The only other alternative was to perish.[29]

On the positive side, the captivity did deal a mortal blow to the dogma propagated by such false prophets as Hananiah and others. This false doctrine was based on two misconceptions. The first was the belief that Jehovah would never allow His temple to fall. Just what precedents caused the people to believe and the false prophets to propagate this idea are unknown, but the common proverb was "The temple of the Lord, The temple of the Lord, The temple of the Lord, are these" (Jeremiah 7:4), meaning that as long as the temple stood, God would protect the people. Jeremiah castigated the Jews for believing "in lying words, that cannot profit. Will ye steal, murder, and commit adultery, and swear falsely, and burn incense unto Baal, and walk after other gods whom ye know not," asked his God, "and come and stand before me in this house, which is called by my name, and say, We are delivered to do all these abominations?" (Jeremiah 7:8–10).

It would not work, the Lord testified, and urged them to go to "Shiloh, where I set my name at the first, and see what I did to it for the wickedness of my people Israel" (Jeremiah 7:12). Judah should have understood the idiocy of the position taken by these pseudoprophets, for Shiloh, the chief sanctuary of Jehovah for centuries, now lay in ruins. Their own hymn mourned the extent of that loss, saying that God "forsook the tabernacle of Shiloh, the tent which he placed among men; and delivered his strength into captivity, and his glory into the enemy's hand. He gave his people over also unto the sword; and was wroth with his inheritance. The fire consumed their young men; and their maidens were not given to marriage. Their priests fell by the sword; and their widows made no lamentation" (Psalm 78:60–64). Still, few seem to have gotten the message, and its echoes must have haunted those in Babylon.

The second misconception lay in the false belief that God would uphold the Davidic dynasty no matter what. Here we can see how the Jews came to believe this idea. Nathan, the prophet, had told David that "thine house and thy kingdom shall be established for ever before thee: thy throne shall be established for ever" (2 Samuel 7:16). David himself exulted that Jehovah "hath made with me an everlasting covenant, ordered in all things, and sure: for this is all my salvation, and all my desire" (2 Samuel 23:5).[30] The theology quickly developed that each king, as Jehovah's anointed "son" (Psalm 2:7–11), would be protected from his foes and lead Israel to an ever-expanding kingdom (see, for example, Psalm 72:8–11).

As Jeremiah had worked to redirect Israel's thinking about the temple, Micah had earlier tried to make a course correction concerning God's covenant with her princes. He stated in no uncertain terms that he had full authority to "declare unto Jacob his transgression, and to Israel his sin. Hear this, I pray you, ye heads of the house of Jacob, and princes of the house of Israel, that abhor judgment, and pervert all equity. They build up Zion with blood, and Jerusalem with iniquity. The heads thereof judge for reward, and the priests thereof teach for hire, and the prophets thereof divine for money: yet will they lean upon the Lord, and say, Is not the Lord among us? none evil can come upon us. Therefore shall Zion for your sake be plowed as a field, and Jerusalem shall become heaps, and the mountain of the house as the high places of the forest" (Micah 3:8–12).

Micah did not stand alone in his testimony. Isaiah also assailed the nobles, judges, and priests for their unscrupulous willingness to rob from the poor and defenseless. God would not allow prince, priest, or prophet to lead Judah astray without severe consequences. Indeed, Judah, with all her seeming splendor, would fall.[31]

But Judah ignored these clear warnings. The false dogma proved too intoxicating because of the acute sense of security it offered. It further allowed Judah to reject Jehovah's laws and His true prophets and foolishly believe that the scion of David's line—the Messiah— would soon come and establish His world-embracing kingdom over which the Jews would triumphantly rule.

Babylonian battering rams destroyed that belief as surely and completely as they breached Jerusalem's walls. Those who had put trust in it now found their spiritual lives in peril, much as their ancestors' physical lives had been in danger under the Egyptian pharaohs. What Judah desperately needed was another Moses to lead her out of the way not of physical harm but of spiritual harm. And she had one in the form of the prophets.

Judaism in Babylon survived because of three interconnected phenomena. First, the spiritually weak apostatized, leaving the ranks of the faithful more pure and determined; second, the spiritually strong repented and became more orthodox; and, finally, those who remained in the faith began to listen with hearing ears to the voices of the prophets. They quickly found that these inspired men had answered and continued to answer Judah's most pressing questions. The prophets carefully and fully identified her problems and gave counsel on how to correct them, promising that the people could once again return to God's covenant and the land tied thereto.

Through the prophets, Judah became convinced that God's judgment had been righteous and well deserved.[32] Her job was to repent; then God would restore the covenant. Hosea's gracious act of taking to himself a wife who had turned to prostitution (see Hosea 1:1–2:23) must have given the Jews comfort and hope. The prophets' love, mirroring that of Jehovah for Judah, testified that God would gladly welcome back the penitent with full forgiveness.

The prophets did not underplay the tragedy that had occurred. Nonetheless, they offered hope in Jehovah's redemptive purpose. Judah would not stay in captivity. She was but a stranger in a strange land, a sojourner in a foreign country from which she would eventually be released. Jeremiah even supplied the parameters of her stay, promising Judah that she would "serve the king of Babylon seventy years. And it shall come to pass, when seventy years are accomplished, that I [God] will punish the king of Babylon, and that nation, saith the Lord, for their iniquity, and the land of the Chaldeans, and will make it perpetual desolations" (Jeremiah 25:11–12). Therefore, Judah's challenge was to make sure that she did not become integrated into the culture of this foreign land or she might forget her true home and temple.

An important task of the prophets was to assure Judah that, even in Babylon, Jehovah was with her. They did that by reinforcing the idea that Jehovah governed and controlled the destiny of all nations, including Babylon. Here the writings of Daniel were particularly poignant. The historical portion of his work contains two stories that bear directly on the point.[33] The first dealt with Nebuchadnezzar's dream of the great image. The important point of the story was not only that Daniel interpreted the king's dream but also that he had the ability to do it. The story really plays upon the latter point. The king insisted that his auditors, consisting of many of his wise men, astrologers, magicians, and soothsayers,[34] tell him the dream before they interpreted it, as insurance that their interpretation was true. His demand brought forth the excuse that "there is none other that can shew it before the king, except the gods, whose dwelling is not with flesh" (Daniel 2:11). Here the Babylonian priests admit that they could not get in contact with their own local gods on such matters. Daniel, however, was able to tell the king the dream because his God, who possessed both wisdom and might, also "giveth wisdom unto the wise, and knowledge to them that know understanding: he revealeth the deep and secret things: he knoweth what is in the darkness, and the light dwelleth with him" (Daniel 2:21–22). The irony is important; the response of the Babylonian wise men underscores their belief that their own gods were distant and impersonal, while Daniel's shows that Jehovah, even in Babylon, was immediate and personal.

So that his readers would not miss the point, Daniel further testified that Jehovah was also the one who "changeth the times and the seasons: he removeth kings, and setteth up kings" (Daniel 2:21). Nebuchadnezzar's dream emphasized the last point. It was Jehovah who chose Nebuchadnezzar to be king and who would set up all the kingdoms to follow until God's own eternal kingdom overmastered and ruled the rest (see Daniel 2:36–45).

Daniel's second point, showing that the Lord governed Babylon, centered on Jehovah's work in convincing its kings that He was the living God. We see the progression in four events. The first, already noted, was Daniel's ability to tell Nebuchadnezzar both his dream and its meaning. Daniel ascribed the power to "the God of heaven" (Daniel 2:19, 44). The Jews used this term to designate the almighty and true God.[35] The point Daniel may have been making with the king is that the prophet's God overmastered the whole heaven, including the stars that the Babylonians worshipped as symbols of their gods. As a result, the king concluded that "your God is a God of gods, and a Lord of kings, and a revealer of secrets, seeing thou couldest reveal this secret" (Daniel 2:47). We see in this admission the king allowing Jehovah a place among the pantheon of Babylonian gods and even according Him the special place as revealer. But to have the Lord as one among the many gods would not do, so Jehovah instituted the next step.

The king set up an idol and wanted all to worship it. When Shadrach, Meshach, and Abednego refused, he ordered them burned (see Daniel 3:13–22). When they emerged from the fire, not only unharmed but not even smelling of smoke, the king exclaimed, "There is no other God that can deliver after this sort" (Daniel 3:29). Jehovah had definitely climbed a few more rungs up the ladder of the pantheon. Still, that was not far enough. The next event would push His position all the way to the top.

The king again had a dream that Daniel interpreted. The king, according to the revelation, would go mad for seven years, "till thou know that the most High ruleth in the kingdom of men, and giveth it to whomsoever he will" (Daniel 4:25). Nebuchadnezzar may rule over Babylon and its temples, but Jehovah ruled over him. The malady struck that very hour.[36] Then, as the record reports, "at the end of the days I Nebuchadnezzar lifted up mine eyes unto heaven, and mine understanding returned unto me, and I blessed the most High, and I praised and honoured him that liveth for ever, whose dominion is an everlasting dominion, and his kingdom is from generation to generation" (Daniel 4:34). It is hard to know from the text if Nebuchadnezzar moved from polytheism to henotheism or monotheism. One thing is sure: he reckoned Jehovah as "the King of heaven, all whose works are truth, and his ways judgment: and those that walk in pride he is able to abase" (Daniel 4:37).

Darius took the last step, which occurred when Daniel's enemies tricked the king into throwing Daniel into the lions' den. The king confessed his belief that Daniel's God could save him (see Daniel 6:16). When He did, Darius made a decree commanding, "That in every dominion of my kingdom men tremble and fear before the God of Daniel: for he is the living God, and stedfast for ever, and his kingdom that which shall not be destroyed, and his dominion shall be even unto the end" (Daniel 6:26). Jehovah no longer stood as one of the many gods nor as the head of the gods: He was *the* living God whose kingdom and dominion were everlasting.

It would be helpful to know when Daniel, or an editor, composed and circulated his works. Because his record does not conclude until the reign of Cyrus the Persian, the book as we know it probably did not come into being until the Jews either had departed or were preparing to depart for the land of Judea. But because Daniel was a high official—second only to the king some of the time, according to the record (see Daniel 6:1–3)—his teachings and experiences should have been well known to his fellow Jews. If that is the case, his testimony would have reinforced the idea that God was with them and directing the affairs not only of Babylon but also of all nations through time. Further, it promised the Jews that even in Babylon, Jehovah could and did sustain and protect those who remained true to the faith.

We are on firmer ground dating the work of Jeremiah. His prophecies were written down throughout his long ministry, beginning under the reign of Josiah (626–608 B.C.) and concluding after Zedekiah's fall in 586 B.C. Though his messages made him unpopular with some of the most influential and powerful people in Jerusalem, to the point where he was incarcerated and persecuted, others, in addition to his scribe Baruch, were carefully recording and preserving them.[37]

Jeremiah was of the priestly house. He lived in the village of Anathoth, about three miles north of the Jerusalem temple. Shortly before 608 B.C., his fearless voice rang out in clear warning. To the Jews who gathered for worship, he warned:

The Lord said unto me, Proclaim all these words in the cities of Judah, and in the streets of Jerusalem, saying, Hear ye the words of this covenant, and do them.

For I earnestly protested unto your fathers in the day that I brought them up out of the land of Egypt, even unto this day, rising early and protesting, saying, Obey my voice.

Yet they obeyed not, nor inclined their ear, but walked every one in the imagination of their evil heart: therefore I will bring upon them all the words of this covenant, which I commanded them to do; but they did them not.

And the Lord said unto me, A conspiracy is found among the men of Judah, and among the inhabitants of Jerusalem.

They are turned back to the iniquities of their forefathers, which refused to hear my words; and they went after other gods to serve them: the house of Israel and the house of Judah have broken my covenant which I made with their fathers.

Therefore thus saith the Lord, Behold, I will bring evil upon them, which they shall not be able to escape; and though they shall cry unto me, I will not hearken unto them. (Jeremiah 11:6–11)

The warning was clear: Judah must repent and follow her God or the coming evil would bring her great suffering. But she would come to repentance, he warned, one way or another. If she would not do it on her own, then "thine own wickedness shall correct thee, and thy backslidings shall reprove thee" (Jeremiah 2:19). The evil agent, He warned, already gathering to the north, was ready to move against this vile and sinful nation. The agent of destruction, the Lord warned, "is a mighty nation, it is an ancient nation, a nation whose language thou knowest not, neither understandest what they say. . . . And they shall eat up thine harvest, and thy bread, which thy sons and thy daughters should eat: they shall eat up thy flocks and thine herds: they shall eat up thy vines and thy fig trees: they shall impoverish thy fenced cities, wherein thou trustedst, with the sword" (Jeremiah 5:15–17; see also 2:16; 4:5–8, 11–17; 6:22–26). When the destruction came, the Jews would lament, "The Lord our God has put us to silence, and given us water of gall to drink, because we have sinned against the Lord" (Jeremiah 8:14).

Jeremiah did not deny the validity of the Davidic covenant in which so many trusted; however, he pushed it into the future and made its realization contingent on the righteousness of the people (see Jeremiah 23:5–8). For now, he warned David's heir, "Execute ye judgment and righteousness, and deliver the spoiled out of the hand of the oppressor: and do not wrong, do no violence to the stranger, the fatherless, nor the widow, neither shed innocent blood in this place. . . . But if ye will not hear these words, I swear by myself, saith the Lord, that this house shall become a desolation" (Jeremiah 22:3–5).

Jeremiah's message must have haunted those captives on the way to Babylon who had heard and spurned it. Yet it still took them some time before they accepted it and were finally healed by it. This spiritual balm of Gilead, once applied, worked upon the captives and those living in Judah and elsewhere. The message made sense and found reinforcement in other scriptures. But the powerful voice of another prophet backed up Jeremiah and acted to fulfill the divine law of witnesses:[38] Ezekiel.

Like Jeremiah, Ezekiel was a priest (see Ezekiel 1:3). That explains in part why he became one of Nebuchadnezzar's many hostages, the Babylonians concentrating on children of the gentry, clergy, and aristocracy. His captors would have taken him into Babylon about 597 B.C. with a group of Jewish exiles deported about a decade before Jerusalem was destroyed.[39] Because Jeremiah had been prophesying for more than ten years by that time, it is very likely that Ezekiel would have heard his testimony and caught the same fire. God called him to carry the message into the streets of the Babylonian captives as Jeremiah did in the streets of Jerusalem.

He used the prophetic *'ot,* rather exaggerated symbolic acts, as the means of drawing attention to his message. Among other things, he symbolized the coming fate of Jerusalem by drawing a picture of the city on a brick and then, while eating rationed foods, simulating a siege against it (see Ezekiel 4:1–15).

A little later, he shaved off his hair and beard. That act alone, especially shaving his beard, would have brought him a great deal of attention. Men in both the Babylonian and the Jewish cultures wore beards, and the Jews viewed them as a sign of adult male vitality and glory.[40] The prophet's clean-shaven face would have startled those who viewed it. But they would have sensed his message, for the shaved beard symbolized a radical change in the state of affairs.[41] He did not leave his audience guessing as to which way affairs were going to change. One-third of his hair he burned with fire, another he hacked with the sword, and the last he scattered to the wind. He did retain a few strands, which he tied to the hem of his robe (see Ezekiel 5:1–5).

This ritual act he followed with a stern warning. "This is Jerusalem," he explained, and because "she hath changed my [that is, God's] judgments into wickedness more than the nations," God "will execute judgments in the midst of thee in the sight of the nations." The judgment would be horrible, for "fathers shall eat the sons in the midst of thee and the sons shall eat their fathers; and I [God] will execute judgments in thee, and the whole remnant of thee will I scatter into all the winds." Underscoring the reason for such severe judgment, the Lord chastised, "Surely, because thou hast defiled my sanctuary with all thy detestable things, and with all thine abominations, therefore will I also diminish thee; neither shall mine eye spare, neither will I have any pity" (Ezekiel 5:5–7, 9–11).

Ezekiel clearly preached against the idea that the temple alone would save the people. He recounted a vision in which he saw the Lord's Spirit lift from the sanctuary, hover over the temple for a moment, and then depart to the east (see Ezekiel 9:8; 10:18; 11:23). His message was both clear and simple: It was not the temple but righteousness that would be Judah's only shield. Where there was no righteousness, there was no hope.

Ezekiel's words stung the Jews of the captivity, but they refused, at least initially, to respond. Jehovah castigated them because "they hear thy words, but they do them not." But they would soon learn a stern lesson, for "when this [the fall of Jerusalem] cometh to pass (lo, it will come,) then shall they know that a prophet hath been among them" (Ezekiel 33:32–33).

Not many months later, the captive Jews received a startling witness that they, indeed, had a prophet among them. An escapee from the siege of Jerusalem was able to make his way to the captives and testify, "The city is smitten" (Ezekiel 33:21). The shock of that testimony and, a short time later, the confirmation by several thousand refugees moving into the area, stirred the Jews to listen to Ezekiel. He assured them that God took no pleasure in His people's pain but that it was the only way He could get Judah to turn from her wicked ways (see Ezekiel 33:11). Ezekiel moved to allay their fears with as much energy as he had used to provoke their righteousness.

Again his voice was not alone. Former and present prophets continually assured the people that there would be a homecoming. Even the most dire prophecies were tempered by the assurance that Zion would be delivered, God's temple would stand again, and Israel would be restored (note particularly Jeremiah 32:6–15). Ezekiel's famous vision of the dry bones testified to not only the eventual resurrection of Israel but also the more immediate restoration of Judah:

> Then he said unto me, Son of man, these bones are the whole house of Israel: behold, they say, Our bones are dried, and our hope is lost: we are cut off for our parts.
>
> Therefore prophesy and say unto them, Thus saith the Lord God; Behold, O my people, I will open your graves, and cause you to come up out of your graves, and bring you into the land of Israel.
>
> And ye shall know that I am the Lord, when I have opened your graves, O my people, and brought you up out of your graves, and shall put my spirit in you, and ye shall live, *and I shall place you in your own land:* then shall ye know that I the Lord have spoken it, and performed it, saith the Lord. (Ezekiel 37:11–14; emphasis added)

God commanded Ezekiel to "take thee one stick, and write upon it, For Judah, and for the children of Israel his companions: then take another stick, and write upon it, For Joseph, the stick of Ephraim, and for all the house of Israel his companions" to show that the whole house of Israel, not just Judah, would be restored (Ezekiel 37:16). Therefore, the Lord said:

> Join them one to another into one stick; and they shall become one in thine hand.
>
> And when the children of thy people shall speak unto thee, saying, Wilt thou not shew us what thou meanest by these?
>
> Say unto them, Thus saith the Lord God; Behold, I will take the stick of Joseph, which is in the hand of Ephraim, and the tribes of Israel his fellows, and will put them with him, even

with the stick of Judah, and make them one stick, and they shall be one in mine hand.

And the sticks whereon thou writest shall be in thine hand before their eyes.

And say unto them, Thus saith the Lord God; Behold, *I will take the children of Israel from among the heathen,* whither they be gone, and will gather them on every side, *and bring them into their own land.* (Ezekiel 37:17–21; emphasis added)

Though this scripture looks to the last days, it had immediate application to Judah's return from captivity. Ezekiel's commission to join together the sticks—or better, writing tablets—became a harbinger of the restoration of all Israel. As Latter-day Saints we understand that the passage referred to the Book of Mormon and the Bible. The captive Jews, however, would have seen it as a plea to accept the message of the prophets of the north (for example, Amos, Hosea, and Isaiah) combined with those of the south (for example, Micah, Jeremiah, and Habakkuk) that Jehovah reigned and would see that His people returned.

Once Judah began to look, the scriptural evidence of her restoration must have been very reassuring. Further, the scriptures even outlined the events that would lead to her return. Isaiah foresaw the fall of her captor Babylon and the coming of her Median liberator, Cyrus.[42] Jehovah's doleful words promised Babylon a tragic end: "I will stir up the Medes against them, which shall not regard silver; and as for gold, they shall not delight in it. Their bows also shall dash the young men to pieces; and they shall have no pity on the fruit of the womb; their eye shall not spare children. And Babylon, the glory of kingdoms, the beauty of the Chaldees' excellency, shall be as when God overthrew Sodom and Gomorrah" (Isaiah 13:17–19).

The reaction of the exiles after the fall of Jerusalem to the promises of deliverance and restoration brought to the prophets all they could have hoped for. The people confessed their sins and turned to their Lord. Solomon's inspired prayer had seen them "repent, and make supplication unto thee [Jehovah] in the land of them that carried them captives, saying, We have sinned, and have done perversely, we have committed wickedness" (1 Kings 8:47). Then would they "return unto thee with all their heart, and with all their soul, in the land of their enemies, which led them away captive, and pray unto thee toward their land, which thou gavest their fathers" (1 Kings 8:48). Isaiah quoted their prayer for restoration. They would ask the Lord to "return for thy servants' sake, the tribes of thine inheritance. The people of thy holiness have possessed it but a little while: our adversaries have trodden down thy sanctuary. We are thine: thou never barest rule over them; they were not called by thy name" (Isaiah 63:17–19). To their prayer the Lord would respond, "I will bring forth a seed out of Jacob, and out of Judah an inheritor of my mountains: and mine elect shall inherit it, and my servants shall dwell there" (Isaiah 65:9).

The promise seemed sure. Judah's job was to turn to her God with full purpose of heart and the reward would come. Yet there was tension between those who desired to establish the new nation on the basis of its old Davidic theology (see Ezekiel 34:23–27; 37:24) and those with the grander vision of an idealized confederation based on the old pattern of the tribal league. These saw the nation presided over by the Zadokite priesthood with the restored Davidic monarchy playing the reduced role of protector of the state and the religion[43] (see Ezekiel 43–45; especially 43:1–7; 44:4–31). The difference of opinion, however, could not be resolved while the Jews were in Babylon, but it does illustrate their growing faith in the prophecies. They hoped that they would have the opportunity to create a distinctly Jewish society in the land of Palestine.

The promises of the scriptures and the hope that they generated moved Judah to place high value upon them. She began to prize God's law as the means of salvation in both a temporal and a spiritual sense. As a result, she embarked upon a kind of "operation salvage," collecting, editing, compiling, and copying the Law and the Prophets. Details are unknown of how the Jews proceeded, but the movement was unstoppable once it began.[44] How the Jews in Babylon happened to have quite a collection of scriptures remains somewhat of a mystery. The Book of Mormon indicates that an extensive collection was kept by one of Jerusalem's generals (see 1 Nephi 3:3; 5:10). We don't know if other copies existed, but it seems reasonable that there were other collections as well as individual pieces treasured by their owners. The wealth of source material in the Bible, especially the historical records and writings of the early prophets, suggests that the records were composed in Jerusalem well before 587 B.C.[45] Many of these records may have been taken to Babylon by various hostages, especially those of priestly and royal rank, and finally, by the last deportees. At any rate, the Jews in Babylon were able to collect and begin to duplicate a large number of scriptures, further evidence of their growing trust in God's word through His prophets.

Thus, while the Jews were still in captivity, the voice of their former and present prophets provided the answers to Judah's questions and gave her hope and direction for the future. Under their auspices, she was able to keep her integrity in Babylon and prepare for the realization of the blessings of her restoration. In the meantime, the prophets gave her a role to play even in Babylon. They allowed her to see herself as the servant of Jehovah responsible for carrying His law to later generations. By encouraging Judah to see herself in this role, the prophets gave a most profound interpretation to both her present distress and her eventual destiny.[46] By doing so, they gave meaning to the whole and reinforced the need for total loyalty to her God. This bound the people to a common ideal and kept many of them from becoming lost in Babylon. When proper circumstances arose, she had the will and determination to appeal to her captors for her freedom. Under the guidance of her leaders, she returned home and began to rebuild her national identity.

NOTES

1. John Bright, *A History of Israel,* 3rd ed. (Philadelphia: Westminster Press, 1981), 343.

2. Such has been done by Charles C. Torrey, *The Chronicler's History of Israel* (New Haven, CT: Yale University Press, 1954).

3. H. H. Ben-Sasson, *A History of the Jewish People* (Cambridge: Harvard University Press, 1976), 160.

4. Cecil Roth, *A History of the Jews* (New York: Shocken Books, 1970), 57–60.

5. Bright, *History of Israel,* 343.

6. Epigraphic sources for the sixth and fifth centuries are meager. Even so, a fairly clear picture can be drawn from Jeremiah, Daniel, Ezekiel, 2 Kings, 2 Chronicles, Ezra, Nehemiah, Esther, 1 Esdras, the postexilic prophetic books, and the few extrabiblical sources that exist.

7. On the extensive damage done to Jerusalem, see Kathleen M. Kenyon, *Jerusalem* (London: Thames and Hudson, 1967), 78–104.

Jerusalem was completely pillaged and much was destroyed, but little of it, including the temple mount, was actually leveled. Until 1925, scholars did not realize the extent of the catastrophe. Archaeology has shown that the Babylonians razed virtually every fortified town in Judea (see Hugh Nibley, *Lehi in the Desert/The World of the Jaredites/There Were Jaredites*, ed. John W. Welch [Salt Lake City: Deseret Book, 1988], 9–10).

8. Amihai Mazar, *Archaeology of the Land of the Bible, 10,000–586 B.C.* (New York: Doubleday, 1990), 548–50.

9. See Ezekiel 33:24–29 in light of Isaiah 57:3–13; 65:1, 11, for example.

10. Peter R. Ackroyd, *Exile and Restoration: A Study of Hebrew Thought of the Sixth Century B.C.* (Philadelphia: Westminster Press, 1968), 18–25; Bright, *History of Israel*, 345.

11. See Hosea 4:6, 12–13; 8:11, for examples. Less devout and more ignorant Jews moving into the area would likely have been influenced by them. These areas also contained non-Israelites, many of whom had been moved here by the Assyrians in the late 700s (see 2 Kings 17).

12. Bright, *History of Israel*, 345.

13. Ben-Sasson, *History of the Jewish People*, 160–61.

14. James B. Pritchard, *Ancient Near Eastern Texts Relating to the Old Testament*, 3rd ed. (Princeton, NJ: Princeton University Press, 1969), 491–92.

15. Ben-Sasson, *History of the Jewish People*, 161–62; Ackroyd, *Exile and Restoration*, 20–23.

16. Bright, *History of Israel*, 346–47.

17. Bright, *History of Israel*, 347. On the demise of the Philistines, see *The Anchor Bible Dictionary*, ed. David Noel Freedman (New York: Doubleday, 1992), s.v. "Philistines."

18. See Ackroyd, *Exile*, 20–23; Ezra Janssen, "Judah in der Exilszeit," *Forschungen zur Religion und Literatur des Alten und Neuen Testaments* (Göttengen: Vandenhoeck and Ruprecht, 1956), 25–39, for further discussion and source material.

19. Adolf Alt, *Kleine Schriften zur Geschichte des Volkes Israel* (Munich: C. H. Beck'she Verlagsbuchhantlung, 1953–59), 2:326, argues persuasively that the Babylonians placed the Jews under a very different internment than that used by the Assyrians.

20. See Ezra 3:15; 2:59; 8:17; Jeremiah 29:5–7, for example.

21. See Ezekiel 8:1; 14:1; 33:30, for examples.

22. Bright, *History of Israel*, 346.

23. Bright, *History of Israel*, 345.

24. Ben-Sasson, *History of the Jewish People,* 163–64; Bright, *History of Israel,* 347. For a discussion of the whole issue, see David Noel Freedman, "Son of Man, Can These Bones Live?" *Interpretation,* 29 (1975): 171–86.

25. Mazar, *Archaeology,* 348–52.

26. Jeremiah 44:15–19 and Ezekiel 20:32 show how acutely some Jews were tempted to leave the old faith (see also Bright, *History of Israel,* 347).

27. See, for example, Ezekiel 18:2, 25; Lamentations 5:7.

28. Isaiah 63:19 reflects the idea that the covenant could be lost, and Ezekiel 33:10; 37:11 shows that some of the Jews were really concerned about it.

29. Bright, *History of Israel,* 348.

30. The same idea is expressed in a number of the hymns. See, for example, Psalms 2; 18; 20; 21; 45; 72; 89; 101; 110; and 132. For discussion on the development of the kingship theology within Israel, see Hans J. Kraus, *Worship in Israel: A Cultic History of the Old Testament* (Richmond: John Knox Press, 1966); R. E. Clements, *Abraham and David: Genesis XV and Its Meaning for Israelite Tradition* (London: SCM Press, 1967), 4–96; and Bright, *History,* 224–25, 289–98.

31. See, for example, Isaiah 1:21–23; 3:13; 5:8, 23; 10:1.

32. Bright, *History of Israel,* 349.

33. Because the apocalyptic portion has been sealed (see Daniel 12:4, 9) and no prophet of the Restoration has opened it, much that is there remains a mystery. As a result, it requires too much speculation to be of worth for the purposes of this paper.

34. The Aramaic word designated "magicians" but would have included all those claiming ability to understand mysteries. Though Daniel would not have been viewed as a magician, he would have been viewed as one with powers of God and therefore would have been caught in the king's net.

35. The title designated the high place of Jehovah and stressed His rank above all things (see Genesis 24:7; Ezra 1:2; 6:10; Nehemiah 1:5; 2:4; Psalm 136:26).

36. Nabonidus may have suffered also from a period of madness. A fragment from Qumran shows that a Jewish tradition existed ascribing his long absence from Babylon to mental illness as a vengeance which came upon him from God (see Joan Oates, *Babylon* [London: Thames and Hudson, 1979], 133).

37. The Book of Mormon suggests there were record keepers in charge of preserving prophecies among the people. The brass plates, taken by Nephi from Laban, contained "prophecies of the holy prophets,

from the beginning even down to the commencement of the reign of Zedekiah; and also many of the prophecies which have been spoken by the mouth of Jeremiah" (1 Nephi 5:12). Because Jeremiah continued to prophesy for some time after 600 B.C., someone was collecting and recording his prophecies while they were being given.

38. See the biblical instruction in Deuteronomy 17:6 and in Matthew 18:16.

39. Because of Ezekiel's call while he was in Babylon about 593, some date his captivity to that point; however, the Babylonians took quite a few of the priestly families captive five years earlier. That seems the better date (see Harold H. Rowley, "The Book of Ezekiel in Modern Study," *Men of God* [London: T. Nelson, 1963], 169–210).

40. In most ancient Near Eastern languages, the word describing an adult male was a cognate of the word for beard (see *The New Bible Dictionary,* ed. J. D. Douglas [Grand Rapids, Mich.: Eerdmans, 1962], s.v. "Beard").

41. Merrill C. Tenney, *The Zondervan Pictorial Encyclopedia of the Bible* (Grand Rapids, MI: Zondervan, 1976), s.v. "Beard."

42. Isaiah 44:28; 45:1 mentions Cyrus by name.

43. See Martin North, *The Law in the Pentateuch and Other Studies* (Philadelphia: Fortress Press, 1967), 67–70.

44. Bright, *History of Israel,* 350. Note 2 Kings 25:27–30, which had to be added to the text by the Babylonian Jews. The addition shows that the Jews were actively working on their records during the captivity.

45. Martin North, *Üuml-berlieferungsgeschichtliche Studien I* (Halle, Germany: M. Niemeyer, 1943), argues that material had been written down from at least the tenth century and that more than one collection existed between 622 and 587. See that study for sources and background material.

46. H. H. Rowley, *The Servant of the Lord and Other Essays,* rev. ed. (Oxford: Blackwells, 1965), 1–60, has completed an excellent study on this motif and its effects on the Jews of the captivity and afterward.

CHAPTER EIGHTEEN

"Hast Thou Considered My Servant Job?"

JOHN S. TANNER

"Hast thou considered my servant Job, that there is none like him?" the Lord asked Satan (Job 2:3). The same question might well be rephrased to us: "Have you considered the book of Job? There is none like it." None indeed. Job is a unique book: uniquely disturbing and uniquely empowered to deepen our faith. Both its answers and its questions about the problem of suffering help clarify gospel truths and are themselves illuminated by the Restoration's light. Well should Latter-day Saints consider the Lord's servant Job—consider him often and well.

If you are like me, you can scarcely keep your mind off Job. His trials come to my mind almost daily as I read or hear or experience fresh instances of unaccountable misery—especially the suffering of innocent victims. The book of Job is as timely as today's headlines telling of blameless children starving in the Sudan or beaten, raped, and murdered in Midvale. It is as timeless as the cry of the widow and the fatherless, whose collected tears over the course of world history would fill a great sea of grief. When life forces us "to feel what wretches feel" (*King Lear* 3.4.34), the book of Job stands as a permanent scriptural referent for our anguish. This power to sensitize us to suffering is alone reason enough to "consider Job," long and hard. For in our quest to become more compassionate disciples of Him who "hath borne our griefs, and carried our sorrows" (Isaiah 53:4), it

John S. Tanner is academic vice president at Brigham Young University.

266

is good for us, like Him, to be "touched with the feeling of [others'] infirmities" (Hebrews 4:15).

No book in the Bible touches us quite like Job. That its power has been universally felt is evident by the countless references to Job from a chorus of sensitive voices over thousands of years: Augustine, Calvin, Kierkegaard, Kant, and Jung; Bacon, Blake, Pascal, Montesquieu, Milton, Melville, Dostoyevsky, and Goethe. These readers and many more, both great and small, have all, after their fashion, considered Job. Civilization's wrestle with Job, no less than Jacob's wrestle with the angel, has left the Judeo-Christian world forever changed. Even today, the book of Job frames the terms of discussion for certain fundamental and permanent questions with which every generation of believers must grapple.

IS JOB HISTORY OR STORY?

One question with which many readers grapple as they consider Job is its historicity: Is the book of Job history or story? Personally, I am not persuaded that the answer to this question makes much decisive difference for the interpretation of the text. My own way of dealing with the question, however, is to adopt a compromise position. In the absence of clear pronouncements by scripture or Church leaders to the contrary, I accept the fact of Job's existence. At the same time, I recognize that the text bears the marks of evident literary fashioning. It has, for instance, a definite three-part structure consisting of prose prologue, poetic dialogues, and prose epilogue. A prose frame thus encloses poetic dialogues. Its central poetic dialogues, moreover, are further neatly divided into three cycles of speeches, alternating between Job and each of his three comforters. I cannot conceive of these long, formal passages of poetry being transcribed *verbatim* from actual conversations. They are clearly literary constructions.

This does not mean, however, that Job is pure fiction. Both the prose narrative frames and the poetic dialogues may be based on the actual experiences of a real man—a good man who lost everything, was pressured to confess to hidden sins but maintained his integrity, implored God for answers and vindication, and finally received revelation and renewed prosperity. I personally think of the book as mixing both fact and fable. Some elements seem fabulous to me (e.g., the wager between God and Satan, the neatly symmetrical doubling of Job's wealth at the end). But elements of fable do not prove that the entire text is fictional, any more than the existence of an actual king named Macbeth is disproved by the fabulous features of Shakespeare's play. There may be much more fact behind even patently literary texts than moderns sometimes suppose. For many years scholars thought the city of Troy to be a fiction and ridiculed Schliemann when he went to dig for Homer's "fabled" Troy—until he found it.[1] We need to be skeptical of our own modern skepticism.

Nevertheless, the book of Job does not make as strong a claim to historicity as do most biblical texts. For example, all we learn of Job's background is that he hails from the land of Uz—a region of uncertain identification and, consequently, no geopolitical consequence in the narrative. Apparently not an Israelite but a foreigner, Job is not given a genealogy, causing the Babylonian Talmud and later Maimonides to speculate that Job is a parable.[2] The tradition appears uncertain as to Job's relation to historical books; this is indicated in the way it has been grouped at different times with various different Old Testament books. The book of Job has, however, always been accepted in the canon.[3]

Modern scholars classify the book of Job as wisdom literature (or *hokmah),* in concert with Proverbs and Ecclesiastes in the Bible, and with Ecclesiasticus (a.k.a. the Wisdom of Jesus Ben Sirach) in the Apocrypha.[4] Unlike prophetic and historical biblical texts, wisdom texts are less concerned with the unfolding history of a covenant people through time than they are with the timeless truths of the individual's relationship to moral and religious principles. Wisdom literature, moreover, belongs to an international movement. Egyptian and Babylonian sages also composed prudential maxims (such as Proverbs) and skeptical reflections on life (such as Ecclesiastes). There also exist Babylonian and Egyptian dialogues about suicide and divine justice similar to those in the book of Job.[5] In short, Job seems not to lay the same claim to historicity as do, say, the great patriarchs or Israel's kings and prophets; in addition, the text bears the marks of a historical genre or literary type known as wisdom literature.

Conceding all these reasons to be cautious about Job's historicity, we still ought not dismiss him out of hand as fictional. For we recall that Job is referred to three times in other scriptures: first in the Old Testament (see Ezekiel 14:14), then in the New Testament (see James 5:11), and last in the Doctrine and Covenants (see D&C 121:10). (No mention of Job is made in either the Book of Mormon or the Pearl of Great Price.) The extratextual references that do occur in scripture, it should be noted, underscore the following specific details from the text: that Job was righteous (see Ezekiel 14:14); that Job was "patient," which might better be translated "steadfast" (see James 5:11); and that Job suffered and was accused by his friends of evil (see D&C 121:10). None of these allusions absolutely guarantees the historicity of all the text's details; none, for example, makes reference to a wager with the adversary. Nor do they even necessarily confirm Job's historical existence, for in principle it is possible to allude to the patience or sufferings of Job *without* his being a real character, just as we might to the beauty of Adonis or the agony of King Lear.[6] Still, these extratextual references to Job ought to make Latter-day Saints hesitant simply to dismiss the notion of a historical Job. They lend additional credibility to Job's existence and to essential facts of his story.

So, too, do most allusions to Job by Church leaders, according to Keith H. Meservy, who concludes that "the Brethren, also, when they have referred to Job, have regarded him as a real person."[7] Granting this, however, still an element of cautious restraint is called for in extending this conclusion to the entire book of Job. Allusions to Job by the Brethren do not necessarily mean that every aspect of the text must be taken as literally historical.

The LDS Bible Dictionary seems to me to provide exactly the right focus on the book of Job by remaining silent about historical questions, by ignoring the prose prologue and epilogue altogether, and by concentrating on the profound questions raised and answers provided in the central poetic dialogues. Perhaps the Bible Dictionary should guide our attention as well, which perhaps for too long has been occupied with the text's historicity rather than with the larger question of its meaning.

WHAT DOES JOB SAY ABOUT RETRIBUTIVE JUSTICE?

The Bible Dictionary states, simply, that the book of Job "narrates the afflictions that befell a righteous man, and discusses the moral

problem such sufferings present." Whether Job is a particular man or
an Everyman, whether the book of Job is history or, simply "his
story," the text still raises the same searching questions about "the
moral problems such sufferings present." Further, no one can doubt
that Job's essential story is true, painfully true, for Job's predicament
has been recapitulated countless times over in history all too real.
Good people have suffered, do suffer, and this for no clearly apparent
reason. Through Job's experience, we explore our faith in a universe
that operates under a system of rewards and punishments—a notion
sometimes called the doctrine of retributive justice.

Many commentators detect in the book of Job an implied challenge to the doctrine of retributive justice. We see this doctrine
debated many times between Job and his interlocutors, as in chapters 20 and 21 where Zophar asserts the standard line that the "tri-
umphing of the wicked is short" and Job answers that the wicked
often enjoy long life, "spend their days in wealth, and in a moment
go down to the grave" (Job 20:5; 21:13). This searching examination
of rewards and punishments in Job is often seen as challenging
Israel's prophets' and historians' unshakable faith in a system of retributive justice. To read the oracles of judgment pronounced by
Isaiah, Jeremiah, Hosea, Amos, and like prophets is to encounter
absolute confidence in retributive justice. Likewise, to read
Deuteronomy is to confront history whose contours are shaped by a
covenant whereby God metes out blessings and cursings according
to the principle of retributive justice: "Behold, I set before you this
day a blessing and a curse; A blessing, if ye obey the commandments
of the Lord your God, which I command you this day; And a curse, if
ye will not obey the commandments of the Lord your God"
(Deuteronomy 11:26–28).

In Latter-day Saint scripture we see this same historical thesis oper-
ating in the Book of Mormon. I call it "Lehi's theme" because Lehi
first received the covenant that his posterity will prosper or suffer in
the new land according to their faithfulness (see 2 Nephi 1:5–10),
though a similar promise of rewards and punishments had been
given to the Jaredites well before Lehi (see Ether 2:8–12). Book of
Mormon history is covenant history *par excellence*. It insists that the
history of the promised land is one of divine punishments and

rewards hinged on the obedience or rebellion of the Lord's covenant people.

Modern revelation also confirms a correlation between blessings and obedience, punishment and transgression. For example, "I, the Lord, am bound when ye do what I say" (D&C 82:10), and "There is a law, irrevocably decreed in heaven . . . upon which all blessings are predicated" (D&C 130:20). These and similar modern oracles provide the basis for our belief that God today still enters into covenants, as He did with Abraham. They lend further weight to faith in divine rewards and punishments.

How can we understand the book of Job in connection with the doctrine of retributive justice? Can Job help us understand the true nature of our belief about the correlation between suffering and sin? I believe so. Perhaps these few points might suggest how:

First and foremost, the book of Job makes clear that suffering is not necessarily a sign of punishment. As the Bible Dictionary states, though "The book of Job does not entirely answer the question as to why Job (or any human) might suffer. . . . It does make it clear that affliction is not necessarily evidence that one has sinned." This is a great comfort, for many people blame themselves when tragedy befalls them. When a child is accidentally killed, when cancer strikes, when a job is lost—our immediate response often is, "what have I done to deserve this punishment?" Job implies that there can be "no fault" tragedy.

Second, Job warns us against trying to reason backward from peoples' external circumstances to the condition of their souls. To do so traps us in a logical fallacy of an "if-then" argument called "affirming the consequent." If-then sequences are not reversible: If A then B does not permit the reverse conclusion, B therefore A. If a man is a millionaire, then he may buy a Mercedes, but if he buys a Mercedes, he is not necessarily a millionaire. Or, to apply the same principles to Job, if a man is wicked then he may (and ultimately will) suffer, but if he suffers he is not necessarily wicked. Sinfulness may result in suffering, but suffering does not necessarily imply sinfulness. The same holds true for the corollary: virtue may result in prosperity, but prosperity does not necessarily imply virtue. You cannot reason backwards from the fact of prosperity or suffering to the state of the soul, as Job's comforters try to do. "Affliction is not necessarily evidence that one has sinned," the Bible Dictionary wisely concludes.

Third, Job implies that neither prosperity nor suffering can be easily or routinely interpreted. It may be that *suffering* is the blessing and *prosperity* the trial. From personal experience no less than from scripture, we know that prosperity may test our faith while suffering may ready us for salvation. As Francis Bacon said, "Prosperity is the blessing of the Old Testament; Adversity is the blessing of the New."[8]

And fourth, the book of Job may serve to remind us that individuals often live out personal tragedies quite apart from the general prosperity and happiness of the larger community. Job addresses itself to the plight of a particular individual, not a covenant people. Most of the Old Testament and Book of Mormon promises, on the other hand, pertain to an entire covenant community. If we look carefully at the Bible or Book of Mormon we can find many instances of good individuals who, like Job, suffer. Think, for example, of the martyred women and children Alma and Amulek witnessed burn to death, or of the wives and children forced to feed upon the flesh of their husbands and fathers just before the final destruction of the Nephites (see Alma 14:7–11; Moroni 9:7–8). Complicating an oversimplified view of history is the knowledge that "the Lord suffereth the righteous to be slain that his justice and judgment may come upon the wicked" (Alma 60:13; compare Alma 14:11).

Righteousness does not insulate us from suffering or assure us of material rewards. As Christians, we need not look only to Job to confirm this fact. The supreme proof of this is Christ, who suffered more than has any man. The mortal Messiah intimately knew poverty, pain, hunger, thirst, fatigue, betrayal, and agonizing death (see Mosiah 3:7). If the Lord, who was perfect, had to endure affliction, should we, who are imperfect, expect to be spared from it? As the Lord reminded the Prophet Joseph, "The Son of Man hath descended below them all. Art thou greater than he?" (D&C 122:8). The only reward for righteousness that the Lord holds out unfailingly to individuals is peace in this life and eternal life in the life to come—and even this peace must be found *amid* persecutions, not in the *absence* (see John 14:27; 15:20).

How Is Job about Man's Relationship to God?

These and other insights into the problem of evil may be drawn from Job. In my opinion, however, the book is not primarily a repository of philosophical or theological answers as to why God permits suffering. The book of Job is not a rational "theodicy," a term coined by the German Enlightenment philosopher Leibnitz, nor does it pretend to be.[9] Theodicies are philosophical attempts to reconcile the goodness and omnipotence of God with the brute reality of human suffering—or the so-called "problem of evil." I'm convinced that strictly speaking, the book of Job's central concern lies not with the philosophical problem of evil but with the personal problem of despair; not with God's relationship to evil but man's relationship to God out of the midst of "evil." Job's sense of godforsakenness is the real problem he must endure and overcome. To put the matter succinctly, the problem Job treats involves *relationship;* the answer it provides entails *revelation.* The book of Job teaches us how to endure suffering, not the reason for it.

Let me explain. If we look at the text, we observe that Job is never told the reason for his afflictions. We also note that the text devotes but a few brief (albeit vivid) verses to the description of Job's physical pain. To be sure, Job's boils are deeply etched upon our memories, but they are not the main source of his suffering. In fact, Job endured physical pain in silence. When he finally cried out, after abiding seven days and seven nights in complete silence, Job complained not of boils but of betrayal: "Wherefore is light given to him that is in misery, and life unto the bitter in soul" (Job 3:20). It is as if Job's cancerous skin disease ate its way inward during his long week of brooding, ulcerating his spirit until he became "bitter in soul." However difficult to bear, Job's physical pain was most embittering for what it seemed to him to betoken: a violated relationship with God.

Job's relationship to God remains the focus throughout the dialogues. Physical affliction forms but the occasion, not the main topic, of the ensuing dialogues, which make no further reference to Job's specific personal losses or boils. Instead, Job's friends come with glib explanations about why Job suffered. Their pious advice—accept your suffering, Job, as punishment for your sins—not only provide him cold comfort but, if accepted, would have perverted Job's absolutely honest relationship with the Almighty. To follow their counsel would have forced Job to live a lie by confessing to the Lord that he felt he deserved his affliction—which he did not, and *should not* feel. Such "comfort" exonerates God by charging man with depravity, so that no matter what happens to man, the pious religionist can always say, "God exacteth of thee less than thine iniquity deserveth" (Job 11:6). One sees why defenders of original sin have found so much fodder in the speeches of Job's self-righteous friends.[10] Such easy explanations for suffering have continued to be foisted on believers by overly simplistic doctrines of retributive justice and depravity. In consequence, many innocent victims have been pressured to confess to the lie that they merit their misfortune—that whatever evil befalls them is less punishment than they deserve.[11]

But Job refuses such false wisdom and stoutly maintains that, even weighed in the balance scales of ordinary justice (see Job 6:2; 31:6), his suffering is disproportionate to any sin that could be laid to his charge. Repeatedly, Job cries out for an encounter with the Lord in order to bring God into the docks and prove his own innocence: "O that one might plead for a man with God, as a man pleadeth for his neighbor" (Job 16:21); "Oh that I knew where I might find him! that I might come even to his seat! I would order my cause before him, and fill my mouth with arguments" (Job 23: 3–4); "Oh that one would hear me! behold, my desire is, that the Almighty would answer me" (Job 31:35). Though heaven might kill him for so doing, Job vows to entrust his life in the hands of a God whom he believes prefers honesty to hypocrisy, while maintaining the injustice of his suffering before God's very face: "Wherefore do I take my flesh in my teeth, and put my life in mine hand? Though he slay me, yet will I trust him: but I will maintain mine own ways before him. He also shall be my salvation: for an hypocrite shall not come before him" (Job 13:14–16). Such is the shocking boldness of Job before his friends and his Lord, and such is his stunning trust in a God who, Job knows, does not want man to come before Him as a hypocrite, feigning to comprehend suffering that he cannot fathom.

In such speeches as these, we glimpse a man whose relationship with the Lord is as powerfully felt as it is powerfully tested—and, to repeat, the text's central concern lies in man's proper relationship to God. The text propounds few, if any, theoretical reasons for suffering, though the so-called comforters advocate many. Rather, it offers a memorable example of how to suffer suffering. Recognizing that man's relationship to Deity is central, we can better sense why Job stands both condemned *and* approved by the Lord in the final chapters, while the comforters stand merely condemned. Out of the Lord's mouth, Job is described as both one who "darkeneth counsel by words without knowledge" (Job 38:2; see also 40:2–8), and also one who has "spoken of me the thing that is right." By contrast, of Eliphaz and Job's other two dogmatic friends, so smugly doctrinaire, the Lord says only, "My wrath is kindled against thee, and against thy two friends: for ye have not spoken of me the thing that is right" (Job 42:7). Thus, the text reminds us that one can say something that is formally wrong but personally right (as did Job), and something formally correct but personally wrong (as did the comforters). The *relationship* of the speaker to the speech matters utterly.

HOW IS JOB ABOUT THE NEED FOR REVELATION?

We can learn much from Job's "friends" about how to comfort those suffering tragedy-induced crises of faith. We learn that it is not enough to have all the right answers. We must also speak the truth in love.[12] We learn that we risk divine condemnation when we cease to comfort and start to accuse. Joseph Smith taught that those who accuse place "themselves in the seat of the Satan."[13] Truly, the very word "devil" derives from "diabolos," meaning "accuser, calumniator, slanderer, traducer."[14] Further, we learn that the only abiding comfort must come from the Comforter. The solution to a sense of godforsakenness is, obviously, the revelation that God has not forsaken us. Again, the problem in the book of Job is one of relation; the answer is one of revelation. Job is a wisdom text about the limits of wisdom.

The comforters' failure to reason Job out of his anguish provides a striking illustration of the impotence of human wisdom alone to solve a Job-like crisis. The advice of Job's first comforter, Eliphaz the Temanite, typifies the posture they all adopt. You were ready, Eliphaz reminded Job, to encourage others in their suffering: "Now it is come upon thee, and thou faintest; it toucheth thee, and thou art troubled" (Job 4:5). Suffering is not arbitrary, this dogmatist continued, but constitutes a sure sign of divine judgment upon sin, for "who ever perished, being innocent? or where were the righteous cut off?" (Job 4:7). Further, if suffering is divine correction, Eliphaz reasons, then "happy is the man whom God correcteth: therefore despise not thou the chastening of the Almighty" (Job 5:17). Although the Temanite momentarily entertains the possibility that the Lord's judgment may not be so easy to read, for the Lord "doeth great things and unsearchable" (Job 5:9), in general Eliphaz remains certain that if you live righteously, the Lord will deliver you from famine, war, and destruction, and you will die peaceably of old age: "Thou shalt come to thy grave in a full age, like as a shock of corn cometh in his season" (Job 5:26).

All these points may have elements of truth, but they are also untrue. Why? First, they were uttered without compassion. "To him that is afflicted pity should be shewed from his friend," Job protests (Job 6:14; compare 19:21). Next, they were glib. Those who suffer are *not* happy, at least not until they have been allowed to be unhappy first. And last, they are counsels based on human reason about suffering in general—upon hearsay, as it were—not upon revelation about Job's particular predicament. This is clear when Eliphaz proudly discloses the source of his knowledge as he concludes his counsel, seeming to speak for all the comforters: "Lo this, we have searched it, so it is; hear it, and know thou it for thy good" (Job 5:27).

Such smugness is roundly condemned in the book of Job. All of us who are called upon to comfort those working through their own personal Job-like trials should take note not only of the comforters' failure to solve Job's problem but of the Lord's divine displeasure with them. Even Elihu, the fourth and final comforter, whose speeches echo those issuing from the whirlwind, had no impact on Job and, in my opinion, stands under the same divine disapproval as the other comforters.[15] For reason alone cannot solve Job's crisis, which is a crisis in his relationship with God. Job makes no reply to Elihu, but well might he have responded to the arrogant young man in the language of a character in a novel by Charles Williams: "As a mere argument there's something lacking perhaps in saying to a man who's lost his money and his house and his family and is sitting on the dustbin, all over boils, 'Look at the hippopotamus.'"[16] The point is that Elihu's answer remains "mere argument;" the Lord's is a revelation.

As a personal revelation from the Lord to the long-suffering, steadfast Job, the voice from the whirlwind had authority and meaning that no merely human voice could match. Apart from *what* the Lord said, simply the fact *that* he spoke at all, and spoke directly to Job, relieved the man of Uz's deepest need—his hunger for reassurance that God has not forsaken him. Intellectual answers can never provide this knowledge. Kenneth Surin recently observed that "for those who experience godforsakenness there can be no answer except the stammeringly uttered truth that God himself keeps company with those who are oppressed."[17]

This is very wise, but it does not go quite far enough. To human utterance must be added the witness of the Spirit. We can testify to the truth that the Lord loves and pities His children in the midst of their sharpest sorrows. We can offer scriptural and personal insights about the various purposes served by suffering. But only the Lord can confirm His continuing love through the voice of the only unfailing comforter, His Comforter. This revelation is, ultimately, the *sine qua non* for resolving a Joban crisis. It is the essential comfort every Job requires. Not "mere argument;" not philosophical theodicies; but the revealed reassurance that the Lord has not forsaken us in our suffering, however obscure this may seem in our distress.

The book of Job, then, is at bottom about the need for personal revelation. Revelation is the key to human crises of faith brought on by suffering. This interpretation, little recognized in biblical scholarship, fits LDS theology, which stresses the need for both general and personal revelation. Again, the Bible Dictionary touches upon this distinctively Latter-day Saint interpretation of the book of Job: "There is a mystery in the incidence of suffering that only a fresh revelation can solve."

WHAT DOES JOB IMPLY ABOUT GOD'S EQUITY AND LOVE?

There is indeed a mystery in suffering. Job is overwhelmed by mystery in the theophany as the enigma of his own suffering is engulfed by the larger mystery of creation. Job never does receive an answer as to why he suffered; nor, often, do we. It remains inexplicable, mysterious. Yet one can overstate the mystery. Beyond the mystery, Latter-day Saint readers must affirm the continuing presence of divine justice and love. Overemphasis upon the Lord's transcendence and sovereignty can sever Him from the concept of equity. A good instance of this misreading may be seen in an article by Matitiahu Tsevat. Tsevat draws the figure of a triangle, labeling the three corners for God (G), Job (J), and Retributive Justice (R). Job's dilemma, argues Tsevat, stems from his inability to reconcile G, J, and R; the theophany overcomes the impasse by eliminating R: "He who speaks to man . . . is neither a just nor an unjust God but God."[18] Others have made similar unwarranted claims. For example, the eminent authority on wisdom literature, James Crenshaw, writes of the theophany that "the putative principle of order collapsed before divine freedom."[19] In the same spirit, but more colloquially, Robert Frost portrays a droll character of the Lord returning to thank Job for "releasing me from moral bondage to the human race. . . . I had to prosper good and punish evil. You [Job] changed all that. You set me free to reign."[20]

But does the theophany in Job in fact reveal a God cut loose from justice, order, or morality? LDS theology, certainly, does not endorse such absolute divine sovereignty, which from a human vantage appears indistinguishable from caprice. Nor does the climax require the collapse of divine justice so the Lord may reign sovereign. We believe that the Almighty Himself subscribes to law (see Alma 42:22). Our innate demand for fairness, order, law, and justice doubtless is a legacy from our divine parentage. In the words of the eminent Jewish scholar Abraham Herschel, "Even the cry of despair—There is no justice in heaven!—is a cry in the name of justice that cannot come out of us and be still missing in the source of ourselves."[21]

Traces of divine law—higher perhaps than man's human wisdom can reach, but still within divine control—are everywhere inscribed in the revelation Job receives from the whirlwind. Tellingly, the theophany's imagery recalls that of Genesis 1 when the Lord imbues form and light upon that which was "without form, and void," and dark (Genesis 1:2). The very first question the Lord asks Job requires both him and us, as readers, to remember that God is the great Artificer of all earthly and cosmic order: "Where wast thou when I laid the foundations of the earth? . . . When the morning stars sang together, and all the sons of God shouted for joy?" (Job 38:4, 7). This is the God of Creation, not the voice of a mercurial being who rejects the "putative principle of order."

Nor is it the voice of one detached from justice. As we have seen, the Lord's equity reaches so deep that it penetrates beneath the superficial morality of the comforters and the sometimes reckless cynicism of Job to honor the one who is most truly faithful. This is the voice of one who looks not on the outward appearance "but looketh on the heart" (1 Samuel 16:7).

It is, furthermore, the voice of a being who clearly continues to care about human suffering. That the Lord responds at all assures us that He is not a *deus absconditus,* as Job feared (Job 23:1–9), but a God who condescends to reveal Himself to mankind in its darkest hours of need. As the great Job scholar Samuel Terrien so eloquently phrases it: "A God who concerns himself for man is a God who loves. There is not love without sharing and a God who loves is a God who suffers. Underneath the high notes, a *De Profundis* of God's own agonies is audible."[22]

Here Terrien adumbrates what is also a distinctively Latter-day Saint view regarding the Lord's outlook on the "problem of evil"; namely, that evil is a problem for Him too. In any world of both natural law (where apples and parachutists fall according to the same law of gravity) and of agency (where people are free to do good and evil), suffering will occur. But on the whole, Heavenly Father neither wants nor wills suffering. In fact, He grieves over it: the heavens thunder and they weep in emotional solidarity with the innocent who suffer (see Moses 7:29–40). Enoch wondered how this can be so: "How is it that the heavens weep" (Moses 7:28). But he finally came to share the Lord's view of human misery: "Wherefore Enoch . . . looked upon their wickedness, and their misery, and wept and stretched forth his arms, and his heart swelled wide as eternity; and his bowels yearned; and all eternity shook" (Moses 7:41). Surely, as we respond to the invitation to consider Job, this is our faith about God's nature: that though we do not fully comprehend all His ways, He is just and good.

Job is a provocative and profoundly rewarding book—one that, as we have seen, both clarifies gospel principles and is itself best understood in the light of modern revelation. It is a book that refuses to offer us ready answers to the so-called problem of evil, for it acknowledges how inexplicably cruel life can be. At the same time it points to a way of enduring. In Samuel Terrien's fine phrases, it proposes "not a speculative answer . . . but a way of consecrated living;" it presents to us a world that is "not [wholly] intelligible, but [is] livable."[23]

And Job teaches even more. It says something unforgettable about honesty in our relationship with God; something about compassion in comforting those in spiritual distress; something about tentativeness in offering them ready explanations. Finally, it says something about the absolute need for revelation to solve the problem of faith that encompasses the problem of understanding. As Latter-day Saints, we should welcome a text that finally throws us back, just as it does Job, upon the necessity of seeking understanding through personal revelation from an often inscrutable, but nevertheless living and loving God.

Notes

1. For a highly readable, popular account of Schliemann's biography, see C. W. Ceram's *Gods, Graves, and Scholars,* trans. E. B. Garside and Sophie Wilkins, rev. 2nd ed. (New York: Bantam Books, 1967), 30–67.

2. E. Dhorme, A *Commentary on the Book of Job,* trans. Harold Knight (London: Thomas Nelson & Sons, 1926; Trans. & Rpt. 1967), xv.

3. Dhorne, *Commentary,* vii–xii.

4. Bernhard Anderson, *Understanding the Old Testament,* 2nd ed. (Englewood Cliffs: Prentice-Hall, 1966), 487–521.

5. See, for example, "Dispute over Suicide" [Egyptian], and "I Will Praise the Lord of Wisdom" and "A Dialogue about Human Misery" [Babylonian] in J. B. Pritchard's standard collection, *Ancient Near Eastern Texts Relating to the Old Testament,* 2nd ed. (Princeton: Princeton University Press, 1955).

6. I disagree with Keith Meservy that an allusion by the Lord to a fictional Job would constitute a cruel mockery of Joseph's nonfictional suffering. The Lord's purpose here is simply to remind Joseph that things could be worse, not to verify Job's existence (see Keith Meservy, "Job: 'Yet Will I Trust in Him,'" Sixth Annual Sperry Symposium, January 1978).

7. Meservy, "Job," 29.

8. Francis Bacon, "Of Adversity."

9. Immanuel Kant recognized this and therefore excepted the book of Job in his 1791 essay "On the Failure of All Attempted Philosophical Theodicies," trans. Michel Despland (Montreal: McGill—Queens University Press, 1973), 283–97. The book of Job does not fail as a theodicy, Kant claims, because it does not

approach the question of evil philosophically but puts the whole discussion on an entirely different plane.

10. We should remember that the dark vision of depravity the friends sometimes unfold, such as that in Job 11:6 or in 15:14–16, form planks in arguments framed with the intent to prove all men sinners (and hence worthy of punishment). They do not represent either the book of Job's or the Lord's view of human nature.

11. The book of Job provides a classic instance of what we now call "blaming the victim." For the seminal treatment of this phenomenon, see William T. Ryan, *Blaming the Victim* (New York: Random House, 1972).

12. See Russell M. Nelson, "Truth and More," *On the Lord's Errand*, address given at the Brigham Young University Annual University Conference, August 27, 1985.

13. *Teachings of the Prophet Joseph Smith*, comp. Joseph Fielding Smith (Salt Lake City: Deseret Book, 1938), 212. See also Hugh Nibley's discussion of accusing in "Brigham Young and the Enemy" (Provo, UT: FARMS Report, 1972), 12.

14. *Oxford English Dictionary*, s.v. "devil."

15. The young man Elihu is not mentioned until late in the drama (chapter 32), and no one responds to him. His speeches about God's wonderful works and unfathomable ways in some respects anticipated the theophany. For these reasons, most commentators see his discourse as a later interpolation in the text, a later scribe's effort to give Job a proper answer from a human companion.

16. From *War in Heaven*, quoted by Samuel Terrien in *Job: Poet of Existence* (Indianapolis: Bobbs-Merrill, 1958), 238.

17. "Theodicy?" *Harvard Theological Review* 76, no. 2 (1985): 246. Surin argues that the problem of evil must locate itself in the victim's "space," and not presume to answer the question from a purely "cosmic" vantage. I concur with Surin that the book of Job takes the side of the sufferer. The sympathy the text displays for Job— evidenced by God's commendation—is also asserted in a fine recent essay by Rene Girard, who argues that in casting Job as scapegoat, his comforters take a satanic stance, while the scripture sides with the victim, Job (see "Job et le Bouc Emissaire," *Bulletin du Centre Protestant D'Etudes*, 6 [1983]: 3–33).

18. "The Meaning of the Book of Job," in *Studies in Ancient Israelite Wisdom: The Library of Biblical Studies,* ed. James L. Crenshaw (New York: KTAV Publishing House, 1976), 373.

19. *Old Testament Wisdom Literature: An Introduction* (Atlanta: John Knox Press, 1981), 125.

20. "A Masque of Reason," rpt. in *The Voice out of the Whirlwind: The*

Book of Job, ed. Ralph E. Hone, rev. ed. (San Francisco: Chandler Publishing, 1972), 261.

21. *Poet of Existence,* 241. On the whole issue of the Old Testament image of a suffering God, see Terrence E. Fretheim's *The Suffering of God* (Philadelphia: Fortress Press, 1984), and also Kazoh Kitamori, *Theology of the Pain of God,* trans. M. E. Brachten (Richmond: John Knox Press, 1965).

22. "Introduction and Exegesis to Job," *Interpreter's Bible* (Nashville: Abingdon Press, 1954), 3:902; *Poet of Existence,* 248.

23. *Essays on Biblical Interpretation,* ed. Lewis S. Mudge (Philadelphia: Fortress Press, 1980), 86–87.

CHAPTER NINETEEN

ELIJAH'S MISSION: HIS KEYS, POWERS, AND BLESSINGS FROM THE OLD TESTAMENT TO THE LATTER DAYS

E. DALE LeBARON

In this, the dispensation of the fulness of times, when there is to be a "restitution of all things" (Acts 3:21), the mission of Elijah, the last prophet in the Old Testament to hold the keys of the priesthood, is vital. This is evidenced by the prophetic promise of his return to the earth (see Matthew 17:1–4) and the fact that each of the standard works contains prophecies of Elijah's important work.

Interestingly, like two prophetic bookends, the last words of the Old Testament (Malachi 4:5–6) and the earliest revelation recorded in the Doctrine and Covenants (D&C 2) give prophetic promise of Elijah's mission. This prophecy is spoken of in the New Testament,[1] the words of the Savior to the Nephites in the Book of Mormon (see 3 Nephi 25:5–6), and the words of Moroni to the youthful prophet Joseph Smith as recorded in the Pearl of Great Price. Moroni's rendition was slightly different from other passages of the same prophecy, as he stated: "Behold, I will reveal unto you the Priesthood, by the hand of Elijah the prophet, before the coming of the great and dreadful day of the Lord. . . . And he shall plant in the hearts of the children the promises made to the fathers, and the hearts of the children

E. Dale LeBaron is professor emeritus of Church history and doctrine at Brigham Young University.

shall turn to their fathers. If it were not so, the whole earth would be utterly wasted at his coming" (Joseph Smith—History 1:38–39). Compare this with the biblical account: "Behold, I will send you Elijah the prophet before the coming of the great and dreadful day of the Lord: and he shall turn the heart of the fathers to the children, and the heart of the children to their fathers, lest I come and smite the earth with a curse" (Malachi 4:5–6).

The New Testament records that Elijah bestowed the keys of the sealing power on Peter, James, and John when they were with the Savior on the Mount of Transfiguration (see Mark 9:1–9).[2] Jesus later taught these three Apostles that Elijah would return in the last days to "restore all things" (Matthew 7:11; see also 7:1–13; Mark 9:2–13; Luke 9:28–36).[3]

The Book of Mormon records that the Savior quoted Malachi's prophecy of Elijah (see 3 Nephi 25:5–6). He told the Nephites, "These scriptures, which ye had not with you, the Father commanded that I should give unto you" (3 Nephi 26:2).

Malachi's prophecy of Elijah is also found in the Pearl of Great Price, as it was part of Moroni's instructions to the Prophet Joseph Smith (see Joseph Smith—History 1:38–39).

Elijah's mission is discussed several times in the Doctrine and Covenants (see D&C 2:1–3; 27:9; 35:4; 110:13–16; 128:17; 138:46–47). Doctrine and Covenants 2:1–2 states: "Behold, I will reveal unto you the Priesthood, by the hand of Elijah the prophet, before the coming of the great and dreadful day of the Lord. And he shall plant in the hearts of the children the promises made to the fathers, and the hearts of the children shall turn to their fathers." According to the headnote, this is "an extract from the words of the angel Moroni to Joseph Smith the Prophet . . . on the evening of September 21, 1823." It is noteworthy that during this eventful night Moroni visited young Joseph three times, quoting many scriptures and giving much revelation. But of all the passages of scripture Moroni quoted that night, the only verses we know of that the Lord had the Prophet Joseph Smith include in the Doctrine and Covenants were the verses prophesying of Elijah's mission.

The last verses of the Old Testament and the earliest passage of scripture recorded in the Doctrine and Covenants are both prophecies of Elijah's mission. Malachi's prophecy of Elijah's mission forms a scriptural and a spiritual bridge between the last prophet of the Old Testament and the first prophet of this dispensation.

The Importance of Elijah's Mission

Events that occurred in the Kirtland Temple were very important. The temple was dedicated March 27, 1836. It was a season of pentecost, with an outpouring of the Spirit of the Lord. Before Elijah and other heavenly messengers restored vital priesthood keys on April 3, 1836, the Savior Himself appeared to Joseph Smith and Oliver Cowdery to accept the temple and the sacrifices the Saints had made.

Earlier the Lord had declared that if Elijah's mission were not accomplished as prophesied, "the whole earth would be utterly wasted at his coming" (D&C 2:3). The Prophet Joseph Smith taught, "How shall God come to the rescue of this generation? He will send Elijah the prophet. . . . Elijah shall reveal the covenants to seal the hearts of the fathers to the children, and the children to the fathers. . . . What is this office and work of Elijah? It is one of the greatest and most important subjects that God has revealed. . . . The power of Elijah is sufficient to make our calling and election sure."[4]

President Joseph Fielding Smith explained: "Elijah restored to this Church . . . the keys of the sealing power; and that sealing power puts the stamp of approval upon every ordinance that is done in this Church and more particularly those that are performed in the temples of the Lord. . . . Some members of the Church have been confused in thinking that Elijah came with the keys of baptism for the dead or of salvation for the dead. Elijah's keys were greater than that. They were the keys of sealing, and those keys of sealing pertain to the living and embrace the dead who are willing to repent."[5] President Smith further stated, "This priesthood holds the keys of binding and sealing on earth and in heaven of all the ordinances and principles pertaining to the salvation of man, that they may thus become valid in the celestial kingdom of God."[6]

Without the keys that Elijah conferred upon the Prophet Joseph Smith in the Kirtland Temple, no ordinance of the gospel would be binding beyond this life. All sealings would be null and void, including eternal marriages and eternal families. And because eternal marriage is a prerequisite for exaltation, our purpose for coming to this earth would be thwarted. The Lord has stated that marriage and families are necessary for the earth to "answer the end of its creation" (D&C 49:15–17). Thus, without the sealing powers Elijah restored, truly "the whole earth would be utterly wasted at [the Lord's] coming" (D&C 2:3; Joseph Smith—History 1:39).

Soon after the keys were restored in Kirtland, the Saints were forced to flee, leaving their beloved temple. Elder Boyd K. Packer gave us this perspective on those events: "You might think the Lord would protect His temple with thunderbolts or earthquakes, if necessary. He did not! The Saints lost the Kirtland Temple. . . . The Church does not have the Kirtland Temple now. *But we have the keys we received within it.*"[7]

FATHERS, CHILDREN, AND PROMISES

The words of Malachi's prophecy concerning Elijah's return vary somewhat in the several scriptural records, but their essence is the same in all, for they speak of fathers, children, and hearts of children turning to their fathers. In addition, Moroni's words to Joseph Smith refer to promises made to the fathers by the children.

Who are the fathers and the children referred to? President Joseph Fielding Smith said: "The fathers are our dead ancestors who died without the privilege of receiving the gospel, but who received the promise that the time would come when that privilege would be granted them. The children are those now living who are preparing genealogical data and who are performing the vicarious ordinances in the temples."[8]

What are the promises? The prophets have taught that we made sacred covenants before we came to this earth. President Spencer W. Kimball said, "We made vows, solemn vows, in the heavens before we came to this mortal life. . . . We have made covenants. We made them before we accepted our position here on earth. . . . We committed ourselves to our Heavenly Father, that if He would send us to the earth and give us bodies and give to us the priceless opportunities that earth life afforded, we would keep our lives clean and would marry in the holy temple and would rear a family and teach them righteousness. This was a solemn oath, a solemn promise."[9]

Elder John A. Widtsoe said of the specific promises we made to our fathers: "In our preexistent state, in the day of the great council, we made a certain agreement with the Almighty. The Lord proposed a plan, conceived by him. We accepted it. Since the plan is intended for all men, we become parties to the salvation of every person under that plan. We agreed, right then and there, to be not only saviors for ourselves but measurably, saviors for the whole human family. We went into a partnership with the Lord. The working out of the plan became then not merely the Father's work, and the Savior's work, but also our work. The least of us, the humblest, is in partnership with the Almighty in achieving the purpose of the eternal plan of salvation."[10]

Moroni's account of Elijah's mission is especially significant. Moroni says: "And he shall *plant in the hearts* of the children the promises made to the fathers, and the hearts of the children shall turn to their fathers" (D&C 2:2; emphasis added). Because we do not remember our experiences before birth, the verb *plant* should be given careful consideration. The mission of Elijah plants in our hearts the awareness of our responsibilities to be saviors to our fathers. It then becomes our responsibility to nourish the tender plant so that it grows and produces fruit. Some of us excuse ourselves from genealogical and temple work, saying, "I just can't get interested" or "Others in the family have done it all."

Alma used a powerful analogy that can be applied here. He taught that after the seed is planted, we should desire to believe and not cast it out. He promised:

> If ye nourish it with much care it will get root, and grow up, and bring forth fruit.
>
> But if ye neglect the tree, and take no thought for its nourishment, behold it will not get any root; . . . and ye pluck it up and cast it out.
>
> Now, this is not because the seed was not good, neither is it because the fruit thereof would not be desirable; but it is because your ground is barren, and ye will not nourish the tree, therefore ye cannot have the fruit thereof. . . .
>
> But if ye will . . . nourish the tree as it beginneth to grow, by your faith with great diligence, and with patience, looking forward to the fruit thereof, it shall take root; and behold it shall be a tree springing up unto everlasting life. (Alma 32:37–41)

With respect to planting promises in our hearts—promises made to our forefathers—the growth is up to us. There are specific things we can do to cause this growth, as President Ezra Taft Benson stated:

When you attend the temple and perform the ordinances that pertain to the House of the Lord, certain blessings will come to you:

You will receive the spirit of Elijah, which will turn your hearts to your spouse, to your children, and to your forebears.

You will love your family with a deeper love than you have loved before.

Your hearts will be turned to your fathers and theirs to you.

You will be endowed with power from on high as the Lord has promised.

You will receive the key of the knowledge of God (see D&C 84:19). You will learn how you can be like Him. Even the power of godliness will be manifest to you (see D&C 84:20).

You will be doing a great service to those who have passed to the other side of the veil in order that they might be "judged according to men in the flesh, but live according to God in the spirit" (D&C 138:34).[11]

ELIJAH'S MISSION MANIFEST

There are many ways in which the power and spirit of Elijah are manifest today. We may not even be aware when they happen. Let me share a few of them.

Missionary work on the earth. Because of Elijah's mission, missionaries are led to descendants of those who have accepted the gospel in the spirit world. Elder Melvin J. Ballard observed: "It was made known to me that it is because the righteous dead who have received the Gospel in the spirit world are exercising themselves, and in answers to their prayers elders of the Church are sent to the homes of their posterity so that the Gospel might be taught to them, and that descendant in the flesh is then privileged to do the work for his dead kindred. I want to say to you that it is with greater intensity that the hearts of the fathers and mothers in the spirit world are turned to their children now in the flesh than that our hearts are turned to them."[12]

A pair of missionaries in the South Africa Johannesburg Mission had an experience that demonstrates this principle. While driving near the outskirts of town, they passed an elderly gentleman standing at the side of the road. The missionaries felt strongly impressed to stop and speak to him. They told him that Jesus Christ had sent them to him with an important message. The elders bore strong testimony of Joseph Smith and the Restoration. They gave him a pamphlet with their names and phone number and urged him to read the material and contact them.

About three weeks later, the elderly gentleman phoned the missionaries. He asked them to come to his home and pray for his wife, who was very ill. At the home, which was so far out of town that they never would have stopped at that house during their regular proselyting, the elders administered to the wife, and she was healed immediately. She then asked the missionaries to teach her and her husband. Three weeks later, the couple were baptized. The elderly sister told the missionaries the following story:

> Some time ago my husband came home and told me that he met two young men who said that the Lord had sent them to him.
>
> Three days later I had a dream. I dreamed that I was with my mother, who died thirty-five years ago. I have never before dreamed of my mother. The dream was vivid, just as if it was real.
>
> My mother said to me, "My child, I cannot rest." I replied, "Why, Mom, why can't you rest?" She answered, "Because you don't belong to the right church." I was surprised because I am in the church which my mother and father raised me in. Then the scene changed, and we were standing next to a beautiful clear pool of water that had three steps leading down into the water. My mother said, "My child, go down into the water, and I will follow." I hesitated and said, "No, Mom, you go first and then I will follow." Then my mother said, "No, my child, you must go first! Then I will come after."
>
> When I woke, I wondered what the dream meant. Then I became sick, and you came out and blessed me. You taught us the gospel. I learned about the spirit world and that my parents may have heard the gospel. Then we were baptized. When I

stood before the steps of the baptismal font, I remembered my dream. It was the same pool of water that I had seen in my dream.[13]

Missionary work in the spirit world. There may be occasions when missionary work and mission calls are correlated on both sides of the veil. President Joseph F. Smith said, "I beheld [in a vision] that the faithful elders of this dispensation, when they depart from mortal life, continue their labors in the preaching of the gospel . . . in the great world of the spirits of the dead" (D&C 138:57).

As the work expands in the spirit world, specially qualified servants may be required to move the work forward there, as President Wilford Woodruff explained: "I have felt of late as if our brethren on the other side of the veil had held a council, and that they had said to this one, and that one, 'Cease thy work on earth, come hence, we need help,' and they have called this man and that man. It has appeared so to me in seeing the many men who have been called from our midst lately."[14]

A statement Elder Neal A. Maxwell made at the dedication of the Toronto Ontario Temple helps explain how missionary work on the earth is connected with missionary work on the other side of the veil. "'[The Lord] will hasten [His] work in its time' (see D&C 88:73). When He hastens His work, He hastens it on both sides of the veil. This is why, of course, the holy temples are so crucial especially at this time in human history. The constituency in the spirit world, by the way, is many times larger, numerically, than here. Whenever we open new nations on this side of the veil, as is now happening, we have simultaneously opened the door to thousands beyond the veil. The temple provides the precious spiritual linkage."[15]

It was while I was presiding over the only mission on the continent of Africa in June of 1978—the South Africa Johannesburg Mission—that the revelation on the priesthood was received. Shortly after that historic announcement, many African nations were dedicated to the preaching of the gospel and the floodgates were opened. The growth of the Church on that continent has accelerated at a phenomenal pace.

Over a period of 125 years after the arrival of the missionaries in South Africa in 1853, to the time of the revelation in 1978, membership grew to about 7,600 white Latter-day Saints within one stake and one mission in southern Africa. However, within the twenty-six years following the revelation, Church membership soared to 197,454 in fourteen missions and forty stakes. This explosive growth, which has come almost exclusively among the blacks of Africa, might be compared to a horse and buggy moving at five miles per hour before to the revelation to a racing car making a rapid acceleration to one hundred twenty-five miles per hour.

In addition to this rapid growth it is important to note that the faithfulness of these converts is reflected by their dedication in keeping their covenants. It is reported that the two African areas are among the highest in the Church in sacrament meeting attendance and that they are the only areas of the Church in which there are more brethren than there are sisters on the membership rolls. It is also significant that the Lord has blessed Africa with two temples—in Accra, Ghana, and Abba, Nigeria—within the record number of twenty-seven years after the arrival of full-time missionaries.

Sacred records. The Lord preserves and makes available treasured records so that saving ordinances can be performed for His children. Inspired leaders are instruments in God's hands in preserving these records.

In October 1976, Ted Powell, from the Church Family History Department, was preparing to leave on a trip to the Orient when Elder Boyd K. Packer, who had responsibility for the family history work in the Church, asked him to change his plans and leave immediately for southern Africa. Elder Packer had received a strong prompting that genealogical records in Rhodesia, now known as Zimbabwe, needed to be microfilmed as soon as possible. The nation of Rhodesia was in the terrible throes of a civil war. As president of the South Africa Johannesburg Mission, which included Zimbabwe, I was asked to assist Brother Powell in this endeavor.

The Saints in southern Africa held a special fast that this urgent and important project might be completed. I recorded in my journal: "Indeed, this is the most crucial time in the history of this great part of the world as far as genealogy is concerned. The momentous decisions about to be made will determine whether the records are preserved."[16]

Brother Powell and I traveled to Rhodesia to meet with prime minister Ian Smith, but as he was attending peace talks in Europe, we met instead with the acting prime minister. A letter of introduction from President Ezra Taft Benson, who knew the prime minister personally, helped increase our credibility. The acting prime minister agreed that microfilming the records was a good idea, but he did not feel he had authority to approve it. For three frustrating days we talked with other high government officials who also agreed with the acting prime minister.

It seemed hopeless. We pleaded with the Lord for help. After a day of pondering and prayer, Brother Powell heard the voice of the Spirit say: "Ted Powell, do you understand who you are and whose errand you are on?" He was then directed about what to do and say. We once more met with the acting prime minister, and the Spirit touched his heart. Approval was given.

Although official approval was given for the records to be micro-filmed, we now faced another major obstacle. How could the Church obtain the needed equipment for microfilming in Rhodesia? Due to heavily imposed sanctions from the international community, such equipment could not be imported. Another miracle occurred as a company that had all of the needed equipment went into bank-ruptcy at that time and the Church was able to obtain the cameras and other equipment needed.

Through a sequence of miracles, the way was opened for micro-filming to begin. The project moved along quickly, considering the limited equipment and the lack of skilled personnel available. Within days of the last roll of microfilm being safely stored in the Church vaults in Cottonwood Canyon, the government of Ian Smith col-lapsed and a Marxist government took over the country. The national archivist and government officials who had been very coop-erative and friendly during the project were immediately removed from office. The new government destroyed many of the records that had just been microfilmed and made it extremely difficult for the Church to operate in that country, which became known as Zimbabwe.

Temple ordinances. Temple ordinances are at the heart of Elijah's mission. It is believed that those in the spirit world who have accepted the gospel may be allowed to witness their ordinances as they are performed for them in the temple. Elder Melvin J. Ballard tells of observing baptisms for the dead performed in the Logan

Temple, at which time he saw a vision of a great congregation of spirits witnessing their ordinances. He says that he had never seen such happy people in his life. From that time Elder Ballard taught that departed spirits are permitted to witness and accept the ordinances performed in their behalf.[17]

We are given to understand that there are many manifestations of spirits witnessing their ordinances being performed by proxy in temples. One example is recorded from the life of President Edward J. Wood, who was the first president of the Cardston Alberta Temple. In 1931 a group of Saints traveled from Portland, Oregon, to the Cardston temple. One sister, a convert to the Church, brought her children to be sealed to her and to her husband who had passed away. A friend was acting as proxy for the husband. As President Wood began the ordinance to seal the children to their parents, he stopped and asked the sister if the information he had been given was complete. After being assured that it was, he began the ceremony again. Before finishing, he once again stopped and asked the sister if she had other children whose names should be included. She said she had other living adult children who were not members of the Church, but that was all. A third time President Wood started the ceremony, but again he stopped, explaining that he had heard a voice quite distinctly say, "I am her child." Once more he asked the mother if she had another child who was not listed on the sheet. She began weeping as she explained that she did indeed have another daughter, one who had died twelve days after her birth, and had been overlooked in the preparation of the information. All in the room shed tears of joy to realize the closeness of kindred dead.[18]

ETERNAL FAMILIES TODAY

Building an eternal family is surely our ultimate partnership with our Heavenly Father, but doing so depends upon each family member's responding to the spirit of Elijah. President Harold B. Lee said:

> When the full measure of Elijah's mission is understood, . . . the hearts of the children will be turned to the fathers, and the fathers to the children. It applies just as much on this side of the veil as it does to the other side of the veil. If we neglect our families here in having family home night and we fail in our responsibility here, how would heaven look if we lost some of

those [we love] through our own neglect? Heaven would not be heaven until we have done everything we can to save those whom the Lord has sent through our lineage. So, the hearts of you fathers and mothers must be turned to your children right now, if you have the true spirit of Elijah, and not think that it applies merely to those who are beyond the veil. Let your hearts be turned to your children, and teach your children; but you must do it when they are young enough to be schooled. And if you are neglecting your family home evening, you are neglecting the beginning of the mission of Elijah just as certainly as if you were neglecting your research work of genealogy.[19]

All things that help turn the hearts of children to their parents and the hearts of parents to their children are of great importance. Recent, as well as historical family records, can help us reach that eternal goal and thus are important to the Lord. I learned that through an experience we had while I was presiding over the South Africa Johannesburg Mission.

One Sunday afternoon, following a stake conference, Sister LeBaron became ill. She took some medicine and went to bed while I took the children to sacrament meeting. As I was leaving the meeting, I received an urgent phone message that the mission home was on fire. I raced the three or four miles to our home. I could see the smoke rising above the trees. I was terrified, not knowing whether my wife was still asleep in the upper level of the home.

By the time I arrived, the fire was spreading through the upper part of the beautiful mission mansion. I raced into it, shouting my wife's name. I ran up the circular staircase to our bedroom, where she had been sleeping. It was filled with smoke and the fire was raging, but thankfully she was not there. Feeling assured that she was safe, I raced back down the winding staircase and across the large entrance area toward my office. At that moment there was a loud explosion above me, sending the huge chandelier crashing to the hardwood floor and splattering glass against the back of my legs as I dashed into my office. I felt panic. My mind was racing and in my panic I thought, "What should I do? What should I try to save?"

I knew that there were many church records and documents that were housed in the mission home and office. They were invaluable.

The firemen were ineffective in putting out the fire, and I feared that we might lose everything.

Then the thought came to me that I should use my priesthood to pronounce a blessing upon all that was of great value, and irreplaceable, to the Church and to our family. They were the Lord's. I must leave them in His hands. And so, I offered a priesthood blessing upon all things of great value and irreplaceable, to the Church or to us, that they would be preserved.

As I said amen, I felt a spirit of peace and calm that was every bit as powerful and wonderful as my feelings of terror and fear that I had felt a few moments earlier. I took pictures of my family from my desk, put them into my briefcase, and calmly walked out to join my family and endeavor to comfort them.

That night we comforted the children by pointing out that we still had everything that was important in our lives. Their mother's life had been spared, we had the gospel, our family was together, and we had not lost anything of great value to us or the Church. I shared with them my experience in giving the priesthood blessing and assured them that the irreplaceable things of great value had not been lost. I told them that the Lord had granted that blessing and that none of the valuable Church records had been burned.

Then my oldest son, Curtis, asked, "What about our family photo album?" This was a beautiful large leather album that contained portraits of our children at various ages. Like the Church records, it was of great value and irreplaceable. Had it been preserved? I did not have an answer.

The next morning we went back to view the remains of the mission home. It was painful and pitiful to see this once-beautiful mansion now a shell with no roof. Our children tried to be as positive as they could. Curtis, trying to lighten up a sad and serious situation, said, "Dad, you can tell the Brethren that last night we had a fireside and today we have an open house."

My main objective in returning to the destroyed mission home was to answer my son's question from the night before—what about the family photo album? I got a digging fork and carefully went up the concrete stairs to the family room where our photo album had been. The heat had been so intense that the television set had melted. The roof had collapsed and burned, and I could see nothing

but blackened walls and about four to five feet of ashes and rubble. I
went to the area of the room where the album had been lying on a
table. I began to dig. As I got down near the floor level, the fork hit
something solid. I carefully dug around it and lifted it up with the
fork. It was a large black blob. Although I could not recognize any
part of it, I felt that I knew what it was. I gingerly carried it down the
stairs and outside into the cool morning. I called my family together.
They were puzzled as to what I had. Carefully I removed the layers
of blackened and burned material on the outside until we saw the
photographs. Every picture had been preserved, although some of
the edges were singed. Our children were ecstatic and one exclaimed,
"Dad, look! Our pictures have been antiqued!"

I am so grateful that a loving Heavenly Father cared about our
family portraits and preserved them for us. Today, nearly thirty years
later, our "antiqued" family portraits are a testimony and reminder
of Heavenly Father's love and concern for each of His children. But
more miraculous and meaningful even than that experience has been
the spirit and power that touched a precious daughter's heart and
brought her back to our eternal family. Although too personal and
sacred to relate, that has brought a witness and gratitude to each family member's heart of the power and blessing of Elijah's mission and
the Savior's Atonement.

CONCLUSION

Truly, the more clearly we are able to see eternity, the more mon-
umental Elijah's mission becomes. President Benson has said: "God
bless us to receive all the blessings revealed by Elijah the prophet so
that our callings and election will be made sure."[20] Some years ago,
at the dedication of the temple in Buenos Aires, Argentina, Elder
Boyd K. Packer said: "We are dedicating a monument to [the] resurrection and exaltation of the human family. If the outside world
knew about what was happening here, the cars would stop, planes
would not take off, and people would gather to see what the Lord
hath wrought. This work we have a part in; it is cause for great rejoic-
ing."[21] Indeed it is. Of this I testify.

NOTES

   1. Joseph Smith, *Teachings of the Prophet Joseph Smith,* comp. Joseph
      Fielding Smith (Salt Lake City: Deseret Book, 1938), 172.

2. Joseph Fielding Smith, *Doctrines of Salvation* (Salt Lake City: Bookcraft, 1955), 2:108–11.

3. Smith, *Doctrines of Salvation,* 2:108–10.

4. Smith, *Teachings of the Prophet Joseph Smith,* 323, 337–38.

5. Smith, *Doctrines of Salvation,* 3:129–30.

6. Smith, *Doctrines of Salvation,* 2:117.

7. Boyd K. Packer, *The Holy Temple* (Salt Lake City: Bookcraft, 1980), 174; emphasis added.

8. Smith, *Doctrines of Salvation,* 2:127.

9. Spencer W. Kimball, devotional address given at the Salt Lake University Institute of Religion, January 10, 1975.

10. *Utah Genealogical and Historical Magazine,* October 1934, 189.

11. Ezra Taft Benson, "What I Hope You Will Teach Your Children about the Temple," *Ensign,* August 1985, 10.

12. Melvin R. Ballard, *Melvin J. Ballard, Crusader for Righteousness* (Salt Lake City: Bookcraft, 1977), 219.

13. Copy in author's possession.

14. Wilford Woodruff, in *Journal of Discourses* (London: Latter-day Saints' Book Depot, 1882), 22:334.

15. Neal A. Maxwell, in *Church News,* September 1, 1990, 7.

16. Copy in author's possession.

17. *Church News,* January 5, 1980, 12.

18. Melvin S. Tagg, "The Life of Edward James Wood: Church Patriot" (master's thesis, Brigham Young University, 1959), 118–19.

19. Harold B. Lee, banquet speech delivered at the Eighth Annual Priesthood Genealogical Seminar, August 3, 1973; printed in "Syllabus for the Ninth Annual Priesthood Genealogy Seminar," 529–30, typescript.

20. Benson, "What I Hope You Will Teach Your Children," 10.

21. *Church News,* January 26, 1986, 6.

CHAPTER TWENTY

THE LORD WILL REDEEM HIS PEOPLE: ADOPTIVE COVENANT AND REDEMPTION IN THE OLD TESTAMENT

JENNIFER C. LANE

In singing the hymn "Redeemer of Israel," I have always enjoyed the message of the Lord's sustaining and protecting power, but until recently I had never asked myself, What does it mean that the Lord is the Redeemer of Israel? What does it mean to be a redeemer? Why is He the Redeemer of Israel? When and how did He become Israel's redeemer?

Likewise, biblical scholarship has not often addressed these questions. Some scholars have briefly noted a correlation between redemption and covenant, but questions such as why, when, and how the Lord became the Redeemer of Israel are not frequently asked. The Lord's characterization as redeemer is usually seen by scholars as a vague reference to His desire to help His people. More specific study of His role as redeemer is rarely made.

An examination of the text of the Old Testament, however, suggests that the Lord's acts of redemption involve far more than simply an exercise of strength for a people He loves. The role of a redeemer in ancient Israelite society carried with it specific responsibilities and a very specific relation to the person redeemed. To the Israelites, a

Jennifer C. Lane is assistant professor of Religious Education at Brigham Young University—Hawaii.

redeemer was a close family member responsible for helping other family members who had lost their property, liberty, or lives by buying them out of their bondage or avenging them. The family relationship was the reason the redeemer acted on behalf of his enslaved kinsman.[1]

The Old Testament further indicates that those people for whom the Lord acts as redeemer likewise have established a familial relationship with Him. Covenants in the Old Testament are repeatedly associated with the giving of a new name, which indicates a new character and a new relationship. Those covenants are the means by which individuals, or Israel as a people, are "adopted" into a new relationship and receive a new name. They become part of the family of the Lord and, as their kinsman, He becomes their redeemer. I refer to this idea of familial ties being created by covenant and expressed in the giving of a new name as adoptive redemption.

As Latter-day Saints, we recognize that we are the spirit children of our Father in Heaven. Through our own sins, we separate ourselves from our Father and enslave ourselves spiritually. Christ, also known as Jehovah, the God of the Old Testament, can act as our intermediary to redeem us from spiritual bondage if we make and keep covenants with Him. When we covenant with Christ and take His name upon us, we become His "adopted" children and He becomes our spiritual Father. King Benjamin explained, "Because of the covenant which ye have made ye shall be called the children of Christ, his sons, and his daughters" (Mosiah 5:7). Thus, the Book of Mormon supports the Old Testament connection between the making of a covenant and the receiving of a new name, whereby the Lord allows people to enter into an adoptive relationship with Him so that He can act as their redeemer. An overview of the use of *redemption, name,* and *covenant,* combined with an examination of critical biblical passages, demonstrates how the covenantal relationship between the Lord and His people binds the two parties together and permits the Lord to act as the Redeemer of Israel.

REDEMPTION IN THE OLD TESTAMENT: DEFINITIONS AND USAGE

In the Old Testament, two words, *ga'al* and *padah,* are usually translated as *redeem* in English. Both express the idea of "buy[ing] back" or "releas[ing] by the payment of a price"[2] and are often used interchangeably, illustrating the concept of salvation through a commercial or legal transaction. Both verbs also imply a mortal danger or a fatal situation from which one needs to be redeemed.[3]

Although these two terms are often used interchangeably, there are several clear differences in connotation between the two. *Padah* is essentially a commercial term that shares a common root with words in other Semitic languages, such as the Arabic *fidan* ("ransom money") or the Akkadian *padû* ("to set free").[4] *Padah* refers only to the change of ownership from "evil" ownership (slavery) to "good" ownership (being repurchased by a family member) and freedom. The motive for the redemption is not essential to the meaning of the word; this idea of redemption does not suggest prerogative, right, or duty.[5] The classic distinction between *ga'al* and *padah* is that *ga'al* is used in connection with family law, whereas *padah* is linked mainly with commercial law.[6]

Unlike *padah, ga'al* has no Semitic cognates; therefore, the base meaning cannot be traced etymologically. Some have suggested root meanings such as "to cover," "to protect," "to lay claim to someone or to something," "to redeem," and "to repurchase."[7] *Ga'al* carries a sense of duty (for the redeemer) or right (for the person redeemed). This duty is based on familial ties to the person or object (usually land) to be redeemed and can be understood as a recuperation or a restoration.[8] The person who carries this responsibility is known as the *go'el,* which is the participle form of *ga'al.*

THE ROLE OF THE *GO'EL*

The *go'el* was a person's closest relative who was "responsible for standing up for him and maintaining his rights,"[9] a responsibility based on feelings of tribal unity. In a sense, the *go'el* represents the clan, exemplifying the ancient Hebrew concept of vicarious solidarity.[10] Basic duties of the *go'el* were to buy back sold property; to buy back a man who had sold himself to a foreigner as a slave; to avenge blood and kill a relative's murderer; to receive atonement money; and, figuratively, to be a helper in a lawsuit.[11] Michael S. Moore makes several perceptive observations about the spiritual implications of the role of redeemer. He suggests that the *go'el*'s temporal responsibilities can be understood only in light of spiritual relationships. He argues that "all the legal material which deals with the duties of the *go'el* is predicated by Israel's relationship to Yahweh."[12]

Moore describes the *go'el* as the "cultural gyroscope" of Israel, whose purpose is to restore equilibrium, and claims that the social and economic situations of Israel must be seen in light of their relationship with the Lord. Israel's responsibility is to obey the Lord's statutes and ordinances; in return for their obedience, they will be blessed with economic and social equilibrium. Events that disrupt the social equilibrium, such as manslaughter, the death of one's husband or male children, or the obligation in time of poverty to sell one's ancestral estate, affect the whole of the kinship group. Thus "the *go'el* functions as a restorative agent whenever there is a breach in the clan's corporate life."[13]

The need to restore the social equilibrium can help us understand the role of the *go'el* as the avenger of blood (*go'el ha-dam*). It has been argued etymologically that the root meaning of *ga'al* is "to revenge" or "to protect" and that the basic duty of the family was to avenge the death of a kinsman.[14] Moore insists that what western minds may see as excessive vengeance must be understood in an Israelite context. He writes that whereas "western societies restore justice by means of external laws imputed by the State, ancient Israelite society restored justice by means of the divinely appointed agent of restoration (Leviticus 25:25ff)."[15] Another scholar claims that the "vengeance of blood . . . acts less as a vengeance than as a recuperation,"[16] suggesting that the blood of the murderer acts as compensation for the life of his victim.[17]

THE LORD AS THE *GO'EL* OF ISRAEL

All of the various duties of the redeemer are at different times assumed by the Lord, who acts as the *go'el* of Israel in the Old Testament. The idea of intimate kinship, essential to the role of the *go'el,* is connected with the Lord in Isaiah 63:16, where Isaiah cries out, "Doubtless thou art our father, though Abraham be ignorant of us, and Israel acknowledge us not: thou, O Lord, art our father, our redeemer; thy name is from everlasting." The Lord's protection of orphans and widows is described in Proverbs 23:10–11 and Isaiah 54:4–5. He is also portrayed as the redeemer of individuals, as the worshipper in Lamentations 3:52–58 states: "Mine enemies chased me sore, like a bird, without cause. They have cut off my life in the dungeon, and cast a stone upon me. Waters flowed over mine head;

then I said, I am cut off. I called upon thy name, O Lord, out of the low dungeon. Thou hast heard my voice: hide not thine ear at my breathing, at my cry. Thou drewest near in the day that I called upon thee: thou saidst, Fear not. O Lord, thou hast pleaded the causes of my soul; *thou hast redeemed my life*" (emphasis added).

REDEMPTION AS A SUBCLASS OF SALVATION

In addition to questions about meaning and usage of *ga'al* and *padah*, there is a confusion about the use of the English words *save* and *redeem*. Although they seem to be used interchangeably and are sometimes assumed to be synonyms because they both do convey the meaning of "deliver," nonetheless *redeem* is a subclass of *save*. In both English and Hebrew, there is a clear difference in meaning: *save* means any kind of deliverance, and *redeem* means, specifically, deliverance based upon a payment. The English word *save* is from the Latin *salvare* ("to save") and *salvus* ("safe"), and its basic meaning is "to deliver or rescue from peril or hurt; to make safe, put in safety."[18] There is no intrinsic indication of how this rescue is performed. With *redeem,* on the other hand, the Latin root specifically means "to buy back," *re(d)* + *emere*. Accordingly, the basic meaning in English is "to buy back (a thing formerly possessed); to make payment for (a thing held or claimed by another)."[19]

Although the meaning of Hebrew words may not be as clear as English words because of our limited information on etymology and usage, the words used to express the general concept of salvation are different from those used to refer to salvation through a specific means. The most common Hebrew root meaning "save" is *yasa*.

W. L. Liefeld notes that "whereas other terms describe specific aspects of salvation (e.g., redemption), *yasa* is a general term. . . . The root idea seems to be that of enlargement . . . removing that which restricts."[20] Other Hebrew words that express a general concept of delivering include *nasal, palat,* and *malat*. Those terms clearly differ from *ga'al* and *padah,* which refer to deliverance through the payment of a ransom.

NAME GIVING AND COVENANT MAKING

To understand the significance in the Old Testament of giving a name, it is essential to appreciate the importance of names to the

Israelites.[21] The Hebrew word *sem,* usually translated *name,* can also be rendered *remembrance* or *memorial,* indicating that the name acts as a reminder to its bearers and others. The name shows both the true nature of its bearer and the relationship that exists between people. The Old Testament records several instances when names were changed to indicate a corresponding change in character and conduct, thus illustrating the Hebrew belief that names represent something of the essence of a person. A new name, therefore, shows a new status or a new relationship. That new relationship may express the dependent state of the person who receives a new name; at the same time, renaming may also indicate a type of adoption.[22]

To the Israelites, covenant making symbolized the formation of a new relationship. In a discussion of the establishment of the covenant at Sinai—and the associated ritual meal of Moses and the elders of Israel with the Lord—in Exodus 24:9–11, Dennis J. McCarthy comments: "To see a great chief and eat in his place is to join his family in the root sense of that Latin word [*gens*]: the whole group related by blood or not which stood under the authority and protection of the father. One is united to him as a client to his patron who protects him and whom he serves. . . . Covenant is something one makes by a rite, not something one is born to or forced into, and it can be described in family terms. God is patron and father, Israel servant and son."[23]

By making a covenant with the Lord, the people of Israel enter into His family and protection. That concept is explicitly expressed in terms of adoption when the Lord tells Moses: "I will take you to me for a people, and I will be to you a God" (Exodus 6:7).

OLD TESTAMENT EXAMPLES OF ADOPTIVE REDEMPTION

An examination of biblical passages that include redemption, covenant making, and name giving illuminates the adoptive aspect of covenantal redemption and demonstrates that it is this creation of an adoptive relationship by covenant that is the basis for the Lord's acts of redemption. The story of the covenant of Abraham, for example, is central both to the Old Testament and to subsequent religious traditions. It gives a sense of identity to many religious groups that look to Abraham as their father. Even the Lord repeatedly refers to that covenant, calling Himself the God of Abraham, Isaac, and

Jacob. The central text for this covenant and the name change from Abram to Abraham is found in Genesis 17:1–8. This passage does not touch on redemption specifically, but it contains two elements that are central to the covenant-redemption relationship: renaming and adoption.

In this passage, as part of the covenant, Abram is called by a new name, Abraham, "father of a multitude," denoting a change in nature and character. In addition, there is a specific promise of adoption. The Lord says, "I will establish my covenant between me and thee and thy seed . . . to be a God unto thee, and to thy seed after thee" (Genesis 17:7). This adoptive covenant makes Abraham and his descendants the people of the Lord. It establishes a sense of possession, a familial relation that allows the Lord to act as a *go'el* and redeem, or buy back, His people from slavery. Though the concept of redemption is not specifically related to Abraham in this passage, it may have been understood, as we infer from a statement made hundreds of years later by Isaiah, who referred to God as the redeemer of Abraham: "Therefore thus saith the Lord, *who redeemed Abraham,* concerning the house of Jacob" (Isaiah 29:22; emphasis added).

These same elements—renaming and establishing a covenant—are combined with the idea of redemption in the story of Jacob and the angel. The texts that relate this story are found in both Genesis 32:24–30 and Genesis 48:14–16. The first passage tells of Jacob's wrestling with the angel and receiving a new name. The second passage is the blessing that Jacob (Israel) gave to his grandchildren Ephraim and Manasseh, in which he referred to his experience with the angel when he received his new name. In the second passage, which represents Jacob's commentary on the original incident, Jacob clearly identifies his experience as an act of redemption. When Jacob refers to "the Angel which redeemed me from all evil" (Genesis 48:16), it could be argued that he is referring to the Lord Himself. He "called the name of the place Peniel: for I have seen God face to face" (Genesis 32:30) and declared that his life had been preserved. In the Hebrew text, the angel is called *ha-go'el,* "the redeemer" or "the one redeeming." In both passages, the concept of renaming or passing on a name is central. In the original description, Jacob is blessed in response to his request by being given the new name *Israel.* Then, in Genesis 48, Jacob blesses his grandsons Ephraim and Manasseh, recalling his redemption, and asks for the angel's blessing to be upon the boys, giving them his name and the names of Abraham and Isaac.

In the account of the deliverance out of Egypt, we find another clear connection between redemption and covenant. In Exodus 5, Moses speaks to the Lord, reporting on his unsuccessful efforts to convince Pharaoh to release the children of Israel. The Lord responds that He has "heard the groaning of the children of Israel" (Exodus 6:5) and remembered the covenant that He made with Abraham, Isaac, and Jacob. Because of this covenant, He promises to act as a redeemer: "I will bring you out from under the burdens of the Egyptians, and I will rid you out of their bondage, and I will redeem you with a stretched out arm, and with great judgments" (Exodus 6:6). This connection between covenant and redemption is clearly explained in Deuteronomy 7:8: "Because he would keep the oath which he had sworn unto your fathers, hath the Lord brought you out with a mighty hand, and redeemed you out of the house of bondmen, from the hand of Pharaoh king of Egypt."

After the promise of redemption from bondage in Egypt because of previous covenants, the Lord promises to establish that adoptive relationship with the house of Israel as a people. The phrase "I will take you to me for a people, and I will be to you a God" (Exodus 6:7) is reminiscent of a sense of adoption in the individual covenants the Lord made with Abraham and Jacob. The adoption to become the people of the Lord suggests a sense of family obligation that is the basis of the redemption provided by the *go'el* in Hebrew legal practice. Interestingly, because the *go'el* has the responsibility to both redeem family members out of slavery and also to restore land to those who have lost it, this passage contains the promise that the land will be given as "a heritage" by the Lord.

The story of the redemption from Egypt remained a powerful image to later Old Testament prophets. In Psalm 74:1–2, the Psalmist cries out to the Lord for help and recalls the memory of His redemption and adoption of Israel: "O God, why hast thou cast us off for ever? why doth thine anger smoke against the sheep of thy pasture? Remember thy congregation, which thou hast purchased of old; the rod of thine inheritance, which thou hast redeemed; this mount Zion, wherein thou hast dwelt." Here again, the purchase of Israel is cited as a source of connection with the Lord that allows present-day Israel to call for divine help.

The Lord is repeatedly identified as the *go'el* of Israel in the writings of Isaiah, where the redemption of Israel is portrayed as both a past and a future event. In Isaiah 43:1–3, the redemption and adoption of Israel are cited as sources of comfort for present fears: "But now thus saith the Lord that created thee, O Jacob, and he that formed thee, O Israel, Fear not: for I have redeemed thee, I have called thee by thy name; thou art mine. When thou passest through the waters, I will be with thee; and through the rivers, they shall not overflow thee: when thou walkest through the fire, thou shalt not be burned; neither shall the flame kindle upon thee. For I am the Lord thy God, the Holy One of Israel, thy Saviour: I gave Egypt for thy ransom, Ethiopia and Seba for thee." Here again the redemption of Israel is connected with both the giving of a name and the creating of a tie between the Lord and Israel: "Thou art mine" (Isaiah 43:1). The mention of the Lord's position as redeemer assures that He will be with Israel in future troubles and trials.

The comfort of past redemption and the promise of future deliverance are combined in Isaiah 63. To demonstrate the goodness and mercy of the Lord for the house of Israel, Isaiah refers to the redemption out of Egypt: "In all their affliction he was afflicted, and the angel of his presence saved them: in his love and in his pity he redeemed them; and he bare them, and carried them all the days of old. . . . As a beast goeth down into the valley, the Spirit of the Lord caused him to rest: so didst thou lead thy people, to make thyself a glorious name" (vv. 9, 14). Isaiah specifically refers to this act of the Lord as a redemption rather than simply a deliverance. He explains the motive for this action twice, once speaking about the Lord and the other time in direct address, saying that the Lord did it "to make himself an everlasting name" (v. 12). Even though this particular phrase does not specifically connect to the common theme of giving Israel a name, that concept is part of the fundamental role of the *go'el*, who was to redeem his kinsmen in order to protect the family name. Isaiah's mention of "the angel of his presence" that saved them is reminiscent of Jacob's reference to the "Angel which redeemed me from all evil" (Genesis 48:16). More likely, however, Isaiah refers to the angel in the promise the Lord made to Israel as they left Egypt: "I send an Angel before thee, to keep thee in the way, and to bring thee into the place which I have prepared. Beware of him, and obey his voice . . . for my name is in him" (Exodus 23:20–21). Interestingly, in both situations—Jacob's struggle and the deliverance of the house of Israel—there is an association with angels, a name, and redemption.

In all of these Old Testament passages, whether descriptions of original events or commentaries by later prophets, the Lord's acts of redemption are connected to covenant making and name giving. Like an ancient Israelite *go'el,* by whose title He is called, the Redeemer of Israel acts to save His adoptive kinsmen from bondage. Those adoptive family ties with both individuals and the house of Israel are created by the "rebirth" provided by covenant and indicated in the giving of a new name.

ADOPTIVE REDEMPTION IN THE BOOK OF MORMON

The distinctive Israelite concept of a redeemer as a close family member is seen in the Book of Mormon as well as in the Old Testament.[24] As in the Old Testament, redemption is a central theme of the Book of Mormon. The concept of redemption in the Book of Mormon fits the ancient Near Eastern practice of buying someone out of slavery and bondage. That redemption is often expressed in spiritual terms, as seen in references to the "chains of hell" (Alma 5:7), "the captivity of the devil" (1 Nephi 14:4), and others. Just as the writers of the Book of Mormon saw captivity in spiritual terms, so they also saw redemption as a spiritual matter and sought to persuade people that Jesus Christ is the Redeemer (see Alma 37:5–10).

The concept of a redeemer in the Book of Mormon clearly matches the Israelite concept of the *go'el,* a family member who had the responsibility to redeem his kinsmen from bondage. The Lord's acts of redemption are connected to covenants that establish an adoptive relationship with a person or a people; when they enter into an adoptive covenantal relationship and receive a new name, Christ becomes their *go'el* and is able to redeem them from spiritual captivity.

One clear and concise textual example of the connection between covenant and redemption is found in Mosiah 18, in which Alma talks to the subjects of King Noah who have come into the wilderness to hear him teach the words of Abinadi. We are told that, in the city, Alma taught the people "concerning the resurrection of the dead, and the redemption of the people, which was to be brought to pass through the power, and sufferings, and death of Christ, and his resurrection and ascension into heaven" (Mosiah 18:2). Those who believed his teachings went to the waters of Mormon, where he "did preach unto them repentance, and redemption, and faith on the Lord" (Mosiah 18:7). When they were ready to enter into a covenant with the Lord, Alma addressed them in a famous discussion of the duties of the Saints associated with the baptismal covenant.

Alma's speech is even more interesting when we notice the explicit connections between covenant, adoption, and redemption. In Mosiah 18:8–9, Alma mentions the people's desire "to come into the fold of God, and to be called his people" and "to bear one another's burdens, that they may be light; . . . that ye may be redeemed of God, and be numbered with those of the first resurrection, that ye may have eternal life." This passage explicitly states that coming "into the fold of God" and being "called his people" (v. 8) are necessary in order to be redeemed of God. In Mosiah 18:10, Alma explains how this adoption is possible, saying that "if this be the desire of your hearts, what have you against being baptized in the name of the Lord, as a witness before him that ye have entered into a covenant with him." The baptismal covenant acts here as an adoption, which allows the Lord to become the redeemer, or *go'el*, of the individual who has taken His name upon him and covenanted with Him.

CONCLUSION

Knowing that an Israelite redeemer was a close family member fulfilling family responsibility gives a new perspective on the Lord's actions as the Redeemer of Israel. It is through covenants and the reception of a new name that individuals are adopted into the family of the Lord and are eligible to be redeemed. Paralleling the Israelite concept of the *go'el* as a close relative whose responsibility was to redeem his kinsmen, this adoptive covenant can be understood as the basis for the Lord's redemptive actions as the *go'el* of Israel.

An understanding of the role of covenants in creating an adoptive relationship with the Lord, allowing Him to act as *go'el*, is more than a scriptural or historical footnote. The concept of adoptive redemption explains the importance of making covenants to qualify for redemption through the Atonement of Christ. This understanding is crucial for Latter-day Saints as a modern covenant people. To fully appreciate the importance of covenants, we must recognize that we are in bondage and that, like the ancient Israelites, we need a *go'el* to redeem us. We need Christ to become our spiritual father and ransom us from spiritual bondage, understanding that "were it not for the redemption which he hath made for his people, which was prepared from the foundation of the world, . . . all mankind must have perished" (Mosiah 15:19). To appreciate the power of our covenants, we must recognize not only that we are in bondage but also that our *go'el* has already paid the price of redemption, that "he suffer[ed] the pains of all men, yea, the pains of every living creature, both men, women, and children" (2 Nephi 9:21). With the knowledge that our *go'el* has paid the ransom price, we can claim the redemptive power of the Lord because we have established an adoptive relationship with Him through our covenants. We must believe in the reality of that relationship and "exercise faith in the redemption of him who created [us]" (Alma 5:15).

NOTES

1. "*Ga'al*," in *Theological Dictionary of the Old Testament,* ed. G. Johannes Botterweck and Helmer Ringgren (Grand Rapids, MI: Eerdmans, 1975), 351–52.

2. J. Murray, "Redeemer; Redemption," *The International Standard Bible Encyclopedia,* ed. Geoffrey W. Bromiley (Grand Rapids, MI: Eerdmans, 1979), 4:61.

3. Evode Beaucamp, "Aux origines du mot 'rédemption' le 'rachat' dans l'ancien testament," *Laval Théologique et Philosophique* 34 (1978): 50–51.

4. Gerhard Kittel, ed., *Theological Dictionary of the New Testament* (Grand Rapids, MI: Eerdmans Publishing, 1967), 330–31, s.v. "Luo."

5. Beaucamp, "Aux origines," 53.

6. Johann Jakob Stamm, *Erlösen und Vergeben im Alten Testament* (Bern: A. Francke A.-G, 1940), 30.

7. Botterweck and Ringgren, *Theological Dictionary of the Old Testament,* 351. An interesting discussion of these different root meanings is found in Michael S. Moore, "*Haggo'el:* The Cultural

Gyroscope of Ancient Hebrew Society," *Restoration Quarterly* 23, no. 1 (1988): 27–28.

8. Beaucamp, "Aux origines," 53.

9. Botterweck and Ringgren, *Theological Dictionary of the Old Testament*, 351.

10. Cuthbert Lattey, "Vicarious Solidarity in the Old Testament," *Vetus Testamentum* 1 (October 1951): 267–74.

11. Botterweck and Ringgren, *Theological Dictionary of the Old Testament*, 351–52.

12. Moore, *"Haggo'el,"* 29.

13. Moore, *"Haggo'el,"* 31.

14. Mario Cimosa, "Translating *Go'el Ha-dam*," *The Bible Translator* 41 (July 1990): 319–26.

15. Moore, *"Haggo'el,"* 33. "Such total vengeance is difficult for western minds to comprehend and may underlie much of the Occidental world's attempts to see a different God in the Old Testament from the God revealed in the pages of the New Testament."

16. Beaucamp, "Aux origines," 54. "Il s'agit moins d'une vengeance, que d'une récupération." Translation mine.

17. Beaucamp, "Aux origines," 54.

18. *Oxford English Dictionary*, 2nd ed., s.v. "Save."

19. *Oxford English Dictionary*, 2nd ed., s.v. "Redeem."

20. W. L. Liefeld, "Salvation," *International Standard Bible Encyclopedia*, 4:288.

21. G. F. Hawthorne, "Name," *International Standard Bible Encyclopedia*, 3:481–83; D. Stuart, "Names, Proper," *International Standard Bible Encyclopedia*, 3:483–88.

22. Bruce H. Porter and Stephen D. Ricks, "Names in Antiquity: Old, New, and Hidden," in *By Study and Also by Faith* (Salt Lake City: Deseret Book, 1990), 504–5.

23. Dennis J. McCarthy, *Treaty and Covenant: A Study in the Ancient Oriental Documents and in the Old Testament* (Rome: Biblical Institute Press, 1978), 266.

24. For a further discussion of adoptive covenant and redemption in the Book of Mormon, see my paper, "The Lord Will Redeem His People: 'Adoptive' Covenant and Redemption in the Old Testament and the Book of Mormon," *Journal of Book of Mormon Studies* 2 (Fall 1993): 39–62. For my study of New Testament implications, see "Hebrew Concepts of Adoption and Redemption in the Writings of Paul," in *The Apostle Paul: His Life and Testimony*, ed. Paul Y. Hoskisson (Salt Lake City: Deseret Book, 1994), 80–95.

CHAPTER TWENTY-ONE

THE RESTORATION AS COVENANT RENEWAL

DAVID ROLPH SEELY

The Lord, in His preface to the Doctrine and Covenants, says that because the world has "broken mine everlasting covenant" the Restoration was necessary, "that mine everlasting covenant might be established" (1:15, 22). Thus, the concept of covenant is central to understanding the restored gospel. Covenant is a central and unifying theme of the scriptures beginning in the Hebrew Bible and reflected in the very title of the book in Christendom—the Old Testament. The English word "testament" ultimately derives from the Hebrew word for "covenant,"[1] whereas the term "old" is used to designate the Mosaic covenant—in effect until the time of Christ—and contrasted with the terminology of Jeremiah, who prophesied the future establishment of a "new" covenant (Jeremiah 31:31). The Apostle Paul confirmed that Jesus Christ fulfilled Jeremiah's prophecy and was the "mediator of the new testament [covenant]" (Hebrews 9:15).[2] Therefore, the record of the ministry of Jesus and the early covenant community became known as the New Testament, and the titles of both parts of the Christian Bible, the Old Testament and the New Testament, refer to the two significant stages of biblical covenant. The covenant document of the new and everlasting covenant is called the Doctrine and Covenants.

Covenant is an eternal principle that defines the relationship between God and His children. It is a process by which God

---

David Rolph Seely is a professor of ancient scripture at Brigham Young University.

administers the plan of happiness. The Lord for His part promises His children redemption from their fallen state, and the direction and the sacred ordinances necessary for salvation and exaltation while preserving the conditions in which agency can be exercised. The covenant children, in turn, voluntarily commit themselves to remember and obey their Father and to accept and apply the power of the Atonement in their lives in order to fulfill the measure of their creation—to find joy in mortality and eternal life in the world to come. Covenant thus provides purpose, meaning, and direction to mortality, as a time of probation, and defines the various degrees of glory in the hereafter as the promised rewards of the covenant relationship.

From modern revelation we learn that the Lord has administered His covenant to His children from the very beginning and that Adam was the first to accept the gospel of Jesus Christ and enter into the covenant through the ordinance of baptism (see Moses 6:62–67). The scriptures record the restoration, or renewal, of this same covenant at pivotal times in history, through Noah, Abraham, Moses, and in the meridian of time through Jesus Christ, who fulfilled the Mosaic covenant and established the "new covenant" (see Hebrews 8–9). In this, the last dispensation, the Lord has once again restored the fullness of the gospel and renewed the new and everlasting covenant (D&C 1:17). Since the basic principles of the covenant are eternal, every time the covenant is revealed to an individual or a community it is in a real sense a "restoration" or "renewal" of this special relationship between God and man. The renewal aspect of covenant may be referred to in the phrase "new and everlasting covenant." The covenant is "everlasting" in that it is the same "from the beginning" (D&C 22:1), and yet it is "new," both in the sense that it is a fulfillment of the "old covenant" or law of Moses, and it is always "new" to each dispensation in which it is restored and to each individual who enters into it.

The Old Testament provides crucial information for those who have entered into the new and everlasting covenant by helping us to understand the significance of the covenant, its promised blessings and curses, and how God has dealt with His children in the past. Furthermore, it recounts the historical consequences of obedience or disobedience to the conditions of the covenant. A careful reading of the well-known scriptural accounts of the actual giving of the covenant to Adam, Noah, Abraham, and Moses, and its fulfillment through Jesus Christ, is essential for a study of this important concept. In addition to these texts, however, there is a series of often overlooked passages that further illuminate our understanding of covenant. These are the accounts of the periodic covenant-renewal assemblies and ceremonies, when the covenant children—typically following periods of apostasy, or at times of crisis or transition—are assembled by their leader to publicly rededicate themselves to the conditions of the covenant. Among these accounts are the assemblies recorded in Joshua 8:30–35 and chapter 24 when Joshua called the people together at Shechem; 2 Kings 22–23 when King Josiah, after the discovery of the book of the law, gathered the people to the temple; and Ezra 9–10 and Nehemiah 9–10 when Ezra recommitted the postexilic community at Jerusalem to the laws of the Mosaic covenant. In addition to the Old Testament, a detailed account of a similar covenant renewal assembly is found in the Book of Mormon in Mosiah 1–6 when the people are gathered together by King Benjamin to renew their commitment to the Mosaic covenant.

The "restoration of all things" is covenant renewal on a grand scale and bears with it an obligation to study the scriptural history of the covenant and covenant-renewal. This study will attempt to demonstrate the importance of the scriptural accounts for an understanding and appreciation of the Restoration in two steps. First, a review and summary will be made of the biblical evidence in order to arrive at a definition of covenant and covenant renewal. This will be done by first examining in some detail the account of the establishment of the Mosaic covenant in Exodus 19–24 and then two examples of covenant renewal found in Joshua 24 and 2 Kings 22–23, as well as the account of the fulfillment and establishment of the new covenant by Jesus Christ In the course of this discussion we will identify the seven elements of biblical covenant. Second, the events and teachings of the Restoration will be presented as covenant renewal, and the same seven elements corresponding to the biblical covenant pattern will be identified and discussed in light of the restored gospel. In this discussion we will demonstrate the value of the study of ancient covenants for an understanding of the Restoration and, at the same time, the value of the more fully

documented account of covenant renewal through the Restoration
for a comprehension of covenant in antiquity.

THE STRUCTURE AND CONTENT OF BIBLICAL COVENANT

Scholars have long recognized the importance of covenant in the
Bible, and it has been the focus of much research through the years.
The scholarly discussion in the past has basically been centered on:
(1) a description of the historical setting and the content of the
covenant—particularly the Mosaic covenant—as described in the biblical text; and (2) an examination of the function of covenant in the
religious institutions of the Israelite community.

For the most part, the attempts to describe the setting and content
of covenant have been based on the texts of the Pentateuch and
other relevant legal, historical, and prophetic passages that describe
the establishment and conditions of the covenant. Most recently can
be cited the work in this regard of Albrecht Alt, Walther Eichrodt,
and Gerhard von Rad.[3] The most extensive of these studies on
covenant is Eichrodt's two-volume *Theology of the Old Testament,* in
which he proposed that the "covenant-idea" is the central theme of
the Old Testament (as well as the New Testament), and attempted to
interpret all of biblical history and thought as it relates to this important concept.

The study of covenant in the religious institutions of Israel has its
origins in Sigmund Mowinckel's *The Psalms in Israel's Worship* and
has been carried on by others with varying conclusions, such as
Claus Westermann and H. J. Kraus.[4] Mowinckel argued, for example,
from the evidence in the various enthronement psalms, that a
covenant-renewal ceremony was an integral part of an annual New
Year's festival associated with what we know today as the Feast of
Tabernacles.[5]

In 1955, George E. Mendenhall published his seminal study *Law
and Covenant in Israel and the Ancient Near East,*[6] which had a major
impact on the study of biblical covenant. Comparing the structure
of a relatively large and detailed corpus of Hittite international
suzerainty treaties/covenants (meaning a treaty or covenant between
a king or ruler and a vassal) from 1450–1200 B.C. (approximately the
period of the Mosaic covenant), Mendenhall set forth a typology of
seven elements that regularly appear in such covenants. Although

some of these had previously been identified in the Bible, this study provided a much wider context for discussion and, with minor variations, these seven elements of the covenant have been accepted by most scholars as the major structural elements of biblical covenant.[7]

These elements can be summarized as follows: (1) *Preamble:* An introductory statement which identifies the author of the covenant, in the case of the Hittite treaties the suzerain (the ruler), and his titles, attributes, and authority; (2) *Historical Prologue:* This section describes the past relations between the two covenanting parties with special emphasis on the benevolent acts of the suzerain toward the vassal, implying reciprocal obligation; (3) *Stipulations:* This part sets forth the conditions of the covenant; (4) *Provisions for Deposit and Public Reading:* A clause providing for a safe deposit (often in the sanctuary of the vassal) and a requirement that it be regularly read to the public; (5) *List of Witnesses:* Usually the local deities, but often natural phenomena as well (mountains, rivers, springs, heavens, earth, etc.), are cited as witnesses to the covenant; (6) *Blessings and Curses:* This section contains the blessings predicated on obedience to the covenant and the curses threatened in the case of disobedience.

In addition to these six elements, Mendenhall recognizes that there must have been a formal oath by which the vassal pledged his obedience, and a solemn ceremony that accompanied such an oath with "symbolic actions" to dramatize various aspects of the agreement and sometimes acting out or otherwise indicating the punishment promised for disobedience.[8] Thus the seventh element is (7) the *Covenant Oath Ceremony.* The actual ceremony is lacking in the Hittite documents but is represented in the biblical texts by accounts of the assembly of the people to formally accept the law contained in the conditions of the covenant. However, Mendenhall notes that even in the accounts of these ceremonies we lack the exact language of the oath itself and the accompanying symbolic act.[9]

Focusing on a similar covenant assembly found in Mosiah 1–6, several Latter–day Saint scholars—Hugh Nibley, John Tvedtnes, John Welch, and Stephen Ricks[10]—have compared the account of the covenant-renewal ceremony in the Book of Mormon to the biblical accounts. Arguing both from the structure of the covenant and the covenant assembly, and from the similarities that the Book of

Mormon account shares with the Feast of Tabernacles, they have persuasively demonstrated that King Benjamin's address, and the accompanying assembly, fit the biblical pattern remarkably well. Ricks has adopted the general pattern of seven elements suggested by Mendenhall with some slight variations, and has provided an excellent discussion of the covenant ceremony in Mosiah as well as a useful chart of these specific elements in the treaty-covenant pattern in Exodus 19:3–8; Exodus 20–24; the book of Deuteronomy as a whole; Joshua 24; and Mosiah 1–6.[11]

The present study will survey these seven basic elements as a way of describing and defining the structure, and hence the content, of biblical covenant. While the historical setting and some of the specific details of each covenant and covenant ceremony are different, these seven elements are almost always present in the scriptural accounts. Identifying the common elements can help us to understand the structure and dynamics of covenant and recognize the meaning of important covenantal passages that otherwise may appear difficult and randomly organized.

THE MOSAIC COVENANT

The Old Testament account of the revelation of the Mosaic covenant is recorded in Exodus 19–24.[12] The words of the formal *Preamble* of the covenant identify God as the initiator and suzerain of the covenant: "And God spake all these words" (Exodus 20:1). Biblical covenants must identify not only the title of God but also the authority of the mortal agent that God has appointed to deliver the covenant to the future covenant people. Although Moses' authority had been well established by that time among the children of Israel, the *Preamble* contains the ratifying statement, "And Moses went up to God, and the Lord [said], Thus shalt thou say to the house of Jacob" (Exodus 19:3).

The *Historical Prologue* is a concise reference to God's mighty act of delivering Israel from Egypt: "I am the Lord thy God, which have brought thee . . . out of the house of bondage" (Exodus 20:2). Accounts of God's relationship with His children, which document His love and divine intervention in history to preserve and deliver them (and at the same time His divine wrath and punishments for disobedience) are an essential part of the scriptures. These accounts provide a sacred history that serves as an everlasting witness of the indebtedness of God's children to their maker, and in a sense, all of the historical accounts found in the Bible function as a *Historical Prologue* to covenant. An understanding of the mutual relationship of history and covenant helps us to better understand and appreciate why the scriptures are composed of a constant interweaving of law and historical narrative. The *Stipulations* (the Law) are referred to in the well-known Decalogue (the Ten Commandments in Exodus 20; compare 19:5–6) and establish for the children of Israel regulations for the proper relationship of humans to God and each to his neighbor.

The account of the Mosaic covenant is accompanied by a formal assembly of the people and a covenant ceremony in which they publicly acknowledge their acceptance of the conditions of the covenant and their commitment to abide by them. The remaining elements of the covenant are intertwined with this ceremony. The *Deposit and Public Reading* occurs when Moses "wrote all the words . . . and . . . took the book of the covenant, and read in the audience of the people" (Exodus 24:4–7). The covenant itself is recorded on the tablets of stone (see Exodus 31:18) and eventually deposited in the ark of the covenant (see Exodus 40:20). Although no *Witnesses* are specifically indicated, it is possible that the altar and the twelve stone pillars erected earlier by Moses (see Exodus 24:4) were invoked to stand as witnesses much as the stone later erected by Joshua (see Joshua 24:27). Furthermore, it is likely that the people themselves were accounted as witnesses to the covenant (also in Joshua 24:22) as they publicly declare, before God and their peers, "All that the Lord hath said will we do, and be obedient" (Exodus 24:7).

The *Blessings and Curses* contingent on the obedience or disobedience to the stipulations are outlined in Exodus 23:20–33. The *Covenant Oath Ceremony* is also described. Moses gathered the people together, built an altar and offered sacrifice and read to the people the words out of the book of the law in which he had written the words of the Lord he received on Mount Sinai. The people in turn agreed to the conditions of the covenant as read by Moses, saying together, "All that the Lord hath said will we do, and be obedient." Moses then sprinkled the people with the blood of the sacrifices, proclaiming, "Behold the blood of the covenant" (see Exodus 24:3–8).

Just before being taken to God, Moses commanded the children of Israel to renew their commitment to the covenant—as soon as they passed over the Jordan to take possession of the promised land—in a formal covenant-renewal ceremony that was to take place at Shechem and on the mountains of Ebal and Gerizim that rise on either side of this town. Moses describes the particulars of this ceremony in great detail with special emphasis on the accompanying blessings and curses of the covenant (see Deuteronomy 27–28). This is one of the first references to a covenant-renewal ceremony in the Bible, typically recorded at a time of crisis or transition, in which the people publicly recommitted themselves to the covenant in a ceremony similar to that of the initial establishment of the covenant. This passage, as well as the short account of its fulfillment in Joshua 8:30–35, can be profitably studied in regard to covenant.

Two direct results of covenant and covenant renewal are: (1) the formation of a covenant community, including all those who have accepted the covenant; and (2) the collection of the "words of the book of the law" that are binding on the covenant community and thus function in the community as scripture. The children of Israel, since they had publicly committed themselves to the covenant, became responsible both as individuals as well as a community to obey its stipulations. This corporate responsibility is the foundation for the enforcement of the Mosaic law, since the entire community would bear the consequences of the sin of an individual that went unresolved (see, for example, the story of Achan in Joshua 7). At the same time, the community shared the common objective of becoming "a kingdom of priests, and an holy nation" (Exodus 19:6) and could look forward to the promised blessings of obedience to the law. The words of the covenant that had been publicly read, agreed to, and deposited became legally binding on the community and thus constituted canonized scripture.

JOSHUA AND COVENANT RENEWAL AT SHECHEM

Joshua, just before his death, called for an assembly of the people at Shechem as prescribed by Moses, between the twin mountains of Ebal and Gerizim, in order to renew the covenant. The *Preamble* "thus saith the Lord God of Israel" (Joshua 24:2) is followed by the *Historical Prologue* (see Joshua 24:2–18) in which Joshua recounted

God's mighty acts in behalf of the children of Israel from the calling of Abraham to the miraculous deliverance from Egypt and the conquest of Canaan. The *Stipulations* (see Joshua 24:14, 18, 23) call for the people to repent and put away their strange gods and renew their exclusive allegiance to the Lord God. The *Blessings and Curses* are alluded to in Joshua 24:19–29, and the *List of Witnesses* includes the people themselves (see Joshua 24:22) and the great stone that Joshua erected there (see Joshua 24:26–27). The *Deposit and Public Reading* is referred to when "Joshua wrote these words in the book of the law of God" (Joshua 24:26). After Joshua introduced the stipulations of the covenant, he dramatically challenged the people, "Choose you this day whom ye will serve" (Joshua 24:15), and a few verses later we read the rest of the *Covenant Oath Ceremony* when the people responded to Joshua's challenge, "The Lord our God will we serve, and his voice will we obey" (Joshua 24:24).

KING JOSIAH AND THE REFORMATION

Another instructive example of a covenant-renewal ceremony can be found in the account of the reforms of Josiah in 622 B.C. (see 2 Kings 22–23). During the course of renovation of the temple, Hilkiah, the high priest, found "the book of the law" in the house of the Lord (2 Kings 22:8), which had apparently been lost or forgotten. King Josiah, upon hearing the contents of the book, was distressed and sent for a representative of the Lord—the prophetess Huldah— to ascertain the validity of the covenant contained in the law. In a sense, Huldah provides the *Preamble* to the covenant ceremony when she declared that in fact the Lord was the author of the *Stipulations* contained therein (see 2 Kings 22:16). Furthermore, Huldah prophesied the destruction of Israel, declaring that the *Blessings and Curses* associated with the stipulations "even all the words of the book which the king of Judah hath read" would stand as a *Witness* against Israel's disobedience and would all be fulfilled (2 Kings 22:16–17). Josiah immediately gathered the people "both small and great" to Jerusalem, where he *Publicly Read* "the words of the book of the covenant" (2 Kings 23:1–2) to the people. Then the king led the people in covenanting before the Lord to "perform the words of the covenant that were written in the book" (2 Kings 23:3). Israel's apostasy and the need for covenant renewal are graphically illustrated in the almost incredible description of the abominable objects that were brought out of the temple of the Lord and the idolatrous and immoral practices that were once again outlawed (see 2 Kings 23:4–20).

As a sign of the people's recommitment to the covenant, Josiah commanded them to observe the Feast of the Passover (see 2 Kings 23:21–22), which recounts God's miraculous deliverance of Israel from Egypt and provides a sort of *Historical Prologue* to the covenant-renewal process. At the end of the event King Josiah conducted the *Covenant Oath Ceremony* when he "stood by a pillar, and made a covenant before the Lord, to walk after the Lord, and to keep his commandments and his testimonies and his statutes with all their heart and all their soul, to perform the words of this covenant that were written in this book. And all the people stood to the covenant" (2 Kings 23:3).[13]

Unfortunately, Israel's commitment did not outlive the nationalistic fervor brought about by Josiah's reforms. Within a few short years Israel reverted to a state of apostasy, eloquently documented by the writings of Jeremiah and the Book of Mormon (see 1 Nephi 1), which led to their destruction and exile in 598 and 586 B.C.

Many other passages could be cited showing that the basic elements of covenant and covenant renewal continued to serve as the framework for Israelite religion in the Old Testament.[14] Baltzer has further demonstrated that these same elements are present in the intertestamental and early Christian literature with some notable examples from Qumran.[15] The prominence of covenant language in the Book of Mormon (especially Mosiah 1–6) affirms that this tradition continued in the New World as well as the Old World.

JESUS, THE MEDIATOR OF THE NEW COVENANT

The focal point of all covenant making from the beginning was the coming, in the meridian of time, of the promised Messiah who would fulfill the law of Moses by the actual shedding of His own blood. Through His suffering, death, and Resurrection, He would atone for the sins of the world and would break the chains of death. It was Jesus Christ who would fulfill the "old" and establish the "new" covenant.

In the search for the elements of the actual covenant in the New

Testament it becomes apparent that indeed "the Word was made flesh" (John 1:14) and that the covenant was embodied in the personage of its author, Jesus of Nazareth. The Gospels present a powerful *Preamble* to the covenant by reciting the prophecies of His coming and the miraculous events surrounding His birth into the world—all testifying of His divine origin. The narratives of His ministry attest that He "taught with authority" and performed miraculous acts of compassion and carefully provide adequate *Lists of Witnesses* of the events of His ministry, death, and Resurrection.

The *Stipulations* of the new covenant are presented throughout the teachings of Jesus but were perhaps best summarized when He said, "A new commandment I give unto you, That ye love one another; as I have loved you" (John 13:34), and when, at the end of His discourse on love in the Sermon on the Mount, He commanded the children of the covenant, as He had commanded Abraham two thousand years before, "Be ye therefore perfect" (Matthew 5:48; compare Genesis 17:1). At the same time, evidence of the promised *Blessings and Curses* can be found throughout His teachings. The blessings are notably apparent in the Beatitudes, where covenantal language "blessed are those" is found, and the curses are frequent in the "woe unto you" passages pronounced by Jesus on those who were breaking the covenant (compare Matthew 23:13–39). The *Covenant Oath Ceremony* of the new covenant, like the old covenant (see D&C 84:27) consisted of repentance and the ordinance of baptism. This ordinance was required of all—including the Savior (John 3:5).

Besides the baptism of Jesus and an enigmatic account of the events of the Transfiguration, there is little detail about early Christian covenant ordinances in the New Testament. Some, noting the scarcity of direct references to the covenant and its attendant ordinances in the New Testament, have suggested that perhaps the authors of the New Testament realized that the covenantal language would have been threatening to the Romans;[16] others have suggested that, due to the sacredness of such things, they were either omitted or through time deleted from the record.[17]

The actual covenant-renewal ceremony, however, is preserved in the simple yet profound accounts of the Last Supper (see Matthew 26:26–29; Mark 14:22–24; Luke 22:19–20).[18] The *Historical Prologue* to the new covenant is presented to the disciples in the symbolically rich setting of the Passover feast that commemorated the mighty act of God in the past when He delivered His people from bondage and death in Egypt. Then "Jesus took bread, and blessed it, and brake it, and gave it to the disciples, and said, Take, eat; this is my body. And he took the cup, and gave thanks, and gave it to them, saying, Drink ye all of it" (Matthew 26:26–27). With these words Jesus dramatically pointed ahead to the mightiest of the mighty acts of God, the greatest event in all of sacred history, which would deliver His children from the bondage of sin and death for all eternity. "For this is my blood of the new *covenant* [KJV, "testament"], which is shed for many for the remission of sins" (see Matthew 26:26–29). In this simple declaration Jesus alludes to the passage in Exodus when Moses initiated the old covenant while sprinkling the people with the blood of the sacrifices and declaring, "Behold the blood of the covenant" (Exodus 24:8), as well as to Jeremiah's prophecy of the future establishment of the "new covenant" found in Jeremiah 31:31. Partaking of the bread and wine, the disciples symbolically became *Witnesses* to the new covenant, and in the ensuing weeks they were to become literal witnesses to Jesus, the Mediator of the new covenant, as they beheld the Resurrection of the Word. In addition the publication and distribution of the Gospels (see John 20:31) and the institution of the sacrament as an ordinance in the Church served the function of the *Deposit and Public Reading* of the covenant known from the Old Testament tradition of reading the law at the Feast of Tabernacles (Deuteronomy 31:10–11).[19]

The reality of the blood atonement that Jesus Christ accomplished is represented in the sacrament by the symbols of flesh and blood just as they were in the blood sacrifices of the law of Moses. Paul, in his teachings of how the old covenant was fulfilled and done away with by the new, carefully points out this symbolism and repeatedly makes reference to the sacred ordinance of the sacrament as one of the most significant signs of the covenant in the early Church (see 1 Corinthians 11:25–32; Ephesians 2:12–13; and Hebrews 7–9).

Probably the most complete and comprehensive description of the covenant as established by Jesus Christ can be found in the account in the Book of Mormon when He appeared to His covenant people in the New World and, through a covenant-making assembly, established the new covenant among the Nephites (see 3 Nephi 9–28).

Although an adequate study of this passage as covenant renewal is beyond the scope of the present study, a brief outline will show the basic elements. The dramatic *Preamble* can be seen both in the words "Behold, I am Jesus Christ the Son of God" (3 Nephi 9:15) uttered by the heavenly voice at the end of the first message from heaven after the destruction, and in the Father's formal introduction, "Behold my Beloved Son, in whom I am well pleased, in whom I have glorified my name—hear ye him" (3 Nephi 11:7). The *Historical Prologue* is given several times as Jesus' act of redemption (3 Nephi 9:15–22; 11:10–11), and it is clearly explained how the old covenant is done away with in the new (3 Nephi 9:19–21; 15). The *Stipulations* of faith, repentance, baptism, and the Holy Ghost, as well as the basic law of the kingdom (much as it had been presented in the Sermon on the Mount in the Old World), are presented along with their respective *Blessings and Curses* and are accepted by the people in the *Covenant Oath Ceremony* through the covenantal ordinances of baptism and sacrament (see 3 Nephi 11–26). Jesus chose twelve disciples to serve as His authoritative agents and to stand as *Witnesses* of the covenant (see 3 Nephi 12:1–2), and the covenant community was formally organized into the Church (see 3 Nephi 26–27). The sacred history and doctrines from the Nephite scriptures were added to and presumably accepted by the people as scripture (see 3 Nephi 23:7–26:11) which filled the function of *Deposit and Public Reading*. Thus, the Book of Mormon account of the visit of Jesus Christ to the New World provides another witness to "the covenants of the Lord" and to Jesus as the Christ, and is a record that was sealed up to come forth to the covenant people of the last dispensation.

THE RESTORATION AS COVENANT RENEWAL

The same seven elements well known from biblical covenants can be clearly seen, both in the events of the Restoration of the fullness of the gospel, and in the document that contains the covenant itself, not surprisingly entitled the Doctrine and Covenants. This study of covenant renewal in the Restoration will limit itself to events of 1820–44 and will focus on the Doctrine and Covenants as the primary document of the new and everlasting covenant.[20]

The *Preamble* to the new and everlasting covenant can be seen in the event of the First Vision, with the appearance of the Father and the Son to Joseph Smith, and in the events of the following decade up to the formal organization of the Church. The pronouncement that pierced the silence of the centuries, "This is My Beloved Son. Hear Him!" (Joseph Smith—History 1:17), can be seen as the initiation of covenant renewal in the last dispensation. In response to Joseph's inquiry as to which sect to join, the Lord revealed that he should join none of them. The words of the Lord to young Joseph, "They draw near to me with their lips, but their hearts are far from me" (Joseph Smith—History 1:19), revealed that it was indeed a time of crisis—of total apostasy from the covenant—and implied that it was time for restoration, by covenant renewal, of the new and everlasting covenant. Just as was noted in the biblical covenants, the work of restoration was entrusted to a mortal agent of God, and the *Preamble* therefore contains numerous references to the sources of divine authority received by this modern-day prophet, justifying his claim to represent the author of the covenant in the covenant-renewal ceremony. Passages in Joseph Smith—History and numerous references in the Doctrine and Covenants attest to the restoration of the necessary instruction and priesthood authority by divine messengers: Moroni (see Joseph Smith—History 1:27–54); John the Baptist (see Joseph Smith—History 1:68–73; D&C 13); Peter, James, and John (see D&C 27:12); and later Moses, Elias, and Elijah (see D&C 110:11–16).

THE DOCTRINE AND COVENANTS AS THE DOCUMENT OF THE COVENANT

Along with the restoration of the necessary priesthood authority (both Aaronic and Melchizedek) and baptism—the first covenant ordinance—Joseph Smith's first great task was to record and "recite" for the children of the covenant in the latter days the *Historical Prologue* of the new covenant. By 1830, when the Church was formally organized, Joseph Smith had restored to the covenant community the lengthy sacred history recorded in the Book of Mormon containing a record of God's relationship with His covenant peoples of old from the Tower of Babel to AD 421. The importance of the Book of Mormon as a part of the *Historical Prologue* to the covenant-renewal process is explicitly stated on its ancient title page where it declares that its purpose is "to show unto the remnant of the House of Israel what great things the Lord hath done for their fathers; and that they may know the covenants of the Lord," as well as serving "to the convincing of the Jew and Gentile that Jesus is the Christ." In addition, the Book of Mormon preserves a prophecy of the latter-day covenant renewal made by Joseph of old, that a latter-day Joseph would come from his seed and would "do a great work . . . for his brethren that would bring them to a knowledge of the covenants" the Lord had made with his father (2 Nephi 3:7). In 1830–31, Joseph restored the book of Moses, a sacred record that recounts the history of the covenant people from Adam to Noah. By the end of his life, including his inspired additions and revisions to the Bible, the book of Abraham, and the account of his own relationship with God (Joseph Smith History), Joseph Smith had presented to the latter-day covenant community an extensive account of sacred history from the beginning of time, much of which had been lost from the scriptures of his own day. Just like the covenant accounts found in the Old Testament, the scriptural legacy restored by Joseph Smith is characterized by an interweaving of sacred history and law.

In the year 1831, the year after the organization of the Church, Joseph Smith was in the process of preparing the major document of the latter-day covenant itself—the Book of Commandments (later to be called, more precisely, Doctrine and Covenants). In this collection of revelations, Joseph Smith would complete the restoration of the covenants with provisions for the *Deposit and Public Reading* of the covenants, the *List of Witnesses,* and the *Stipulations* of the covenants with their attendant *Blessings and Curses.* The Doctrine and Covenants also provides specific instructions for the actual *Covenant Oath Ceremonies,* by which individuals are to be admitted to the new and everlasting covenant (baptism, the oath and covenant of the priesthood, and celestial marriage), as well as instructions for its periodic renewal through the sacrament.

Like Exodus 19, which precedes the giving of the Decalogue, Section 1 serves both as a formal *Preamble* to the covenant contained in the Doctrine and Covenants as well as a complete summary—with all of the characteristic elements—of the covenant itself. The *Preamble* of this summary can be seen in D&C 1:1–5, where the participants of the covenant are identified—the Lord as the sovereign, and the entire world as the potential members of the covenant. The entire world is exhorted to hearken to "the voice of him who dwells on high, and whose eyes are upon all men" (D&C 1:1). Besides identifying Himself as the author and initiator of the new and everlasting covenant, the Lord, as in the other covenants discussed above, clearly identifies His chosen agents to carry His voice of warning to all people as His "disciples, whom I have chosen in these last days" (v. 4). The Lord declares that this voice of warning can be heard in the words of the Book of Commandments that was shortly to be published (v. 6). The Lord specifically identifies Joseph Smith as the chief agent of the covenant-renewal process (v. 17) and refers to his role in bringing forth the sacred history found in the Book of Mormon (v. 29) (the *Historical Prologue* of the covenant) in order to establish the new and everlasting covenant (v. 22). The history of God with His people is briefly reviewed in the past, present, and future, and it is clear that the people have strayed and will continue to stray from the ordinances of the everlasting covenant and "seek not the Lord" but rather walk after the way of the world (vv. 15–16), and that this will cause great calamity on the earth in the future. To stem this calamity, the Lord has once again called a prophet to hear and proclaim the voice of the Lord so that the everlasting covenant might be established, the fullness of the gospel proclaimed (vv. 17–23), and the Church restored (v. 30). The *Stipulations* are to be found by hearkening to the voice of the Lord, found in the Book of Commandments (v. 6, 37), Book of Mormon (v. 29), and the voice of His servants—prophets and apostles (v. 14). The *Blessings and Curses* of obedience and disobedience are found in verses 14, 32, and 33. *Provisions for Deposit and Public Reading* of the covenant are made by the command to publish the book of the covenant (v. 6). The commandments, contained in the book, function as *Witnesses* to the covenant in that "the prophecies and promises which are in them shall all be fulfilled" (v. 37).

The elements of the covenant are found on a much larger scale throughout the Doctrine and Covenants. The publication of the Book of Mormon in 1830, the Book of Commandments in 1833, and the initial publication of the expanded Doctrine and Covenants in 1835 (see D&C 1; 42:56–60; 104:58) seem to fit the element of the *Deposit* of the covenant in a public place. The accompanying provision for the *Public Reading* of the covenant is an ongoing duty given to the leaders of the Church as well as to each individual (see D&C 24:5, 9; 42:12–15, 56–60; 71:1).

In the Revelation on Church Organization and Government (see D&C 20), the Lord revealed that the great *Witness* to the renewal of the covenant is the Book of Mormon, "which was given by inspiration, and is confirmed to others by the ministering of angels" (D&C 20:10). In addition to the book itself, the Lord made provisions for three specific witnesses to the reality and divinity of the plates from which the Book of Mormon was translated (see D&C 17), and later, for eight more men to actually see and handle the plates. The Doctrine and Covenants also indicates that the Holy Ghost functions as a witness (see D&C 14:8) in a general sense to all truth, and that the Twelve Apostles are designated as special witnesses for "the name of Christ" (D&C 27:12; 107:23). Section 135:1–7 of the Doctrine and Covenants eloquently states that the blood of Joseph and Hyrum serves as a witness of the Doctrine and Covenants and the Book of Mormon as well.

The Doctrine and Covenants consists (as its title suggests) of the *Stipulations* (commandments) of the new and everlasting covenant and of doctrine revealed to individuals and the Church that explains the significance of the stipulations. Some of the basic *Stipulations* of the covenant are baptism, priesthood, sacrament, church organization, Sabbath observance, the law of consecration, the Word of Wisdom, tithing, and temple ordinances (see the chart at the end for scriptural references).

The *Stipulations* of the covenant in the Doctrine and Covenants were revealed over a period of time that spans from 1823 to 1978 (for the purposes of this study, 1844) and reflect the dynamic growth and change in the covenant community as the Lord revealed the tenets of the covenant. The necessity of baptism, for instance, by one holding proper authority, for the remission of sins, was revealed as early as 1829 (see JS—H 1:72–73; D&C 18:21–24) and confirmed in April 1830 as it related to the formal organization of the Church (see D&C 20:37–38; 22:1–4). Thus, baptism, preceded by faith and repentance, and followed with the bestowal of the Holy Ghost, becomes the first ordinance and the gate by which one enters into the new and everlasting covenant and into the covenant community of the Church. The law of consecration was also given as early as 1831 (see D&C

38:32; 42) as an essential part of the new and everlasting covenant, but because many were unable to abide by it the Lord revealed to the Church in 1838 the law of tithing (see D&C 119).

The *Stipulations* of the covenant are most often accompanied by their respective *Blessings and Curses,* contingent on acceptance and obedience or rejection and disobedience. (See the chart at the end of this article for specific references.) The covenant mechanism of blessings and curses is also clearly set forth as an eternal principle: "There is a law, irrevocably decreed in heaven before the foundations of this world, upon which all blessings are predicated—And when we obtain any blessing from God, it is by obedience to that law upon which it is predicated" (D&C 130:20–21).

The Prophet Joseph Smith, in addition to the covenant itself, restored the formal covenant ceremonies and oaths: baptism, sacrament, priesthood, celestial marriage, and other temple ordinances. While instructions for the ordinances of baptism and the sacrament and, to a limited degree, the covenant of the priesthood are contained in the Doctrine and Covenants—the covenantal ceremonies of priesthood, the endowment, celestial marriage, and other temple ordinances are only to be had by the individual in sacred places. The Doctrine and Covenants, like the books of the covenant of old, teaches that these ordinances are part of the covenant, but the actual account of the covenant ceremony and the oaths themselves are considered sacred and are only learned in the holy places. It can, however, be noted that the scriptural accounts of covenant and covenant renewal enhance and elucidate the structure and content of these ceremonies as well.

Two important results of covenant renewal, just as in the biblical passages, are the establishment of the covenant community—the Church—and the canonization of the ancient and modern scripture—the standard works. An understanding of these concepts as direct results of the covenant process helps us to understand their function and importance in the life of an individual who enters into the new and everlasting covenant. Thus, baptism for the remission of sins, and as a formal entrance into the covenant, also functions as an initiation rite into the Church—the covenant community. The individual submitting to this ordinance becomes like the children of Israel in ancient times declaring before God and their peers "all that the Lord has spoken I will do." The standard works serve as the binding record containing both the sacred history of the mighty acts of God in delivering His children from sin and death, and the laws of the covenant. The constant study of these books causes the individual in the covenant community, like King Josiah of old, to "rend his garments" and to cleanse his "temple" of the abominations found therein, and to cry out to God like the Nephites in the time of King Benjamin, "O have mercy, and apply the atoning blood of Christ that we may receive forgiveness of our sins, and our hearts may be purified" (Mosiah 4:2). Covenant renewal has occurred throughout history as disobedience and disbelief have caused the covenant community to abandon the covenant, and the Lord has called forth His servants to restore and renew the covenant. But the principle also applies to each individual member of the Church who must liken the scriptures unto himself and institute periodic covenant renewal into his or her own life.

One of the poignant and perplexing questions posed by Jeremiah as he watched the approaching Babylonians and the destruction of the disobedient and hard-hearted covenant people, and by Ezekiel as he, already exiled to Babylon, watched in vision the destruction of Jerusalem and the expulsion of the people from their "promised land" (a great symbol of the covenant), was how any future people would ever be able to maintain the conditions of the covenant. Based on the past history of Israel, it must have seemed impossible. The answer to this question, however, was eloquently expressed by Jeremiah and Ezekiel as they prophetically foresaw the future gathering and restoration of the covenant people. Jeremiah records: "Behold the days come, saith the Lord, that I will make a new covenant with the house of Israel, and with the house of Judah: not according to the covenant that I made with their fathers in the day that I took them by the hand to bring them out of the land of Egypt; which my covenant they brake, although I was an husband unto them, saith the Lord: but this shall be the covenant that I will make with the house of Israel; After those days, saith the Lord, I will put my law in their inward parts, and write it in their hearts; and will be their God, and they shall be my people" (Jeremiah 31:31–33). And Ezekiel, in much the same language, says: "And I will give them one heart, and I will put a new spirit within you; and I will take the stony heart out of their flesh, and will give them an heart of flesh: that they may walk in my statutes, and keep my ordinances, and do them: and they shall be my people, and I will be their God" (Ezekiel 11:19–20).

May we as latter-day children of the covenant benefit from an understanding of the Restoration of the fullness of the gospel—the new and everlasting covenant. May we remember the divine origins as the *preamble* of the covenant and recognize God as its initiator. May we read, study, and appreciate the sacred history contained in the scriptures—both ancient and modern—that have been preserved and published in our day as a *historical prologue* to the covenant, containing a record of God's continuing relationship with His children. May we acknowledge the list of *witnesses* that accompany the restoration of the covenant. May we seek to fulfill the *stipulations* of the covenant and commit ourselves to continuously repent, and may we gain, through our obedience to the commandments, faith in their attendant *blessings and curses*. May we participate often in the *covenantal oath ceremonies*—the sacrament for periodic covenant renewal for ourselves, and temple work for our dead, and may we find joy in our membership in the Church—the covenant community.

But most of all, may we always remember that salvation and exaltation are only to be had through "the redemption of him who created us" (Alma 5:15) and that the ability to respond to and faithfully abide by all of the conditions of the covenant are not within our mortal capacity, but, as prophesied by Jeremiah and Ezekiel, are attained through being spiritually born of Him and receiving His image in our countenances (see Alma 5:14). May we be "willing to take upon [us] the name of [the] Son, and always remember him and keep his commandments which he has given [us]; that [we] may always have his Spirit to be with [us]" (D&C 20:77).

THE STRUCTURE OF BIBLICAL COVENANT

1. *Preamble:* Introduces God as the author and initiator of the covenant.
2. *Historical Prologue:* Describes the past relations between the covenanting parties, especially God's mighty acts in preserving His people.
3. *Stipulations:* The formal conditions of the covenants.

4. *Provisions for Deposit and Public Reading:* A clause providing for a safe place of deposit and a requirement for a regular public reading.
5. *List of Witnesses:* Provisions for witnesses to the covenant.
6. *Blessings and Curses:* The consequences of obedience or disobedience.
7. *Covenant Oath Ceremony:* Formal public acceptance of the conditions of the covenant.
   (Source: George E. Mendenhall, *Law and Covenant in Ancient Israel and the Ancient Near East* [Pittsburgh: Biblical Colloquium, 1955]).

MOSAIC COVENANT (EXODUS 19–24)

1. *Preamble:* "And God spake all these words, saying, I am the Lord thy God" (Exodus 20:1–2). Identification of Moses as the Lord's agent, "And Moses went up unto God, and the Lord called unto him out of the mountain, saying, Thus shalt thou say to the house of Jacob" (19:3).
2. *Historical Prologue:* "Ye have seen what I did unto the Egyptians, and how I bare you on eagles' wings, and brought you unto myself" (19:4). "I am the Lord thy God, which have brought thee . . . out of the house of bondage" (20:2).
3. *Stipulations:* "And ye shall be unto me a kingdom of priests, and an holy nation" (19:6). The Ten Commandments and Covenant Code are set forth (20:3–26; 20:22–23; 33).
4. *Deposit and Public Reading:* Moses "wrote all the words . . . and . . . took the book of the covenant, and read in the audience of the people" (24:4, 7). The covenant was recorded on tablets of stone (31:18) and eventually deposited in the ark of the covenant (40:20).
5. *List of Witnesses:* No specific witnesses, but it is likely that the people themselves serve as witnesses when they publicly declare "all that the Lord hath said will we do, and be obedient" (24:7).
6. *Blessings and Curses:* The blessings and curses are represented in statements such as: "And ye shall serve the Lord your God, and he shall bless thy bread, and thy water, and I will take sickness away from the midst of thee" and "Behold, I send an Angel

before thee, . . . provoke him not; for he will not pardon your transgressions" (23:20–33).

7. *Covenant Oath Ceremony:* Moses took the blood of the sacrifice and sprinkled it on the altar and on the people, he read the covenant to the people and they answered, "All that the Lord hath said will we do, and be obedient" (24:7–8). The oath itself is not mentioned. For examples of other biblical oaths, see 1 Samuel 3:17 and 25:34.

COVENANT RENEWAL: JOSHUA AT SHECHEM (JOSHUA 24)

1. *Preamble:* "Thus saith the Lord God of Israel" (Joshua 24:2).
2. *Historical Prologue:* Joshua recounts God's mighty acts in behalf of the children of Israel from the calling of Abraham to the miraculous deliverance from Egypt and the conquest of Canaan (24:2–18).
3. *Stipulations:* Calls for the people to repent and put away their strange gods and renew their allegiance to the Lord God of Israel.
4. *Deposit and Public Reading:* "Joshua wrote these words in the book of the law of God" (24:26).
5. *List of Witnesses:* "Ye [the people] are witnesses against yourselves that ye have chosen you the Lord, to serve him. And they said, We are witnesses" (24:22). Also the stone which Joshua erected was accounted as a witness (24:2–27).
6. *Blessings and Curses:* "If ye forsake the Lord, and serve strange gods, then he will turn and do you hurt, and consume you, after that he hath done you good" (24:19–20).
7. *Covenant Oath Ceremony:* In response to Joshua's challenge, "Choose you this day," the people respond, "God forbid that we should forsake the Lord, to serve other gods. . . . Therefore will we also serve the Lord; for he is our God" (24:15–16, 18). Joshua records the covenant and sets up a stone under the oak near the sanctuary of the Lord in commemoration (24:25–27).

THE DOCTRINE AND COVENANTS AS THE DOCUMENT OF THE COVENANT

1. *Preamble:* First Vision (1820); D&C 1; Book of Mormon Title Page. Authority: Aaronic Priesthood (1829), D&C 13; Melchizedek Priesthood (1829), D&C 27:1–13; 110; etc.

2. *Historical Prologue:* Book of Mormon (1830); Book of Moses (Adam, Enoch, Noah) (1831); Book of Abraham (1842); Joseph Smith Translation (1830–44).

3. *Deposit and Public Reading:* Publication of the Book of Commandments (1833); Doctrine and Covenants (1835), D&C 1; 42:56–60; 104:58.

4. *List of Witnesses:* Three Witnesses (1829), D&C 5, 6, 17; Apostles (1835), D&C 27:12; Book of Mormon as witness of the new covenant (1830), D&C 20:8–16.

5. *Stipulations—Blessings/Curses:*
   Baptism (1829), D&C 22; 18:22–25; 84:74.
   Priesthood (1829), D&C 20, 84, 107, 110, 121, etc.; 84:33–40; 84:41–42.
   Sacrament (1830), D&C 20, 27—see also Baptism.
   Church Organization (1830), D&C 20, 21, 42, 46, 90, 102, 115—see also Baptism.
   Sabbath (1831), D&C 59:9–19, 68:29; 59:9–19.
   Consecration (1831), D&C 38:32, 42, 104; 42; 104:1–10.
   Word of Wisdom (1833), D&C 89:18–21.
   Tithing (1838), D&C 119; 64:23–25; 119:6–7.
   Temple (1830–1844), D&C 45; 57; 58; 84; 93; 95; 109; 127; 128; 131; 132.
   Endowment (1836–42), D&C 38:32, 38; 95:8–9; 105:11–12; 110:9; 124:39.
   Work for the Dead (1842), D&C 127; 128.
   Celestial Marriage (1831–43), D&C 131:1–3; 132:19–25; 132:4, 26–27, 41–44.

6. *Covenant Oath Ceremony:*
   Baptism, D&C 20:43, 72–74.
   Sacrament, D&C 20:75–77.
   Priesthood Oath and Covenant, D&C 84; 107—no ceremony described, probably related to those in the temple.
   Endowment, celestial marriage, and other sacred oath

ceremonies are administered in the temples—explicit discussion of these sacred ordinances is confined to the temple.

7. *Covenant Community = The Church of Jesus Christ of Latter-day Saints (April 1830).*

8. *Canonization = Standard Works:*
   Book of Mormon (April 1830).
   Doctrine and Covenants (April 17, 1835).
   Pearl of Great Price (October 10, 1880).

NOTES

1. The Hebrew word for "covenant" (*berit*) was translated by the LXX as *diatheke,* a Greek word usually referring to a "will" or "testament," but which can also mean "covenant." It was thus rendered *testamentum* in Latin and then as *testament* in English (see G. E. Mendenhall, "Testament," *The Interpreter's Dictionary of the Bible,* 4:575).

2. Jesus Himself alluded to this throughout His ministry as recorded in the New Testament. The clearest explanation of the "new" and the "old" covenant, however, is found in 3 Nephi 15.

3. See A. Alt, "The Origins of Israelite Law," in *Essays on Old Testament History and Religions,* trans. R. A. Wilson (Oxford: Basil Blackwell, 1966); W. Eichrodt, *Theology of the Old Testament,* 2 vols., trans. J.A. Baker (Philadelphia: The Westminster Press, 1961); and G. von Rad, "The Problem of the Hexateuch," in *The Problem of the Hexateuch and Other Essays* (New York: McGraw-Hill Book Company, 1966).

4. S. Mowinckel, *The Psalms in Israel's Worship,* trans. D. R. Ap-Thomas (Nashville: Abingdon, 1967); C. Westermann, *The Praise of God in the Psalms,* trans. K. R. Grim (Richmond, 1966); and H. J. Krause *Worship in Israel,* trans. G. Ruswell (Richmond: 1961).

5. Mowinckel, *The Psalms* 1:129–92.

6. G. E. Mendenhall, *Law and Covenant in Israel and the Ancient Near East* (Pittsburgh: Biblical Colloquium, 1955). He originally published this work in *Biblical Archaeologist* 17 (1954): 26–46, 49–76. See also his article entitled "Covenant," *The Interpreter's Dictionary of the Bible,* 1:714–23. Mendenhall based his study on the previous work on the Hittite treaties of Viktor Korosec, *Hethitische Staatsvertrage: Ein Beitrag zu ihrer juristischen Wertung* (Leipzig: Verlag von Theodor Weicher, 1931).

7. The major works on the subject at the present are D. J. McCarthy, S. J., *Treaty and Covenant* (Rome: Biblical Institute Press, 1978), a comprehensive study of treaties and covenants throughout the ancient Near East, including the biblical covenants; and Klaus

Baltzer, *The Covenant Formulary,* trans. David Green (Philadelphia: Fortress Press, 1971) which traces the covenant pattern from the Old Testament through the intertestamental and early Christian literature.

8. Mendenhall, *Law and Covenant,* 34–35.

9. Mendenhall, "Covenant," 720. Mendenhall points out that the Old Testament preserves many such oaths in other contexts, including the purely verbal forms like "God do so to thee, and more also, if thou hide anything from me" in 1 Samuel 3:17, 25:34; and the symbolic actions of Genesis 15 and Jeremiah 34, where one taking an oath would pass through the parts of an animal that was cut in two—presumably symbolizing the punishment for breaking the oath.

10. Hugh W. Nibley, *An Approach to the Book of Mormon* (Salt Lake City: Deseret Book Company, 1964), 243–56; John A. Tvedtnes, "The Nephite Feast of Tabernacles," in *Tinkling Cymbals: Essays in Honor of Hugh Nibley,* ed. John W. Welch (n.p.: 1978), 145–77; John W. Welch, compiler, "King Benjamin's Speech in the Context of Ancient Israelite Festivals," (Provo, Utah: FARMS, 1985); and Stephen D. Ricks, "The Treaty/Covenant Pattern in King Benjamin's Address (Mosiah 1–6)," *BYU Studies* 24 (1984): 151–62.

11. Ricks, "King Benjamin's Speech," 161.

12. The Joseph Smith Translation indicates that in fact the first time the law was given it was the higher law and that the passage in Exodus 34 is the actual giving of the lower law, or law of Moses, without "the words of the everlasting covenant of the holy priesthood" (JST, Exodus 34:1–2, Deuteronomy 10:2). For the sake of discussion we will refer to this passage throughout the study as the giving of the law of Moses, with the understanding that the first time it was the higher law. Also we should note why we are beginning this study with the Mosaic rather than the Abrahamic covenant. The accounts of the covenant given to Abraham, although demonstrating the basic elements of the later biblical covenants, have unique features that deserve a more complete treatment than is possible in the present study. Many scholars believe that this covenant doesn't fit the suzerain-vassal treaty structure because it is a series of unconditional promises/blessings (promised by the suzerain rather than the vassal), and that the conditions—although surely implicit in the covenant—are not specifically stated (see, for example, David N. Freedman, "Divine Commitment and Human Obligation: The Covenant Theme," *Interpretation* 18 [1964]: 419–31).

13. It is possible that the sacrifice in Exodus 24:5 and the ensuing ritual of sprinkling the blood of the sacrifice on the altar and on the

people (see Exodus 24:6–8) was part of the oath-swearing ceremony and had symbolic meaning specifically related to the taking of the oath, but the oath itself is not specifically stated.

14. Baltzer, *The Covenant Formulary,* 39–62, further lists as possible covenant-renewal ceremonies Exodus 34; 2 Chronicles 29:5–11; Ezra 9–10; Nehemiah 9–10; and Jeremiah 34:8–22.

15. Baltzer, *The Covenant Formulary,* 99–112, discusses the Qumran Manual of Discipline, which contains the initiation ceremony for the Qumran community and shows remarkable similarity to the biblical covenant process (see also Mendenhall, "Covenant" 721–22).

16. Mendenhall notes that there is "a surprising infrequency to covenant in the New Testament" and suggests that specific references were purposely avoided because it may have been threatening to the Romans. For a succinct discussion of the New Testament references, see Mendenhall, "Covenant," 722–23.

17. Nibley suggests that Jesus presented many of His important teachings after His Resurrection that were originally preserved in the "forty-day" literature (see Nibley, "The Forty-day Mission of Christ—The Forgotten Heritage," originally in *Vigiliae Christianae* 20 (1966):1–24; reprinted in *When the Lights Went Out* [Salt Lake City: Deseret Book, 1976], 32–54).

18. It is interesting that the Gospel of John does not contain an account of the Last Supper. The teachings about the sacrament in John appear in the passage of the feeding of the five thousand, in which Jesus declares, "I am the bread of life" (John 6:35, 48, 51). In other words, where the emphasis in the Last Supper accounts culminates in the blood, in John there is a powerful image of the bread as well as the flesh which Jesus gave for the life of the world (see John 6:51–58).

19. For a more detailed discussion of the sacrament as the establishment of the new covenant, see David R. Seely, "The Last Supper According to Matthew, Mark, and Luke," in *From the Last Supper through the Resurrection: The Savior's Final Hours,* ed. Richard Neitzel Holzapfel and Thomas A. Wayment (Salt Lake City: Deseret Book, 2003), 99–103.

20. A similar discussion of this pattern can be found in David J. Whittaker, "A Covenant People: Old Testament Light on Modern Covenants," *Ensign,* August 1980, 36–40.

CHAPTER TWENTY-TWO

SYMBOLIC ACTION AS PROPHECY IN THE OLD TESTAMENT

DONALD W. PARRY

Ancient Israelite religion featured groups and individuals who expressed themselves with symbolic actions. For example, Moses and Joshua removed their shoes while standing upon holy ground (see Exodus 3:5; Joshua 5:15); Saul cut up two oxen and sent the pieces throughout Israel as a warning that individuals who failed to rally around the king would be similarly destroyed (see 1 Samuel 11:7); Solomon spread his hands toward heaven during the dedicatory prayer of the temple (see 1 Kings 8:22); Elijah divided the waters of the Jordan River by smiting them with his mantle (see 2 Kings 2:8); Elisha cast salt into a spring to heal its bitter waters (see 2 Kings 2:19–21); and Abraham took a heifer, a she-goat, and a ram and "divided them in the midst, and laid each piece one against another" (Genesis 15:10), after which he may have passed through the two parts (see Jeremiah 34:18). Several Old Testament prophets, including Abraham, Moses, Ahijah, Elijah, Isaiah, Jeremiah, and Ezekiel used such symbolic actions to prophesy, without words, of future events.[1] Their unconventional action, gesture, movement, or posture of itself may not have had an immediate practical purpose but had symbolic meaning or metaphoric application. The future action was the typological fulfillment of the first, original action.

Donald W. Parry is professor of Hebrew Bible at Brigham Young University.

Although the symbolic actions of prophetic characters of the Old Testament occurred during various gospel dispensations, within different geographic locations, and under varying circumstances and contexts, there are commonalities among them. First, a prophet played a major role in the symbolic actions as prophecy. On one hand, it was common for the prophet himself to dramatize the prophecy, as was the case with Melchizedek breaking the bread and blessing the wine (see Joseph Smith Translation, Genesis 14:17), Moses casting the tree into the bitter waters (see Exodus 15:22–25), or Jeremiah breaking the clay vessel (see Jeremiah 19). On the other hand, the prophet gave directions to or witnessed a second party who enacted the prophecy, as was the case with Jeremiah, who watched a potter create two vessels (see Jeremiah 18:1–12) and who caused several nations to drink from the wine cup of fury (see Jeremiah 25:15–29).

Second, the prophetic symbolic action originated from God. In most cases, the scriptural record sets forth in a straightforward manner that the prophets received direct revelation from God. Such a revelation was given in the texts with one of two common formulaic expressions or revelatory speech forms—the messenger formula and the revelation formula.[2] "Thus saith the Lord," "For thus saith the Lord God of Israel unto me," and "Thus saith the Lord God of Hosts" are variations of the messenger formula. The revelation formula features various expressions that indicate the prophet's reception of God's word, for example, "the word of the Lord came also unto me, saying," "the Lord said unto the prophet," "God . . . said unto him," and so on. Generally recorded at the beginning of a new revelation, the formula introduces prophetic language; its primary purpose is to manifest the authority and origin of the revelation. Because the revelation originates with God and thus carries the authority of God through His prophet, the message (whether verbal or nonverbal) should therefore be accepted. Both the messenger and the revelation formulas "are indicative of prophetic authority and prerogative."[3] The formulas demonstrate that the symbolic actions conducted by the prophets originate from Deity and did not stem from the imaginations of the prophets.

Third, prophetic symbolic actions include either a ritualistic gesture, a movement, a posture, or a dramatized act. For example,

Joshua stretched a spear toward the city of Ai (see Joshua 8:18–19); Ahijah tore a new garment into twelve pieces (see 1 Kings 11:29–31); Isaiah wrote the name *Mahershalalhashbaz* upon a scroll and then united with his wife (see Isaiah 8:1–4); Jeremiah placed stones in a brick kiln (see Jeremiah 43:8–13); and Ezekiel ate a scroll (see Ezekiel 2:8–3:6).

Fourth, the dramatized action represents something other than what is visible to onlookers or participants. For example, the Lord instructed Ezekiel to perform a certain action, which in turn became a nonverbal prophecy. On one occasion, God told Ezekiel to shave his beard and to cut the hair of his head with a razor and a knife and divide the cut hair into three parts. Next God commanded, "Thou shalt burn with fire a third part [of the hair] in . . . the city, . . . and thou shalt take a third part, and smite about it with a knife: and a third part thou shalt scatter in the wind" (Ezekiel 5:2). The Lord interpreted these strange acts by drawing direct parallels between the three portions of Ezekiel's cut hair and the inhabitants of Jerusalem: "A third part of [the inhabitants of Jerusalem] shall die with the pestilence, and with famine shall they be consumed in the midst of thee; and a third part shall fall by the sword round about thee; and I will scatter a third part into all the winds" (Ezekiel 5:12). Ezekiel's symbolic prophetic actions were fulfilled when the Jews were scattered or destroyed—some were consumed by famine, others by the sword, and still others were scattered upon the face of the earth.

Other scriptural objects serve as symbols and representations: Jeremiah's yoke signified bondage (see Jeremiah 27–28); Ezekiel's journey from home symbolized an exile of Israel (see Ezekiel 12:1–16); Hosea and his wife represented Jehovah and unfaithful Israel respectively (see Hosea 1; 3:1–5); Ezekiel's two sticks referred to the Bible and the Book of Mormon (see Ezekiel 37:15–28); Jeremiah's book of evil represented the destruction that would come upon Babylon (see Jeremiah 51:58–64); and the serpent of brass pointed to Jesus Christ and His Atonement (see Numbers 21:6–9). On occasion, the prophet himself served as the symbol. Such was the case with Ezekiel, of whom the Lord explained, "For I have set thee for a sign unto the house of Israel" (Ezekiel 12:6). Similarly, Isaiah stated, "I and the children whom the Lord hath given me are for signs and for wonders in Israel from the Lord of hosts" (Isaiah 8:18). Many times the prophet's explanation of the symbolic action is included alongside prophecy (see 1 Kings 11:29–31; Isaiah 20:1–6; Jeremiah 18:1–12; Ezekiel 4:9–17).

Fifth, prophetic symbolic actions often required the participation of two or more individuals, or, if there were no actual participants, the symbolic action may have been conducted in the presence of an audience. In at least two instances in the Old Testament, the symbolic action included participation of the prophet and one or more other individuals—Elisha and Joash together shot an arrow (see 2 Kings 13:14–19), and Zechariah and others participated in a symbolic coronation ceremony (see Zechariah 6:9–15). Other examples demonstrate audience observation. Ahijah ripped the garment as King Jeroboam looked on, and then Jeroboam received ten pieces of it (see 1 Kings 11:29–31); Ezekiel was not permitted to mourn the loss of his wife so that those who observed this act would inquire "wilt thou not tell us what these things are to us, that thou doest so?" (Ezekiel 24:19); Moses smote the rock from which water flowed "in the sight of the elders of Israel" (Exodus 17:6); Jeremiah was told to break a vessel "in the sight of the men that go with thee" (Jeremiah 19:10); he also hid stones in the clay of a brick kiln "in the sight of the men of Judah" (Jeremiah 43:9).

Finally, because nonverbal prophecies originated with God, therefore they have been or will be fulfilled, according to the prophetic word. Yet false prophets imitated true prophets even in making nonverbal prophecies. Two false prophets,[4] Zedekiah and Hananiah, attempted to imitate the actions of the true prophets of God when they created dramatizations that did not originate with God. Zedekiah made horns of iron and then prophesied that kings Ahab and Jehoshaphat would push (like the horns of a ram) the Syrians "until they be consumed" (2 Chronicles 18:10). Hananiah removed and broke a yoke that was upon the neck of Jeremiah, prophesying that God would break the yoke (bondage) of the kings who were subject to the governance of the king of Babylon. In doing so, Hananiah contradicted an earlier prophecy made by Jeremiah (see Jeremiah 27–28). Both of the false prophets, counterfeiting the true prophetic word, used revelatory language as they introduced their symbolic actions by uttering the formula "thus saith the Lord" (1 Kings 22:11; Jeremiah 28:11).

Of course, the "prophecies" of neither "prophet" were fulfilled. Very little is known of the end of Zedekiah (see 1 Kings 22:24–25). The fate of Hananiah, however, was prophesied by Jeremiah: "Hear now, Hananiah; The Lord hath not sent thee; but thou makest this people to trust in a lie. Therefore thus saith the Lord; Behold, I will cast thee from off the face of the earth: this year thou shalt die, because thou hast taught rebellion against the Lord. So Hananiah the prophet died the same year in the seventh month" (Jeremiah 28:15–17).

Two themes constantly recur in the nonverbal prophecies—the theme of God's judgment against an individual, community, or nation and the theme of the mission, attributes, goals, or atoning sacrifice of Jesus Christ.

PROPHECIES OF GOD'S JUDGMENT

A judgment of God or divine retribution is the "process of God's meting out merited requital—punishment for evil or reward for good."[5] For example, Isaiah was commanded by the Lord to "go and loose the sackcloth from off thy loins, and put off thy shoe from thy foot" (Isaiah 20:2). The prophet obeyed the Lord's command and walked for three years "naked and barefoot" (v. 2). The expression "naked and barefoot" may signify that Isaiah walked with no foot-gear nor clothing on the upper portion of his body. Such an action on the part of Isaiah gave him no practical or materialistic benefit; rather, the dramatization held a symbolic, prophetic message for those who beheld the prophet in such a state.

Isaiah explained his symbolic action. His walking "naked and barefoot three years" was for a "sign and wonder upon Egypt and upon Ethiopia; So shall the king of Assyria lead away the Egyptians prisoners, and the Ethiopians captives, young and old, naked and barefoot, even with their buttocks uncovered, to the shame of Egypt" (Isaiah 20:3–4). Isaiah's walking naked and barefoot was an unspoken prophecy, in the form of an action, that pointed to the time when the Egyptians and Ethiopians would be taken captive by the Assyrians, who would lead them away like slaves, without clothing or footgear. The prophecy was probably fulfilled in 667 B.C. when Ashurbanipal, king of Assyria, crushed an Egyptian rebellion and forced his captives to march like slaves to Nineveh.[6] Although God does not act directly in the judgment upon the Egyptians and Ethiopians, His role in the scene is understood.

The judgment upon the Egyptians and Ethiopians is but one of many prophecies connected with divine retribution. Joshua's stretching out of the spear toward the city of Ai spelled out an ominous judgment against the city, which was immediately fulfilled when the Israelites ambushed the city and "slew the men of Ai" (Joshua 8:21). An instance of judgment that was prophesied against a nation occurred when Jeremiah wrote in a book of the destruction that would come upon Babylon. Jeremiah afterwards tied the book to a rock and then tossed the book and the rock into the Euphrates River. His action signified impending judgment against Babylon, pointing to the time when Babylon would be destroyed (see Jeremiah 51:58–64). Other instances of heaven-sent judgments against groups are common in the dramatized acts of Ezekiel. He drew a picture of Jerusalem upon a tile (see Ezekiel 4:1–3); lay on his left and right side (4:4–8); baked bread that contained dung (4:9–17); trembled as he ate and drank (12:17–20); sighed, groaned, and beat his breast (21:6–7); and made sweeping movements with a sword (21:8–17). All such actions prophesied of impending doom, destruction, and hardship upon various groups in the region.

PROPHECIES REGARDING JESUS CHRIST

Many prophetic symbolic actions look forward to a future event that has greater significance than does the original symbolic action. For instance, the binding and offering up of Isaac by Abraham on Mount Moriah anticipated the atoning sacrifice of Jesus Christ. According to the book of Jacob, in this symbolic action Abraham represented Father in Heaven, and Isaac was an archetypal representation of Jesus. Abraham was "obedient unto the commands of God in offering up his son Isaac, which is a similitude of God and his Only Begotten Son" (Jacob 4:5). Abraham and Isaac were, of course, shadows when compared to Heavenly Father and His Son and their dramatized prophecy, a miniature model of the true and real moment when Jesus accomplished the Atonement.

In another example, Zechariah's actions connected with the making of the crowns are replete with Christ-centered symbolism (see Zechariah 6:9–15). The scripture begins with the formula "And the word of the Lord came unto me, saying" (Zechariah 6:9). Zechariah is commanded to "take silver and gold, and make crowns, and set [one] upon the head of Joshua the son of Josedech, the high priest; and speak unto him, saying, Thus speaketh the Lord of hosts, saying, Behold the man whose name is The Branch; and he shall grow up out of his place, and he shall build the temple of the Lord: even he shall build the temple of the Lord; and he shall bear the glory, and shall sit and rule upon his throne; and he shall be a priest upon his throne" (Zechariah 6:11–13). Several symbols in this passage have Jesus as their referent. The name *Jesus* is associated with the Hebrew *Joshua*.[7] Joshua, the high priest, has reference to Jesus, the "great high priest" (Hebrews 4:14; see also 3:1). The Branch identified in the passage is Jesus (see Jeremiah 23:5–6; Isaiah 11:1–5; Zechariah 3:8–10). The references to regalia—the crowns and the throne—and the statements regarding bearing the glory and sitting and ruling upon the throne point to Jesus as the "King of Zion" (Moses 7:53), "King of glory" (Psalm 24:7), and the "King of Kings, and Lord of Lords" (Revelation 19:16). In addition, the duplicated reference to the temple speaks of the crowned and enthroned Jesus Christ. It is evident, then, that Zechariah's participation in the coronation of Joshua, the high priest, prophesied of the future coronation of Jesus Christ.

PURPOSE OF NONVERBAL PROPHECIES

One obvious purpose of prophetic drama is that dramatic acts serve to pique the interest of the participants in the action, the audience of the action, or subsequent generations who would learn of the action. Drama is often much more interesting than the spoken word, for it appeals to both the ear and the eye. It is colorful, vivid, and three-dimensional. Dramatized action can be much more shocking than the spoken word—one prophet marries a harlot, and another one breaks a vessel while the public watches—causing the audience to pay great heed to the actions being performed. As with any theatrical production, symbolic actions tend to involve the audience, causing them to question the movements and postures and moving them to a higher plane of understanding. As with visual aids used in the classroom, the prophetic drama served to make the harsh message of judgment—or the sacred prophecy concerning Christ's Atonement—both easier to understand and more memorable.

CONCLUSION

Understanding the environment and significance of symbolic actions in the Old Testament can aid Latter-day Saints in four ways. First, our religious tradition embraces a number of sacred ordinances, including baptism, the sacrament of the Lord's Supper, administrations on behalf of the sick, ordinations, confirmations, and temple ordinances. Within this system of ordinances are numerous movements, gestures, and actions (for example, the laying on of the hands, burial in water, the anointing with consecrated oil) that coincide in an approximate manner with the sacral movements of religious individuals of the Old Testament. As we study the symbolic actions of the Old Testament, both those conducted by the prophets and those performed by the community of Israel in the temple and in their religious festivals, we may learn of the meaning and symbolism of sacred movement in The Church of Jesus Christ of Latter-day Saints.

Second, a careful examination of the lesser-known dramatized actions of the Old Testament will increase our understanding of the more celebrated scriptures. For instance, we can now reread Ezekiel 37:15–28 (the sticks of Judah and Ephraim) and obtain new insights into why Ezekiel dramatized such an act, where he received his authority to do so, and in what manner the prophecy may be fulfilled.

Third, several of the nonverbal prophecies prefigure specific aspects of Jesus' atoning sacrifice. Consider the lifting of the serpent of brass by the prophet Moses. As he *lifted up* the brazen serpent in the wilderness on a pole, even so Jesus was *lifted up* on the cross. As Jesus was *lifted up* on the cross, those who look to Jesus on the cross will be *lifted up* into heaven. Again, as ancient Israel looked up at the serpent and were healed of the poison of the fiery serpents and thereby retained physical life, "even so as many as should look upon the Son of God with faith, having a contrite spirit, might live, even unto that life which is eternal" (Helaman 8:15).

Finally, the individual daily actions, movement, and posture of each member of the Church prophesy in a real sense what will become of that individual in the eternities. Righteous actions prophesy of the opportunity to dwell with Heavenly Father in the eternal world; wicked actions prophesy of the possibility of living outside of the realm of Heavenly Father, both in this sphere of existence and in the eternities.

TABLE 1. EXAMPLES OF NONVERBAL PROPHECIES

Source: Joseph Smith Translation, Genesis 14:17
Prophet: Melchizedek
Prophetic speech formula: None
Object or person used as a symbol: Bread and wine
Symbolic action: Melchizedek breaks bread and blesses wine
Prophecy: Looks forward to Christ's Atonement, His broken body, and blood sacrifice

Source: Genesis 22
Prophet: Abraham
Revelation formula: "God . . . said unto him, Abraham" (Genesis 22:1)
Object or person used as a symbol: Isaac
Symbolic action: Abraham prepares to sacrifice Isaac
Prophecy: Looks forward to the atoning sacrifice of Jesus Christ (Jacob 4:5)

Source: Exodus 7:8–12
Prophet: Aaron
Revelation formula: "And the Lord spake unto Moses and unto Aaron, saying" (Exodus 7:8)
Object or person used as a symbol: Rod
Symbolic action: Aaron casts down his rod, and it becomes a serpent
Prophecy: Points to the regal power and priesthood authority of Jesus

Source: Exodus 15:22–25
Prophet: Moses
Prophetic speech formula: None
Object or person used as a symbol: Tree and waters
Symbolic action: Moses throws a tree into waters of bitterness

Prophecy: The tree typifies and points forward to Jesus Christ, who is the Tree of Life

Source: Exodus 17:1–6
Prophet: Moses
Revelation formula: "And the Lord said unto Moses" (Exodus 17:5)
Object or person used as a symbol: Water, rock, and rod
Symbolic action: Moses smites a rock, and water gushes out
Prophecy: All three symbols—water, rock, and rod—point to Jesus

Source: Numbers 21:6–9
Prophet: Moses
Revelation formula: "And the Lord said unto Moses" (Numbers 21:8)
Object or person used as a symbol: Serpent of brass on a pole
Symbolic action: Moses lifts a brazen serpent in sight of Israel
Prophecy: The future lifting of Christ on the cross and the subsequent healing of believers (John 3:14–15; Helaman 8:14–15; Alma 33:19)

Source: Joshua 8:18–19
Prophet: Joshua
Revelation formula: "And the Lord said unto Joshua" (Joshua 8:18)
Object or person used as a symbol: Spear
Symbolic action: Joshua stretches the spear toward Ai
Prophecy: Joshua and his army will conquer the city

Source: 1 Kings 11:29–31
Prophet: Ahijah
Prophetic speech formula: None
Object or person used as a symbol: New garment
Symbolic action: Ahijah rips the new garment into twelve pieces and gives ten pieces to Jeroboam
Prophecy: Jeroboam will soon take possession of the ten tribes as king

Source: 1 Kings 19:19–21
Prophet: Elijah
Prophetic speech formula: None
Object or person used as a symbol: Mantle

Symbolic action: Elijah casts his mantle upon Elisha

Prophecy: Elisha will succeed Elijah as prophet and wear the prophetic mantle

Source: 2 Kings 13:14–19
Prophet: Elisha
Prophetic speech formula: None
Object or person used as a symbol: Bow and arrow
Symbolic action: Elisha and Joash shoot an arrow
Prophecy: Joash will receive deliverance from Syria

Source: Isaiah 8:1–4
Prophet: Isaiah
Revelation formula: "The Lord said unto [Isaiah]" (Isaiah 8:1)
Object or person used as a symbol: Mahershalalhashbaz
Symbolic action: Isaiah writes the name *Mahershalalhashbaz* upon a scroll, unites with his wife (the prophetess), and she bears a son, whom they name Mahershalalhashbaz
Prophecy: With Isaiah 7:14–16, prophesies of the birth of Jesus Christ

Source: Isaiah 20:1–6
Prophet: Isaiah
Revelation formula: "Spake the Lord by Isaiah the son of Amoz, saying" (Isaiah 20:2)
Object or person used as a symbol: Isaiah
Symbolic action: Isaiah removes his clothes and walks naked like a slave
Prophecy: The Assyrians will take the Egyptians and Ethiopians captive and cause them to walk naked

Source: Jeremiah 13:1–10
Prophet: Jeremiah
Messenger/Revelation formula: "Thus saith the Lord unto me . . . And the word of the Lord came unto me the second time, saying" (Jeremiah 13:1, 3)
Object or person used as a symbol: Linen girdle
Symbolic action: Jeremiah clothes himself with a linen girdle, removes the girdle, and then hides it in the hole of a rock
Prophecy: Just as the people of Judah were once whole like the

linen girdle, so will they become marred and rotten like the
girdle that was placed in the rock

Source: Jeremiah 16:1–12

Prophet: Jeremiah

Revelation formula: "The word of the Lord came also unto me,
saying" (Jeremiah 16:1)

Object or person used as a symbol: Jeremiah

Symbolic action: Jeremiah was commanded to refrain from marrying and having children and from feasting in a joyous
manner

Prophecy: Israel will be destroyed and not enjoy familial relations,
and they, like Jeremiah, will be unable to mourn for the loss of
family life

Source: Jeremiah 18:1–12

Prophet: Jeremiah

Revelation formula: "The word which came to Jeremiah from the
Lord, saying" (Jeremiah 18:1)

Object or person used as a symbol: Potter and his clay

Symbolic action: In the presence of Jeremiah, the potter creates
two separate vessels—one marred and one pleasing in the eyes
of the potter

Prophecy: God is the potter, and Israel is like clay in His hands. If
they repent of their sins, they will become a good vessel; if they
do not repent, they will become a marred vessel

Source: Jeremiah 19

Prophet: Jeremiah

Messenger formula: "Thus saith the Lord" (Jeremiah 19:1)

Object or person used as a symbol: Potter's vessel

Symbolic action: Jeremiah breaks the vessel in the presence of men
at Tophet, near the east gate of Jerusalem

Prophecy: "Thus saith the Lord of hosts; Even so will I break this
people and this city, as one breaketh a potter's vessel, that cannot be made whole again: and they shall bury them in Tophet,
till there be no place to bury" (v. 11)

Source: Jeremiah 25:15–29

Prophet: Jeremiah

Messenger formula: "For thus saith the Lord God of Israel unto me" (Jeremiah 25:15)

Object or person used as a symbol: Cup

Symbolic action: God commands Jeremiah to cause many nations to drink from the wine cup of fury

Prophecy: Many nations will be destroyed by the sword

Source: Jeremiah 27–28

Prophet: Jeremiah

Revelation/Messenger formula: "Came this word unto Jeremiah from the Lord, saying, Thus saith the Lord to me" (Jeremiah 1:1–2)

Object or person used as a symbol: Yoke

Symbolic action: Jeremiah makes yokes and bonds, places one around his neck (Jeremiah 27:2; 28:10), and sends the remaining yokes and bonds to neighboring kings

Prophecy: The kings and kingdoms who do not submit to the governance of Nebuchadnezzar will be destroyed

Source: Jeremiah 32

Prophet: Jeremiah

Revelation formula: "The word that came to Jeremiah from the Lord" (Jeremiah 32:1)

Object or person used as a symbol: A field in Anathoth and an accompanying deed of land

Symbolic action: Jeremiah buys a field in Anathoth and accepts the deed of land

Prophecy: Although Israel is experiencing calamity and destruction, the time will come when they will once again enjoy prosperity and peace, such as buying and selling land

Source: Jeremiah 35

Prophet: Jeremiah

Revelation formula: "The word which came unto Jeremiah from the Lord" (Jeremiah 35:1)

Object or person used as a symbol: Pots and cups of wine

Symbolic action: Jeremiah accompanies the Rechabites into the temple and offers them wine

Prophecy: The obedient Rechabites will remain (symbolically) in the temple forever; on the other hand, the disobedient men of Judah and inhabitants of Jerusalem will be cursed

Source: Jeremiah 43:8–13
Prophet: Jeremiah
Revelation formula: "Then came the word of the Lord unto Jeremiah in Tahpanhes, saying" (Jeremiah 43:8)
Object or person used as a symbol: Great stones and brick kiln
Symbolic action: Jeremiah hides stones in a brick kiln near the entry to Pharaoh's house
Prophecy: Nebuchadnezzer's throne will be set upon rocks and will burn the houses of the gods of Egypt

Source: Jeremiah 51:58–64
Prophet: Jeremiah
Messenger formula: "Thus saith the Lord of hosts" (Jeremiah 51:58)
Object or person used as a symbol: A book with a stone bound to it
Symbolic action: Jeremiah writes in a book the evil that will come upon Babyon; the book is tied to a stone and thrown into the Euphrates
Prophecy: Evil and destruction will come upon Babylon, and it will sink and not rise again

Source: Ezekiel 2:8–3:6
Prophet: Ezekiel
Revelation formula: "But thou, son of man, hear what I say unto thee" (Ezekiel 2:8)
Object or person used as a symbol: Scroll
Symbolic action: Ezekiel eats the scroll
Prophecy: As the eaten scroll contains lamentations, mourning, and woe, so Ezekiel's prophecies and revelations will consist of lamentations, mourning, and woe

Source: Ezekiel 4:1–3
Prophet: Ezekiel
Prophetic speech formula: None
Object or person used as a symbol: Clay tile
Symbolic action: Ezekiel places tile in front of him, draws a picture

of Jerusalem on it, and creates details of a siege with mounds,
a wall, battering rams, and camps

Prophecy: Jerusalem will be besieged by an army that will build
mounds and use battering rams to break through the wall and
take the city captive

Source: Ezekiel 4:4–8
Prophet: Ezekiel
Prophetic speech formula: None
Object or person used as a symbol: Ezekiel
Symbolic action: Ezekiel lies on his right and on his left side
Prophecy: Meaning uncertain

Source: Ezekiel 4:9–17
Prophet: Ezekiel
Prophetic speech formula: None
Object or person used as a symbol: Bread, water, and dung
Symbolic action: Ezekiel bakes bread with a mixture of dung, eats
measured portions of it, and drinks measured portions of water
Prophecy: Israel will have to "eat bread by weight" and "drink
water by measure" because God will make food and drink
scarce. Also, Israel will "eat defiled bread among the Gentiles,
whither [the Lord] will drive them" (Ezekiel 4:10–11, 13)

Source: Ezekiel 5
Prophet: Ezekiel
Prophetic speech formula: None
Object or person used as a symbol: Hair
Symbolic action: Ezekiel shaves the hair of his head and his beard,
divides it into three parts, and then burns one-third, strikes
one-third, and scatters one-third
Prophecy: One-third of Jerusalem's inhabitants will be burned
with fire and destroyed with pestilence, one-third will be smitten with the sword, and one-third will be scattered to the four
winds

Source: Ezekiel 12:1–16
Prophet: Ezekiel
Revelation formula: "The word of the Lord also came unto me,
saying" (Ezekiel 12:1)
Object or person used as a symbol: Personal belongings of Ezekiel

Symbolic action: Ezekiel packs his bags and goes forth from his
  home

Prophecy: The children of Israel will pack their personal effects
  and be led away captive to Babylonia

Source: Ezekiel 12:17–20

Prophet: Ezekiel

Revelation formula: "Moreover the word of the Lord came to me,
  saying" (Ezekiel 12:17)

Object or person used as a symbol: Food and drink

Symbolic action: Ezekiel trembles as he eats his food and drinks
  his drink

Prophecy: Israel's land will be stripped of its produce, and the
  inhabitants of Israel will eat and drink with great trembling
  because of their fearful hearts

Source: Ezekiel 21:6–7

Prophet: Ezekiel

Prophetic speech formula: None

Object or person used as a symbol: Ezekiel

Symbolic action: Ezekiel sighs, groans, and beats his breast

Prophecy: Bad news is coming that will cause hearts to melt,
  hands to become feeble, spirits to faint, and knees to become
  weak as water

Source: Ezekiel 21:8–17

Prophet: Ezekiel

Revelation formula: "Again the word of the Lord came unto me,
  saying" (Ezekiel 21:8)

Object or person used as a symbol: Sword

Symbolic action: Ezekiel strikes his hands together (around the
  sword?) and then makes several movements with the sword,
  moving it to the right and left and so on

Prophecy: In every direction that Ezekiel points and slashes with
  the sword, so will the Lord cause slaughter and destruction
  upon the people

Source: Ezekiel 21:18–24

Prophet: Ezekiel

Revelation formula: "The word of the Lord came unto me again,
  saying" (Ezekiel 21:18)

Object or person used as a symbol: Two roads

Symbolic action: Ezekiel marks out two roads and places a sign-post where the two roads branch out

Prophecy: The king of Babylon will stand at the head of the two roads with his sword and choose through divination one of the two roads

Source: Ezekiel 24:15–24

Prophet: Ezekiel

Revelation formula: "Also the word of the Lord came unto me, saying" (Ezekiel 24:15)

Object or person used as a symbol: Wife of Ezekiel

Symbolic action: Ezekiel's wife dies, and he does not mourn for her

Prophecy: Just as Ezekiel does not mourn the loss of his wife, even so the children of Israel will not be permitted to mourn the loss of their spouses and children whom they will lose during wars and tribulations

Source: Ezekiel 37:15–28

Prophet: Ezekiel

Revelation formula: "The word of the Lord came again unto me, saying" (Ezekiel 37:15)

Object or person used as a symbol: Two sticks or two pieces of wood

Symbolic action: Ezekiel takes two sticks, writes upon them, and then joins them together in one hand

Prophecy: The Bible and the Book of Mormon will come forth together for the use of humanity; the two scriptures will result in the union of the twelve tribes of Israel with Jesus Christ as their king

Source: Hosea 1:2–11

Prophet: Hosea

Revelation formula: "The beginning of the word of the Lord by Hosea. And the Lord said to Hosea" (Hosea 1:2)

Object or person used as a symbol: Hosea and Gomer, his wife of whoredoms, and their children

Symbolic action: Hosea marries Gomer, and they have three children

Prophecy: A prophecy that Israel (Jehovah's wife) will commit whoredoms by departing from Jehovah (Hosea) and chasing after false deities (spiritual adultery). The children represent different aspects of the Lord's relationship with Israel

Source: Hosea 3
Prophet: Hosea
Revelation formula: "Then said the Lord unto me" (Hosea 3:1)
Object or person used as a symbol: Hosea and Gomer
Symbolic action: Hosea is once more commanded to demonstrate love to his wife, the adulteress
Prophecy: As Hosea once more shows love for his wife, so the Lord will once more show love to Israel

Source: Zechariah 6:9–15
Prophet: Zechariah
Revelation formula: "And the word of the Lord came unto me, saying" (Zechariah 6:9)
Object or person used as a symbol: Gold and silver crowns
Symbolic action: Zechariah makes crowns of silver and gold and sets them upon Joshua the high priest and others
Prophecy: The coronation of the Branch, who is Jesus Christ

TABLE 2. EXAMPLES OF FALSE PROPHETS' NONVERBAL PROPHECIES

Source: 1 Kings 22:11
False prophet: Zedekiah
Messenger formula: "Thus saith the Lord" (1 Kings 22:11)
Object or person used as a symbol: Iron horns
Symbolic action: Zedekiah makes iron horns
Prophecy: Prophesies (falsely) that kings Ahab and Jehoshaphat will conquer the Syrians

Source: Jeremiah 28:10–11
False prophet: Hananiah
Messenger formula: "Thus saith the Lord" (Jeremiah 28:11)
Object or person used as a symbol: Yoke
Symbolic action: Hananiah removes the yoke from the neck of Jeremiah and breaks it

Prophecy: Prophesies (falsely) that God will break the yoke of the kings from the captivity of King Nebuchadnezzer

NOTES

1. Symbolic action as prophecy is but one legitimate type of prophecy in the scriptures. Other types of prophecy include single fulfillment (the prophecy has but one legitimate fulfillment or accomplishment), multiple fulfillment (the prophecy has more than one legitimate fulfillment or accomplishment), conditional (the prophecy is not absolute but contains a condition or stipulation), unconditional (no conditions are attached to the prophecy), and type (a symbol that looks forward in time and is attached to a typological meaning).

2. See my article, "'Thus Saith the Lord': Prophetic Language in Samuel's Speech," *Journal of Book of Mormon Studies* 1 (Fall 1992): 181–83.

3. Parry, "'Thus Saith the Lord,'" 183.

4. Beyond the world of the Old Testament, wherein both true prophets of God and false prophets acted out prophecies, David E. Aune, in *Prophecy in Early Christianity and the Ancient Mediterranean World* (Grand Rapids, MI: Eerdmans Publishing, 1983), 100, claims that pagans of the Greco-Roman world also possessed similar types of prophecy.

5. Trent C. Butler, ed., *Holman Bible Dictionary* (Nashville, TN: Holman Publishers, 1991), 373.

6. John D. W. Watts, *Word Biblical Commentary, Isaiah 1–33* (Waco, TX: Word Books, 1985), 265.

7. O. Odelain and R. Seguineau, *Dictionary of Proper Names and Places in the Bible* (Garden City, NY: Doubleday, 1981), 222.

APPENDIX

Ludlow, Victor L. "Jeremiah's Prophecies Concerning the Gathering of the Jews in the Last Days."

Matthews, Robert J. "Toward a Better Understanding of the Old Testament as a Result of Joseph Smith's 'New Translation' of the Bible."

1978 Sperry Symposium on the Old Testament, Brigham Young University, soft cover

Brandt, Edward J. "The Hebrew Background of the New Testament."

Craner, Max Wells "How to Teach the Scriptures."

King, Arthur Henry "Skill and Power in Reading the Authorized Version."

Matthews, Robert J. "The Mosaic Law in Ancient and Modern Scripture."

Meservy, Keith H. "Job: Yet Will I Trust in Him."

Nibley, Hugh "Great Are the Words of Isaiah."

Patch, Robert C. "Wisdom Literature."

Petersen, Mark E. "Moses, Man of Miracles."

The Old Testament and the Latter-day Saints, Randall Book Company, 1986

Brown, S. Kent "Trust in the Lord: Exodus and Faith."

Christianson, James R. "Noah, the Ark, the Flood: A Pondered Perspective."

Cowan, Richard O. "The Latter-day Significance of Ancient Temples."

Flinders, Neil J. "Ancient Hebrew 'Psychology'": A Radical Option for Educators in the Latter Days."

Garrard, LaMar E. "The Last Shall Be First and the First Shall Be Last."

Garrett, H. Dean "Daniel: Ancient Prophet for the Latter Days."

Horton, George A. "The Old Testament: An Indispensable Foundation."

Hoskisson, Paul Y. "A Latter-day Saint Reading of Isaiah in the Twentieth Century: The Example of Isaiah 6."

Matthews, Robert J. "The Old Testament: Voice from the Past and Witness for the Lord Jesus Christ."

McConkie, Joseph F. "Prophets: How Shall We Know Them?"

Millet, Robert L. "The Brass Plates: An Inspired and Expanded Version of the Old Testament."

Nyman, Monte S. "Micah, the Second Witness with Isaiah."

O'Driscoll, Jeff "Kibroth-hattaavah: The Graves of Lust."

Parrish, Alan K. "Your Daughters Shall Prophesy: A Latter-day Prophecy of Joel, Peter, and Moroni Examined."

Reeve, Rex C., Jr. "Malachi and the Latter Days."

Ricks, Stephen D. "The Restoration of the Tribes of Israel in the Writings of Jeremiah and Ezekiel."

Riddle, Chauncey C. "Justification, Ancient and Modern."

Seely, David R. "The Restoration as Covenant Renewal."

Skinner, Andrew C. "Genesis 22: The Paradigm for True Sacrifice in Latter-day Israel."

Tanner, John S. "Hast Thou Considered My Servant Job?"

Van Orden, Bruce A. "The Seed of Abraham in the Latter Days."

A Witness of Jesus Christ, Deseret Book Company, 1990

Adams, L. LaMar "Isaiah: Disciple and Witness of Christ."

Brandt, Edward J. "The Law of Moses and the Law of Christ."

Christenson, Allen J. "The Waters of Destruction and the Vine of Redemption."

Dahl, Larry E. "The Abrahamic Test."

Garrett, H. Dean "A Major Change in Israel: Effects of the Babylonian Captivity."

Holzapfel, Richard N. "The 'Hidden Messiah.'"

Johnson, Clark V. "Job's Relevancy in the Twenty-First Century."

Ludlow, Daniel H. "The Old Testament, a Witness for Jesus Christ."

Matthews, Robert J. "Beyond the Biblical Account: Adam, Enoch, Noah, Melchizedek, Abraham, and Moses in Latter-day Revelation."

Meservy, Keith H. "Isaiah 53: The Richest Prophecy on Christ's Atonement in the Old Testament."

Millet, Robert L. "The House of Israel: From Everlasting to Everlasting."

Top, Brent L. "The Marriage of Hosea and Gomer: A Symbolic Testament of Messianic Love and Mercy."

Turner, Rodney "The Two Davids."

Van Orden, Bruce A. "Redeeming the Dead as Taught in the Old Testament."

Wilcox, S. Michael "The Abrahamic Covenant."

Woods, Fred E. "The Waters Which Make Glad the City of God: The Water Motif of Ezekiel 47:1–12."

Thy People Shall Be My People and Thy God My God, Deseret Book Company, 1994

Ball, Terry B. "Isaiah's Imagery of Plants and Planting."

Lane, Jennifer Clark "The Lord Will Redeem His People: 'Adoptive' Covenant and Redemption in the Old Testament."

LeBaron, E. Dale "Elijah's Mission: His Keys, Powers, and Blessings from the Old Testament to the Latter Days."

Matthews, Robert J. "Our Heritage from Joseph of Israel."

Parry, Donald W. "Symbolic Action as Prophecy in the Old Testament."

Pike, Dana M. "Seals and Sealing Among Ancient and Latter-day Israelites."

Redd, J. Lyman "Aaron's Consecration: Its Nature, Purpose, and Meaning."

Skinner, Andrew C. "Jacob in the Presence of God."

Strathearn, Gaye "The Wife/Sister Experience: Pharaoh's Introduction to Jehovah."

Thomas, M. Catherine "The Provocation in the Wilderness and the Rejection of Grace."

Valletta, Thomas R. "The Exodus: Prophetic Type and the Plan of Redemption."

Voices of Old Testament Prophets, Deseret Book Company, 1997

Ball, Terry B. "Isaiah and the Great Arraignment."

Draper, Richard D. "The Prophets of the Exile: Saviors of a People."

Gillum, Gary P. "Obadiah's Vision of Saviors on Mount Zion."

Huntington, Ray L. "The Prophetic Ministry of Haggai: The Blessings of the Temple."

Millet, Robert L. "Prophets and Priesthood in the Old Testament."

Ostler, Craig J. "Isaiah's Voice on the Promised Millennium."

Owen, Carolyn Green "The Habakkuk Principle: Abigail and the Minor Prophet."

Rivera, Anthony "Jethro, Prophet and Priest of Midian."

Tvedtnes, John A. "Ezekiel's 'Missing Prophecy.'"

Wright, Dennis A. "The Prophet's Voice of Authority."

Covenants, Prophecies, and Hymns of the Old Testament, Deseret Book Company, 2001

Allred, Philip A. "Moses' Charge to Remember."

Ball, Terry B. "Isaiah and the Gentiles."

Bokovoy, David E. "The Calling of Isaiah."

Draper, Richard D. "I Have Even from the Beginning Declared It."

Durkin, Timothy W. "Deuteronomy as a Constitutional Covenant."

Eastmond, Mark E. "Images of Mercy in the Writings of Isaiah."

Hardison, Amy "Being a Covenant People."

Hauglid, Brian M. "Temple Imagery in the Psalms."

Hoskisson, Paul Y. "The Witness for Christ in Psalm 22."

King, Michael L. "Isaiah's Vision of God's Plan to Fulfill his Covenant."

Madsen, John M. "A Precious and Powerful Witness of Jesus Christ."

Peterson, Kim M. "Psalms of the Heart, Prayers unto God."

Richardson, Matthew O. "The King's Law: A Framework of Leadership."

Simon, Jerald F. "Researching Isaiah Passages in the Book of Mormon."

Swift, Charles L. "The Power of Symbol."

Tvedtnes, John A. "Ancient Israelite Psalters."

Van Dyke, Blair G. "Profiles of a Covenant People."

Wayment, Thomas A. "Jesus' Use of the Psalms in Matthew."

INDEX

Aaronic Priesthood, 58–62, 58–62

Abandonment of Israel, 202

Abraham: scriptural mentions of, 15; covenant of, 41–42; taught by Melchizedek, 56–57; age of, 98; god of, 100–101; calls Sarah his sister, 101–2; non-marital relationship to Sarah of, 102–4; commanded to call Sarah his sister, 104–6; introduced to Pharaoh, 106–7; cures plague, 110–12; as example of adoptive redemption, 303–4

Abrahamic covenant, 7–8

Abrahamic test, 85–88; purpose of, 83–85, 94–97; not all trials are, 88–89; collective, 89–92; individual, 93–94; enduring, 97; Isaac's age at, 98; Joseph Smith on, 126

Abuse, stopping cycle of, 231–32

Accusation, 275

Actions, 337–41

Adam, 49–53

Adoptive redemption, 303–8

Affirming the consequence, 271–72

Affluence, 90–92

Agency, 279

Alma, 307–8

Angels, 125

Apathy, 198–99

Apocrypha, 36

Apostasy, 175

Assyria, 191–92

Atonement: Cain and Abel and, 51–53; symbols of, 140–41

At-one-ment, 172–74

Babylon: Jews in, 247–48; Judaism survives in, 252–53

Bacon, Francis, on prosperity and adversity, 272

Ball, Terry B., 196–205

Ballard, Melvin J.: on missionary work and Elijah, 288; baptisms for dead and, 292–93

Baptism: law of Moses and, 144–46; dream of, 289–90; for dead, 292–93

Bath, 145–46

Beard, 257–58, 265

Beasts, 212–13, 221–22

Beauty, 101–2, 184–85

Benson, Ezra Taft: on Adam, Eve, and priesthood, 49–50; on Zion, 72; on temples in city of Enoch, 74–75; on entering order of Son of God, 75–76; on generational trials, 90; on blessings of temple work, 240, 288; on mission of Elijah, 296

Bible: study aids in, 46–47; structure of covenant in, 314–16, 330–31

Blessing(s): of Jacob's lineage, 120; Jacob wrestles for, 124–29; temple work and, 240–41;

obedience and, 270–71; of temple work, 288

Bones, 259

Book of Mormon: as link between ancient and modern Israel, 5–7; manuscripts of, 15; plan of salvation and, 22–23; law of Moses in, 140–42; exodus and, 157–58; as covenant history, 270–71; adoptive redemption in, 307–8

Brandt, Edward J., 133–51

Bridegroom, 206

Broderick, Carlfred, on stopping cycle of abuse, 231

Brown, Hugh B., on Abrahamic test, 95–96

Brown, S. Kent, 154–62

Buenos Aires Temple, 296

Burton, Theodore M., 234

Cain and Abel, 51–53

Capitivity of Israel, 202

Cardston Alberta Temple, 293

Carnal commandments, 135–39

Catholic Old Testament, 36–37

Chasten, 84–85

Children: decisions of, 118; teaching, 230–31; dream of abused, 231–32; turning hearts of, toward fathers, 286–88

Choke, 183–84

Church of Jesus Christ of Latter-day Saints: members of, called Saints, 2; connection between Old Testament and, 2–14; membership of, 14; growth in Africa of, 290–91

City of Enoch, 74–75

Clean hands, 193–94, 201

Clean lips, 214

Cleansing, 214

Clothes, 185

Coal, 214

Collapse, 186–87

Comfort, 275–77, 281

Comforter, 130

Commandments, contradictory, 105–6

Commerce, 189–90

Consider, 239–40

Contradictory commandments, 105–6

Covenant(s): of Abraham, 7–8, 41–42; Jacob and, 120; reminders of Israelites', 139; in premortal existence, 286–87; redemption and, 299; names in Old Testament and, 302–3; Restoration and renewal of, 311–14; structure of biblical, 314–16, 330–31; Mosaic, 316–18, 331–32, 335; Joshua and renewal of, 318–19, 332; King Josiah and renewal of, 319–20; Jesus Christ as mediator of new, 320–23; Restoration as renewal of, 323–24; Doctrine and Covenants and renewal of, 324–28, 333–34; results of renewal of, 328–29; translations of, 334; in New Testament, 336

Covenant history, Book of Mormon as, 270–71

Cowdery, Oliver, 21–22

Cowley, Matthias, on missionary work, 230

Crenshaw, James, 278

Culture, 209, 218–19

Dahl, Larry E., 83–97

Daniel, 253–55, 264

Dates, determining, 210–11, 219

Daughters of Zion, 200

Davidic dynasty, 251–52, 255–57

Day of the Lord, 207

Dead, temple work for, 230

Death of Isaiah, 206

Degrees of glory, 121

Deity, ancient concepts of, 100–101

Deseret News, 42

Desolation of Israel, 202–3

Dispersed, 8–9

Divine investiture, 33, 171–74, 176

Divine messengers, 124–29
Doctrine and Covenants: plan of salvation and, 25; covenant renewal and, 324–28, 333–34
Doors, 213, 222
Doubt, 158
Draper, Richard D., 245–62
Dream: of Abraham, 105; of abused children, 231–32; Daniel interprets, 253–55; of mother and baptism, 289–90
Dry bones, 259

Ears, 215–16
Ease, 90–92
Ebers Papyrus, 108
Edomites, 226–33
Edwin Smith Papyrus, 108
Egypt, medical practices of, 108–9
Elihu, 281
Elijah: keys of priesthood and, 62–65; prophecies on, 283–85; importance of mission of, 285–86; manifestation of mission of, 288–93; eternal families and, 293–96; Ezra Taft Benson on mission of, 296
Endowment of Jacob, 120–21
Enduring, 273–75
Enoch: priesthood and, 53–55, 70–72; life and ministry of, 72–74; temple blessings and, 74–76; as type of Christ, 78–81
Equity, 277–80
Esau, 117–18, 122–24
Estates, 189
Eternal family, 293–96
Evil: called good, 188–89; problem of, 279; Job and, 281
Example, 70
Exodus: as link between ancient and modern Israel, 10–12; Spencer W. Kimball on Brigham Young and, 16–17; faith and, 154–62
Eyes, 215–16
Ezekiel, 257–60; covenant renewal and, 329–30; symbolic action of, 339, 342

Failure to thrive, 200–201
Faith: of Abel, 51–53; of Abraham, 85–88; of Jacob, 118–22; exodus and, 154–62
False doctrine, 250–52
False prophets, 340–41, 354–55
Family: Charles W. Penrose on saviors and, 230–31; Ezra Taft Benson on protecting, 240; Elijah and, 293–96
Fashion, 185
Fathers, turning children's hearts toward, 286–88
Feasts, 140–41
Fire, 294–96
First Presidency, on Jesus Christ, 19
First Vision, 134, 323–24
Frost, Robert, 278

Ga'al, 299–300
Gather, 9–10, 15
Genealogy, 287
Genesis, 40–41
Genesis Apocryphon, 110–12
Gillum, Gary P., 226–33
Ginzberg, Louis, on Obadiah, 229
Go'el, 300–302
God, 49; Jesus Christ represents, 33; plans and purposes of, 42–43; of Abraham, 100–101; dematerialization of, 169–72; Jesus Christ is one with, 171–74, 176 Moses speaks with, 175; of Isaiah, 178; pleasing and displeasing behavior for, 183–87; virtues desired of, 192–95; Isaiah sees, 212, 220; smoke as metaphor for, 213–14; seraphim attend, 221; intervenes to stop cycle of abuse, 231; man's relationship with, 273–75; equity and love of, 277–80; preserves sacred records, 291–92; prophetic symbolic action and,

338; prophecies on judgment of, 341–42
Godhead, 171–74, 176
Good, called evil, 188–89
Gospel truths, 12–13
Government: unified pattern of, 11–12; corruption of, 188–89
Grace, 164–75
Great Arraignment, 197–205
Greatness, 190–91
Greed, 199–200

Haggai, 236–40
Haight, David B., on temple, 242
Hands: clean, 193–94, 201; laying on of, 109–12
Healing, 110–12
Heart: pure, 193–94, 201; as organ of perception, 215–16
Heavenly Father. *See God*
Heave offering, 138–39
Hebrew, 209, 223–24
Hebrew Old Testament, 36–37
Herodotus, on Egyptian physicians, 108
Herschel, Abraham, on divine justice, 278
Hezekiah, 190, 206
Hinckley, Gordon B., on blessings of temple work, 240–41
Holiness, 242–43
Homer, on Egyptian physicians, 108
Homes, 238
Hoskisson, Paul Y., 209–19
Humiliation of Israel, 203–4, 206
Huntington, Ray L., 236–43

Idolatry, 179–80, 200
If-then arguments, 271–72
Ignorance, 198–99
Isaac, 117
Isaiah: Saints admonished to study, 7; aversion to, 177–80; chapter 1 of, 180–82; vices and, 183–87; societal woes and, 187–90; pride of nations in, 190–92; desired virtues in, 192–95; importance

and uniqueness of, 196–97; as spiritual physician, 197–205; forsees last days, 205; death of, 206; dualistic prophecy of, 207; six impediments in studying, 209–10; measuring time in, 210–11; sees God, 212, 220; cleansing of, 214; mission of, 215–18, 224; stepping blocks to understanding, 218–19; poetry of, 219; premortal council and, 223; symbolic action of, 341–42
Iscah, 113–14
'ish, 124
Israel(ites): Joseph as link between ancient and modern, 3–5, 9–10; Book of Mormon as link between ancient and modern, 5–7; House of, as link between ancient and modern, 7–10; Exodus as link between ancient and modern, 10–12; gospel truths as link between ancient and modern, 12–13; latter-day, 41–42; priesthood and children of, 58–62; faith of, 154–62; recitations and, 162; reject grace, 164–75; pride of, 183–87; spiritual maladies of, 198–201; spiritual prescription for, 201; prognosis for, 201–5; as political entity, 211; Jesus Christ as life substance of, 217–18; tree as symbol of, 224–25; remnant of, 225; term *redeemer* and, 298–99; Jesus Christ as go'el of, 301–2; as example of adoptive redemption, 305–7

Jacob, 35–36; faith of, 118–19; vision of, 119–21; endures trials, 121–22; prepares to meet Esau, 122–24; wrestles with visitor, 124–29; as example of adoptive redemption, 304–5
Jehovah: Jesus Christ as, 19–22; as god of Abraham, 100–101;

engineers exodus, 156–57; exiled
Jews' belief in, 248–50; Daniel's
prophecies on, 253–55. *See also*
Jesus Christ

Jeremiah, 255–57, 329–30

Jerusalem: Zion and, 208; at time of
Haggai, 237; destruction of,
245–47, 262–63

Jesus Christ: scriptures testify of,
18–19; as Jehovah of Old
Testament, 19–22; salvation
comes through, 22–25; titles of,
23; Old Testament bears witness
of, 25–26, 37–39; Law of Moses
bears witness of, 27–28; prophets
testify of, 28–31; Psalms bear
witness of, 31–32; represents
Father, 33; priesthood traced
from Moses to, 58–62; Enoch
and Melchizedek as type of,
78–81; Joseph Smith on
receiving, 130; law of Moses and,
139–51; is one with Father,
171–74, 176; writings of Isaiah
and, 196; as bridegroom, 206; as
life substance of Israel, 217–18;
will visit temples, 241–42; as
go'el of Israel, 301–2; as
mediator of new covenant,
320–23; prophecies on, 342–43.
See also Jehovah

Jews: views of, on Obadiah, 229,
235; urged to consider their
ways, 239–40; scattering of,
245–47; in Babylon, 247–48;
belief of, in Jehovah, 248–50;
false doctrine of, 250–52; survive
in Babylon, 252–53; prophets
warn, 253–62

Job, 266–67; as history or story,
267–69, 280; retributive justice
in, 269–72, 281; relationship
with God and, 273–75; need for
revelation and, 275–77; love and
equity of God and, 277–80; as
theodicy, 280–81

John Calvin, on restoration, 228

Joseph: as link between ancient and
modern Israel, 3–5, 9–10;
definition of term, 9; age of, at
death, 15; added to Rachel's
family, 15–16

Josephus, on temples in Zion, 75

Joshua: covenant renewal and,
318–19, 332; symbolic action of,
342

Josiah, King, 319–20

Journey, 167–68

Judd, Frank F., Jr., 69–81

Judgment: by if-then reasoning,
271–72; prophecies on, 341–42

Justice: retributive, 269–72, 281;
divine law and, 278–79

Justification, 193–94

Kant, Immanuel, 280–81

Kay, F. Arthur, 233

Keys: Joseph Smith on, 56; Elijah
and, 62–65; ordinances and,
285–86

Kimball, Spencer W.: on Brigham
Young and pioneers, 16–17; on
Jesus Christ and Old Testament,
19; on scripture study, 43; on
Zion, 54; on misusing worldly
resources, 238–39; on premortal
covenants, 286

Kingdom of God, 49

King Hezekiah, 190, 206

King James Old Testament, 36–37

King Josiah, 319–20

Kings, 254

Kirtland Temple, 285; Jesus Christ
appears in, 21–22; loss of, 286

Kiss, 35–36

Ladder, Jacob's vision of, 119–21

Land, 189

Lane, Jennifer C., 298–309

Language, from Old Testament, 35

Last days, 205

Last Supper, 321–22, 336

Latter-day Saints: views of, on

Obadiah, 229–31; symbolic actions and, 344–45
Law, 278–79
Law courts, 188–89
Law of Christ, 139–51
Law of Moses: bears witness of Jesus Christ, 27–28; priesthood and, 133–35; as fundamental of gospel, 135–39; law of Christ and, 139–51
Laying on of hands, 109–12, 115
LeBaron, E. Dale, 283–96
Lee, Harold B.: on luxury, 91; on sophistication, 92; on Elijah and eternal families, 293–94
Leprosy, 116
Liefeld, W. L., on terms *salvation* and *redemption,* 302
Lips, 214
Literature, wisdom, 268
"Living Christ, The," 19
Lord's work, 237–39
Love of God, 277–80
Luxury, 90–92

Madness, 254, 264
Madsen, John M., 18–32
Magician, 264
Man, theomorphic, 175
Manna, 161–62, 167–68
Marriage: priesthood and, 49–50; metaphor of, 206
Martyrdom of Isaiah, 206
Matthews, Robert J., 35–47; on priesthood principles, 65
Maxwell, Neal A.: on individual trials, 93; on missionary work in spirit world, 290
McCarthy, Dennis J., on covenants, 303
McConkie, Bruce R.: on book of Genesis, 40; on Adam and priesthood, 50; on Melchizedek Priesthood and Mosaic Law, 62; on Melchizedek and Zion, 70; on Zion, 77, 79; on Melchizedek's establishment of peace, 74; on

prophets as types of Christ, 80; on Saints as types of Christ, 81
Medical practices, of Egypt, 108–9
Meekness, 192–95
Melchizedek, 69–70; teaches Abraham, 56–57; priesthood and, 70–72; life and ministry of, 72–74; temple blessings and, 74–76; as type of Christ, 78–81
Melchizedek Priesthood, 49–53; as timeless gospel truth, 12–13; eternal nature of, 49; Enoch and, 53–55; degrees of, 60; Joseph Smith on, 63; laying on of hands and, 110; Jacob holds, 120; Israelites reject, 166–67; Israelite prophets had, 175
Mendenhall, George E., 314–16
Meservy, Keith H., on Job, 269
Microfilm, 291–92
Mikveh bath, 145–46
Military power, 191–92
Millet, Robert L., 48–66
Miracles: of pioneers, 17; of Melchizedek Priesthood, 71–72
Mission: of Isaiah, 215–18, 224; of Elijah, 285–86, 288–93; Ezra Taft Benson on Elijah's, 296
Missionary work: Matthias Cowley on, 230; as manifestation of Elijah's mission, 288–91
Mission home, 294–96
Mixing, 139
Moore, Michael S., on term *go'el,* 300–301, 310
Mortal testing, 83–85
Mosaic covenant, 316–18, 331–32, 335
Moses, 15; priesthood traced from, 58–62; exodus and, 158–60; speaks with God, 175
Mother, dream of baptism and, 289–90
Mountain, 207–8
Mount Zion, 226–33
Movement, 338–39

Music, 184–85
My Parents Married on a Dare, 231

Nabonidus, 264
Name, 128; of God, 171, 176; covenants in Old Testament and, 302–3
Nations, pride of, 190–92
Nebuchadnezzar, 253–55
Nelson, Russell M., 1–14, 234; on Adam, Eve, and priesthood, 49
Nephites, Melchizedek Priesthood and, 62
New Testament: plan of salvation and, 24–25; law of Moses in, 142–43; covenant in, 336
Nibley, Hugh W., 177–95
Noah, priesthood and, 55–56

Obadiah, 226–33
Obedience: of Jacob, 120; blessings and, 270–71
Offerings, 136–39
Old Testament: connection between Church and, 2–14; testifies of Jesus Christ, 18–19, 25–26, 37–39; Jesus Christ as Jehovah of, 19–22; plan of salvation and, 22–24; well-known phrases from, 35; different versions of, 36–37; latter-day revelation and, 40, 45; as book for latter-day Israel, 41–42; laying on of hands and, 109–10; redemption in, 299–300; name giving and covenant making in, 302–3; adoptive redemption in, 303–7; Mosaic covenant in, 316–18, 331–32; preserves oaths, 335; symbolic actions in, 337–41
Oppression, 183–84, 192–95, 207
Ordinances, 52; priesthood and, 61–62; offerings and, 136–39; priesthood keys and, 285–86; temple, 292–93; as symbolic actions, 344
Organs, 215–16

Packer, Boyd K., 291–92; on individual trials, 93; on blessings of temple work, 240; on loss of Kirtland Temple, 286; on dedication of Buenos Aires Temple, 296
Padah, 299–300
Parenting, 118
Parry, Donald W., 337–55
Parties, 184–85
Passover, 140–41
Paul, 2
Peace, 72–74
Peace offering, 137
Penrose, Charles W., on family and saviors, 230–31
Persecution, 16, 89–90
Pharaoh: Abraham meets, 106–7; healing of, 110–12; sickness of, 116
Philo, 170
Physician, Isaiah as spiritual, 197–205
Picture album, 294–96
Pioneers, 1–2, 9; as link between ancient and modern Israel, 10–12; persecution of, 16, 89–90; care and protection of, 17
Plague, 110–12, 116; Israelites spared from, 160–61
Plan of salvation: as God's plan, 42–43; Cain and Abel and, 51–53; premortal covenant on, 286–87
Planting, 287–88
Poetry, 209, 218, 219, 267–69
Polytheism, 180
Poverty, 192–95
Powell, Ted, 291–92
Power, military, 191–92
Pratt, Orson: on scripture study, 43–44; on latter-day Zion, 79
Premortal council, 223
Premortal existence, covenants made in, 286–87
Preparatory gospel, 135–39

Pride, 183–87; of nations, 190–92; in book of Obadiah, 228
Priesthood, 49–53, 58–62, 285–86; as timeless gospel truth, 12–13; Adam and, 49–53; Noah and, 55–56; Abraham receives, 56–57; three orders of, 57; traced from Moses to Jesus Christ, 58–62; Elijah and keys of, 62–65; principles of, 65; Melchizedek and order of, 70–71; miracles and, 71–72; temple blessings and, 74–76; law of Moses and, 133–35
Priests, offerings and, 138–39
Problem of evil, 279
Procrastination, 237–39
Promised land, 11
Promises, premortal, 286–88
Prophecy: Isaiah's dualistic, 207; of Obadiah, 226–33; recording, 264–65; on Elijah, 283–85; symbolic actions as, 337–41; fulfillment of, 340–41; of God's judgment, 341–42; on Jesus Christ, 342–43; purpose of non-verbal, 343–44; examples of non-verbal, 345–54; examples of false prophets' non-verbal, 354–55; legitimate types of, 355
Prophet(s), 354–55; testify of Jesus Christ, 28–31; order of, 37; of Old Testament acquainted with gospel, 38–39; as types of Christ, 80; Jacob as, 120; Isaiah as, 197, 210, 219; of Judah, 246; of exiled Jews, 248–50; Jews ignore warnings from, 251–52; give warnings to Judah, 253–62; symbolic actions of, 338
Prosperity, 90–92, 272
Provocation, 164–75
Psalms, 31–32
Punishment, 271
Pure heart, 193–94, 201

Rabbis, 6

Real estate, 189
Realpolitiks, 191
Rebellion of Israel, 202
Recitations, 162
Redeemer, 298–99
Redemption: covenants and, 299; in Old Testament, 299–300; salvation and, 302; adoptive, 303–7
Reflexive, 223–24
Reformation, 319–20
Relationship: of Abraham and Sarah, 102–4; with God, 273–75
Repentance: Isaiah and, 179; Israel urged to, 201; promises for, 204–5
Representation, 339–40
Restoration, 234; technology and, 47; of old Church, 48–49; as theme in book of Obadiah, 228; of Judah, 259; as covenant renewal, 311–14, 323–24
Retributive justice, 269–72, 281
Revelation: comes through Jesus Christ, 18–19; Old Testament clarified by, 40; explains why, 45; Job and need for, 275–77; prophetic symbolic action originates from, 338
Rhodesia, 291–92
Richards, Franklin D.: on power of Melchizedek, 57; on temples in city of Enoch, 74
Richards, LeGrand, 234; on prophecy on transportation, 208
Riches, 186–87
Righteousness: promises for, 204–5; suffering and, 272
Robinson, Stephen E., on Zion, 76
Rock, 167–68
Romney, Marion G., on endowment of Jacob, 120–21

Sabbath day, 12
Sacred records, 291–92
Sacrifice: Joseph Smith on

priesthood and, 63–64; oaths and, 335–36

Saints, 2; term found in New Testament, 14; persecution of, 16, 89–90

Salt, 147–48

Salvation: comes through Jesus Christ, 22–25; redemption and, 302

Sanctification: chastening and trying and, 84–85; Jacob and, 120

Sarah, 113–14

Satan: as example in Isaiah, 186; as god of underworld, 192–93; accusation and, 275

Saviors, Obadiah's vision of, 226–33

Scattered, 8–9

Scriptures: saints admonished to study, 7; testify of Jesus Christ, 18–19; teaching aids in, 46–47; technology and, 47; Ray C. Stedman on, 227; of exiled Jews, 261–62, 265; preserving, 264–65; prophecies on Elijah in, 283–85

Scripture study, 7, 43–45

Sealing, 293

Second Coming, 224

Security, 191–92

Seed, 287

Seely, David Rolph, 311–34

Seraphim, 212–13, 218, 220–21

Serpents, 221

Seventy-one, 229

Sex, 185

Shavuoth, 162

Shechem, 318–19, 332

Shiloh, 250–51

Sill, Sterling W., on agreeing with Lord, 42

Sin offering, 137–38

Sister, Abraham calls Sarah, 101–6

Skinner, Andrew C., 117–31

Slave, 96–97

Smith, Ian, 291–92

Smith, Joseph: as link between ancient and modern Israel, 3–5; sees Jesus Christ in Kirtland Temple, 21–22; on Church organizaton, 48; on kingdom of God, 49; on priesthood as everlasting principle, 49; on Cain and Abel, 51–53; on Noah's place in priesthood hierarchy, 55–56; on keys of priesthood, 56; on power of Melchizedek, 57; on three orders of priesthood, 57; on government of children of Israel, 58; on degrees of Melchizedek Priesthood, 60; on Elijah and priesthood keys, 62; on Melchizedek Priesthood, 63; on priesthood and doctrine of translation, 63; on priesthood and sacrifice, 63–64; on restoration of priesthood, 64; on building Zion, 79; on Abrahamic test, 83, 87, 126; on generational Abrahamic tests, 89–90; on contradictory commandments, 106; on vision of degrees of glory, 121; on angels and ministering spirits, 125; on translated beings, 125; on wrestling, 127; on receiving Comforter, 130; on curse of Israelites, 166–67; on oneness of Father and Son, 176; Second Coming and, 224; on prophecy of Obadiah, 230; on accusing, 275; on importance of Elijah, 285; covenant renewal and, 324–28

Smith, Joseph Fielding: on revelation coming through Jesus Christ, 18–19; on Adam and priesthood, 51; on withdrawal of priesthood, 59–60; on importance of Elijah, 285; on fathers as ancestors, 286

Smoke, 213–14

Societal woes, 187–90

Soddom and Gomorrah, 185

Solomon's Temple, 222

Sophistication, 92

South Africa Johannesburg Mission: missionary work in, 289–90; growth of Church in, 290–91; fire in mission home of, 294–96

Spirits, witness ordinances, 292–93

Spiritual death, 168

Spirit world, missionary work in, 290

Stedman, Ray C., on scriptures, 227

Strathearn, Gaye, 100–113

Study aids, 46–47

Submission, 96–97

Success, 183–87

Suffering, 271–75, 279

Surin, Kenneth, on being forsaken, 277

Symbolic actions, 337–41; as prophecies of God's judgment, 341–42; as prophecies of Jesus Christ, 342–43; purpose of, 343–44; Latter-day Saints and, 344–45; examples of, 345–54

Symbols: of Atonement, 140–41; of provocation, 167–68

Tanner, John S., 266–80

Taylor, John: on Adam and priesthood, 51; on Noah's ordination to priesthood, 55; on patriarchal order, 55; on translated residents of Zion, 55; on conferral of Melchizedek Priesthood, 60–61; on Nephites and priesthood, 62; on translation of Zion, 77–78; on translation of city of Enoch, 80; on submitting to God, 96–97

Teaching aids, 46–47

Technology, 47

Temple: as timeless gospel truth, 13; mountain as metaphor for, 207–8; Solomon's, 222; Haggai's message on, 237–39; Spirit resides in, 241–42; holiness and uncleanness and, 242–43; Jewish misconceptions on, 250–51; ordinances, 292–93

Temple blessings, during establishment of Zion, 74–76

Temple work: prophecy of Obadiah and, 226, 230; blessings and, 240–41; Ezra Taft Benson on blessings of, 288

Tenth, 224

Terrien, Samuel: on love of God, 279; on book of Job, 279–80

Test(s): purpose of, 83–85, 94–97; causes and timing of, 88–89; collective, 89–92; individual, 93–94; enduring, 97; prosperity as, 272. *See also* Abrahamic test

Teven, 163

Thank offering, 137

Theodicy, 273, 280–81

Theomorphic, 175

Thomas, M. Catherine, 164–75

Thriving, 200–201

Time, measuring, 210–11, 219

Tithing, 12–13

Titles of Jesus Christ, 23

Topical guide, 46

Trade, 189–90

Translated beings, 125

Translation: as power of Melchizedek Priesthood, 54–55; Joseph Smith on priesthood and, 63; of Zion, 76–78

Transportation, 208

Tree, 224–25

Trespass offering, 137–38

Trials: purpose of, 83–85, 94–97; causes and timing of, 88–89; collective, 89–92; individual, 93–94; enduring, 97; Jacob endures, 121–22

Trinity, 176

Truth: as link between ancient and modern Israel, 12–13; teaching children, 230–31

Tsevat, Matitiahu, 278

Uncleanness, 242–43

Understanding, organs as symbol of, 215–16
Unworthiness, 214

Vices, 183–87
Vineyard, 200–201
Virtues, desired of God, 192–95
Vision: of Jacob, 119–21; Joseph Smith on, 121; of Obadiah, 226–33; of dry bones, 259
Visitor, Jacob wrestles with, 124–29
Vow offering, 137

Washings, 144–46
Water, 161; as symbol, 167–68
Wealth, 90–92
White House prayer breakfast, 6
Why, 45
Wickedness, 187–90
Widtsoe, John A.: on scripture study, 44; on gifts of temple, 239; on premortal covenants, 286–87
Wife/sister motif, 101–6
Wilderness: Israelite provocation in, 164–75; as symbol, 167–68
Williams, Charles, 276
Wings, 212–13

Wisdom literature, 268
Wood, Edward J., 293
Woodruff, Wilford: on saviors on Mount Zion, 233; on missionary work in spirit world, 290
Word of Wisdom, 13
World: collapse of, 186–87; as it should be, 194–95
Worldliness, 199–200
Wrestle, 124–29

Young, Brigham: prepared for exodus, 10–12; Spencer W. Kimball on exodus and, 16–17; on searching after God's plan, 42; on temples in city of Enoch, 74; on building Zion, 79; on wealth as trial, 90; on laying on of hands, 112; on wrestling, 127

Zimbabwe, 291–92
Zion, 53–55; establishment of, 72–73; temple blessings and, 74–76; translation of, 76–78; building, 78–81; daughters of, 200; Jerusalem and, 208
Zoramites, 183–8